MORAL VALUES
AND THE SUPEREGO CONCEPT
IN PSYCHOANALYSIS

MORAL VALUES

AND THE

SUPEREGO CONCEPT

IN

PSYCHOANALYSIS

Edited by

SEYMOUR C. POST, M.D.

INTERNATIONAL UNIVERSITIES PRESS, INC.

NEW YORK

Manufactured in the United States of America

Table of Contents

Preface

THIS BOOK has been published under the auspices of the Society of Medical Psychoanalysts. It was upon the occasion of its twenty-first anniversary that the Society held a Symposium, the substance of which was to form the nucleus of the current volume. The Symposium was the most recent in a series of triennial symposia sponsored by the Society, each of which has constituted an important scientific episode in the history of the Society.

The Society is a multiorientational group, where customarily the widest range of psychoanalytic thought exists side by side. It is an expression of the academic freedom which is the hallmark of the group that on this occasion, paradoxically, the editor was able to approach his subject from primarily one orientation, the Freudian, and to develop his theme in what some of the members of the Society considered a relatively narrow focus.

I wish to thank the members of the committee of the Society who worked with me in planning the Symposium. This committee composed of Malvina W. Kremer, M.D. (co-chairman), Paul Dince, M.D., Joseph Merin, M.D., Lilly Ottenheimer, M.D., Salo Rosenbaum, M.D., and Nathan Roth, M.D., acted in a consulting capacity as the book was being edited.

My publishers were unusually patient, understanding that volumes of this kind present unique problems. I should like to extend thanks to Miss Norma Fox, my editor, for her assistance which has been of immense value.

I am especially grateful to Dr. Jacob Arlow, who served as an unofficial adviser and consultant to the editor from the beginning of this project. Though not a member of the Society, he gave much to this volume out of his unsparing interest in seeing a scientific project carried through.

S.C.P.

Contributors

SILVANO ARIETI, M.D.: Clinical Professor of Psychiatry, New York Medical College; Training Analyst, Psychoanalytic Division, Department of Psychiatry, New York Medical College; Member of the Faculty of the William Alanson White Institute.

IRVING BIEBER, M.D.: Clinical Professor of Psychiatry, New York Medical College; Training Psychoanalyst, Psychoanalytic Division, Department of Psychiatry, New York Medical College.

VICTOR CALEF, M.D.: Associate Chief, Psychiatric Department, Mount Zion Hospital and Medical Center, San Francisco; Training Analyst, San Francisco Psychoanalytic Institute.

PATRICIA CARRINGTON, Ph.D.: Member, Faculty, Postgraduate Center for Mental Health, New York City.

HARMON S. EPHRON, M.D.: Associate Clinical Professor in Psychiatry, New York Medical College; Training Analyst (emeritus) Psychoanalytic Division, Department of Psychiatry, New York Medical College.

AARON H. ESMAN, M.D.: Chief Psychiatrist, Jewish Board of Guardians; Lecturer in Psychiatry, Columbia University School of Social Work; Member of the Faculty, New York Psychoanalytic Institute.

VIVIAN FROMBERG, M.D.: Member of the Faculty, Department of Psychiatry, New York University School of Medicine; Member, New York Psychoanalytic Institute.

MANUEL FURER, M.D.: Faculty, New York Psychoanalytic Institute; formerly, Director of Research, Masters School, New York City.

MARTIN GROTJAHN, M.D.: Clinical Professor of Psychiatry, University of Southern California, Los Angeles.

ROBERT JAY LIFTON, M.D.: Foundations' Fund Research Professor of Psychiatry, Yale University School of Medicine. Author of *Death in Life: Survivors of Hiroshima*, awarded the National Book Award in the Sciences in 1969.

HENRY LOWENFELD, M.D.: Training Analyst, New York Psychoanalytic Institute.

YELA LOWENFELD, M.D.: Training Analyst, New York Psychoanalytic Institute.

HYMAN MUSLIN, M.D.: Professor of Psychiatry, Abraham Lincoln School of Medicine, University of Illinois, College of Medicine, Clinical Associate, Chicago Institute for Psychoanalysis.

Contributors

MORTIMER OSTOW, M.D.: Visiting Professor of Pastoral Psychiatry, Jewish Theological Seminary; Preceptor, Department of Psychiatry, Mount Sinai Hospital School of Medicine, New York; Member, New York Psychoanalytic Institute.

LILLY OTTENHEIMER, M.D.: Associate Clinical Professor of Psychiatry, New York Medical College. Training Analyst, Psychoanalytic Division, Department of Psychiatry, New York Medical College.

SEYMOUR C. POST, M.D.: Assistant Clinical Professor of Psychiatry, Columbia University, College of Physicians & Surgeons; Member, Society of Medical Psychoanalysts, New York.

ISHAK RAMZY, M.A., Ph.D.: Training Psychoanalyst, Topeka Institute for Psychoanalysis. Instructor, Department of Psychoanalytic Training, The Menninger Foundation, Topeka, Kansas.

SAMUEL RITVO, M.D.: Professor of Psychiatry, Yale University School of Medicine; Training Analyst, Western New England Psychoanalytic Institute.

PAUL ROAZEN, Ph.D.: Associate Professor, Division of Social Science, York University, Ontario, Canada; formerly, Faculty, Department of Government, Harvard University; Guest at the Boston Psychoanalytic Society and Institute; Author of *Freud: Political and Social Thought* and *Brother Animal: The Story of Freud and Tausk.*

SALO ROSENBAUM, M.D.: Assistant Clinical Professor of Psychiatry, New York University School of Medicine; Member, Society of Medical Psychoanalysts, New York.

MARTIN H. STEIN, M.D.: Training Analyst and Chairman of the Faculty, New York Psychoanalytic Institute; formerly Chairman, Board on Professional Standards, American Psychoanalytic Association.

ALAN A. STONE, M.D.: Lecturer in Law, Harvard Law School; Associate Professor of Psychiatry, Harvard Medical School; Member, Boston Psychoanalytic Society and Institute.

ARTHUR VALENSTEIN, M.D.: Assistant Clinical Professor of Psychiatry, Harvard Medical School; Training Analyst and Faculty Member, Boston Psychoanalytic Institute.

ALEXANDER WOLF, M.D.: Associate Clinical Professor of Psychiatry, New York Medical College; formerly, Training Analyst, Psychoanalytic Division, Department of Psychiatry, New York Medical College.

NORMAN ZINBERG, M.D.: Scholar in Residence, Tufts University; Field Foundation Fellowship; formerly Assistant Clinical Professor in Psychiatry, Harvard Medical School; Lecturer on Social Relations, Harvard University; Faculty, Boston Psychoanalytic Institute.

Editor's Foreword

SEYMOUR C. POST, M.D.

FREUD has shown us that we are capable in our mental functioning of developing moral ideals and imperatives, derived from the biologically required and lengthy period of childhood dependence, during which time powerful psychological forces operate between parent and child, while the latter attempts to deal with sexual and aggressive development (Hartmann, 1960).

After Freud, a number of authors, notably Flugel (1945), whose monograph stands as a classic, and more recently Hartmann (1960), have addressed themselves to the subject. However, for some considerable period of time, psychoanalysts, having been preoccupied with ego functioning, had paid lesser attention to the superego. To some extent, this selective inattention has served, to create the impression that problems raised at an earlier time had all been settled. It is clear though, that there are still ambiguities, confusions and misconceptions clinging to the subject.

The general public, on the other hand, has never really grasped that psychoanalysis had something to say concerning man as a creature with *unconscious moral forces.* Their accedence to the concepts derived from psychoanalytic formulations of the id has been considerable, and in fact, quite one-sided. For it is no secret among psychoanalysts that there is almost universal misunderstanding by the public about those elements in psychic functioning which, as has been revealed by psychoanalysis, operate to *limit* the direct expression of the drives. In an era when questions about morality and values have both assumed greater importance and yet seem less easily answered, a great deal of confusion and uncertainty exists, as people struggle to understand what appears to them to be changing life styles, and increasing turmoil and violence in the relationship between individuals and groups. There is particular concern about what is thought to be marked shifts in the values of youth.

Authors from other scientific and intellectual disciplines have been much preoccupied by this apparent shift in the moral climate, while expressing sharp disagreement as to its meaning and portents. Daniel Bell (1970), for example, believes that a crisis of confidence in the moral structure of our society is not merely a very recent phenomenon, but is a function of the era of "modernism," which he conceives as being roughly concurrent with the present century. The prophets of modernism have been represented in art by Picasso, Braque, Pollack, Kline and the cubist, abstract-expressionist, pop and minimalist, as well as other of the avant-garde art schools. This trend has been expressed in literature by Pound, Woolf, Joyce, Genet, Mallarmé, Mailer and others. Bell describes the undermining and replacement of the small-town, Protestant, bourgeois, capitalist cultural model by antinomian, antiestablishment, anti-intellectual, voluptuarian trends that characterize this new cultural model of modernism, which he says has set the standards for our society and moral concepts. Robert Lifton, on the other hand, while noting much the same factual data, is hardly appalled by the emergence of this new cultural model, but in a series of papers, one of which ("The New and the Old, Notes on a New History") is included in this volume, has set forth his conviction that these same forces represent the wave of the future, and far from being destructive in their essence, are a constructive and beneficial change from the sterile patterns of the past.

What does psychoanalysis have to contribute towards an understanding of values and morality in the individual and in the group? It was with this question in mind that the current volume was conceived. The nucleus consists of papers delivered at a weekend symposium sponsored by the Society of Medical Psychoanalysts in 1968. Some of the chapters have been revised from papers presented at that meeting, while a number of others were written expressly for this volume. The authors were asked to address themselves to issues that seemed to be heretofore unresolved, unclear or not yet the subject of attention by the profession.

Authors were encouraged to take a fresh view of the superego and moral values in all its aspects. What, for example, is the relationship between the superego and morality? Beres (1965) distinguishes between ethics and morality, morality being defined as the response of the individual to the ethical demands of his time. But do we have a misconception in identifying the superego of the patient with the mores of the community? Could this imply a hypothetical norm which may not always exist? What of the conflicts one observes in patients where the role played by the superego does not permit of analogy to the world, as in cases of pathological ego-ideal and unusual superego formations? To what extent did the fact that in analysis we deal with a primitive child-like superego influence our concepts? Then also, concerning the nature of the superego, we speak of *the* superego when in point of fact it is a conglomerate structure and yet related to specific conflict. Thus, for example, the same moral problems may be dealt with in two different ways by two different individuals.

What about the idea that the superego is attributable to identification with the parent of the same sex, upon the resolution of the Oedipus complex? (Note the difficulty Freud got into when he said that the boy identified with the father at the time of the Oedipus complex, since the *loss* was of the mother. Reason might suggest, by virtue of what Freud had said about identification with the lost object, that identification should have been with *her*.) The question of whether or not the superego antedates the Oedipus complex, and whether identifications come not only from object loss but also might be a concomitant of normal development, also suggests itself. What about the ego-ideal—which has been so meticulously placed in the psychic apparatus? Recent considerations made it seem much more difficult to place in the ego, superego or id.

Then there is the weighty matter of moral values in psychoanalysis. We know they are there but are they distinct from the psychoanalytic situation or different? Are the moral values implicit in psychoanalysis different from the moral values of society, in general, and specifically from the analyst-analysand relationship? What about the equation of morality and mental health: if it exists, then what about class conflicts and conflicts of interest as they affect our patients? We speak of the analyst as a remolder of the personality: does he or does he not introduce new moral values? Are the values those of the analyst, those that stem from analysis as a therapy, societal mores or none of these? To what extent does the analyst offer himself as a model for the patient? Is there, for example, anything immoral in the analyst's analyzing away a reaction-formation—such as he might do with a person who became involved in civil rights as a reaction-formation to the wish to kill a sibling? How do we distinguish what is illegal from what is immoral, or mentally unhealthy? If the patient takes an immoral stand, at what point do we get involved, as for example, in adultery? What about fee morality: when do we charge, when don't we, and does this imply some sort of morality?

In matters affecting adolescents there are many questions which appear to require clarification. What stand does one take on promiscuity, the drug culture, conflicts with responsibility as against freedom in the individual, values which are not yet determined; for example, how much should a student body have to say in the matter of parietal rules?

These were among the questions that the authors were asked to consider, and which resulted in the group of papers constituting this volume. The majority of the contributors, along with the editor, proceeded from the conceptual viewpoint of Freudian psychoanalytic thought. Certain of the papers are included, however, because they derive from viewpoints which, although psychoanalytic, are far removed from classical thought, or in several instances reflect other conceptions which psychoanalysts must become conversant with in their developing thinking in this area. Inevitably, certain matters occur redundantly, while others seemed not to interest any author, and some seemed to present painful difficulty (the question of moral values in the relationship between student and training analyst, for example, was considered for some time by several individuals who ultimately confessed that they were unable to come up with papers they considered suitable, in the time allotted for publication. While two papers contain sections which touch on this subject, the thoroughgoing study which it demands has remained undone.)

The volume opens with Furer's review and summary of the literature. His scholarly paper elucidates and presents in spare and elegant fashion what has been written by leading authors.

Samuel Ritvo, using data from long-term longitudinal studies of infants and children at the Yale University Child Study Center, finds that earlier speculations regarding predictability of superego formation were rather more optimistic than originally thought.

Valenstein investigates the earliest reciprocity between mother and child, in an ethological comparison. Among his conclusions is one that has rather serious implications: he finds that in the disturbances of conscience and morality that appear in certain "disadvantaged" groups, there is impairment at such an early level, and of such profound degree, that therapy or corrective educational procedures, based on assumptions of more malleable causation, may not be to great avail. Here Valenstein gives psychoanalytic support to the pessimistic but perhaps more realistic evaluation also recently made by Lustman (1970).

The vexing aspect of moral values in adolescence is discussed in a timely paper by Esman, whose formulations about the superego, as derived from his clinical data, are both interesting and innovative.

Muslin writes on the feminine superego. He regards it as different from that of the male only in origin and mental content, not in function, and derived largely from preoedipal anxieties, in particular fear of loss of love and separation from or destruction by the mother. Since the superego also contains societal restrictions particular to the culture's model for the woman, Muslin sees in our changing culture the possibility of the internalization of precepts not only for mothering, but for achievement in other areas as well.

The paper by Bieber, on the concept of the superego, represents a revision of that concept insofar as the author's approach to adaptational thinking has been influenced by a neurophysiological background and exposure to the work of Rado and Kardiner. Though some readers may not agree with his critique of classical formulations, his plea for a more clinically based concept of the superego mirrors a widely felt need. His paper represents an attempt in this direction, also made by Esman in his paper on adolescence.

Calef's paper is a speculation upon the theory of therapeutic results in psychoanalysis. Its relevance to the volume lies in Sterba's comments that the therapeutic process has as its prototype the formation of the superego.

The next section of the book takes up the interaction between patient, psychoanalyst and culture in the thorny arena of moral values. Particular emphasis is placed on the problem of values in the one-to-one psychoanalytic situation. Zinberg opens this section with a thoughtful essay that touches upon many aspects of the matter, among them the psychoanalyst's relationship to social change and the psychoanalyst as derived from his social milieu. Roazen also addresses himself to this question, but does so from his vantage point as an interested and informed layman, who looks at the psychoanalyst and asks him to carefully assess his relationship with his patient and with the social environment that forms his value matrix. His views may appear somewhat abrasive and his criticism unjustified to some, but his comments represent a view from outside the profession that commands significant attention. Ramzy's controversial paper regarding values in psychoanalysis, reprinted with certain modifications, is included here because of its significance to the current discussion. Stein uses a clinical example, finely dissected, to delineate what occurs between psychoanalyst and patient concerning a specific value problem: truth-telling by the analyst. He demonstrates the close relationship between ego and superego, namely, that an activity regarded primarily as an ego function must be described in terms of superego function as well.

Two brief discussions by Bieber and Ottenheimer which touch upon the special contributions that psychoanalysis has made to the understanding of human value systems conclude this section.

Three clinical papers follow. Post's paper on a special type of defense to be found in certain Don Juan-micro-impostor cases is a contribution to the elaboration of superego functioning described by Reich (1953, 1954, 1960) in her series of studies on the narcissistic neuroses. Arieti links catatonia to conscience-produced inhibitory factors. Ephron and Carrington have had a unique opportunity to attempt psychotherapy in a would-be juvenile murderer.

The next section is a psychoanalytic study of value problems in the culture. The Lowenfelds' paper, expanded and revised with additional clinical material, is a clear and uncompromising psychoanalytic confrontation with "the new morality" of the Age of Aquarius. The perceptive understanding it provides should be of considerable help to clinicians and laymen alike. Ostow's paper on religion and morality offers further illumination on the turmoil of the day as expressed in the behavior and symptomatology of normal and neurotic individuals. Lifton, who writes not as a psychoanalyst, but as a "psychohistorian," is in sharp contrast, not only in his methodology and intellectual approach, but in his conclusions as to the meaning of manifest characterological transformations in today's adolescents and their parents.

Stone, writing from the experience gained in recent years from the combined study undertaken at Harvard by the Law School and the Department of Psychiatry of the Medical School, discusses the interaction of psychoanalysis with the law. In the course of his paper he considers "principled" (i.e., moral) disobedience of the law as an example of the kind of difficulty that may come about when psychoanalytic concepts are inexpertly applied in the course of jurisprudence. He concludes that the law cannot lightly set policy by "either ignoring or hiding in the dark forest of the psyche."

Rosenbaum and Fromberg make an attempt to analogize the cultural development of the superego throughout history to its development in the individual. Grotjahn sees similarities between Luther and Freud, which emerge from a study of Freud's close relationship with the Swiss pastor, Pfister.

Wolf, in a light, engaging style, deals with a subject that troubles him deeply, and shows how mental functioning can influence value judgments made by the individual which have profound implications for the culture and the environment.

It remains to thank the contributing authors for their courage and integrity in attacking their respective tasks. Their willingness to subject themselves as well as their patients to close scrutiny has made this volume possible.

BIBLIOGRAPHY

Bell, D. (1970), The cultural contradictions of capitalism. *The Public Interest,* No. 21, Fall 1970.

Beres, D. (1965), Psychoanalytic notes on the history of morality. *J. Amer. Psychoanal. Assn.,* 13:3–37.

Flugel, J. C. (1945), *Man, Morals and Society.* London: Duckworth.

Hartmann, H. (1960) *Psychoanalysis and Moral Values.* New York: International Universities Press.

Lustman, S. L. (1970), Cultural deprivation: a clinical dimension of education. *The Psychoanalytic Study of the Child,* 25:483–503.

Reich, A. (1953), Narcissistic object choice in women. *J. Amer. Psychoanal. Assn.,* 1:22–44.

———— (1954), Early identifications as archaic elements in the superego. *J. Amer. Psychoanal. Assn.,* 2:218–238.

———— (1960), Pathologic forms of self-esteem regulation. *The Psychoanalytic Study of the Child,* 15:215–232.

PART I

THEORETICAL PAPERS

1. The History of the
Superego Concept in Psychoanalysis:
A Review of the Literature

MANUEL FURER, M.D.

THIS PAPER presents a survey of the psychoanalytic literature on the superego. Freud's thought in this area is summarized in Part I, which is focused particularly on those aspects of his writings on the subject that have subsequently led to controversy. Part II summarizes the major trends in the literature, since the publication in 1923 of Freud's most definitive statement on the superego. Part III deals with some of the literature on psychoanalysis and moral values.

The tasks for theory that will be brought out in this review include: (1) the integration of the original theory of the formation of conscience out of ambivalence, as set forth in *Totem and Taboo* (1913), with Freud's later formulations, which involve psychic structure and the theory of anxiety; (2) the integration of that portion of the theory that has to do with the role of the superego as the savior of narcissism, with the essentially prohibiting nature of the superego, such as might be emphasized, for example, in a theory of the regulation of self-esteem; (3) the relation of the superego to reality testing, including self-observation; (4) the economics of the superego in general, especially the problem of the libidinal energies that may be available to it; (5) the nature of the ego-superego relationship, in terms of their interdependent functioning; (6) the relationship between psychoanalysis and ethics.

A portion of this paper was read at the Symposium on Moral Values and Superego Functioning in New York City on March 4, 1968.

Manuel Furer

I

In Freud's earliest writings on psychic conflict—the chapter on psychotherapy in *Studies on Hysteria* (1893–1895), the paper on "The Neuropsychosis of Defense" (1894), and the "Further Remarks" (1896)—there are repeated statements on the role of what we would today call superego functioning in relation to repression. The reason why pathogenic ideas have been put out of consciousness, he said then, is that they arouse the distressing affects "of shame, of self-reproach, of psychical pain and the feeling of being harmed" (1893–1895, p. 269). A new idea has to submit to what he called a process of censorship, arising out of the "trend of the ideas already united in the ego" (1893–1895, p. 269). The belief that such self-reproaches can also be repressed became the keystone of his theory of obsessional neurosis: obsessions, he maintained, are always reproaches re-emerging in a transmuted form under the impact of repressions. They can also be transformed, Freud indicated, into *shame,* lest another person should come to hear about the action that evoked the self-reproach; *hypochondriacal anxiety,* lest some bodily injury should result from it; fear of punishment for it by the world at large; religious anxiety; delusions of reference; dread of betraying the deed; and dread of the temptation to perform the deed. In the somewhat later paper, "Obsessive Actions and Religious Practices" (1907), Freud used the phrase "unconscious sense of guilt" to explain why the compulsive patient behaves as if he were dominated by a guilt of which he nevertheless seems to know nothing.

The first full discussion of the genesis and content of what Freud (1913) was later to call the superego appears in the monograph *Totem and Taboo.* Here he deals with the origin of conscience, in the history both of the individual and of mankind, as a manifestation of consciousness, internalized and independent, "with no need to appeal to anything else for support." The argument is that the source of conscience is emotional ambivalence, a conflict between hatred toward the father and love and admiration for him, as had already been demonstrated in the case of Little Hans.

In the primal crime of parricide, the band of brothers satisfied that hatred and at the same time realized their wish to identify with their father. The affection in which they held the father afterwards made itself felt "in the form of remorse"; in the individual this made its appearance as a sense of guilt, which coincided with the remorse felt by the group as a whole. In accordance with the mechanism of "deferred obedience," ". . . They revoked their deed by forbidding the killing of the totem, the substitute for the father, and they renounced its fruits by resigning their claim to the women who had now been set free."

In the totemic system, the substitute for the father offered the clan "protection, care and indulgence . . . while on their side they undertook to respect his life, that is, not to repeat the original deed." Periodically, however, in the festival of the totem meal, the crime was relived and the prohibitions against it thrown off. In discussing the taboo of the dead, Freud says that in order to maintain the repression of the hostile current in the ambivalence, it is projected onto the tabooed object, which thereby becomes a demon threatening the mourners.

In the paper "On Narcissism," Freud (1914) brings his ideas about the functioning of conscience together with those having to do with the cultural and ethical ideals that lie at the base of repression. Repression, he says, proceeds from the "self-respect of the ego that has been set up as an ideal in himself, by which he measures his actual ego." Conscience is the "special psychical agency" that observes the actual ego and measures it against its own ideal. The actual source of the ego-ideal, however, lies in the child's narcissism.

Freud explains that the actual ego is at first conceived of as the target of self-love, as well as being the possessor of every perfection. When this conception is called into question by the admonitions of others and by the awakening of the child's own critical judgment, however, he then seeks to recover this narcissistic satisfaction by setting up the ego-ideal, "the substitute for the lost narcissism of his childhood, in which he was his own ideal."

Another source of the conscience that is represented, for example, in paranoid delusions of being observed and criticized is "the critical influence of his parents, conveyed to him by the medium of voice." This new agency (which does not appear to be separated into parts, but rather includes a variety of different contents) has a number of functions assigned to it, in addition to those of self-observation and self-criticism. These include the dream censorship and also, in keeping with what was on Freud's part at that time a leaning toward the more conscious topographic position of the agency, such functions as subjective memory and the time factor. In the paper on "The Unconscious" (1915), the latter aspects of the reality sense and the secondary process were assigned to the "system preconscious."

The part played in the formation of the ego-ideal by idealization and by the attribution of omnipotence to the parents, along with the subsequent devaluation of these objects—later emphasized by Jacobson and Annie Reich—does not seem to have been stressed by Freud. It may be, as in his remarks in the paper on his visit to the Acropolis (see later), that he viewed this devaluation as occurring later in childhood, during the oedipal and latency periods.

In this same paper ("On Narcissism"), Freud says that self-regard has an especially intimate dependence on narcissistic libido, the reasons being: the primary residue of infantile narcissism; that which arises out of the sense of omnipotence, as corroborated by experience, and is here called the "ego ideal"; and finally, that which results from the satisfaction of object libido —the return of love. The feeling of inferiority that is found in neurotics, Freud believed, was the result of the impoverishment of the ego, which was in turn due to the withdrawal of libidinal cathexis from the self and its displacement onto the loved objects. The neurotic, being at one and the same time incapable of fulfilling his ego-ideal, and possessed of an impoverished ego, seeks a way back to narcissism (self-regard) by choosing an object on a narcissistic basis—that is, someone who possesses the excellences that he himself has never had. In reference to the choice of a narcissistic love object, Freud described a "cure by love" which, he said, entered into the transference.

In 1916 Freud published a paper on "Some Character Types Met with in Psychoanalytic Work"; characteristic of these "types" was that conscience had played a major role. In the first of these—the exceptions—the neurosis was always connected with some experience to which the patient had been subjected in early childhood; in regard to it he knew himself to be guiltless, and he could therefore look upon it as a disadvantage that had been unjustly imposed upon him. Like Richard III, he could thus either justify the wrong that he now did, or else he could refuse altogether to accept the reality principle, on the grounds that he had already suffered enough. In keeping with his view of feminine psychology, Freud added that the claim by women "to exemption from so many of the importunities of life" rests upon the same foundation, although he did not use this argument later in explaining the difference he felt existed in the feminine superego. In the second type, "Those Wrecked by Success," the fantasy that has all along been tolerated at length becomes intolerable to the ego, precisely when it is approaching fulfillment. It is the "forces of conscience which forbid the subject to gain the hoped-for advantage." In the paper on his visit to the Acropolis, Freud compared the feeling of something being "too good to be true" with this sense of guilt about success. In the third type, called "Criminals from a Sense of Guilt," a preexisting feeling of guilt finds relief in the commission of a forbidden act; this relief is also due to displacement of the occasion for guilt onto a lesser crime.

The main thread of the argument is taken up once again in the paper on "Mourning and Melancholia" (1917), the theme of which is that the self-reproaches of the melancholic are in actuality derived from reproaches toward and hatred of the lost object, this being due to the fact there has been an identification of the ego with that object. "The conflict between the ego and the loved person is transformed into a cleavage between the critical activity of the ego and the ego as altered by identification" (p. 249). This critical agency, he says, will be found to show its independence in other circumstances as well, and to become ill on its own. The dynamics of that illness, melancholia—later to be described as being similar to the mechanism of the formation of the superego—is that, from the original ambivalent narcissistic object ca-

· 15

thexis, one part of the libidinal cathexis has regressed to identification and another part to the stage of sadism. Identification, here as later, is regarded as being the preliminary stage of object choice, the first way in which the ego shows its choice of an object—that is, by seeking to incorporate it into the self, in keeping with the oral, cannibalistic phase of libidinal development.

The next important discussion of this question by Freud (1921) is to be found in the book, *Group Psychology and the Analysis of the Ego.* Here Freud concluded that the bond among members of groups is based upon the identification in the ego as well as upon the bond to the leader. The latter has developed through the giving up to him of the function of the ego-ideal—a process that is described as replacing the ego-ideal with the group ideal, which is now embodied in the leader, or as putting the object in place of the ego-ideal.

The postulate of the ego-ideal is here put forth firmly. As in other instances, Freud anticipates that this addition to theory will have to be justified in terms of its explanatory value in all areas of psychology. The sense of guilt, as well as a sense of inferiority must be understood, he says, as an expression of the tension between ego and ego-ideal. In mania the two become fused together as the result of a rebellion on the part of the ego; there is a feeling of triumph when something in the ego corresponds with the ego-ideal. Freud anticipated that much of significance would be derived from the idea that the ego can enter into an object relation with the ego-ideal, and that the interplay between them may duplicate what takes place between the external object and the ego as a whole.

The conception of the formation of the ego-ideal rests upon the concept of identification, to which Freud devotes in this monograph a separate chapter on individual psychology; in it he also brings the ego-ideal into the relationship with the Oedipus complex. "Identification is known to psychoanalysis," he says, "as the earliest expression of an emotional tie with another person" (1921, p. 105); he is here referring to the little boy's wish to grow up and be like his father, a wish that prepares the way for the later emergence of the Oedipus complex. At the same time, or later, the boy

16 ·

develops a sexual object cathexis toward his mother; then when the "irresistible advance toward a unification of mental life" occurs (the synthetic function of the ego), these two are brought together. The original ambivalent attitude in the identification with the father now tends to be narrowed down to the hostile component, and identification behaves on the model of the oral-cannibalistic phase of the libido, in its urge both to annihilate the object and to assimilate it by eating.

To illustrate the pathological operation of identification, Freud uses the case of Dora: on the one hand, she identified with the suffering of her mother under the influence of a sense of guilt arising out of her seeking to fulfill her Oedipal wishes; on the other hand, she imitated her father's cough through an identification that here took the place of object choice, having been brought into being through introjection. Freud asks himself whether or not the presence of identification is an indication that object cathexis has been given up; to this he replies that the choice of answer may rather be between whether the object is put in place of the ego or in place of the ego-ideal. The latter, he says once again, stems from the original narcissism; but now he adds that "it gradually gathers up from the influences of the environment the demands which that environment makes upon the ego and which the ego cannot always rise to."

In some forms of object choice—as, for example, falling in love— in which the object takes the place of an unattained ego-ideal, the functions of the latter agency cease to operate in reference to the object. The functions that are here assigned to the ego-ideal include "self-observation, the moral conscience, the censorship of dreams and the chief influence in repression." Freud adds also that he had previously omitted placing among these functions, but now wishes to include among them, the business of testing the reality of things; he says that he is doing so in order to explain, for example, the absence of criticism toward, and instead the subjection to, the reality sense of the hypnotist. In *The Ego and the Id* (1923), the function of reality testing is attributed without further discussion to the ego.

The Ego and the Id represents the culmination of these formulations. The two discoveries, says Freud, that brought into question the previously accepted coincidence of the ego with the preconscious and with consciousness, and thus led to structural reformulations, were: first, the resistance that stems from the ego during analysis; and second, the unconscious sense of guilt. Chapter III, entitled "The Ego and the Super-Ego (Ego Ideal)," is devoted to Freud's final conclusions about the genesis of the superego, which is here described as being the heir to the Oedipus complex.

As far as the basic processes are concerned, Freud (1923) says, basing himself on the model of the process in melancholia, especially during the early phases of development, "it may be that identification is the sole condition under which the id can give up its objects" (p. 29). However, he also says that there are cases of simultaneous object cathexis and identification, in which the alteration of the ego has been able to survive the emergence of the object relation, and even in a sense to conserve it. From the economic point of view, the transformation of object libido into narcissistic libido implies an abandonment of sexual aims, a "desexualization." In addition, he declares, there is an instinctual defusion, in that the "erotic component no longer has the power to bind the whole of the destructiveness that was combined with it" (p. 54), and the aggression is turned against the ego (self).

The ego-ideal derives, says Freud, from identification with the parents. In this connection, he uses the boy's identification with his father, which takes place earlier than the development of object cathexis, but is then reinforced by the identifications that are the outcome of what Freud calls the object choices of the first sexual period, that of the Oedipus complex. And referring to the intensifying of identification with the mother as being essentially similar, he adds "or the setting up of such an identification for the first time." In this regard he underscores the human being's bisexuality, as well as the existence of the complete positive and negative Oedipus complexes, the outcome of which is the "forming of a precipitate in the ego, consisting of these two identifications with father and mother, in some way united with each other."

The relation to the ego, Freud says, is no longer only in terms of the demanding "you *ought to* be"; it is also, and more momentously, in terms of the forbidding "you *may not* be such-and-such" (for example, "like your father" [1923, p. 34])—a prohibition that results in the repression of the Oedipus complex. He then goes on to say that one consequence which persists even after these conflicts have been mastered is that the ego has "placed itself in subjection to the id." By contrast with the ego, which Freud calls the representative of the external world, the superego is also the representative of the internal world of the id, including its archaic heritage. This closeness to the instincts, he says, explains why the superego remains, to so great an extent, unconscious and hence inaccessible to the ego.

The ultimate source of the birth of the superego, says Freud, is first of all biological; it is a function of the lengthy duration of man's childhood helplessness. The second factor (an historical one) is the Oedipus complex and the interruption of childhood sexuality by the latency period, which is derived from man's cultural past. The special position of the superego, in terms of its power, he says, is based on the fact that it is the *first* identification, the one that takes place at a time when the ego is still feeble.

On several occasions, Freud asks why it is that the superego manifests itself essentially as a sense of guilt or criticism—that is, as a sadistic attitude. He also raises the related question of why it is that the more firmly a man checks his aggression against the external world, the more severe, that is, aggressive, he becomes in his ego-ideal. At this point his answer to both these questions is chiefly in terms of instinctual defusion. In other places (1930), however, he answers in terms of the projection of the child's aggression and his identification with the parents' superego.

With reference to anxiety, he points out that the superior being who has become converted into the ego-ideal had once threatened castration; it is this threat that is probably the nucleus around which the fear of conscience has gathered.

As for the auditory source of the superego, he says that "for the superego, as for the ego, one cannot disclaim its origin from things heard." These structures become accessible to consciousness chiefly by way of word-representations.

In the subsequent paper on "The Economic Problems of Masochism" Freud (1924a) asserts that the unconscious sense of guilt was earlier stated incorrectly, and now should be changed to "a need for punishment." In discussing the negative therapeutic reaction, he separates it from moral masochism. In the latter, he indicates, morality has become sexualized—that is, it has regressed to the Oedipus complex—and he emphasizes that in this case it is the ego's masochism that is important, even though it is kept hidden. The masochistic fantasies are now displaced onto "destiny": one performs sinful actions that must be expiated by way of the reproaches of a sadistic conscience. In order to provoke this punishment, the individual has to act against his own interests (1924a, p. 169).

In the papers on "The Dissolution of the Oedipus Complex" (1924b) and "Some Psychical Consequences of the Anatomical Distinctions Between the Sexes" (1925) Freud asserts that because, in the girl, the Oedipus complex escapes the fate that it meets with in the boy, and is instead only slowly abandoned, the resulting superego is "never so inexorable or so independent in its emotional origins." On the strength of this, he explains that what is ethically normal for women is different from what is ethically normal for men, in that the former reveal less of a sense of justice and are "less ready to submit to the exigencies of life." In this same regard, however, he also says that "variations in the chronological order and in the linking up of these events"—that is, of the Oedipus complex—are bound to have an important bearing on the development of the individual.

In the monograph *Inhibitions, Symptoms and Anxiety,* Freud (1925) defines the final stage in the developmental series of danger situations as being derived from the superego, here called "moral anxiety." He also includes in this category "social anxiety"—the fear of separation and of expulsion from the horde. This fear, he says, applies only to the later portion of the superego, which has been formed on the basis of social prototypes (although in other places he had asserted that such identifications do not form a part of the superego). Fear of the superego is finally transformed into fear of death; this takes place when it is projected onto the powers of destiny. "What the ego regards as danger and responds to with the anxiety signal, is that the superego should be angry with it, punish it, or cease to love it" (pp. 139-140). This conception of anxiety as rooted in the fear of separation, the fear of the loss of love or of abandonment, in addition to castration anxiety, as located in the superego, was derived, as Strachey points out, from Freud's later study of female sexuality.

In discussing obsessional neurosis from a structural point of view, Freud says that the superego, originating as it does out of the id, cannot dissociate itself from anal-sadistic regression or from defusion of instinct, and that it is this fact that explains its harshness in that illness.

In the paper on "Humor," Freud (1927) postulates that there is displacement of a great quantity of cathexis from the ego to the superego, and that the latter, having been thus inflated, is able to look upon the sufferings of the ego as being somewhat trivial, in much the same way as a parent treats lightly the pain its child feels, in an effort to console it. This is described as a temporary regressive phenomenon, which also includes the repudiation of reality by the superego in the service of "an illusion." It is also, Freud says, a triumph of narcissism, underscoring the invincibility of the ego, as in mania. Freud states explicitly that, although in other connections the superego is known as a severe master, in humor it "speaks such kindly words of comfort." This he considers to be not incompatible with the superego's source in the "parental agency."

The next set of Freud's (1930) comprehensive formulations on the superego are found in the book, *Civilization and Its Discontents.* Here he argues that the most important means by which civilization sets itself against the aggression inherent in man, which is so dangerous to it, is by having that aggression taken over by the superego, which then turns it onto the self. The attainment of this mastery of aggression is expressed in the sense of guilt, which cannot stem from the ego itself, since what is prohibited may indeed be pleasurable to the ego. Rather, it has its origins in the fear of loss of the love of those people upon whom the child is dependent—a loss that would not only deprive him of protection against a variety of dangers, but might also entail the danger of punishment from those same powerful persons. The child first attempts to keep himself from doing what is called bad, since to do that may bring upon him both loss of love and punishment; then he feels guilty for having had the *intention* to do exactly that.

The first stage of this sense of guilt, which is derived from fear of the loss of love from the external object, Freud calls "social anxiety"; in his eyes, it is not yet conscience. In a second stage, the authority is internalized and presses for punishment because of the continued existence of the forbidden wishes, despite the fact that they have been renounced. However, Freud asserts that side by side with this second stage of the introjected superego there still persists the original infantile prestage of conscience—which explains why external misfortune can heighten the demands of conscience, since such misfortune supposedly indicates that the person is no longer loved by the parent-substitute, fate or destiny. He explains here that conscience arises through suppression of the child's aggressiveness against the authority that prevents him from fulfilling his wish, and that the superego is subsequently reinforced by each succeeding suppression. The earlier theory that the aggressiveness of the superego was originally the counterpart to the aggressiveness of the object is, he says, not incompatible with this idea, insofar as the child's vengeful aggressiveness will be determined at least in part by the extent of the punitive aggression he anticipates.

Freud maintains that the sense of guilt is rooted in the perception that the ego has of being watched and assessed in relation to the superego's demands. The need for punishment is an instinctual manifestation of the ego, which has become masochistic under the impact of the sadistic superego. That is to say, one portion of the instinctual drive toward self-destruction that is present in the ego is now employed to form an erotic attachment to the superego. Remorse is the ego's reaction to a sense of guilt that contains "the sensory material of the anxiety, in itself a punishment." Remorse, which is conscious, like the fear of external authority, is older than conscience. Before the internalization of the superego, the sense of guilt coincided with remorse, both of them being related to an act of aggression that has *already been carried out.*

In this work *(Civilization and Its Discontents)* Freud presents the view that it is frustration of the *aggressive* drive, not of the erotic drive, that results in a heightened sense of guilt. (In the latter case, what occurs is only that its frustration calls up an aggressiveness that then becomes operative.) However, he says, clinical material can provide no unequivocal answer to this question, because the two categories of instinct hardly ever appear in pure form, isolated from each other. A useful simplification of the theory, he asserts, might be to say that when an instinctual trend undergoes repression, its libidinal elements are turned into symptoms, while its aggressive components are turned into the sense of guilt. The latter, of course, are also always present in the symptom and fortify it by making use of it for purposes of self-punishment.

In Lecture 31 of the *New Introductory Lectures,* Freud (1933b) makes certain statements, in summarizing, that are either ambiguous or have been contradicted in other places in his own writings. He says, for example, in referring to conscience as one of the functions of the superego, that self-observation must be one of its activities, since this is necessary as a preliminary to the "judicial aspect of conscience." Later, he says that "the superego seems to have made a one-sided selection and to have chosen only the harshness and severity of the parents, their preventive and punitive functions, while their loving care is not taken up and continued by it." Still further on he says that "when the Oedipus complex passes away, the intense object cathexis of the parents must be given up," and it is in order "to compensate for this loss of object" that the child's identification with his parents becomes intensified.

At the time of the Oedipus complex, Freud declares, the parents seem to the child to be splendid figures; it is only later on that they lose a good deal of their prestige. While identifications with these "later editions" of the parents affect the ego, they have no influence upon the superego.

Freud concludes that it is exceedingly difficult to distinguish between the sense of inferiority and the sense of guilt, and suggests that one might regard inferiority feelings as being the erotic complement to the sense of moral inferiority, in keeping with the fact that the child feels inferior when it perceives that it is not loved.

Once he has posited this special function of restriction and rejection, he asserted, he would then go on to say that repression is the work of the superego—"either it does its work on its own account, or else the ego does it, in obedience to its orders."

Two specific points are taken up by Freud in later papers. In "A Disturbance of Memory on the Acropolis," Freud (1936) described an unexpected visit to Athens, during which, upon seeing the Acropolis, he thought, "So this really does exist, just as we learned at school" (p. 241). This strange doubt he connected with a thought that he had arrived at prior to his going to Athens, at a time when he had not yet achieved that ambition—namely, that it "would be too good to be true." The latter thought had itself been an attempt to repudiate a piece of reality. When the wish was indeed fulfilled, however, he then needed another such attempt; this said, "What I see here is not real," thereby displacing his disbelief in his actually ever getting to see it onto the question of whether or not it actually existed. He concluded that the impetus for this defense was the guilt he felt about having so outdistanced his father in life, and that this was in turn related to the undervaluation of his father that had replaced his overvaluation of the latter, during his early childhood. In addition, he said, his guilt arose from his piety toward his father, who, being without the necessary education, would not have felt the significance of the Acropolis as he, Freud, did.

In his last work, *An Outline of Psychoanalysis,* Freud (1940) says that, in the transference, the patient gives to the analyst the power that his superego already exercises over his ego and, as a result, "the new superego now has an opportunity for a sort of after-education of the neurotic. It can correct blunders for which his parental education was to blame" (p. 175). Nevertheless, he goes on to warn the analyst not to use this position in such a way as to crush the patient's individuality. Whether we regard a case as light or severe, he says, depends on two factors: the sense of guilt, and the need to be ill (both of which are influenced by "deep-going modifications in its instinctual economy"). The resistance that arises from the superego, he points out, does not interfere with the intellectual work, but rather "makes it ineffective." The analyst, he says, is therefore obliged to restrict himself to making conscious the need to suffer, and "attempting thereby the gradual demolition of the hostile superego."

II

A vigorous discussion, on a subject that still remained a concern of Freud's as late as 1940 in the *Outline*, had already got under way among psychoanalysts about 1925. It seems to have been prominent in the 1930s, but the topic has since then rarely been regarded as self-contained; namely the role of the superego in psychoanalytic treatment, especially in regard to cure.

In 1925, Franz Alexander presented a paper, "A Metapsychological Description of the Process of Cure," in which he stated that the superego, once formed, takes over the function of inner perception, as well as the dynamic task of regulating instinctual life. It acts, he said, in two ways: first, by inhibiting behavior that is at present ego-syntonic, but which it mistakenly equates with past forbidden activity; second, by permitting, through self-punishment, only autoplastic symbolic gratification of the condemned wishes, by way of the symptom.

The superego, which he called "an anachronism in the mind," has to be eliminated and the ego put in its place. This takes place in the transference, by way of the fact that the analyst takes over the role of the superego and then, after "working through," shifts that role back to the patient's conscious ego; in this way the new analyst-superego produces an accurate testing of reality through the reliving of the past.

James Strachey (1923), in "The Nature of the Therapeutic Action of Psychoanalysis," indicated his belief that there are two reasons why the superego occupies the key position in analytic therapy: on the one hand, it is that part of the patient's mind that is especially susceptible to the analyst's influence; on the other hand, it is also that part of the mind whose favorable alteration would be likely to lead to general improvement. He argues that, as a result of the peculiarities of the analytic situation, the introjected imago of the analyst tends to be separated off from the rest of the patient's superego as an "auxiliary superego"; this is milder than the former and, more importantly, it is based upon real and current considerations.

The therapeutic effectiveness of this auxiliary superego—that is, of "the analyst's essential function"—is endangered by the patient's tendency first to project the terrifying superego image onto the analyst and then to reintroject it. According to Strachey, crucial work of analysis lies in what he referred to as "mutative interpretation": the patient is made aware, during the course of the transference, of the fact that an id impulse is being directed toward an archaic fantasy object that has become the harsh superego, rather than toward a real analyst or an auxiliary superego.

The Marienbad Congress in 1936, at which a Symposium took place on the theory of therapeutic results, was concerned chiefly with a discussion of the role of the superego. Glover (1937), in his introduction to the Proceedings, asserted that modification of the superego had long been regarded as the essential factor in therapeutic success; it is brought about essentially by "fresh introjections." Nunberg (1937) argued that identification with the analyst's superego takes place because the patient is seeking an ally against his own superego, at a time when forbidden instinctual derivatives are thrusting themselves into consciousness. He also thought that one important factor was the displacement of aggressive energy from the superego to the ego, and its utilization for mastery of the external world instead of for self-punishment.

Edward Bibring (1937), by contrast with other discussants, argued that the change in the superego is the result of the new solution to childhood conflicts that is arrived at through the analysis of the ego's resistances; this entails secondarily the coming into existence of a healthier superego. He described the analytic situation as the creation of a group of two, in which the loving and beloved leader takes over the superego's functions, thereby eliminating the necessity for these in the follower. Once this has occurred, the influence of objectivization and of genetic reduction can lead to the resolution of the archaic superego's demands through interpretation.

He further pointed to the contradictions within the patient's superego—for example, between the aggressive and the kindly portions, or between the fantastic and the reality-oriented portions—that require resolution through the analytic work. In the analysis, he says, it is the frustration and the continual experience of separation from the analyst that leads to the reintrojection of the projected superego—an aspect of analysis that was recently considered by Stone (1961), but without his placing any emphasis on the superego.

It was Bibring's opinion that changes in the superego are often difficult to achieve, because it is in the relationship between superego and ego that "every institution can experience gratification to an extent that amounts to a close system." He also believed that too great an aggressive discharge via the superego may prevent the ego from cooperating in the cure.

Lewin (1950), in his monograph on *The Psychoanalysis of Elation,* points out that, in these theories, cure is described as taking place by the same dynamic means as are utilized in recovery from a depression. Freud had, in fact, compared the working-through process in mourning with the process of the same name in analytic therapy. However, the emphasis in the latter, said Lewin, is upon *reality*-testing—separating the *true* from the *false*—rather than as it is in depression, where, despite the fact that the mourner is "in analysis with his superego," it is a *morality*-testing that is involved—separating the *good* from the *bad.* In addition he points out that, in the therapeutic working-through process there may be, as one part of the superego's role in neurosis, an actual depression. He also regards the negative therapeutic reaction as a depressive equivalent.

An area of increased understanding in clinical psychoanalysis that was one consequence of the development of the superego concept was the elucidation of the "fate" or "destiny neurosis" during the '20s and '30s, by such writers as Alexander (1923, 1930) and Helene Deutsch (1932): the self-producing of an unkind fate was found to be linked with the functioning of the superego. A further refinement in this area was supplied by Alexander in his concept of the "corruptibility" of the superego, according to which the superego is bribed, by means of the acceptance of one punitive action, to permit the gratification of another instinctual drive. Subsequently, Loewenstein (1945), in a paper on "A Special Form of Self-Punishment," described an opposite mechanism, in which the achievement of the self-punishment aim of the superego is fulfilled through the ego's arousal of a repressed drive.

Another area of discussion that was stimulated by the developing theory of the superego was concerned with the dynamics and genetics of the related affects. In recent times, these have come to be spoken of as "shame and guilt," but during the 1930s they were referred to as "guilt and inferiority feelings"—the title of a paper written by Alexander in 1937. In that paper he defined guilt feeling as the fearful expectation of deserved suffering for the commitment of certain acts; this results in inhibiting the discharge of the forbidden impulses, which are probably solely of a destructive nature. A fundamental sense of justice is required as a basis for the sense of guilt, in that the punishment is regarded as being deserved only because the outward aggression is unjustified; otherwise, even aggression in the service of self-defense would be impermissible. In contradistinction, inferiority feelings, says Alexander, are based upon the making of a simple comparison in which one fails.

Self-criticism as such does not require a sense of justice; also, its effect on hostile aggression may be stimulating rather than inhibitory. The word "shame," asserts Alexander, can be applied to both feelings, the distinction between them arising out of what is needed to overcome each: increasing one's ambitious competition or atoning and suppressing. Guilt feelings, accordingly, derive from the structural differentiation of the mental apparatus, whereas inferiority feelings stem from deeper or earlier conflicts —the contrast being defined here in terms of the progressive wish to grow up versus the regressive pull toward dependency.

The same issue was taken up once again by Piers and Singer (1953) in a book entitled *Shame and Guilt*. In it they say that shame, to which the greater amount of attention should be given,

ought to be clearly differentiated from guilt: the former arises out
of the tension between ego and ego-ideal, the latter out of the tension between ego and superego. The fear associated with feelings
of shame is the fear of contempt and, on a deeper level, of
abandonment—what they call "death by emotional starvation";
this is contrasted with the fear of castration, which is involved in
the sense of guilt. The ego-ideal, they assert, represents the sum
total of the positive identifications with the parental images and
therefore contains a core of narcissistic omnipotence. Later
identifications, which are especially important in determining
one's *social* role, also enter into the ego-ideal. In addition, it contains certain goals of the ego, which the two authors relate to the
concept of mastery, concluding that the successful exertion of this
drive to mastery, in accordance with the ego-ideal, is accompanied by "pleasure in functioning."

They offer many examples of intrasystemic conflict, in reference
to superego contents as they define them, which show an antago-
nism between guilt and shame; for example, they indicate that the
moral masochist accepts shameful humiliation in order thereby to
buy off the sadistic superego. As do others, Piers and Singer place
the genetic origin of shame at an earlier period of life, and tie it in
with body function and body performance.

Edith Jacobson (1946, 1964) has elaborated an extensive theory
of the superego. She too argues for distinguishing between shame
and guilt, although in her view shame does become partly integrated into the superego—for example, in moral shame. Along
with others she concludes that shame develops at a more
primitive—that is, earlier—time, and consequently involves more
of the individual's narcissistic conflicts and anxieties. In terms of
functioning, her belief is that guilt feelings show greater reference
to our social *relations to the world*, whereas shame has to do
mainly with the *relation to our own selves*, even in the situation
of moral shame. As an affect, shame is induced by dependent,
masochistic, feminine strivings, whereas guilt feelings are more
closely related to aggressive leanings, both sexual and other.

An important point is the distinction she makes between the
ego-ideal, as part of the superego, and what she calls "ego goals."

She considers a moral factor to be a *sine qua non* for ego-ideal superego functioning; if perfectionism or idealization is to be included, it must be distinguished carefully from pure ambition. In pathological states, which can be considered from the standpoint of regression, grandiose ambitious fantasies may invade both the superego and the ego goals. It must be borne in mind that in such states the differentiation of the psychic systems may become less clear; the fantasies referred to can be regarded as forerunners of both superego and ego goals. The superego's regulatory function with regard to the ego also applies to the ego goals, which may be more easily invaded by such fantasies when they are not under stable superego regulation.

Jacobson pointed out that gratification of fantasies of ambitious success may result in self-esteem, which is derived from an ego goal, and yet at the same time arouse moral conflicts in the superego—that is, between the ego goals and the superego. Finally, she states that, in her experience, people with primitive grandiose ambitions tend to suffer from both shame and identity conflicts, and that, in this regard, a stable and effectively functioning superego seems to be protective. She illustrates this last point by calling attention to the fact that manic-depressive persons tend not to suffer from fear of the loss of identity; by contrast, in schizophrenics, among whom such fears are quite prominent, there is often regressive dissolution of the superego—which may be externalized and completely transformed, for example into homosexual conflicts, even in cases where ego functioning remains good.

What some call an "ideal," as Annie Reich (1960) does—for example, to be the most potent lover or the wealthiest person of all—Jacobson would call an ambitious ego-ideal, which is not part of the superego, and may give rise to conflicts with it. Such ambitious fantasies as these, Jacobson feels, are kept in check by the superego. It is her opinion, by contrast with Reich, that these early fantasies do not normally survive; when they do, they still remain undifferentiated within the ego. She regards both ego-ideal and superego as reactive formations, rather than viewing them in terms of the fulfillment of wishes. Freud too, she believes, held that the ego-ideal is entirely a moral institution, once it is fully formed. In his (1914) paper on "Narcissism," Jacobson emphasizes, Freud said that the ego-ideal contains the old narcissism of the child; he himself, as his ideal, may survive in the ego-ideal, and he may choose an object on these grounds. In the mature superego, on the other hand, idealization is based on moral grounds and not on the grounds of power.

While a sense of primitive power is the forerunner of both ego goals and superego, Jacobson believes that confusion is likely to arise if one does not distinguish between them. Guilt, she says, represents a conflict between the superego and the ego, including the latter's ego goals. The regulations of self-esteem and inferiority feelings can stem wholly from the ego, and they may or may not produce a conflict with the superego. Intrasystemic conflicts also exist in the superego among various moral demands; in pathological instances, the forerunners of such conflicts may enter into the superego, and there may then be conflict between these regressive contents and the rest of the superego.

Herman Nunberg (1932) presented a theory of the superego that is somewhat at variance with more recent formulations: he prefers to make a distinction between feelings of guilt and the need for punishment. For the origins of the superego, which is involved in both, he goes back to the discussion in *Totem and Taboo;* this is based upon the ambivalence toward the father, together with his destruction and incorporation via an actual cannibalistic act. Nunberg seems to postulate equivalent fantasies or methods of functioning in the developing child, both prior to and following the resolution of the Oedipus complex.

From the fact that the schizophrenics he studied showed an *increase* in the sense of guilt during the phase of identification, which then *diminished* during the phase of restitution, he concluded that, in the earlier phase, the sense of guilt arose out of the fantasy of destroying and incorporating, which has its counterpart in the child's incorporation of the parents into the superego by way of all his sense organs. This incorporation then gives rise to a feeling of guilt which Nunberg defines as "ungratified object libido"; the individual seeks reconciliation through a restitutional act, such as making a gift, giving birth to a child, or reviving a destroyed object—the father, in the case of religion—in order to love him again.

The earliest onset of the feeling of guilt, he says, takes place during the anal phase, when the child gives up his cherished possession, the feces, out of fear of the loss of love; the feeling of guilt is here closely linked with the fear of loneliness. This is originally, Nunberg suggests, an intestinal sensation, which occurs at the same time as the process of identification. By contrast, the need for punishment is derived from the aggressive-destructive drive and is supposed to produce atonement. The destructive drive, originally fantasied with regard to the father—out of the wish, says Nunberg, to reproduce the crime (that is, the crime of both killing and swallowing the father), to *repeat* the crime rather than to *undo* it—is now turned onto the self. His explanation for this *need for* punishment—he sees it that way rather than as the *fear of* punishment—is that libidinal investment also makes its appearance, with the result that "the ego *enjoys* the sadism of the superego" (italics added). Escape from this need for punishment can be obtained only through labor, he says—for example, by way of the work of analyses.

Nunberg presents a strong argument for the important role of the superego in reality-testing; for example in states of depersonalization, one part of the ego perceives, yet the *reality* of its perception is not accepted by another part of the ego. The recognition of reality and the individual's adaptation to it is, according to Nunberg, dependent on the superego, which takes a position with regard to the ego's experiences and has to sanction them if they are to become fully real. It is for this reason that denial of reality—that is, not telling the truth—is regarded as immoral. Although this agency of the ego obtains its impressions —a kind of perception of the inner life, at second hand—via the ego, it participates directly in the determination of what is real. Something similar, he says, takes place during hypnosis, when the hypnotist, acting from the position of the superego, is able to *dictate reality* to his subject.

Nunberg argues repeatedly for the operation of libidinal forces, as well as aggressive ones, in the superego. The earliest acceptance of restrictions on instinctual life, he says, is based upon love, and consists essentially of identifying with the parents' wishes. The ego-ideal is the image of the loved objects, which is cathected with desexualized libido, and derived predominantly from the child's relationship with the mother. The ego tolerates as much as it does at the hands of the superego because ultimately the latter also furnishes it with love and protection.

These ideas are related to concepts that were originally proposed by Hanns Sachs (1929), in order to explain the role of the superego in women. By contrast with the abrupt end to the Oedipus complex that occurs in the boy with the establishment of the superego, the girl is able, says Sachs, to continue clinging to the father via the positive Oedipus complex. This clinging takes the form of a wish for a child or for the phallus, through oral incorporation. The woman can attain her superego only when she is able to renounce these desires and to accept "deprivation as a lifelong ideal." His case material consisted, in part, of women who had no moral code of their own, but acquired one from their lovers.

Jacobson (1937), in a paper on the female superego, argues against attempting to distinguish between a feminine and a masculine superego, at least on the basis of castration anxiety. She believes that the universal fantasy of an illusory penis results in an equivalent complex. She also raises, as an historical point, the question of whether the phenomena that are generally associated with what has been called the "feminine superego" were not derived from the study of women in an era prior to their emancipation.

The subject is once again pursued by Greenacre (1948) in "Anatomical Structure and Superego Development." She feels that the oral attitude described by Sachs may be a displacement upwards of vaginal sensations, and argues for the probability of early vaginal sensations and of a "castration fear" that is equivalent to that felt by the boy. The differences pointed out by Freud, such as the lesser sense of justice on the part of women, their lesser readiness to submit to the necessities of life and their greater jealousy, as well as the comparative ease with which they can be influenced by their feelings—all these she attributes to the earlier onset of the narcissistic conflicts and also of superego development, during the first phase of the Oedipal struggle involving the mother.

The concept that libidinal energies are available to the superego has been emphasized by several writers in their studies of schizophrenia—in 1949, for example by William L. Pious, in a paper on "The Pathogenic Process in Schizophrenia." His patient's clinical state varied with the mental image held of the analyst at the time. The image was clear and undistorted when the patient was in good contact, but when he was in a psychotic state it became menacing. According to Pious, the earliest source of the superego is the loving and protecting mother image, so needed in childhood to bind aggression. His argument is that, in his patient, it was the superego that had the function of containing aggression, and that it was because the superego was defective that destructive energy flooded the mental apparatus, eventuating in psychosis.

In a paper on hallucinatory experiences by Dr. Arnold Modell (1958), we find the view that hallucinated voices are a reflection of one stage in the prehistory of the superego, and include not only accusatory voices but also helpful and loving ones. The hallucinations seemed to act as substitutes for guilt feelings, which diminished with their appearance as affects. A similar conclusion was reached by Eugene B. Brody (1958) in a paper on "The Superego, Introjected Mother, and Energy Discharge in Schizophrenia." Here the internalized mother image of the preoedipal period, which is considered to be the nucleus of the superego, was predominantly hostile, the loving component being entirely nonexistent.

Paul Kramer (1958), in his "Note on One of the Pre-Oedipal Roots of the Superego," also postulated a benign superego. Without mutual love between the ego and the superego, he says, one would experience *fear* of authority rather than *guilt* toward it (see Alexander, 1938). In the case he presents, there was a developmental absence of this benign superego, which eventuated in a kind of "ignorance in moral matters," a dependence instead upon social convention, and a chronic pessimism. The patient needed the analyst's facial expression, as he had earlier needed his mother's to tell him whether an action was good or bad. During the course of the treatment, however, the patient, who had been until then rather humorless, did develop a sense of humor; the latter, Kramer points out, Freud postulated as being dependent on a loving relationship of superego to ego.

Roy Schaefer (1960) published a paper on "The Loving and Beloved Superego in Freud's Structural Theory," in which he argued for consideration of this neglected aspect of superego functioning. Schaefer says that Freud was compelled to elaborate a theory of a hostile superego primarily because of therapeutic considerations—such as the negative therapeutic reaction—and because of the need to account for the disposition of aggression following instinctual renunciation and frustration. Furthermore, Freud's observations came chiefly, he notes, from cases of obsessional neurosis, melancholia and paranoia, in which both the sense of guilt and the need for punishment are pronounced.

On the other hand, Freud referred specifically to the loving aspect of the superego in three separate areas: in reference to humor, to traumatic neurosis, and to religion. Schaefer (1960) reminds us that guilt is the last in the genetic series of danger situations, and that a traumatic situation can follow from feeling deserted by the superego—for example, in the form of the "powers of destiny." Finally, in his comments on religion and God, Schaefer points out, Freud speaks of a "protection through love, of the need for a protective God-figure who is more powerful than the real father." In *Moses and Monotheism,* Freud (1939 [1934–38]) also says that the ego, after effecting a renunciation, expects to be rewarded for it by being loved all the more; the consciousness of deserving that love is felt as pride.

Schaefer (1960) appears to be suggesting an addition to the content of the ego-ideal, stemming from the conception of the father that is characteristic of the Oedipal period; he quotes Freud to the effect that the father is regarded as being "a great man, decisive in thought, strong of will, self-reliant and independent"—which then becomes an internalized standard. His conclusion is that, in normal development, the superego is not based upon a permanent defusion of libidinal and destructive energies. Furer (1967) discusses identification with the "object-as-comforter" as being a precursor of the benign aspect of the superego.

A special discussion of the superego concept must be reserved for the conception that originated in the English, or Kleinian, school. In "The Early Development of the Conscience in the Child," Klein (1933) says that she discovered that "the superego had been in full operation for some time, in children between 2-¾ and 4 years of age, prior to the dying down of the Oedipus complex." This early superego she found to be immeasurably harsher and more cruel than the one that had been described as developing in later childhood.

Her theory of the superego rests on her theory of anxiety, which says, in brief, that "in order to escape from being destroyed by its own death instinct, the organism employs its narcissistic or self-regarding libido to force the former outward and direct it against objects." The child perceives the anxiety that is produced by this aggression as a *fear* of external objects, both because he has made the object his outward goal and because he has projected onto it. All this occurs during the time when the child is making the earliest oral incorporation of his objects—although, as many critics of Klein have pointed out, this is not clearly distinguished from the formation of the object-representations. These introjects, which are also called superego by Klein, may subsequently be projected and, because of fear of the externalized superego, may cause the child to turn away from the object relationship as such.

At the genital stage, when the child's sadism has been diminished and he has developed some degree of consideration for objects, the superego is altered in the direction of a milder form of conscience, which nevertheless remains able to arouse a sense of guilt. This sense of guilt, however, has its roots in the child's specific unconscious fantasies, during the pregenital phase, of attacking the mother's body; it therefore shows itself later in "tendencies in the child to make good the imaginary damage it has done to its objects." Klein uses an example of this restitution the observation that was made by Spitz (1958) and others—that is, of the two-year-old boy who begins to put together the pieces of wood he has just broken up. This occurs, says Klein, at the time when social feelings are developing.

In many other papers, such as "The Oedipus Complex in the Light of Early Anxieties," Klein (1945) elaborates her ideas of the good and bad imagos, both of the mother's breast and of the father's penis, that enter into what she sees as an intrasystemic conflict within the superego. It is important, however, to take note of the stress she lays upon the importance for the later Oedipus complex of the vicissitudes of preoedipal aggression—specifically, the need for a preponderance of introjections of the "good breast" and "good penis"; this emerges in both sexes as the basis for the establishment of the necessary and beneficial later superego. These arguments are similar to those employed by writers who have studied the superego in schizophrenia.

In a paper on "Psychoanalysis and the Sense of Guilt" (1958), and a subsequent paper on "The Development of the Capacity for Concern", D. W. Winnicott (1963) elaborates upon these theories, returning explicitly to *Totem and Taboo* for his source. Like Klein, he maintains that the capacity for concern and restitution is the product of emotional growth during the preoedipal period; this involves, first, the fusing of love with the primary hatred, and second, the fusing of the image of the object mother—that is, the object of crude instinctual wishes, especially the destructive ones—with that of the environmental mother, who provides security and trust. This then makes for an ambivalence conflict that eventuates in guilt, defined in Winnicott's terms as "the essential fear that hate will overcome love, destruction overcome reparation."

This type of theory of the superego can be combined with the ideas about cure put forward at the Marienbad Symposium, as was done in a discussion of the superego by Edith Weigert (1961). Here the patient's identification with the relatively anxiety-free ego-superego unity of the analyst gradually dissolves the anxieties that are inherent in the images of the original introjected parents. A statement made at this later Symposium on the Superego (1962), by Herbert Rosenfeld of the Kleinian school, accepts the superego and the ego-ideal of the Freudian theory, but argues for the importance of the early superego, pointing out that the complete and uncritical identifications of the latency period—and, I suppose it could also be argued, of the Oedipal period—come into being as ways of warding off the anxiety that would otherwise result from projection of the persecutory early superego.

An interesting paper in this area, by Susan Isaacs (1929), is entitled "Privation and Guilt." In it she quotes Jones (1919), who repeats the same argument in his paper on "The Genesis of the Superego" in 1947, to the effect that the formation of the superego is essentially defensive—that is, it is designed to protect the child from the danger of privation, of lack of gratification, by putting a damper on those wishes that are destined not to be gratified. In his argument and Klein's, it is a wholly internal danger—instinctual tension—and not an external one, such as castration, that is regarded as basic and, in fact, the operative factor in the experiences at the time of superego formation.

In this regard, Isaacs points out that Klein's formulation about the images of the introjected parents being distorted by the projection of pregenital impulses is to be contrasted with Freud's somewhat similar formulations, to the effect that the parental images are altered through the projection of aggressive impulses in the Oedipal situation, and that there is identification with the parents' superegos.

Isaacs raises the question of how guilt can be attributed to functioning in the oral stage—a time when the distinction between the self and the not-self is only rudimentary—by contrast with ego modifications that take place during the phallic phase, as a result of the cathexis of the lost object. She argues that the former introjection is of a different kind, since it is predominantly an aspect of the "me," which may also be reprojected, and also that the privations of weaning and of bowel training heighten the awareness of things "not-me," at the same time that they increase the hatred of the frustrating objects. To quote her explanatory syllogism: "I am afraid of my helplessness before my own sadistic desires because I fear your cruel thwarting."

Let us now turn to some of the more recent contributions to the superego concept. One approach, also present in the study of ego functions and defenses, has been the search for antecedents in the earliest period of childhood. Rene Spitz (1958), in a paper entitled "On the Genesis of Superego Components," expressed his belief that there are three precursors to the later superego: (1) the physical activity of the parent, in attempting to restrict the child or to facilitate its movements; (2) the child's own attempts at mastery, by way of identification with parental actions; and (3) perhaps most important, identification with the aggressor, especially in the form, to begin with, of the "No." These are steps "leading from compliance with parental wishes, via imitation, to the wish to identify with the love object." In reference to these precursors, Spitz also raises the question of why auditory impressions are found to be so important in the superego, since these early precursors tend rather to be involved with those external restrictions and that self-restraining that come about by way of *tactile* and *visual* impressions.

Fundamental to superego functioning, says Spitz, is the function of judgment, the earliest expression of which is the headshaking "No." He traces its development from parental prohibition to a self-directed judgment during the second year of life. At that time one also sees the emergence of role-playing games, representing identification with the idealized powerful parents, as well as other forms of identification with the aggressor. He uses the example Melanie Klein also referred to—the child's not only breaking things into bits, but putting them together again—as the basis for postulating an organizing element of mastery during this age. Spitz emphasizes the ego contribution of mastery in these identifications, as well as the opening of a new avenue for the discharge of aggression and for an increase in autonomy—that is, independence of the objects. Internalization and the sense of guilt, he says, result from the conflict between the aggressive reaction to the prohibition and the libidinal attachment to the love object.

In her discussion in *The Ego and the Mechanisms of Defense*, Anna Freud (1936) pointed out that, at this stage of identification with the aggressor, internalized criticism has not yet been transformed into self-criticism; rather, wrongdoing is dissociated by the child from his own activity, the result being an active assault on the external world. Identification with the aggressor is, at that time, supplemented by the projection of guilt, which she calls a preliminary phase of morality. "True morality begins when the internalized criticism, now embodied in the standard exacted by the superego, coincides with the ego's perception of its own fault" (p. 128).

Another superego precursor that Miss Freud discusses is objective anxiety—that is, anticipation of the suffering that may be inflicted, in the form of punishment, by outside agents. She speaks of "a kind of forepain which governs the ego's behavior, no matter whether the expected punishment always takes place or not." The connection of this pain with reality gradually becomes loosened, and it also comes to be frequently combined with an anxiety that has its origins in fantasy.

In the same work, she also expresses her viewpoint on the role of the superego in defense (repression). She says that a defensive conflict is one in which an instinctual wish that is seeking to enter consciousness is not regarded as dangerous by the ego; yet, since the superego does prohibit its gratification, the ego wards it off: ". . . the ego of the adult neurotic fears the instincts because it fears the superego."

David Beres (1958) discussed early origins in a paper entitled "Vicissitudes of Superego Functions and Superego Precursors in Childhood." In keeping with a very careful definition of the psychic structures in terms of their functions, he points out that the functions of the superego must be regarded in a different light from those of the ego. "Superego is a part of psychic structure that can be defined in terms of attitude, not in terms of action" (p. 327). The superego functions essentially as a way of increasing the ego's capacity for recognizing certain kinds of danger situations.

In presenting cases of severely disturbed children with "arrested psychic development," who show self-attacking behavior, a low self-esteem, and self-accusations, he shows that these are based on mechanisms, derived from disturbances in object relationship, that have resulted in fixation at a level of primitive identification, as well as in a limited capacity for the neutralization of aggression.

In addition to self-punishment, he says, shame, disgust, remorse, unhappiness, humiliation and fear are among the ego responses that may make their appearance with or without the functioning of an internalized superego, although in the developed psychic structure it may not be possible to separate the latter from the ego's defensive reactions.

He would regard these various modifications of the drives, as Freud (1915a) did in "Instincts and Their Vicissitudes," as superego precursors. He also mentions Ferenczi's "sphincter morality," and points out that, at that time in his life, the child, who is learning the difference between the external world and his inner wishes, uses the available ego defenses—such as turning on the self and reversal—to modify his instinctual discharge, because of the danger of loss of love. It is only later in the Oedipal period that a new structure becomes possible. By this time the child has developed the ego functions of reality-testing and thought processes to such an extent that it now becomes possible for him to conceptualize the conflict (he has the concept of time, of the future, and of the consequences of right and wrong—that is, of values). Specific ego functions must first have developed before the structure superego is able to emerge. True depression is rare in childhood, says Beres, precisely because it requires the presence of an intersystemic conflict. While the child may have reactions of great severity, these take other forms, such as profound unhappiness, remorse and apathy.

A similar mode of thinking prevails in a number of earlier papers, such as "On the Exceptional Position of the Auditory Sphere" (1939) and "Spoken Words in Dreams" (1954) by Otto Isakower. In these papers, it is argued that the auditory sphere, "modified in the direction of a capacity for language," is the nucleus of the superego, just as the body ego is the nucleus of the ego. Sense perception and experience, Isakower says, are required for superego formation, and if this were of only an optical sort, without showing the "linguistically ordered structure" that is rooted in language, there could be neither logical nor ethical judgment. These conclusions are based upon his belief that self-observation, which is one form of reality-testing, is "indisputably a superego function," and that, genetically, "correct" or "incorrect," in reference to perception, is not sharply separated from "right" or "wrong," or from "good" or "bad," in the area of self-observation.

The examples he gives are based on experiences of going to sleep; at that time some people hear words of elaborate grammatical structure but with little content, as though the censor or superego was attempting to make its voice heard before being eliminated; also of relevance are the brief auditory phenomena one experiences upon awakening, especially from a dream that had a threatening tone. He further believes that "speech elements in dreams are direct contributions from the superego to the manifest content of the dream," and that the superego is also the carrier of the function of secondary revision. Freud (1914) in his paper "On Narcissism" referred to self-observation as playing a role in dream formation. The role of wakener—or castrator—in reference to sleep and dreams has also been elaborated upon by Lewin (1950).

Some of the most important contributions to clinical psychoanalysis based upon the concept of the superego have been made by Annie Reich, in her studies of narcissistic object choice and self-esteem regulation. These include "Narcissistic Object Choice" (1953); "Early Identifications as Archaic Elements in the Superego" (1954); and "Pathological Forms of Self-Esteem Regulation" (1960). Starting from Freud's conceptions in "On Narcissism," she argues for a stage in the formation of the ego-ideal that is derived from the longing to become like the parents, who are regarded as being omnipotent; this takes place during that period when the child, who has by this time come to recognize his own weakness, endows his parents with the omnipotence he himself has had to forego. These early identifications—especially with envied parental qualities, as represented by a body part (the maternal breast and the paternal phallus)—take place in order to undo narcissistic injuries. They do not, Reich says, lead to a change in the self, nor do they become integrated into the ego; they are instead differentiated from it.

This structure enters later into the structure of the superego that is derived from the Oedipus complex; yet there may be a fixation of the ego-ideal to this stage, or a regressive reactivation of it, especially under the impact of strong castration anxiety. Such superego regression, which Reich observed in her patients, is also accompanied by an ego regression, in which the fluidity of the differentiation between ego and ego-ideal parallels the "easy revival of the mechanism of undoing the separation between self and powerful object." A temporary disintegration of reality-testing accompanies this form of narcissistic functioning, in which the maintenance of self-esteem requires a "total identification" with the fantasied idealized paternal phallus, or the maternal breast. "In cases of insufficient acceptance of reality, the differentiation between ego and ego-ideal may remain diffuse and, under certain conditions, magic identification with the glorified parent, and megalomaniac feeling may replace the wish to be like him" (1953, p. 29).

The drama is enacted through projection of the ego-ideal onto an object; yet the inherent ambivalence also sets in motion a process of devaluation of the object, along with a new cycle, which results in the choice of another object, thereby warding off a depression. Reich makes the point that these early ego-ideal formations are often derived from "openly sexual aspects of the objects," whereas in normal development they are supplanted by ego identifications that contain objective qualities of the object.

It is with regard to these ideas, which contain many references to Ferenczi, that one should quote the relevant portions of the latter's remarks about the oft referred to "sphincter morality." They appear in his paper, "Psychoanalysis of Sexual Habits" (1925):

> The child's identification with its parents has in fact a pregenital preliminary stage, prior to the attempt to measure his genital capacities with that of the parents. He endeavors to out-rival them by means of anal and urethral exploits. The anal and urethral identification with the parents appears to build up in the child's mind a sort of physiological forerunner of the ego-ideal or superego, not only in the sense that the child compares his achievements with the capacities of the parents, but in that a severe sphincter morality is set up which can only be convened at the cost of bitter self-reproach and punishment by conscience [p. 267].

Manuel Furer

There have recently been a number of *comprehensive* formulations of the superego concept—by Edith Jacobson, Jeanne Lampl-de Groot, Joseph Sandler, and Heinz Hartmann and Rudolph Loewenstein.

Following her earlier studies on the effect of disappointment on ego and superego development, Jacobson (1954) says in *The Self and the Object World* that one particular form of aggression—that which has as its aim the devaluation of the object—is of the greatest significance when it is turned upon the self, in the development of the ego-ideal and the superego. She believes that it is the ubiquitous answer to infantile experiences of frustration, having its earliest genetic source in the child's spitting out of unwanted food. This depreciating form of aggression is then enhanced by cleanliness training, as it shifts from the frustrating breast to the child's own feces and from there to his bad behavior. Feelings of disgust and shame, she says, which originate as reaction formations to exhibitionistic wishes, now assist the child in his struggle against forbidden pregenital (and later genital) wishes.

She postulates a developmental hierarchy of values in the child, and believes that it is important to distinguish those modifications of these values that come about under the influence of standards intended for the achievement of instinctual control, from modifications that are connected with the child's narcissistic strivings. The infant's first notions of a "good" or "bad" mother—that is, of a valued or valueless one—are formulated in relation to gratifying or depriving experiences. These notions are then replaced by a new concept of value—that of power versus weakness—as the child comes to recognize his dependency. Pregenital notions of strength revolve around maternal power and oral-anal property; during the Oedipal phase, these give way to the valued phallus. Oedipal strivings finally come to an end because the child's wishes for phallic intactness have become paramount.

Jacobson also points out that this series of disillusionments, as well as the hostility released thereby, can at the same time be used by the ego for the expansion of realistic perceptions of the self and the world, "especially in relinquishing the magic fantasies about the object." The final development of the mature superego

44 ·

is dependent upon maturation of the ego, and especially of its functions of judgment and discrimination—in particular, between self and object. It is also dependent upon drive neutralization, without which the superego "can hardly be distinguished from the magic, unrealistic object- and self-representations" that are its forerunners.

In agreement with Greenacre, Jacobson asserts that the girl child develops a nucleus of the true ego-ideal at an earlier age. This is because of the early onset of the castration conflict, which leads to depreciation both of herself and of her mother. When the girl enters into the feminine Oedipus complex, there is a regressive process in the direction of introjective fantasies about the paternal phallus. These delay the establishment of that internalization and abstraction of ideals that is requisite to ethical codes; instead, there is a reattachment of the ego-ideal to the idealized phallic father.

She disagrees, however, with Freud's (1923) formulations in *The Ego and the Id*, to the effect that the mother is primarily an anaclitic object for the boy. Instead, she declares that, for both boy and girl during the preoedipal period, the mother is the central object of both love and identification. Instead of bisexuality, Jacobson concludes, it is the child's narcissistic strivings that exercise the decisive influence on the direction and choice of ego and superego identifications. These, as has been noted, are first centered on the omnipotent phallic mother and only later upon the powerful phallic father. Furthermore, by contrast with Freud's later formulations, she stresses superego formation as the solution to the ambivalence conflict.

Since the little boy's hostility is greater toward the father, the paternal image is the one that is internalized in the boy. She believes that one can thereby avoid the problems Freud faced in having to regard the giving up of the Oedipal love object as crucial for superego development. Instead, she points out, the child does *not* lose the object but rather preserves it, even though he does give up his previous sexual and aggressive aims with regard to it. Fear of the loss of the rival on whom he depends, as well as narcissistic strivings, determine that the superego will show the impact of paternal influence in both boy and girl; eventually, maternal influence appears in the latter.

With the passing of adolescence, Jacobson believes, there is a further modification, based on the ego's increased capacity for inner reality testing. As a result, self-evaluation may become more and more a function of the ego, and self-esteem may be "expressive of the discrepancy or harmony between the self-representations and the wishful concept of the self, not the same as an ego-ideal. Once established, the affect signal of guilt establishes an even more severe, certainly more universal and uniform power over the ego than castration fear" (p. 131). The superego is also a safety device of the highest order in the regulation of object relations and instinctual forces. She therefore ascribes to it a special contribution to our general character, in its regulating of both self- and object-directed discharge processes, which produces a characteristic mood or level of self-esteem.

Lampl-de Groot (1962) distinguishes between the ego-ideal, which she regards as a gratifying agency, and the conscience, which she considers to be a restricting, prohibiting agency. Both have their origin in "ego functions"—the ego-ideal in hallucinatory wish fulfillment, and the conscience in all forms of internalized parental restrictions. At each step of development, she emphasizes the reality sense that is involved, in that it is recognition of the hopelessness of instinctual wishes that eventuates in superego types of identifications.

Sandler (1960), in a paper "On the Concept of the Superego," reminds us of the contributions of child analysis in this area, especially the point made by Anna Freud (1946)—namely, that the detachment of superego functioning from the actual parents is far from complete, even after the termination of the Oedipal phase. In latency, and certainly in adolescence, said Miss Freud, changes in real object relationships can give rise to very marked changes in the superego. She also referred to the well-known "double standard" of morality maintained by children—one for grownups, the other for their own peers.

Sandler describes the preoedipal, imitative and self-restricting behavioral organization of the child as a "differentiated part of the child's own reality, since, though influenced by the inner world of drives and fantasies, the conflict is based rather upon the child's predictions, often distorted, of parental reaction." The feeling of well-being comes about through the child's identification with the parents, in which there is a conjoining of obeying them and being like them—which also brings their love. While the warning signal of impending punishment, he says, does not deserve to be characterized as guilt, nevertheless the affective state it produces may be identical with what is later referred to as guilt. With the passing of the Oedipus complex, the introjections of the parents become different from the internal parental schema that is already present, because of their ability now to substitute, in whole or in part, for the real object as a source of narcissistic gratification. He also believes that the reason why tender feelings toward the parents can be maintained is that those destructive urges that do enter into this new structure are directed against the self.

The review by Hartmann and Loewenstein (1962), "Notes on the Superego," which was preceded by the paper, "Comments on the Formation of Psychic Structure" by Hartmann, Kris and Loewenstein (1946), presents many carefully considered points of view, aimed at clarification as well as amplification of their theoretical formulations. They emphasize a number of factors with regard to the ego that they regard as important in superego formation: the degree of maturity of the ego at the time, and particularly the development of language; the capacity for self-observation and for objectivization of inner and outer perception; and the potential for sublimation or neutralization. Resolution of the problem of the feminine superego, approached from this point of view, would also emphasize its earlier origin; yet it would stress the lesser degree of ego autonomy, especially in regard to such functions as integration and objectivization. Also believed to be of great importance is the earliest history of aggression; that drive is closely linked, in their theory, with the disposition of the ego to intrasystemic conflicts.

As far as identification is concerned, they make the point that there are probably thresholds of integration—that is, degrees to which identifications become part of "one's own." They state further that the desexualization and the setting free of aggression that Freud said accompanied identification probably does not occur in cases of early identification—for example, in identification with the aggressor—as compared with the sort of identification that involves superego formation.

They call for a careful distinction between superego contents and superego functions, each of which has its own cathexis. They also point out that Freud finally assigned reality-testing unequivocally as a task of the ego, but they insist that this does not imply that fulfillment of that task is not in any way influenced by the superego. While they accept Freud's formulations about the precursors of the ego-ideal, they point out that some degree of importance may be attached to the degree of idealization of the self that survives, as compared with the idealization of the object. However, they hold that these idealizations—which they term "rescue operations for narcissism"—do not have the characteristics that would permit one to call them a system or an agency; they become part of a system in the mental apparatus, and at that only when the superego is already formed.

Applying the concepts of autonomy and change of function to the superego, they assert that the aims finally developed are "to a considerable extent no longer identical with the primitive wishes which played a role in its formation." Autonomy is here being striven for in relation to both the drives and the objects, and, they add, to the ego—as may be seen, for example, in the independence of moral motivation from the ego's self-interest.

In reference to guilt feeling, they emphasize that Freud had originally tried to derive feelings of guilt from ambivalence. While that conflict may help to explain the existence of presuperego guiltlike feelings in the child, this explanation has since been replaced by the more complex formulations in *The Ego and the Id*.

They are reluctant to separate an ego-ideal system from the superego, or to distinguish sharply between such related affects as guilt and shame. Piers and Singer (1953) did make a distinction between the fear of abandonment and the fear of castration, in regard to superego functioning, which was stated in terms of developmental level, but they feel that it can be applied to the dynamics of either affect. They define superego regression as a process in which "early identifications and early object relationships take the place of the contents and the functions of the superego"—as in Freud's description of moral masochism, in which the sexual relationships of the Oedipal phase replace the superego. They add that they would also consider it a regression to a more instinctual mode of energy discharge in the superego, adding the caution that not every submission to the superego is to be taken as an expression of masochism.

In conclusion, although in very recent times consideration of the superego has tended to fall off by comparison with the situation several decades ago, it seems to me that what has been called a conceptual dissolution of the superego has taken place because advances in the theory of ego psychology have shifted our interest rather than because the problems raised earlier in this regard have been resolved.

III

In what follows, an attempt has been made to select some of the psychoanalytic propositions, from Freud and a few others, that have a bearing on questions of ethics—most particularly in regard to those moral issues that involve the larger community, rather than in terms of superego functioning in the individual.

The problem of the nature of moral values is, of course, an ancient one. To paraphrase from Bertrand Russell's (1945) *History of Western Philosophy*: the problem with which *The Republic* begins is that, while Plato thinks he can prove that his ideal Republic is good, a democrat who has accepted the objectivity of ethics may well think that *he* can prove the Republic is bad. Conversely, anyone who agrees with Thrasymachus's position will say that there is no question involved of either proof or disproof; the only real question is whether or not you *like* the kind of State that Plato sets forth. If you do, then it is good for you; if you do not, it is bad for you. If many do while many others do not, the decision cannot be made by reason but only by force, open or concealed.

Russell then goes on to observe that any view that substitutes consensus for an objective standard has, of course, consequences that few would be willing to accept. The ethical innovations that have been introduced by great religious teachers "imply some standard other than majority opinion; but the standard, whatever it is, is not an objective fact, as in a scientific question."

In discussing the Utilitarians, who formulated what is probably the most commonly accepted popular theory of ethics, Russell states by way of summary:

> Ethics is necessary because men's desires conflict. Ethics has a two-fold purpose; first to find a criterion by which to distinguish good and bad desires; second, by means of praise and blame to promote good desires and discourage such as are bad. The specifically ethical part of the Utilitarian doctrine says that those desires and those actions are good which in fact promote the general happiness. This need not be the intention of the action but only its effect [p. 779].

Freud's views in the realm of ethics are to be found no less in his contributions to clinical theory (see Part I) than in his explicit speculations about society and its evolution. His basic moral position is expressed most fully in the discussion of law and society that is contained in his letter, "Why War?" (1933a). The emergence of society under law, he says, came about when domination by the brute violence of a single individual changed to domination by the violence of the community—this latter violence being, as he puts it, "supported by intellect."

What was the path, he asks, that led from one to the other? The violence of the father could be defeated only by the united action of the brothers. For this purpose, however, one psychological condition had to be fulfilled: the union of the majority must be stable and lasting; toward that end it must be maintained by regulations—that is, by laws. But recognition of the community of interests among these rebels, says Freud, at length leads to emotional ties among them, feelings of unity, which then become the true source of their joint strength—that is, of the bonds that sustain society.

Such a community, Freud adds, will undoubtedly be made up of individuals with unequal degrees of power. The "justice" of the community therefore becomes an expression of that inequality: its laws are made by and in the interests of the ruling members. In this situation, the oppressed have to make efforts to achieve greater power, and to see to it that any changes that they succeed in bringing about by this means are incorporated into law.

Referring to the sexual and destructive drives, Freud (1933) remarks that "neither is less essential than the other; the phenomena of life derive from the concurrent or mutually opposing action of both." Anything that encourages the development of emotional, libidinal ties among men must therefore at the same time operate against war. "Thou shalt love thy neighbor as thyself" is one form of expression of such a tie; identification, the sharing of important interests, is another. Freud's hope was, in fact, somewhat akin to Plato's: "The ideal condition of things would, of course, be a community of men [meaning the leaders] who had subordinated their instinctual life to the dictatorship of reason"—a utopian expectation.

Freud concludes his letter with a condensed statement of his ideas about the evolution of culture and, by implication, of his ideals or values. Civilization, for him

> consists in progressive displacement [that is, psychical modifications] of instinctual aims and a restriction of instinctual impulses . . . Of the psychological characteristics of culture, two appear to be most important [that is, in evolutionary development]: a strengthening of the intellect, which is beginning to govern instinctual life, and an internalization of the aggressive impulses, with all its consequent advantages and perils [1933, p. 214].

A cultured or civilized man, Freud says, would of necessity be a pacifist and have a "constitutional intolerance of war."

In his later work, *Civilization and its Discontents*, Freud (1930) says that "Culture obeys an inner impulse which bids it bind mankind into a closely knit mass—which can be achieved only by means of its vigilance in fomenting an ever increasing sense of guilt" (elsewhere, he says, by its directing aggression outward). Eros also aims at "binding together individuals and families, tribes, races and nations into a great unity of humanity." Further, Freud remarks that, during the course of human development, external coercion gradually becomes internalized, and a specific mental agency—the superego—takes over what had previously been the provenance of external commandments. On the other hand, with his customary clear vision, he states that man has not yet reached the level of internalization at which external coercion is no longer necessary, and that therefore one cannot yet rely on man's moral trustworthiness.

It is of interest, in the light of recent experiences in the United States and elsewhere, that Freud points out the necessity of other conditions for internalization. For example, among oppressed people—that is, those who do not share in the wealth of the culture—the internalization of cultural prohibitions is not to be expected. He does, however, add that there is a narcissistic gratification that can be derived from pride in the culture's ideals, and can be shared even by the oppressed, "since the right to despise the people outside compensates them for the wrongs they suffer within their own unit." For this mechanism to operate, however, those in the higher position must be regarded as ideal by those in the lower. This coexistence, in Freud, of pessimism (or realism, as some prefer to call it) and the belief in reason (and in love) is to be found throughout his writing on social matters.

One might say that Freud made three contributions to moral values or ethics. To begin with, as the leader of a dedicated group of therapists and some reformers, he became a model in this regard for those associated with him. His personal character probably still has some influence, even though perhaps an attenuated one, on modern-day analysts and others.

The second area of his influence has to do with the clinical aspects of psychoanalysis itself, and with certain reforming attitudes that necessarily followed from these. The most conspicuous example is his (1908) paper on "Civilized Sexual Morality and Neurosis"; as Hartmann points out, this was written not by a rebel in ethics but rather by a prophet, comparable to one in the Old Testament, who was attempting to make it known that he felt his moral values to be corrupted in his society. The general cultural influence of psychoanalysis in such areas as a more liberal sexual morality, or the child-centered emphasis in modern-day culture, has had its impact upon social ideals. It should be noted, of course, that there were many other influences besides Freud that were instrumental in these same developments.

Freud's third contribution lies in the influence that his clinical insights and his social-historical speculations have had upon ethical thinkers.

In 1957 an eminent teacher of philosophy, Abraham Kaplan, offered the following summary of Freud's impact on moral philosophy: "The critique of conscience as the ground of morality is perhaps the most notable contribution of psychoanalysis to ethics" (p. 220). That contribution is not simply a matter of tracing the development of the moral sense; it is in addition, says Kaplan, the "recognition of its destructive potentialities, both toward the self and toward others, in history under the standard of moral zeal. . . ." Parenthetically Kaplan points out that reductionism— the "genetic fallacy," which says that conscience can be *either* condemned or ignored, once one has unearthed its origins—was hardly an error that can be attributed to Freud, although he has often been accused of just that.

Traditional ethics, as Kaplan describes it, did not take into account the depth and complexity of the conflicts within the personality in matters of morality. At issue here are "the relations between the self which promulgates the moral law, the self which assumes the moral obligation so defined, and the self whose impulses defy these obligations. The integration of these diverse selves cannot be presupposed, as it had been in moral philosophy" (p. 220).

Kaplan thus concludes: "Psychoanalysis allots less freedom than man thought he had, but makes possible more freedom than in fact he had." Man's freedom (by which he means free will) can rest, as Spinoza had earlier insisted, only on self-knowledge, and this is now available through psychoanalysis. Such a formulation, says Kaplan, is in contrast with Kant's dictum that "free will falls outside the realm of scientific reality" (p. 218).

An attempt to arrive at an overall evaluation of the relationship between psychoanalysis and moral values was made in a lecture of that title by Heinz Hartmann (1959). Speaking of Freud himself, Hartmann comments that "He had no urge to go deeper into the question of the validity of moral feelings or judgments" (p. 15). However, "about the necessity of moral codes he repeatedly and clearly expressed his opinion, both in reference to the need for the integration of the individual personality, as well as 'the fact that human society could not live with them' " (p. 15).

Freud's personal moral thinking was characterized by Hartmann as akin to that of the Stoic philosophers, who placed their emphasis on intellectual integrity: "to face reality at all costs." Freud admired, above all, independent, autonomous morality; what he despised was moral weakness and the tendency to compromise. Although Freud himself was a man of remarkably strong moral feelings, and despite the fact that psychoanalysis has had great influence in moral matters, Freud emphatically repudiated any idea that psychoanalysis could itself give birth to a philosophy of life.

Freud's essential contribution in the area of clinical investigation, according to Hartmann, was his delineation of the factors that "bring it about that man is capable of developing directions of a moral nature, ideals or imperatives which are part of his mental functioning." Biologically, this capability rests on the long dependence of the human child on adults; psychologically, it rests on the identifications and object relations that "tie it to its parents," and on the conflicts that arise as a consequence of the child's sexual and aggressive development.

Consistent with the principle of multiple determination is Hartmann's emphasis, not only on the place of the superego in normal functioning, but also on its vulnerability to the drives, especially to aggression. The latter is able to disrupt the integration of the moral system and to turn the individual—depending on many other factors—either to criminality, to self-punishment or to both. From Hartmann's point of view there is, on the one hand, the problem of achieving integration; on the other hand, there is the vulnerability entailed in fixation and in the subsequent regression to sexualization and aggressivization of the superego-ego relationship. As with his theory of the ego, he proposes a concept of *au-*

tonomy of the superego—that is, the "constancy or dependability of morality," vis-à-vis both reality and inner pressures.

A somewhat neglected aspect of moral codes in the work of psychoanalysts has to do with the cultural support of social codes—that is, their support in the society, and not only in adult society but also in that of childhood. In addition, there are complex interrelations between the ego and the environment that influence behavior—for example, conformity to the society may well override a personal ethical code. In what may be an answer to certain philosophies, Hartmann points out that maximal concern with the realization of self-interest does not necessarily provide the most satisfactory solution, from the point of view of psychic effectiveness. As a matter of clinical fact, the resolution of conflict entails taking into account precisely those moral inhibitions that may be directed against what one regards, in terms of the ego, as self-interest and ambition.

He also points out that man's knowledge of his own moral values is derived not from his study of ethical systems, but rather by way of his life experience—including his own analysis. Where individualism finds itself threatened by modern society, Hartmann maintains, it seeks protection in the realization of the individual's ideals as well as of his imperatives; this brings not only an inner sense of being "at one with one's self," but also pleasure or satisfaction. He warns, however, that as a source of motivation, the latter can hardly be compared with the id, in terms of economic or drive power.

Hartmann makes the interesting observation that while, by and large, the general population no longer denies the existence and dynamic significance of the forces of the id, it still does not grasp the psychoanalytic picture of man as including *unconscious moral forces*. One contributing factor to the existence of the latter attitude is the tradition of "considering morals as an unfortunate and burdensome relic of religious or metaphysical systems"; or I may add it may be—to sound a more immediately contemporary note— the abhorrence of ideals that stem from any authority at all.

In reference to ethical theory, Hartmann takes the position that when we say that a good deed has been done, we are making not an empirical statement, but rather a judgment, based on a system of values; further, he believes that one cannot decide the validity of different value systems from any empirical—that is to say, scientific—viewpoint. The same can be said for health values, which are useful in analytic therapy, yet cannot be based on a judgment of validity, in terms of truth of falsity, and cannot be regarded in a purely empirical way as being the most effective basis for a moral system for any given society. He further asserts that, while one cannot determine what is the optimal state of balance between ego interest and moral demands, it is certain that a maximal concern with self-interest does *not* provide the most satisfactory solution. He also points out, in considering the pleasure experiences that are derived from the three subsystems, that moral satisfactions are much less able to replace the gratification of instinctual demands than the other way round.

Hartmann suggests instead that one can speak of values as being authentic or genuine when "in an individual or in a culture they are not only represented in ideas on ethics, but also are recognizable as dynamic factors in the moral aspects of a personality or a culture." Their authenticity is then established as the result of an inner reality-testing, which he calls "value testing." Hartmann points out, as a psychoanalyst, that any system of ethics that disregards the nature of man has much less likelihood of being authentic or, in another sense, effective. In general, the humanistic philosophies have found it easier to integrate analytic findings than have those with taboos against instinctual phenomena.

In discussing why the search for an empirical validation of values nevertheless persists, Hartmann offers a genetic explanation: when moral imperatives are presented to the child, they do not come to him as demands *from one person to another,* but rather as *objectively valid*—and this at a time when the child "is not capable of distinguishing this kind of objectivity from reality."

In sum, Hartmann maintains that psychoanalysis views moral values, imperatives and ideals solely in terms of the processes that went into their making, and with consideration of the interaction of moral valuations with other mental processes and with reality—that is, with sociocultural factors. In this, of course, there is no place for an absolute or objective validity of these values—which necessarily means taking a relativistic position. Viewed in another way, however, psychoanalysis emphasizes the binding power of those individual moral codes that arise out of the individual's history and obtain their dynamic power from that source. The effectiveness or lack of effectiveness of the value systems of any given society ultimately rests upon the results of these genetic developments—which does not rule out a wide range of moral potential for the adult.

In discussing the effects of personal analysis on the power of moral systems, Hartmann says that, in this area, as in other areas of personality, analysis certainly does not obliterate individual differences. The emphasis in the analytic situation is upon integration and effectiveness, which per se calls for making conscious the goals and ideals of the analysand. Clinically, therefore, the tension between ego and superego continues; and the analysis of the previously unconscious fantasies and defenses contributes to the end result, as much as does the analysis of the superego. He quotes Freud (1915) as saying, with regard to the effects of analysis on moral behavior, "Why should analyzed people be altogether better than others? Analysis makes for unity, but not necessarily for goodness" (p. 182). To this Hartmann adds that he believes there are certain commonalities of change in moral codes as a result of analysis—for example, the more relaxed attitude toward sexual behavior, and the placing of a higher value upon the acceptance of outer and inner reality and on intellectual integrity.

Ishak Ramzy (1965), somewhat in contradistinction to Hartmann, and certainly to Freud, feels that psychoanalysis is not only involved in the study of the role that values play in the conflicts of patients; there are also values, either overt or implicit, in various aspects of psychoanalysis itself. For example, psychoanalysis as a science upholds the value of the love of truth, as against submission to authority, and of humility, self-doubt and disinterestedness, as inherent in the scientific method. He regards the belief in determinism—"an act of faith in the human mind"—as analogous to faith in reason and in that sense an intrinsic value, and he quotes Goblot to the effect that the scientific spirit includes such moral qualities as "intellectual courage, sincerity, integrity, humility and tolerance."

Ramzy makes an analogy between what he regards as the moral values that are inherent in the scientific method and those that lie at the basis of the psychoanalytic therapeutic process. "The correction of magical ways of thinking, of feelings of omnipotence and omniscience, the examination of defenses, etc., are an application of those intellectual and moral values which constitute scientific methods" (p. 101).

In speaking of the values implicit in psychoanalysis as therapy, he first takes up the training of students, which involves the evaluation of the candidate. This is implicitly based on a set of values, as noted before, not only in reference to health and intellectual capacities, but more especially in such matters of moral character as "honesty, integrity, and concern for others." From there he turns to the derivation of psychoanalysis from medicine, carrying with it all the values of the healing arts. It also appears to Ramzy to be impossible for the analyst to operate solely with the "benevolent curiosity" that has been urged upon him; in regarding some behavior as pathological, he must take sides with reference to his own conscience and his ego-ideal. In addition, it is to be expected that the "patient has access to the analyst's values" through the many different forms of contact between the two.

In dealing with psychoanalysis as a theory, Ramzy uses as an example the psychoanalytic study of character, and points out the value judgment that is implicitly involved in the ascription of such characteristics as "egotism versus altruism, truthfulness or lying, peaceableness or aggression." He then goes on to say that "it is preposterous to deny that the accumulated evidence of psychoanalysis has already started to show that certain patterns of psychic organization are more conducive to a better way of life than others."

Finally, he points out that Durkheim (1893) had already proposed, as did Freud later, to search out those laws that explain moral phenomena; but he insists that such a study must lead to the establishment of a "Science of Mores" as a separate discipline. He contends that the scientist of morality should be able to define a state of moral health, not in absolutist terms, but rather in connection with the particular culture and its current phase of evolution. What Ramzy insists is that it is precisely psychoanalysis that has the tools and the information to establish such a science, and that it is time for it to "step into this area, which is an integral part of its territory."

There is always the question as to whether such a science will reflect the dominant forces and changes in a society, or will have a role in determining the motivations and values that society claims as its own. I myself believe that the latter occurs not as the result of a science that is directed toward ethics (that may or may not be possible), but whenever profound discoveries are made in science, either in the psychological or in the physical realm.

BIBLIOGRAPHY

Alexander, F. (1923), The castration complex in the formation of character. *Internat. J. Psycho-Anal.*, 4:11–42.
_____ (1925), A metapsychological description of the process of cure. *Internat. J. Psycho-Anal.*, 6:13–34.
_____ (1930), The neurotic character. *Internat. J. Psycho-Anal.*, 11:292–311.
_____ (1938), Remarks about the relations of inferiority feelings to guilt feelings. *Internat. J. Psycho-Anal.*, 19:41–49.
Beres, D. (1958), Vicissitudes of superego functions and superego precursors in childhood. *The Psychoanalytic Study of the Child*, 8:324–351.
Bibring, E. (1937), Symposium on the theory of the therapeutic results of psychoanalysis. *Internat. J. Psycho-Anal.*, 18:170–189.
Brody, E. B. (1958), Superego and introjected mother and energy discharge in schizophrenia. *J. Amer. Psychoanal. Assn.*, 6:481–501.
Deutsch, H. (1932), Hysterical fate neurosis. In: *Psychoanalysis of the Neuroses*. London: Hogarth Press.
Ferenczi, S. (1925), Psychoanalysis of sexual habits. In: *Further Contributions to the Theory and Technique of Psycho-Analysis*. London: Hogarth Press, pp. 259–297.
Freud, A. (1926), *The Psychoanalytic Treatment of Children*. New York: International Universities Press, 1959.
_____ (1936), *The Ego and the Mechanisms of Defense*. (The Writings of Anna Freud, Vol. II) New York: International Universities Press, 1966.
Freud, S. and Breuer, J. (1893–1895), Studies on hysteria. *Standard Edition*, 2:253–307.
_____ (1894), The neuropsychosis of defense. *Standard Edition*, 3:43–71.

Manuel Furer

_____ (1896), Further remarks on the neuropsychosis of defense. *Standard Edition,* 3:159–189.

_____ (1907), Obsessive actions and religious practices. *Standard Edition,* 9:115–129.

_____ (1908), Civilized sexual morality and modern nervous illness. *Standard Edition,* 9:177–205.

_____ (1913), Totem and taboo. *Standard Edition,* 13:1–165.

_____ (1914), On narcissism: an introduction. *Standard Edition,* 14:65–105.

_____ (1915a), Instincts and their vicissitudes. *Standard Edition,* 14:109–141.

_____ (1915b), The unconscious. *Standard Edition,* 14:159–217.

_____ (1915c), Letter to J. J. Putnam, In: *Life and Works of Sigmund Freud,* ed. E. Jones. New York: Basic Books, 1955.

_____ (1916), Some character types met with in psychoanalytic Work. *Standard Edition,* 14:309–337.

_____ (1917), Mourning and melancholia. *Standard Edition,* 14:237–261.

_____ (1921), Group psychology and the analysis of the ego. *Standard Edition,* 18:67–145.

_____ (1923), The ego and the id. *Standard Edition,* 19:3–69.

_____ (1924a), The economic problem of masochism. *Standard Edition,* 19:157–173.

_____ (1924b), The dissolution of the Oedipus complex. *Standard Edition,* 19:173–183.

_____ (1925), Some psychical consequences of the anatomical distinction between the sexes. *Standard Edition,* 19:243–261.

_____ (1926), Inhibitions, symptoms and anxiety. *Standard Edition,* 20:77–179.

_____ (1927), Humor. *Standard Edition,* 21:159–167.

_____ (1930), Civilization and its discontents. *Standard Edition,* 21:59–149.

_____ (1933a), Why war? *Standard Edition,* 22:197–219.

_____ (1933b), New introductory lectures on psychoanalysis, Lecture 31, "The dissection of the psychical personality." *Standard Edition,* 22:57–81.

_____ (1936), A disturbance of memory on the Acropolis. *Standard Edition,* 22:239–251.

_____ (1939), Moses and monotheism. *Standard Edition,* 23:3–141.

_____ (1940), An outline of psychoanalysis. *Standard Edition,* 23:141–209.

Furer, M. (1967), Some developmental aspects of the superego. *Internat. J. Psycho-Anal.,* 48:277–280.

Glover, E. (1937), Symposium on the theory of the therapeutic results of psychoanalysis. *Internat. J. Psycho-Anal.,* 18:125–133.

Greenacre, P. (1948), Anatomical structure and superego development. *Amer. J. Orthopsychiat.,* 18:636–648.

Hartmann, H. (1960), *Psychoanalysis and Moral Values.* New York: International Universities Press.

_____, Kris, E., and Loewenstein, R. M. (1946), Comments on the formation of the psychic structure. *The Psychoanalytic Study of the Child,* 2:11–38.

_____, and Loewenstein, R. M. (1962), Notes on the superego. *The Psychoanalytic Study of the Child,* 17:42–81.

Isaacs, S. (1929), Privation and guilt. *Internat. J. Psycho-Anal.,* 10:335–347.

Isakower, O. (1939), On the exceptional position of the auditory sphere. *Internat.*

J. Psycho-Anal., 20:340–348.

—— (1954), Spoken words in dreams. *Psychoanal. Quart.*, 23:1-6.

Jacobson, E. (1937), Wege der weiblichen Über-Ich-Bildung. *Int. Z. Psychoanal.*, 23:402–412.

—— (1943), Depression: The oedipus conflict in the development of the depressive mechanisms. *Psychoanal. Quart.*, 12:541–560.

—— (1946), The effect of disappointment on ego and superego formation in normal and depressive development. *Psychoanal. Rev.*, 33:129–147.

—— (1964), *The Self and the Object World*. New York: International Universities Press.

Jones, E. (1949), The genesis of the superego. In: *Papers on Psychoanalysis*, Fifth ed. Baltimore: Williams and Wilkins.

Kaplan, A. (1957), Freud and modern philosophy. In: *Freud and the 20th Century*, ed. B. Nelson. New York: Meridian Books, pp. 209–223.

Klein, M. (1945), The oedipus complex in the light of early anxieties. In: *Contributions to Psychoanalysis*. London: Hogarth Press, pp. 339–391.

—— (1946), The Early Development of the conscience in the child. In: *Contributions to Psychoanalysis*. London: Hogarth Press, pp. 67–74.

—— (1949), Early stages of the Oedipus conflict and of superego formation. In: *The Psychoanalysis of Children*. London: Hogarth Press, pp. 179–210.

Kramer, P. (1958), Note on one of the preoedipal roots of the superego. *J. Amer. Psychoanal. Assn.*, 6:38–46.

Lampl-de Groot, J. (1962), Ego ideal and superego. *The Psychoanalytic Study of the Child*, 17:94–106.

Lewin, B. (1950), *The Psychoanalysis of Elation*. New York: Norton.

Loewenstein, R. M. (1945), A special form of self-punishment. *Psychoanal. Quart.*, 14:46–61.

Modell, A. H. (1958), The theoretical implications of hallucinatory experiences in schizophrenia. *J. Amer. Psychoanal. Assn.*, 6:442–480.

Nunberg, H. (1926), The sense of guilt and the need for punishment. *Internat. J. Psycho-Anal.*, 7:420–433.

—— (1932), *The Principles of Psychoanalysis*. New York: International University Press, 1955.

—— (1937), Symposium on the theory of the therapeutic results of psychoanalysis. *Internat. J. Psycho-Anal.*, 18:161–170.

Piers, G. and Singer, M. B. (1953), *Shame and Guilt*. Springfield: Charles C Thomas.

Pious, W. L. (1949), The pathogenic process in schizophrenia. *Bull. Menninger Clin.*, 13:152–159.

Ramzy, I. (1965), The place of values in psychoanalysis. *Internat. J. Psycho-Anal.*, 46:97–107.

Reich, A. (1953), Narcissistic object choice in women. *J. Amer. Psychoanal. Assn.*, 1:22–44.

—— (1954), Early identifications as archaic elements in the superego. *J. Amer. Psychoanal. Assn.*, 2:218–238.

—— (1960), Pathologic forms of self-esteem regulation. *The Psychoanalytic Study of the Child*, 15:215–232.

Rosenfeld, H. (1962), The superego and the ego ideal. *Internat. J. Psycho-Anal.,* 43:258–264.

Russell, B. (1945), History of Western Philosophy. New York: Simon and Schuster.

Sachs, H. (1929), One of the motive factors in the formation of the superego in women. *Internat. J. Psycho-Anal.,* 10:39–50.

Sandler, J. (1960), On the concept of the superego. *The Psychoanalytic Study of the Child,* 15:128–162.

Schafer, R. (1960), The loving and beloved superego in Freud's structural theory. *The Psychoanalytic Study of the Child,* 15:163–188.

Spitz, R. (1958), On the genesis of superego components. *The Psychoanalytic Study of the Child,* 13:375–404.

Stone, L. (1961), *The Psychoanalytic Situation.* New York: International Universities Press.

Strachey, J. (1923), The nature of the therapeutic action of psychoanalysis. *Int. J. Psycho-Anal.,* 15:127–159.

Weigert, E. (1962), Discussion: The superego and the ego ideal. *Internat. J. Psycho-Anal.,* 43:269–272.

Winnicott, D. W. (1958), Psychoanalysis and the sense of guilt. In: *Maturational Processes and the Facilitating Environment.* New York: International Universities Press, 1965, pp. 15–29.

—— (1963), The development of the capacity for concern. In: *Maturational Processes and the Facilitating Environment.* New York: International Universities Press, 1965, pp. 73–83.

2. The Earliest Mother-Child Relationship and the Development of the Superego

ARTHUR F. VALENSTEIN, M.D.

SOME YEARS AGO, I was present in a small scientific group in London when Dr. Ishak Ramzy (1961) of Topeka talked informally about "The Ontogenesis of Human Ethics." [1] In the first place, he very briefly referred to what he called "animal morality" on the basis of "instinct alone." To the best of my recollection, this was formulated largely on the basis of ethological observations of contestual behavior between animals of the same species wherein the survival of the loser is granted by the victor, the specific ritual of submission having been demonstrated by the loser. Data of this sort, which inferentially connect with the man-made concept of morality are liberally documented by Lorenz (1963), who cites many phylogenetic "Behavioral Analogies to Morality" in his book *On Aggression*. [2]

An earlier abridged version of this paper was read at the Symposium on Moral Values and Superego Functioning in New York City on March 2, 1968.

[1] As I understand it, Dr. Ramzy (1961) developed his thesis on the different types of ethics which accompany human development from narcissism through the "maturation of reason," to finally, a postoedipal position of heterosexuality, realism and healthy adaptation.

[2] See K. Lorenz (1966): ". . . cultural evolution of human peoples proceeds analogously . . . [to] . . . those physiological mechanisms which enforce, in animals, selfless behavior aimed toward the good of the community, and which work in the same way as the moral law in human beings.

"An impressive example of behavior analogous to human morality can be seen in the ritualized fighting of many vertebrates (p. 94). . . . [In the case of the dog,] I have repeatedly seen that when the loser of a fight suddenly adopted the submissive attitude, and presented his unprotected neck, the winner performed the movement of shaking to death, in the air, close to the neck of the morally vanquished dog, but with closed mouth, that is, without biting" (p. 114).

I have taken the liberty of condensing references to "animal morality" on an instinctual basis into the term *instinctual morality;* more accurately speaking, it is really *instinctual protomorality.* As I see it, this concept appropriately connects with that innate disposition for survival coincident prenatally with the extraordinary adaptive intrauterine life and development; and postnatally by the preadapted readiness to respond appropriately to the mother's protective and need-fulfilling child-preserving ministrations. The biologically based early active reciprocity between mother and child is the primary organizing experience toward that social value finally known as morality. It actually serves as a forerunner to the "sphincter morality" described by Ferenczi (1925). Thus I was led to consider the quality of the earliest mother-child relationship in its impact upon psychic development, not only with reference to the emergence and crystallization of an intact ego, but also with regard to that part of the ego which differentiates into the superego.

In this paper, I will concentrate on the development of the superego from the psychobiological side, drawing upon the psychoanalytic concept of instinctual drives and Freud's (1912) formulation of the primary object choice being of an "attachment" or "anaclitic type."

To start with, I will briefly take up some phylogenetic mothering parallels consistent with the assumption of a biological substratum in human development, which, in my view, is basic to the ontogenesis of the superego and the inculcation of socially institutionalized moral values. I will then proceed to the ontogenetic aspects, which I will consider with particular reference to the nature of the utterly dependent infant's vulnerability to failure of the mother, during the phase of mother-child symbiosis, to sufficiently meet his prenatally laid down psychophysiological patterns for survival.

Behavior reflecting a so-called "mothering or nurturing" instinct for higher mammals is so common, both for animals in the wild state as well as for domesticated animals and pets, that it hardly calls for specific explication. What is less generally known is the impressive data along similar lines for species further down the phylogenetic scale. Although there are well established instances where the mother forsakes her offspring, or even turns against them aggressively, such occurrences are comparatively rare. The causes of such paradoxically unmaternal behaviors, which are complex and of particular interest to ethologists, shall not be dwelt upon here. For the most part, what is known as the mothering instinct or nurturing instinct is well documented in observable behavior of various species of the animal world. And such protective behavior on the part of the nurturing parent, usually the mother, but for some species the father, even to the detriment of the safety and well being of the parent, is readily confirmable. Anyone who has ever kept a pet dog or cat, knows the extent to which the mother will protectively hide away and give herself over to the care of her litter.

But let me now relate a few examples [3] from different phylogenetic levels. Among mollusks, several different species of octopus are described by Fisher (1923), while Fox (1938) carefully observed one species of octopus in a tank. In all cases, the eggs were laid at night, whereupon the octopus immediately cradled them in her arms, weaving a sort of basket with them. She became oblivious to everything else unless it came too close to the eggs. This included food, which she refused, and removed from the nest area with some violence. Some of the octopi took a little food at night, but most starved while brooding. When the tank would be cleaned, the brooding octopus refused to leave her post in the wall of the tank as the water receded, and remained on the drying wall for the 15 to 20 minutes it took to clean the tank. In contrast, her mate climbed down as the water level dropped, thereby keeping his body wet.

Fox observed a curious distortion of the usual pattern: his little octopus brooded her eggs with caresses and fondling, i.e., speaking anthropomorphically, but which in any case had the effect of keeping them clean and aerated for the 10 weeks before they hatched. After the young departed on their own, she continued the pattern, fondling the shells, and died of starvation.

[3] I am much indebted to Margaret R. Olmsted, M.A., who carefully accumulated and described the various engaging examples cited in this section of the paper.

Arthur F. Valenstein

Omitting arthropods, where many observations are consistent, and passing on to vertebrates: among the teleost fish (Marshall, 1965), mouth-breeders, i.e., marine cat fish, found from Cape Cod to Panama, for instance, lay large eggs which are retrieved by the male, who carries up to 55 in his mouth for about one month. After the young emerge, he continues to shelter them in his mouth for another two weeks.

At mating, female sea horses pass their eggs to the male, who puts them into his brood pouch, fertilizing them as he goes. Having loaded in as many eggs as he can accommodate, from several females, the lining of the pouch then thickens and becomes vascular. Folds develop and grow between the eggs conveying oxygen and food to the developing young. In about three weeks, the young are fully formed, the male gives birth, and the lining of the pouch sheds like a placenta. After birth, the young stay near the male, taking refuge in his pouch if startled, until before long, he is ready to receive the next clutch.

The most famous maternal fish is again a paterfamilias; the stickleback (Tinbergen, 1952) is positively polyphiloprogenitive, and takes his work seriously. First, he builds an elaborate nest of weeds stuck together with an adhesive substance secreted by his kidneys. He then drills a hole in the middle with his snout, and after changing into fancy-dress, a vivid red color, courts females one after another until he has lured three to five into laying eggs in his nest. He fertilizes each clutch before soliciting the next, whereupon his color returns to normal. Hostile to any new females, he settles down to care for his mixed bag of eggs, fanning water over them constantly for ventilation. As they mature, their requirements rise, and so do his activities, reaching a peak just before the young are born. Thereafter, he keeps them together for a day or so, retrieving stragglers with his mouth.

In the interest of brevity, I shall omit specific reference to amphibians and reptiles, other than to note that Mertens (1960), in his book, *World of Amphibians and Reptiles,* gives vivid examples of parental care among frogs, toads, snakes, skinks and crocodiles.

Among cetacea, namely whales, dolphins and porpoises, epimetic or care behavior, is divided into two types by Caldwell and

66 ·

Caldwell (1966), care of the young (or nurturant care) and care of distressed individuals (succorant care). The latter is extremely rare, but takes place in cetacea. Animals in this group express this by staying close by an injured animal, or actively, by attempting aid, rescue, or attack on the injured animal's predator. In the first instance, the whole school remain in a danger area which in normal conditions would be vacated rapidly, and communicate with the injured animal vocally. In the second circumstance, one or more will bite harpoons in two, chew lines apart, and crush attackers' boats. This adult form of care reflects the nurturant care common to cetacea, and is probably an intelligent extension of it, as will be suggested by the data on maternal care.

All cetacea have a very long period of dependency after birth, in spite of a capacity to swim with the herd at speed. An infant dolphin, if born alive, is capable of swimming to the surface to breathe, after which it takes a protected position a little to one side, and above the mother's trunk, where it is immediately capable of keeping up with her. A constant vocal contact is kept up for the whole nursing period, about 16 months. Even after four to six years respectively, young dolphins were observed to seek out their mothers when tired, sleepy or frightened. One pregnant young dolphin spent the latter part of her pregnancy with her own mother, who assisted her in nudging the infant to the surface.

This is a common pattern. At parturition, other adult females stand by, and as soon as the fetus is expelled, one will move into position on one side of the infant, the mother on the other, and together they will lift the baby to the surface for its first breath, although in normal circumstances it is able to do this unassisted. If the infant is weak, or subsequently is hurt, the females continue their supportive help until it is well or has died. In certain species, this instinct is so strong that a dead infant will be supported for several days, and on one occasion, a pair of adults were seen standing by the severed head of a young one which had presumably been killed by a shark.

The succorant behavior of whales, the sperm whale in particular, is famous, and many old prints show pods of whale attacking a whale boat, cutting harpoon lines, biting harpoons in two, and standing by a fast whale. The devotion of whale mothers was much exploited by whalers, who harpooned the baby in order to draw its mother, and often the entire herd, into the area. This behavior is carried out almost exclusively by females for young or other females, although females seldom stand by males, typically scattering when their protector has been hit. Adult males do not stand by each other, but will sometimes remain near a female, particularly if she has young. The whole succorant pattern seems tied up with the nurturant instinct.

Coming finally to primates, Washburn and De Vore (1961) conclude that the young in the baboon world are in an enviable position. The whole troop is structured to give them care, love and protection. Infants at birth become centers of social attraction. The strongest and most dominant males sit with the mothers when the troop is at rest, and travel with them when the troop is on the move. When the troop is resting, adult females and juveniles crowd about the mother and groom her, and try to groom the infant.

According to Washburn and De Vore (1961), "The learning that brings the individual baboon into full identity and participation in the baboon social system, begins with the mother-child relationship. The newborn baboon rides by clinging to the hair on its mother's chest. The mother may scoop the infant on her hand, but the infant must cling to the mother, even when she runs, from the day it is born" (p. 68).

The baby is with his mother 24 hours a day at first, surrounded by interested and responsive relatives, grooming and being groomed. If isolated in the laboratory, instinct carries the infant to clinging, but social behavior requires learning. In the wild, the point where the baby climbs down from his mother's back, where he has ridden since the first few days of clinging to her chest, and begins to play with the other juveniles, is where his social education in troop life begins. If he has been raised in isolation, he is damaged, and unable to play normally with his peers.

Having concluded this limited consideration of phylogenetic parallels, I shall now continue with the ontogenetic aspects. My assumption is that the exceedingly vulnerable and dependent human infant is born in a state of biological expectancy, we might even say "blindly trustful," as it were, on the basis of the intra-uterine situation of having been so extraordinarily fulfilled in its needs. During this prenatal phase wherein biochemical feedback and reflex mechanisms serve admirably to fulfill needs for survival and development, the fetus has biological priority, before the needs of the mother, even including those of a self-preservative instinctual nature. Under the usual satisfactory circumstances, this relationship between the "parasitic" fetus and the "host" mother continues on into the neonatal phase of life, and by reason of her maternal instinctual propensities, the normal mother now volitionally *honors* this obligation, putting her infant's life and well-being before her own.

This pattern parallels Freud's proposal in 1915, in "Instincts and Their Vicissitudes," of a dualistic instinct theory in which he distinguished on biological grounds between the *ego*, or *self-preservative* instincts and the *sexual* instincts. The former, the ego drives, center on the individual, sexuality "being one of its activities and sexual satisfaction one of its needs"; while the latter, the sexual drives center on "the preservation of the species." Thus the individual is "a temporary and transient appendage to the quasi-immortal germ-plasm, which is entrusted to him by the process of generation" [p. 125].

The neonate's initial primary narcissism and primary identification with the mother through the act of nursing, gradually gives way to taking the mother as the primary object on the experiential grounds of intermittent separation from and reunitement with the pleasurable anaclitically libidinized "breast = mother." Concomitant with this vital paradigm of incorporation, the stage is set for the internalization of qualities essential to development, and for an adequate ego formation, at least initially. And consistent with this, in due course one might expect an internalization of qualities associated with the mother and other early objects that have increasingly a social value, and finally a moral connotation.

Arthur F. Valenstein

Writing of "the caretaking mother as the first legislator," Anna Freud (1965) points out:

> . . . the pleasure principle, in spite of being an internal law lodged in the infant himself, has to be implemented from the outside by the caretaking mother who provides or withholds satisfaction. On the strength of this activity, she becomes not only the child's first (ana-clitic need-fulfilling) object but also the first external legislator. The first external laws with which she confronts the infant are concerned with the *timing* and *rationing* of his satisfaction" [p. 168].

But what if something goes wrong? What if the neonate is, in effect, betrayed in its psychobiological attitude of "blind expectancy?" What if this instinctual forerunner to morality is decisively contravened by a major disruption of the mother-child confidence-trust and mutuality of experience? What if the mother, for whatever reason, decisively fails to provide an extension of what she had provided involuntarily for her child, before he was born? Ample clinical evidence has been reported which points to the variety of ego defects which might ensue, including such possibilities as atypical development, major psychosomatic disturbances, later psychosis, etc.—even assuming that the infant does not become marasmic and perish forthwith.

And what of the superego and moral values? In some instances, it appears that the potential for internalization is so deleteriously affected that the result is a developmental limitation in the capacity to internalize social ideals and critique, and those functions of self-observation, self-judgment and self-punishment (potential for guilt) which are essential to the formation of a reasonably intact superego. [4]

Although the term "psychopathic character" is an unsatisfactory one, largely because it has been such a loosely abused, conglomer-

[4] See A. Aichhorn (1948)—"The nucleus of the superego will not develop if children are deprived of needed love. This happens when parents pay little attention to their children, neglect them, or are indifferent to them. It happens when children are shuttled early in life from one foster home to another, as is the case with public dependents, where children do not have time to develop feelings of affection toward foster parents and to identify with them. Such children absorb all later identifications as loose structures that do not really take hold" (p. 232).

70 ·

ate concept, nonetheless, it has not been supplanted for diagnostic purposes. It continues to have a certain usefulness so long as it is supplemented with a further specification of the nature of the disturbance. Various types of impulse disorders might be subsumed under this general diagnostic label, which in terms of the manifest antisocial behavior might not appear too different. However, a searching psychoanalytic evaluation reveals that this similarity in behavior is more at the surface, with significantly different meaning and determination in depth. There would seem to be a continuum of impulse disorders characterized by dissocial behavior. At one extreme of this hypothetical continuum might be those impulse ridden "psychopaths," whose psychopathic acts are clearly of a neurotic nature, essentially being symptomatic of unconscious intrapsychic conflicts originating paramountly during the postverbal phase of development. Such psychopathic neurotics described over 40 years ago by Aichhorn (1925), and subsequently by Glover (1926), Alexander (1930), and Wittels (1937), as "neurotic characters," are possessed of a very active superego, albeit maladaptive in its form and function, often impelling dissocial acts exactly in order to yield punishment from without and thus relieve unconscious guilt. But on the other extreme of the continuum, there would appear to be a group of "psychopaths" of a quite different qualitative order of psychopathology, the so-called "moral imbeciles," the "morally insane" described by Cleckley (1941) and others. [5] Presumably these extraordinarily disturbed and disturbing individuals constitutionally lack a capacity or potential for guilt, even though they may have developed a sophisticated range of talents, skills, etc. In that they have achieved so many ego abili-

[5] See A. Aichhorn (1925): "It cannot be denied that sometimes a faulty ego-ideal is developed on the basis of hereditarily determined structural deficiencies, and delinquency results. To put it in another way, there are dissocial types with inborn defects, who lack the inherited capacity for object cathexis and identification. Whether this is a quantitative or a qualitative lack, whether object cathexis or identification or both do not function properly, is a problem for investigation. It is questionable, however, whether the constitutional lack can be so great that we can assume the individual was criminal from birth" (p. 172).

It is exactly my point that the irrefutable but elusive question of a hereditary diathesis for dissocial development might be narrowed by including among the constitutional determiners, the possibility of postnatal experiential trauma of major degree, occurring within the context of the earliest mother-child symbiotic relationship.

Arthur F. Valenstein

ties, especially those on a cognitive level, and have become so adaptive in respects other than those of a moral nature, they are, if anything, all the more dangerous to society. Apparently their remarkable versatility to act *as if* socially normal, *as if* individuals of conscience, affords them the knack of being utterly deceptive and thoroughly immoral, living as they do, really, outside of traditional ethical considerations. [6]

The disturbances of these individuals have more in common qualitatively with the atypical child or psychotic, than with the neurotic. Such psychopathy might have to be understood predominantly in terms of the earliest phases of development, the preverbal stages and the early diadic mother-child experience. Is it possible that these "psychopaths" might have suffered major trauma at the level of their inborn "instinctual protomorality?" Perhaps a decisive causational factor was the inability or refusal of the mother to meet that inborn psychobiological pretrustful expectancy with which a child comes into the world—biologically confident, pre-adapted to be loved and to be ordinarily but sufficiently fulfilled by the mother, and gradually beyond, by the environment immediate to both mother and child.

And finally, at a more sociological level, one might ponder the growing social trend toward violence and the breakdown of moral and social constraints against aggression in a changing culture, some aspects of which appear more and more to encourage individuals to seek immediate satisfaction of sensual narcissistic needs. Perhaps this trend might be related, not only to disruption of the nuclear family structure and traditions in an increasingly unstable stratification of society, but also to significant disequilibria in the earliest mother-child relationship within the context of these disrupted families.

---

[6] See A. Aichhorn (1925): "Given certain disturbances in the libido organization, the nature of which cannot be discussed here, the child remains asocial or else behaves as if he had become social without having made an actual adjustment to the demands of society" (p. 2).

Anna Freud (1965) also attributes to Aichhorn (1925) the recognition "that delinquents and criminals may reach a high degree of adaptation to reality without placing this capacity in the service of social adaptation" (p. 171).

72 ·

BIBLIOGRAPHY

Aichhorn, A. (1948), Delinquency in a new light. In: *Delinquency and Child Guidance.* New York: International Universities Press, 1964.
—— (1925), *Wayward Youth.* New York: Viking Press, 1935 (republished New York: Meridian Books, 1955).
Alexander, F. (1930), The neurotic character. *Internat. J. Psycho-Anal.,* 11:292–311.
Caldwell M. and Caldwell, D. (1966), Epimetic behavior. In: *Whales, Dolphins and Porpoises,* ed. K. Norris. Berkeley and Los Angeles: University of California Press.
Cleckley, H. (1941), *The Mask of Sanity.* St. Louis: C. B. Mosby Co.
Ferenczi, S. (1925), Psycho-Analysis of sexual habits. In: *Further Contributions to the Theory and Technique of Psychoanalysis.* London: Hogarth Press, 1926.
Fisher, W. K. (1923), Brooding habits of the cephalopod. *Ann. Mag. Nat. Hist.,* 12:147–149.
Fox, D. L. (1938), An illustrated note on the mating and egg-brooding habits of the two-spotted octopus. *S. Diego Nat. Hist.,* 97:31–34.
Freud, A. (1965), *Normality and Pathology in Childhood.* New York: International Universities Press.
Freud, S. (1912), On the universal tendency to debasement in the sphere of love. *Standard Edition,* 11:179–190. London: Hogarth Press, 1957.
—— (1914), On narcissism: an introduction. *Standard Edition,* 14:73–102. London: Hogarth Press, 1957.
—— (1915), Instincts and their vicissitudes. *Standard Edition,* 14:117–140. London: Hogarth Press, 1957.
Glover, E. (1926), The neurotic character. *Internat. J. Psychoanal.,* 7:11–30.
Lorenz, K. (1963), *On Aggression.* London: Methuen and Co., 1966.
Marshall, N. B. (1965), *The Life of the Fishes.* London: Weidenfield and Nicolson.
Mertens, R. (1960), *The World of Amphibians and Reptiles.* New York: McGraw Hill.
Ramzy, I. (1961), The ontogenesis of human ethics. *Unpublished.*
Tinbergen, N. (1952), Curious behavior of the stickleback. *Sci. Amer.,* 187:22–27.
Washburn, S. L. and De Vore, I. (1961), Social life of the baboons. *Sci. Amer.,* 204:62–71.
Wittels, F. (1937), The criminal psychopath in the psychoanalytic system. *Psychoanal. Rev.,* 24:276–290.

3. Outcome of Predictions on Superego Formation: Longitudinal Observations

SAMUEL RITVO, M.D.

T HE PROMINENCE of the genetic point of view in psychoana- lytic metapsychology in recent years, and with it the in- creased focus on child development, has generated interest also in the genetic determinants of the superego. In speaking of the genetic determinants, developmental elements or precursors of the superego, we want to be clear that we do not mean early forms of the superego as a systematic psychic structure. The su- perego as a structure in the psychic apparatus defined by its func- tions of conscience, self-criticism, and the holding up of ideals and moral values arises out of the oedipal conflict, though its content and characteristics are determined in part by the genetic determi- nants. For theoretical clarity and for the guidance of empirical observation it is necessary to keep in mind the distinctions be- tween genesis and function (Hartmann, 1955; Hartmann and Loew- enstein 1962). Those aspects of the ego which oppose and control instinctual discharge, and which play a part in the earliest defen- sive functions of the ego, can be regarded as genetic determinants of the superego by virtue of the basic relatedness of the functions even though the superego as a systematically related group of functions does not exist before early latency.

The early identifications of the child form another group of superego determinants. Because these involve the inherited ego and drive characteristics of the child, and insofar as they occur in the framework of the mother-child relationship, they include the influence of the environment. These early identifications also subject the child to the first influences of the moral standards and values of the culture of his immediate family because they are incorporated in the daily care and handling of the child, via the ways in which the external force of the parents operates in curbing the child's instincts.

The formation of the superego can be viewed also as dependent on the outcome of the processes of internalization, the developments by which regulations that have taken place in interaction with the outside world are replaced by inner regulations (Hartmann, 1939). Observations in a longitudinal study of child development have indicated how the processes of internalization are related to characteristics of the ego apparatus, drive characteristics and the mother-child interaction (Ritvo and Solnit, 1958). The possible implications of the individual features of the internalization process for superego formation were considered in a predictive fashion in another paper (Ritvo and Solnit, 1960). Follow-up observations in adolescence on two of the three children described in that paper provided an opportunity to check further on those predictions.

One of Ernst Kris' basic aims in the longitudinal study of child development at the Yale Child Study Center was to utilize direct observational data in conjunction with reconstructive data, not merely to test and validate psychoanalytic hypotheses, but to supplement and enlarge the psychoanalytic theory of growth and development (Kris, 1950). The other basic aim was rooted in the clinical and therapeutic functions of psychoanalysis. Longitudinal studies which would fully utilize observational and reconstructive data could yield clinically significant knowledge of the range of variations of mental health and make possible the earlier recognition of pathology (Kris, 1957).

Our therapeutic theory and technique, as in any clinical field, involves repeated short-range predictions and checking of their outcome. Diagnosis and decisions about the indications for analysis, particularly in children, require long-range predictions regarding the pathological significance of symptoms and developmental disturbances. Marianne Kris (1957) has demonstrated how predictions, even those that prove to be incorrect, can be used to sharpen and refine our evaluation and interpretation of the data of direct observation. She has also shown how the unpredictable environmental and reality factors in a child's life may be dealt with to test the assumptions of the predicting observer.

The relevant features of Evelyne's family setting and early development have been described in some detail in the earlier publications so that only the salient features related to the predictions on superego formation will be mentioned here. As an infant Evelyne was not vociferous in her initial demands. She was receptive to the ministrations of her mother and was easily pacified and satisfied by the feeding. The mother had a strong empathic tie with her and attempted to observe and respond to the child's needs. Her behavior indicated her intent to mold the child in the form she preferred by imposing a carefully graded system of restrictions and gratifications. The teaching and training aspects of the feeding, for example, had moralistic overtones. According to the mother, at the age of one Evelyne would eat something she did not like if rewarded by something she did like; at 16 months mother and child had an arrangement which granted Evelyne permission to mess in the process of feeding herself one meal daily while the mother was responsible for the fastidious execution of the other two meals. This form of rearing and training, together with the mother's stimulation of a precocious, role-playing fantasy life, fostered in unusually extensive identification with the mother (Kris, 1955). At the time of her entry into nursery school at two years, four months, Evelyne's self-control and organization was strikingly independent of the mother's presence, representing an advanced level of internalization for that age. She was able to take over the mother's attitudes, values and prohibitions and fit them into the satisfaction of her own needs. In the nursery school, where Evelyne was the most predictable child in the group, she also showed a high degree of ego autonomy and resistiveness to regression under stress. At the time, we regarded the identification with the nurturing and protective mother as the forerunner of a superego which itself would be protective of the ego. Given this background, it seemed likely that Evelyne would develop a superego characterized by flexibility, adaptability, and effectiveness in maintaining a balance between control and instinctual discharge.

During the latency years she had difficulty establishing reliable barriers against the breakthrough of infantile instinctual strivings. Her earlier enjoyment of play with messy materials continued and was an activity to which she regressed during analytic hours in the face of aggression or sexual excitement. Despite her attractive features and coloring she had a drab quality which reflected a similar quality in the mother. Although she did not have strong masculine strivings and showed less envy of the male than did her two younger sisters, neither did she find feminine interests a source of much satisfaction. Both parents viewed her as awkward, clumsy and negativistic, finding the other sisters more to their liking, and admiring them for the phallic qualities which they encouraged. In this setting Evelyne lost a great deal of the imaginativeness she had demonstrated earlier. She showed only a moderate interest in her school work and found excuses for the mediocre quality of her performance, which while very much consistent with her parents' expectations for her, was considerably below what her earlier development presaged of her capacities. Her ideal was to be a nurse like the mother's older sister to whom the mother had been closely attached. The mother became pregnant with Evelyne shortly after her sister had moved away with her husband. The ideal of being a nurse drew some of its interest from the attachment and devotion the mother showed for her sister, which for Evelyne was connected with the memories of her own earlier closeness with her mother. Evelyne repeatedly affirmed her intention not to marry and to remain "a Miss," an expression of her disappointment over not being able to win her father's affection and a turning away from her own feminine wishes toward her father. She responded to her father's dislike, criticism and anger by avoiding confrontations with him yet maintaining an evasive but stubborn noncompliance. The stern and harsh qualities of the developing superego were discernible in her startle reaction on the regular occasions when she soiled her dress while playing with the "messy stuff" concoctions she would make during the analytic hours. The flexibility of the old moralistic feeding pattern reappeared once more when she reassured herself by saying, "It's all right. My mother doesn't mind. It's washable!" In this way she revealed a superego corruptible by detergents and reflecting an identification with what the mother termed her own "sneaky ways."

In a follow-up interview at the age of 15 she gave an impression of docility, compliance and inhibition. She contented herself with a constricted life revolving very much around the home and particularly oriented toward being a helper to her mother in domestic and household duties, helping especially with the cooking. The overall impression was one of massive repression of adolescent sexuality with regression to old oral fixations.

At the time of an interview at 19 she had just completed the first year of a college-level nursing program at a college away from home. Although an attractive girl in her physical features, her dress was drab and colorless and her expression and physical bearing were slack and ungainly. She sat in a slumped position with her shoulders hunched forward, and as she talked she shrugged her shoulders in a resigned, helpless fashion. She was sharply critical of herself for her apathy at school, as well as for "not knowing what was going on in the world," both socially and academically. She berated herself for being a "conformist" and for never having been "rebellious" during her adolescence. She said of herself, "I have a very strict superego," a term she acquired from a classroom discussion of Freud which she thought was applicable to herself. Whenever she thought of doing something she wanted to do which would not please someone else she felt guilty and had "pangs of conscience." Her mother would say, "do whatever you feel is best for you," but then, somehow, pressured her into a particular direction. She felt herself to be limited and constricted compared to her next younger sister who was more imaginative and perceptive and took issue more actively with her mother; the mother in turn showed a greater interest in the sister. Evelyne had nothing at all to say spontaneously about her father; it was as though he had no bearing whatsoever on her life.

Jerry, another child in the longitudinal study, has been described from the standpoint of the interaction of constitutional characteristics with environment in the development of personality (Ritvo et al, 1963), and in relation to genetic determinants of superego formation (Ritvo and Solnit, 1960). At birth Jerry was rated by all observers as a very active infant, whose behavior fell within the limits of the normal range of hyperactivity. His parents were poorly controlled in their behavior and emotional expression toward Jerry as well as toward one another. They were markedly inconsistent in their responses to their son. The same behavior in Jerry might bring a strong rebuke or punishment one time, a jovial response another time, and at other times no response at all. He was frequently subjected to excessive and exciting manipulations of his body, including the frequent administration of rectal suppositories from earliest infancy. Control and compliance were achieved at home with threats and spankings. The mother's overstimulation of the child at every erogenous zone and at every level of activity impeded the development of ego functions. The functions emerged but were poorly elaborated or stabilized. Mental and motor activities remained predominantly under the influence of the primary process. Identifications retained an archaic quality in the totality with which they were made and the ease with which they shifted. The psychic representations of the parents were more closely associated with inability to wait and direct instinctual gratification than with prohibition and control. Those superego precursors which are based on the identification with the parents' modes of gratifying or warding off the instinctual drives were underdeveloped in Jerry. The development of ego functions such as concept formation and abstract thinking, later important for superego formation, were impaired in Jerry. It seemed to us that the combination of overstimulation and poor control in the parents, in addition to a predisposition toward hyperactivity and motor discharge in the child, would continue to hamper the processes of internalization necessary for stable ego and superego identifications. Our expectation with Jerry was that the superego functions would retain the characteristics of the instinctualized expressions to a marked degree and that superego functions based on self-observation and memory would be underdeveloped. We were also concerned that with the parents' marginal psychological, social and economic stability, and Jerry's tendency to action and easy seducibility, faulty superego formation might result in serious delinquency.

Jerry was seen in one interview during latency shortly after he had recovered from a fractured leg sustained when he fell from a fence while being chased by a policeman for trespassing on railroad property. It had been a severe compound fracture which required prolonged immobilization in traction in the hospital. Before this accident his mother had expressed concern about him because of his poor school work, his mischievous escapades with older boys in the neighborhood, and her difficulty in controlling and supervising him. At the time of the interview he appeared subdued and depressed and was no longer the quick, mercurial, darting child he had been earlier. Psychological tests administered at that time indicated a depressive mood and, surprisingly, evidence of considerably more fantasy life than had been present earlier.

On a home visit at 15 Jerry was a composed, well-mannered adolescent who took interest and pride in his place in the family and community. The social and economic condition of the family had changed. The father had been steadily employed in the construction trades for some time and his health, which had been precarious during Jerry's early years, was now sound. Because of the mother's concern about the effects of a borderline slum neighborhood on her children, particularly Jerry, they had assumed large financial obligations to move to an attractive new development in the suburbs. To save money they had undertaken to do much of the work in their new house themselves and Jerry took a proud and active part in this. He also had a respected place in his peer group in the community and with his teachers, more for his athletic abilities than his scholastic achievements, which were just passing. The earlier hyperactive disposition seemed to be constructively channeled into organized athletics. His skill and, surprisingly, his sense of responsibility were recognized in his post of playground supervisor in the town recreation program. There was an interesting and suggestive parallel between his devotion to his coach who was also his history teacher, and his earlier relationship to his nursery school teacher who had functioned as his borrowed, almost grafted auxiliary ego during the years when he would become unmanageable if she were not immediately present.

The follow-up interviews indicate that the superego formation in Evelyne and Jerry took a different course from what had been predicted on the basis of our knowledge of them gained from direct observations and analytic therapy. In Evelyne the early, extensive neutralization of instinctual drives, the remarkable early capacity for sublimation, the resistiveness to regression, the identification with the mother which was so much in the service of competent and predictable adaptation to different environments invited the prediction of a protective and nurturing superego.

In the discussion following an earlier presentation of Evelyne which was focused on the influence of mother-child interaction on early identification processes, Dr. Robert P. Knight (1958) independently made this prediction concerning superego formation in Evelyne:

> Could one say that in Evelyne the forerunner of superego formation could be observed as taking place in her in respect to the early and fortunate indications of the protective and nurturing function of the superego to be, through the internalization of a well attuned mother protector and regulator [p. 91].

In a discussion remark at the same meeting, obviously referring to Evelyne, Hartmann (1958) observed astutely that:

> Occasionally a child may possibly as a consequence of identification or for some other reason, acquire a comparatively high degree of neutralization, as to certain of his functions, precociously—where a lower degree might be age-adequate. In such cases it might happen that this state of affairs—we could call it overneutralization—cannot be maintained and leads to regressive sexualization. This possibility, too, we should consider in our attempts at prediction [pp. 120–121].

In fact this is what took place during the oedipal period and latency. During latency the normal feminine wishes were pro-scribed whereas the regressive oral and anal derivatives were permitted. Consequently she became intellectually inhibited and lost her early imaginativeness. Her two younger sisters had taken her earlier favored position with both parents. Evelyne had been heartily welcomed as the first child who established the family. When the other two girls were born the parents were disappointed in not having a son and in their wishes and fantasies, as we know from the analysis of the parents, the younger daughters were endowed with masculine, phallic qualities. The more active disposition of the younger sisters served them well in their adaptation to their roles in the fantasies of the parents. It was for these reasons that Evelyne was taken into analysis again at the age of seven after an earlier period of analysis while she was in nursery school.

The conflict over aggression was a difficulty for Evelyne which probably contributed to the unexpected severity of the superego. She reacted to being supplanted by her sisters in the affection of both parents with resentment, anger, and a deep smoldering feeling of being unfairly treated which, despite her efforts at containment, came out toward her sisters and her friends. Before the interview at 19, she wrote a note to me making a personal request. The only other comment in the note was that the referees of a team game she played were unfair, always favoring the opposing team so that they always won. The feeling of exclusion and being an unwelcome intruder with her father was discernible also with boys. In her first year away from home she did meet one boy whom she liked who also paid her a little attention. However, he stopped spending time with her because he felt she was controlling his life. Although disappointed and rebuffed, she was quite certain it was his problem and that his criticism was not justified. She related all this with a resigned shrug.

In the early years when her capacity for sublimation was so advanced, her achievements were based on an identification with the mother and particularly with what the mother idealized—imagination, creativity and fantasy. Later she was shunted aside by both parents as they turned to the other children to live out their ideals. A strong blow to her development of a feminine ego-ideal was the father's lack of interest in her femininity and his devaluation and rejection of it. One current in his attitude to Evelyne derived from his feelings toward his own older sister who presented a degraded version of femininity and towards whom he had long-standing negative feelings.

Despite the unexpectedly severe features of the superego formation in Evelyne, the characteristics of the early interaction with the mother which, on the child's side, evolved out of her receptive malleability, were observable in Evelyne's comment at 19. That is, her mother would tell her to do as she pleased but would then pressure her to do the right thing, like taking a dull summer job which paid well rather than an interesting, poorly paid job.

Hartmann was correct in his prediction that the early overneutralization in Evelyne, based on the extensive identifications with the mother, could not be maintained and led to regressive sexualization and aggressivization. The later lowering in the quality and efficiency of Evelyne's ego functioning represented an increasing instinctualization of these functions with a lowering of their secondary autonomy as they were involved in conflict. The later identifications, including the superego identifications, contained more elements of her own ambivalence and the ambivalence of her parents towards her.

If Evelyne can be viewed as a child with precocious overneutralization, who later experienced regressive instinctualization of her ego functioning, Jerry can be seen as a child who early showed underneutralization and who later was capable of a higher level of neutralization with a level of ego functioning and capacity for sublimation which was not as poor as had been feared. He also gave indications of a consistency and quality of superego functioning which exceeded what had been predicted. The stabilization of the family during the latency years was a fortunate and positive factor, providing a salutary external structure at a time when the instinctual drives were less intense relative to the maturing ego. The increasing emphasis on control of instinctual expression, particularly aggression, was also related to a change from the mother's more tolerant attitude toward instinctual expression in Jerry as a preschool child, to a sterner, more consistent demand for good behavior and diligent application to learning in a child old enough to attend what the mother regarded as a "real school." She had always regarded the nursery school as a too indulgent, laisseze-faire play setting which, although not too harmful to a young child, was too lax for a school age child who needed sterner discipline. Our impression that the mother was the prime mover in the stabilization of the family may be inaccurate insofar as we had only minimal contact with the father throughout the study and none in connection with the follow-up interviews. He may have had a larger actual role from latency onward. In any case, from the age of three and four Jerry had idealized his father's strength. Doing hard and heavy work was one of his favorite games in nursery school and in the treatment hours. But at that time, as in the case of the father, hard work had to be interspersed with rest or it would make him sick. The father's steady work and good health made the identification with father safer while at the same time nurturing the ideal of skill, strength and work.

In this setting of maturing inner structure and increasing internal regulation, the large quantity of free aggression, which had been present from infancy, was available to the superego for use against the ego (Hartmann, 1958). This formulation is suggested by the fall which resulted in the fracture and immobilization followed by subdued behavior, depression and increased fantasy life. The aggression which he had earlier projected and then defended against by identification with the aggressor was subsequently turned against the self as a castration threat, the manifestations of which were carried out rather extensively in reality. The modality used by Jerry was strikingly consistent with the prominence and persistence of casting behavior in infancy and his later use of his body as a projectile, hurling his own body about as he would a ball, a block or a doll. In nursery school he would frequently climb to the top of the jungle gym or the roof of the toy shed and fling himself off; or he would dart out of the analytic treatment room, race down the corridor and leap off the top landing of the staircase shouting, "I'm Superman!" Later, the idealization of strength and body prowess found suitable functional pleasure in constructive work and athletics, while winning praise and recognition from parents, teachers and peers as well as approval from the superego.

Anna Freud (1958) summarized the chief factors which make clinical foresight or prediction hazardous: (1) the likelihood of unevenness in the rate of maturational progress in ego and drive development; (2) our lack of an approach to the quantitative factor in drive development, a handicap because, in her view, most of the conflict solutions within the personality will be determined by quantitative rather than by qualitative factors; and (3) the unpredictability of the environmental happenings in a child's life.

In Evelyne, the precocious advance in ego development influenced the prediction as though the ego would always be in this relationship to the drives. In Jerry, the drives predominated the picture at first and we forecast this into the future as though this would always be the case.

In our predictions we tended to regard the unevenness in development as though they reflected fixed quantitative factors which would retain approximately the same relations in the future. Of course, we had no way of predicting the future events. Our predictions about Evelyne did not take the consequences of the advent of two younger sisters sufficiently into account and did not forecast the adverse effects of the father's rejection of her femininity. In Jerry we underestimated the potentiality of the family for healthy social adaptation because of the tendency of the parents to indulge their own regressive pregenital strivings via the child's phase-specific and age-appropriate strivings.

BIBLIOGRAPHY

Freud, A. (1958), Child observation and prediction of development. *The Psychoanalytic Study of the Child*, 13:92–124. New York: International Universities Press.
Hartmann, H. (1955), Notes on the theory of sublimation. *The Psychoanalytic Study of the Child*, 10:9–29. New York: International Universities Press.
—— (1958), Discussion of paper by Anna Freud. *The Psychoanalytic Study of the Child*, 13:120–122. New York: International Universities Press.
—— and Loewenstein, R. M. (1962), Notes on the superego. *The Psychoanalytic Study of the Child*, 17:42–81. New York: International Universities Press.

Samuel Ritvo

Knight, R. P. (1958), Discussion of paper by S. Ritvo and A. J. Solnit. *The Psychoanalytic Study of the Child,* 13:90–91. New York: International Universities Press.

Kris, E. (1957), A longitudinal study in child development. Paper originally prepared in 1952 as a report to the Commonwealth Fund, New York. Read in revised form (by S. Provence) at the International Psycho-Analytical Congress, Paris, 1957.

Kris, M. (1957), The use of prediction in a longitudinal study. *The Psychoanalytic Study of the Child,* 12:175–189. New York: International Universities Press.

Ritvo, S. and Solnit, A. J. (1958), Influences of early mother-child interaction on identification processes. *The Psychoanalytic Study of the Child,* 13:64–91. New York: International Universities Press.

Ritvo, S. and Solnit, A. J. (1960), The relationship of early ego identifications to superego formation. *Internat. J. Psycho-anal.,* 41:295–300.

Ritvo, S., McCollum, A. T., Omwake, E., Provence, S. A. and Solnit, A. J. (1963), Some relations of constitution, environment, and personality as observed in a longitudinal study of child development: case report. In: *Modern Perspectives in Child Development,* ed. A. J. Solnit and S. A. Provence. New York: International Universities Press.

4. Adolescence and the Consolidation of Values

AARON H. ESMAN, M.D.

PSYCHOANALYTIC DISCUSSIONS of adolescence have followed an historical progression that reflects developing patterns of thought within psychoanalysis generally. Thus Freud's (1905) first systematic consideration of the subject, in the third of his *Three Essays in the Theory of Sexuality,* dealt with the transformations of puberty from the standpoint of the vicissitudes of libidinal drive and sexual behavior—that is, from what has been subsequently referred to as an "id" approach. More recent studies, such as those by Anna Freud (1958), Spiegel (1958) and especially Erikson (1956), have focussed on the reorganization of defenses and the formation of identity and self-image in adolescence—i.e., on the ego aspects of this developmental phase. Blos (1962), in his comprehensive approach developed in a continuing oeuvre, has sought for a synthesis of drive-centered and ego-centered conceptions, but one rooted in a drive-economic conceptual framework.

It is certainly true that the revolution which occurs in his instinctual life and its consequences are the most salient features of the adolescent's behavior. It is equally true that maturational factors, such as those delineated by Piaget in the cognitive sphere, as well as the massive increase in bulk and power of the musculature and other bodily changes contribute to an enormous expansion of the ego. Further, the organization and stabilization of character structure, most recently described by Blos (1968), represents the crucial achievement of adolescence and is a fundamental building block in identity formation.

Considerably less attention appears to have been paid to the fate of the third of what are generally regarded as the basic psychic structures, the superego. There are several probable reasons for this relative neglect. The first is, as suggested above, the flamboyance of the id and ego transformations that go on during the postpubertal years. The establishment of mature object-cathexes, the delineation of an occupational goal and the formulation of a defined social role are surely the paramount tasks of adolescence as we know it. The expansion and displacement of object ties from parents to peer group and the evolution of an adolescent peer-culture tend further to focus attention on the adolescent's adaptive shifts.

Another factor, however, seems to me to derive from theoretical rather than phenomenological grounds. It has been, since Freud formulated the superego concept, virtually an axiom in psychoanalytic theory that the superego is consolidated as a psychic structure at the point of resolution of the Oedipus complex. Internalization of parental and societal standards and prohibitions has been considered to be crystallized at the onset of the latency period— indeed, to usher it in—and, though reference is often made to further accessions to the superego in later development (e.g., Hartmann and Loewenstein, 1962), only Jacobson (1964) has discussed in detail the dynamics of these accretions to the basic structure of the superego system.[1]

It is, however, a commonplace of clinical observation of adolescents that a general disorganization and realignment of psychic structures is characteristic, at least in Western industrial cultures. This is surely as true of the superego as of the ego and drive-organization. Erikson (1956) defines the processes through which the adolescent tests out new roles and abandons old identifications in the course of formulating his ultimate "ego-identity." It is my proposition that precisely the same processes occur within the framework of the value-system—i.e., the superego. Old value-

---

[1] In the course of completing this paper I have encountered a monograph by Lederer (1964), which presents a similar view of adolescent superego development, though adhering to a more traditional conception of superego structure and function.

identifications—or, in Sandler's (1960) terms, introjects—are subjected to merciless reappraisal. Some of these identifications are abandoned, some are fortified; new identifications/introjections are formed, derived from new—nonparental—models. Indeed, I should suggest that this reorganization and consolidation of values is as central a task of contemporary adolescence as are the finding of permanent love objects and the stabilization of character and defense organization.

This view is rooted in a concept of the superego that, though somewhat at variance with much of current psychoanalytic thought, is consonant, I believe, with Freud's original formulation. Freud (1923) referred to the superego, even as he defined it, as "a grade within the ego"—i.e., as a differentiated segment of the ego, specifically concerned with value judgments related to the self. It seems to me that much of the complexity and uncertainty of superego theory, reflected in such works as those of Sandler and of Hartmann and Loewenstein (1962) would be obviated by an adherence to this view. Indeed, Freud's own failure to do so—i.e., his tendency to conceive of the superego as a separate and semi-autonomous structure with energies borrowed from the id and endowed with its own functional properties—has led to a kind of psychoanalytic neoscholasticism exemplified in the above-mentioned papers.

If the ego is thought of as the organization of adaptive and executive functions within the mental apparatus, [2] I see no reason to assign such functions as "self-criticism," "self-observation" and "the holding up of ideals" to the superego. All these functions are adaptive, clearly geared to the need to survive in and adapt to a specific socioenvironmental system. The young child who cannot conform at least minimally to socially accepted norms of behavior, dependent as he is on adult support and approval, risks serious injury to his self-esteem, if not to his very bodily integrity. Thus the adherence to ideals and prohibitions is but a special case of the overall functions of adaptation assigned, by definition, to the ego.[3]

[2] cf. Klein (1968)
[3] cf. Stein (1966) for a particularly lucid statement of the opposing viewpoint, and Jacobson (op.cit).

Accordingly, I am inclined to the view that the superego is best understood as a specialized group of identifications within the ego itself, related to issues of value. As part of its adaptive function, the ego (or rather that aspect of it devoted to self-observation) "screens" the superego-value reservoir as it does external reality, to assess the appropriateness of any thought or impulse and its consistency with the conscious and unconscious value systems. All *executive* functions—self-criticism, self-punishment, etc.—should be thought of as residing within the ego and carried out according to the dysharmony or harmony between thoughts and acts on the one hand and the value-system on the other. It is ultimately its survival value, [4] as the individual perceives it through the screen of his idiosyncratic history, identifications, etc. that determines the fate of any impulse or action insofar as the role of the superego is concerned. It is in this sense that, as Loewenstein (1966) says, "the superego may partake of certain areas of reality testing."

Such a conception serves, it seems to me, to eliminate the necessity for tortured explanations of the sources of superego "energy" [5] and of complex controversies over the nuances of superego function. It also permits one to avoid the reification and personification that so often attend discussions of the superego. The superego has no more function than does any other body of identifications. It has no more "energy" at its disposal than does any other body of identifications. The peremptory and categorical quality of the "primitive" or "preoedipal" superego is the consequence of the immature cognitive equipment of the young child (Nass, 1966), rather than the intensity of instinctual energies ascribed to it. The superego is thus best understood in terms of its *contents*, rather than in terms of any executive powers.

SOCIOCULTURAL CONSIDERATIONS

Adolescence as we see it today is distinctly a product of industrialization and urbanization; it is, as Stone and Church (1955)

[4] cf. Hartmann & Loewenstein (1962), p. 71.

[5] Schaefer (1968) discusses in detail the problems attendant on the concept of "psychic energy" in relation to questions of internalization and identification.

have said, "a cultural invention." Characteristic of contemporary adolescence is the prolongation of the period from pubescence to the assumption of adult sexual and economic status. Indeed, as our technology becomes more complex and the need for young working hands less urgent, this delay becomes ever greater, and the period of preparation and education ever longer. Today it is tacitly or explicitly assumed that college education is a necessary prerequisite for the assumption of full adult status in American society, and this view is rapidly spreading to other countries as their technology catches up.

Furthermore, the range of occupational possibilities and other social role models expands as traditional class and caste barriers break down. And finally, there are increasing options with regard to sexual object-choice, as such institutions as arranged marriage disappear, and religious and racial bars against intermarriage crumble. These options are also furthered by the proliferation of the European conception of romantic love (itself a product of an earlier age of privilege and leisure).

Coincident with this deterioration in traditional social institutions is the falling away of the systems of values associated with them—values such as submission to authority, veneration of parents and of the elders in the society, chastity, restriction of personal ambition, etc. [6] As in the sphere of ego-identification, so in that of the value system or superego the opening up of a wide range of possibilities confronts the adolescent with not only the potentiality but also the necessity for choice and self-determination. Though this situation provides him with vastly enlarged opportunities, it also becomes the occasion, in many cases, for intense anxiety, identity confusion and personal alienation.

Nothing exemplifies the latter situation more clearly than the current attitudes and behavior of young Negroes in America. Compounding the phase-specific disposition to reject parental values (v.i.) is the opening up of what has been, until very recently, a closed social system (cf. Pierce, 1968). In the past consigned to the limited range of possibilities open to those in a segregated

[6] Within our generation this process can be seen occurring in contemporary Mainland China.

subculture, negro adolescents suddenly find themselves confronted by a relatively open terrain, where educational and commercial institutions vie for their favor with eager and competitive recruitment programs.

Such young people are quick to derogate the "Uncle Tom" values of their parents (submissiveness, resignation, deference to whites and the wish to emulate them) and to espouse new, radical, aggressive values of Negritude, "Black Power" and violence. The ego-ideal of the young Negro is, then, decisively shaped by the dimensions of social and cultural change; he is no longer content to emulate a Joe Louis, a Bill Robinson, or a Booker T. Washington. The new models—Cassius Clay, Malcolm X, Eldridge Cleaver—are new men, born of the revolution of rising expectations and representative of a new system of values that clash, not only with those of the older generation of Negroes, but most decisively with those of the surrounding white community. The negro girl no longer bleaches and straightens her hair to conform to a white ideal [7]; she wears an "Afro" and proclaims that "black is beautiful."

Parallel processes go on in relation to sexual development. There is considerable evidence that pubertal maturation is occurring earlier in this generation than it did in that of its parents (at least in girls); nonetheless, it remains the "official" morality that premarital sexual relations are immoral and injurious. Young people are thus caught in an inevitable conflict between their importunate sexual urges (more intense than they will ever be again) and the values transmitted to them by their parents and the traditional institutions of society. Whatever the reality of the so-called "sexual revolution" of our times, adolescents who do behave as their biology dictates do so in the knowledge that they are flouting the prevailing moral attitudes and thus with a certain inescapable measure of guilt. [8] At the same time, the more reflective of them are engaged in formulating a new system of sexual ethics, if only

[7] Except for the Negro prostitute who, in appealing to a white clientele, is willing to present a degraded self-image.

[8] The cultural basis of these conflicts is made obvious by a comparison with Mead's (1928) description of Samoan pubescence.

to rationalize their own behavior and to overcome this sense of guilt.

INTRAPSYCHIC CONSIDERATIONS

A crucial element in the breakup of the preadolescent value structure is the change that occurs in early adolescence in the mental representations of the parents. Typically, we see a substantial disillusionment set in, particularly where the preadolescent attitude has been one of intense idealization based on an unreal or exaggerated image. This disillusion induces a state akin to that described by Koestler et al. (1950) among European intellectuals of the 30's and 40's whose illusions about Soviet Communism were shattered by such events as the purges, the pact with Hitler and, later, the coups in Czechoslovakia and Hungary. The state of anomie thus created led, in many cases, to desperate searches for other "gods," in the form of formal religions or other political ideologies.

Just so, the adolescent, endowed with sharpened cognitive skills, aware of a wider range of human experience and human possibility, and locked in an intrapsychic struggle to free himself from the cathexis of parental images, perceives—and sometimes constructs —the feet of clay under the idols of his latency years. Often, of course, this process is facilitated by major imperfections and defects in the parents themselves (hypocrisy, income-tax cheating, sexual irregularities, etc.). More often, however, it is an exaggerated reaction to the ordinary human limitations of those whom the child had earlier seen in an heroic mold.

Case 1

Steve came to analysis at 18, after withdrawing from a large Eastern university in order to avoid failing in his freshman year. Exceptionally bright and eager to learn, he had dissipated his time and energies in political activities to the extent that study was omitted from his program. At the outset of treatment he presented a picture of his father as a brilliant, gifted, energetic, highly successful lawyer with whom he actively identified. One of his earliest memories was of riding in a sound truck during a political campaign his father was managing. During the course of the analysis, however, and in the wake of his father's indisposition by a severe illness, Steve began to speak of long-felt disillusionment in his father. He complained of his father's passivity vis-à-vis the mother, of his tendencies to trim and compromise, and of his failure to achieve the political success he had always talked about wanting. It became apparent that Steve's compulsive political activities represented not only an effort at surpassing his father in an oedipal rivalry, but an attempt to restore the shattered ego-ideal by doing for his father (through identification) what his father could not do for himself.

Steve's politics were those of an operator and organizer rather than those of an ideologue; though liberal in orientation he was little engaged with issues as such. He was like an empty political vessel, in need of values to fill itself up. He would attach himself to older, more experienced professionals, as though hoping to learn from them not only how to operate, but also what to believe in. He was, for a time, enamored of the philosophy of Ayn Rand, which despite its profoundly conservative slant, offered him both a ready made set of values and a strong, powerful fictional hero who personified them. In the transference he constantly sought to provoke the analyst into directing, guiding and controlling his behavior.

The typical recourse of the American adolescent to this loss of the idealized parent image is the turn to the peer group as the major object of libidinal cathexis and the major source of values. Thus, one sees younger adolescents using only slightly older ones as idealized value models, exemplified by the appeal of *Seventeen* magazine to 13- and 14-year-old girls, and the progressive downward spread in drug use characteristic of urban school populations today, where junior high school students ape their senior high school peers in using marijuana much as the latter had earlier followed the lead of their collegiate brothers and sisters.

It is indeed in the drug, hippie, yippie and radical-revolutionary phenomena of the current scene, that we can most clearly see the value hunger of contemporary urban adolescents. Most obvious in the United States, the desperate quest of young people for meaningful and relevant values can be seen all over the civilized world. Though for many adolescents the use of marijuana, LSD and other hallucinogenic agents reflects the phase-appropriate wish to experiment with and experience new sensations, for some it is heavily tinged with a longing for new values of quasi-religious character. The rise to prominence of such gurus as Timothy Leary and Ken Kesey is a manifestation of this need. Lacking the guidelines of an increasingly irrelevant traditional religion, cut adrift from the received morality of the now devalued parents (or having failed ever to receive any in the first place), profoundly disgusted with an older generation that has foisted on them the immorality of the Viet Nam War and the unremitting danger of the draft, these adolescents grasp hungrily at new sources of values, new idealized parent surrogates, new religious leaders.

Case 2

Alan, 16, confessed to his parents that he had been using LSD and other drugs for several months. Long-haired, asthenic, extraordinarily intelligent and reflective, he entered psychotherapy eagerly, not so much because of his drug problem (he professed not to consider it much of a problem in itself) as because of other difficulties with which he wanted help. Both parents had recently remarried after their divorce a year earlier. He felt cut off from both parents, though he was living with his mother, and was mildly but clearly depressed. He complained that his father had always been remote and uninvolved; indeed, it was this quality that largely led to the divorce.

Alan's passivity and value hunger were exemplified by the ease with which he was influenced by peers, and his readiness to accept uncritically the modes and standards prevailing among them. He was intensely caught up in the mysticoreligious aura of "psychedelic" drug use. He quoted Leary extensively, read *The Book of the Dead* assiduously, and spoke of the religious experiences associated with LSD "trips." He was scornful of "conven-

Aaron H. Esman

tional middle-class games," but it became evident as he progressed in treatment that he could not fully accept the substitutes offered him by the psychedelic gurus. Gradually he became interested in the ethical aspects of the drug scene, particularly the "love" ethic that dictated, among other things, a kind of communal sharing of drug supplies and that led to a feeling of goodness when one "turned on" a neophyte to the joys of the psychedelicatessen.

Though Alan was ultimately arrested for selling marijuana, it should be emphasized that this "criminal" activity did not represent merely a defiance of conventional values; it was, for him, primarily carried out in the service of another set of values that he prized more highly. This "love" ethic served also to support Alan's unconsciously determined fear of aggression. He was proud that he never got angry (unlike his parents) and he was, of course, militantly pacifist.

Titchener (1969) in a fascinating account of his experiences as a doctor at Woodstock, formulates what he describes as a "new value system," an "empathic revolution," a "cultural standard of openness and emotional understanding of others" that manifested itself amidst the miasma of pot-smoke and the ubiquitous "dropping" of LSD that took place there. To quote:

> I believe that this new value system has developed from the permissiveness and increasing openness of family patterns which have been evolving since the beginning of this century. . . . In addition, social changes, mainly the immense proliferation of communication systems and the availability of information about political and international affairs has played a part in the emergence of empathic understanding and personal openness as a cultural value in young people.

Titchener further speaks of the special role at Woodstock of the "Hog-Farmers," a communal group who have evolved a spiritual system predicated on the role of LSD as a facilitating agent. At Woodstock, they served as guides, caretakers, priests—as parent surrogates who, at least transiently, served as models for the reformulating ego-ideals of the young people with whom they were working.

In his thoughtful study, *The Uncommitted,* Keniston (1965) has

96 ·

described the desperation of the "alienated" youth who, in response to the disillusionment with and rejection of parental models (particularly the father) finds himself bereft of life-directing values to support a quest for ego-identity. In contrast, his (1968) *Young Radicals* presents the picture of the ego strength, dedication and goal-directed identity of a group of youths who have, after a period of disorganization, assimilated their parents' values. Their radicalism and political activism, far from representing a rebellion, was actually an application and elaboration of ethical and political ideals espoused, though not always implemented, by their parents.

Case 3

Mike, a 19-year-old college junior, was a classic specimen of his type. Born to a rich family, reared in an exclusive suburb, educated at expensive private schools, he appeared slovenly and unkempt, with holes in his trousers, long shaggy hair and a droopy blond mustache. He came to treatment because of chronic feelings of self-doubt and inferiority, and intense social and sexual anxiety. He was an ex-drug user, having had three or four years' regular experience with marijuana and LSD and the values attending them before abruptly abandoning them completely after a "bad trip" during which he almost jumped out a window. During the course of his first analytic year, Mike began a fairly intense flirtation with radical politics. He was fascinated by SDS, participated in a couple of campus demonstrations and became friendly with an SDS leader. He was unable, however, to induce himself actually to join SDS or to accept fully its anarchist ideology. He would entertain himself with long, complex fantasies in which, as a radical leader, he would be wounded and jailed or hospitalized, achieving through his martyrdom both gratification of his profound masochistic wishes and a reconciliation with his conservative parents.

The route to such a reconciliation often runs through temporary repudiation and the reinforcing support of peer-group values which sometimes are only superficially at variance with those of

Aaron H. Esman

the older generation they are supposed to be defying. It is usually the adolescent who for one reason or another cannot conform to prevailing values who can elaborate for himself a value system that can be deviant from the norm but truly autonomous. In times of kaleidoscopic social change, this process may appear chaotic and disruptive especially among that segment of youth most actively implicated in change. But it is this quality that underlies the idealism of youth which is, at its best, its most appealing characteristic and is, in our time at least, making its own massive contribution to social change.

It should not be thought that the processes described here are ordinarily conscious. In fact, in the majority of adolescents they appear to exist quite outside consciousness, and to impose no great strain on everyday behavior. This is particularly true where the social surroundings tend to foster and support the process—i.e., where conformity to peer-group norms is taken for granted and supported by adults, and where intellection and reflection are not encouraged (Offer, 1969). It should also not be thought that the results of this process are always a repudiation of parental values and the institution of an autonomous, fully differentiated superego. On the contrary, it appears that most adolescents ultimately come to terms with what has been transmitted to them, and integrate a value system that is, in most particulars, a fairly accurate replica of that of their parents; indeed, cultural continuity requires that this be so. The point of view advanced here, however, is that this does not occur without some discontinuity, without some—at least internal—questioning, and without some transitory disruption of the preexisting value system. The traditional European model of tempestuous adolescence may not, as Keniston has said, be a valid normative picture of American youth, but a break does occur that, however repaired, should be recognized.

Thus it becomes clear that some reformulation of the concept of superego formation is in order. We cannot look upon the superego of the adult simply as "the heir to the Oedipus complex." Malmquist (1968) has recently and convincingly summarized the evidence for preoedipal superego development—data of the sort that have led to what Sandler (1960) has called "the conceptual dissolution

98 ·

of the superego." Though it may still be said that the Oedipal crisis constitutes a critical point in the evolution of the internalized value system, it seems that internalization takes place far earlier, in both ego-ideal and prohibitive aspects of the superego. Solnit and Ritvo (1960) state, ". . . Freud's idea that the superego is the heir to the oedipal situation would imply that the process of internalization has proceeded sufficiently to permit the forming superego to be relatively independent of the ego, *and to be an aid rather than an obstruction to ego function . . .*" (italics mine). Actually, the process of internalization is continuous, and adolescence would seem to be a second nodal point for the definition of internalized values. If heir to anything, then, the superego as we find it in the adult, as a stable guiding system of autonomous values, must be seen as the heir to the adolescent process. As Jacobson (1964) has put it, "When the adolescent has reached this level . . . we may say that he has found himself."

BIBLIOGRAPHY

Blos, P. (1962), *On Adolescence.* New York: The Free Press of Glencoe, Inc.
_____ (1968), Character Formation in Adolescence. *The Psychoanalytic Study of the Child,* 23: 245–263. New York: International Universities Press.
Erikson, E. (1956), The problem of ego identity. *J. Amer. Psychoanal. Assn.* 4: 56–121.
Freud, S. (1905), Three essays on the theory of sexuality. *Standard Edition,* 7:125–245. London: Hogarth Press, 1953.
_____ (1923), The ego and the id. *Standard Edition,* 19:3–68. London: Hogarth Press, 1961.
Freud, A. (1958), Adolescence. *The Psychoanalytic Study of the Child,* 13:255–278.
Hartmann, H., and Loewenstein, R. M. (1962), Notes on the superego. *The Psychoanalytic Study of the Child,* 17: 42–81.
Jacobson, E. (1964), The self and the object world. New York: International Universities Press.
Keniston, K. (1965), The uncommitted. New York: Harcourt, Brace and World.
_____ (1968), Young Radicals. *New York:* Harcourt, Brace & World.
Klein, G. S. (1968), Ego psychology. In: *International Encyclopedia of the Social Sciences.* New York: The Macmillan Co. and The Free Press of Glencoe.
Koestler, A. (1950), The initiates. In: *The God that Failed,* ed. R. Crossman. New York: Bantam, 1965.

Aaron H. Esman

Lederer, W. (1964), *Dragons, Delinquents and Destiny.* [*Psychological Issues,* Monogr. 4] New York: International Universities Press.

Loewenstein, R. M. (1966), On the theory of the superego: A discussion. In: *Psychoanalysis—A General Psychology,* ed. R. M. Loewenstein, L. M. Newman, M. Schur and A. J. Solnit. New York: International Universities Press.

Malmquist, C. (1968), Conscience development. *The Psychoanalytic Study of the Child,* 23:301–331.

Nass, M. (1966), The superego and moral development in the theories of Freud and Piaget. *The Psychoanalytic Study of the Child,* 21:51–68.

Offer, D. (1969), *The Psychological World of the Teenager.* New York: Basic Books.

Pierce, C. (1969), Problems of negro adolescents in the next decade. In: *Minority Group Adolescents in the United States,* ed. E. Brody. Baltimore: Williams & Wilkens Co.

Ritvo, S. and Solnit, A. (1960), The relationship of early ego identifications to superego formation. *Internat. J. Psychoanal.,* 41:295–300.

Sandler, J. (1960), On the concept of superego. *The Psychoanalytic Study of the Child,* 15:128–162.

Schaefer, R. (1968), *Aspects of Internalization.* New York: International Universities Press.

Spiegel, L. (1958), Comments on the psychoanalytic psychology of adolescence. *The Psychoanalytic Study of the Child,* 13:296–308.

Stein, M. H. (1966), Self-observation, reality and the superego. In: *Psychoanalysis—A General Psychology,* ed. R. M. Loewenstein, L. M. Newman, M. Schur and A. J. Solnit. New York: International Universities Press.

Stone, L. and Church, J. (1955), *Childhood and Adolescence.* New York: Random House.

Titchener, J. (1969), A most remarkable gathering. Presented to the American Psychoanalytic Assn., Dec. 1969.

5. The Superego in Women

HYMAN L. MUSLIN, M.D.

T HE SUPEREGO as it develops and functions in women continues to be a considerable source of curiosity in psychoanalysis, an enigma unto itself. This study will reexamine the contributions of various psychoanalytic authors, starting with Freud, and then offer a reappraisal of the subject.

THE CONTRIBUTIONS OF FREUD

Ernest Jones (1926) has written, "There is little doubt that Freud found the psychology of women more enigmatic than that of men. He once said to Marie Bonaparte, 'The great question that has never been answered and which I have not yet been able to answer, despite my thirty years of research into the feminine soul is: What does a woman want?' " (p. 421) Freud (1905) had earlier complained of the obscurity concerning the sexual life and psychology of women in *The Three Essays on the Theory of Sexuality*. He had written that the sexual life of men "alone has become accessible to research. That of women . . . is still veiled in an impenetrable obscurity." Somewhat later in a pamphlet on lay analysis Freud (1926b) had written "we know less about the sexual life of little girls than of boys. But we need not feel ashamed of this distinction, after all the sexual life of adult women is a 'dark continent' for psychology" (p. 212). There are several other references in the years between the Dora case and the case of female paranoia in which Freud alluded to the obscurity and enigma of female psychology. Thus in his (1900) account of the oedipal situation in "The Interpretation of Dreams," he assumed that there was a complete parallel in the development of the two sexes, that a "girl's first affection is for her father and a boy's first childish desires are for his mother." This line of investigation can be further noted in lecture 21 of "The Introductory Lectures" (1916–1917) where he wrote: "as you see I have only described the relation of a boy to his father and mother. Things happen just the same way with little girls, with the necessary changes: an affectionate attachment to her father, a need to get rid of her mother as superfluous" (p. 333). There is yet another allusion to the sameness between the sexes in the discussion on identification in *Group Psychology and the Analysis of the Ego* (1921); "The same holds good with the necessary substitutions of the baby daughter as well" (p. 116). As late as 1923 in *The Ego and the Id* Freud's comments related to the dissolution of the Oedipus complex, and its consequent heir, the superego, again followed the line of sameness between girls and boys.

> Along with the demolition of the Oedipus Complex, the boy's object-cathexis of his mother must be given up. Its place may be filled by one of two things: either an identification with his mother or an intensification of his identification with his father. We are accustomed to regard the latter outcome as the more normal; it permits the affectionate relation to the mother to be in a measure retained. In this way the dissolution of the Oedipus complex would consolidate the masculinity in a boy's character. *In a precisely analogous way,* the outcome of the Oedipus attitude in a little girl may be an intensification of her identification with her mother (or the setting up of such an identification for the first time)—a result which will fix the child's feminine character.
>
> It would appear, therefore, that in *both sexes* the relative strength of the masculine and feminine sexual dispositions is what determines whether the outcome of the Oedipus situation shall be an identification with the father or with the mother [p. 32].

It was from this point on, directly after the investigation into the formation of the superego and the structural theory in general, that Freud denied the existence of a "precise analogy" between the two sexes in their evolution towards the Oedipus complex and the consequent formation of the superego. It is noteworthy, however, that his (1923b) paper, "The Infantile Genital Organization," he had stated: "Unfortunately we can describe this state of things only as it affects the male child; the corresponding processes in the little girl are not known to us" (p. 141). In the following two years he was to write two papers revealing the new understandings about the Oedipus complex and the superego in women. These thoughts were contained in the 1924 paper on "The Dissolution of the Oedipus Complex" and the 1925 paper on "Some Psychical Consequences of the Anatomical Distinction Between the Sexes."

In the paper on "The Dissolution of the Oedipus Complex," Freud (1924) related the convoluted development (the biphasic development) of the girl in her journey from the early object relation with the mother based on a deep and active attachment which inevitably comes to a "tragic" end shortly after the full awareness of the difference in the physical endowments vis-à-vis the penis between boys and girls. This "tragic" perception which then initiates the little girl's search for the penis or its equivalent, the baby, from the father is the beginning of what was now to be called the "positive Oedipus complex" in women. According to Freud, the resolution of the Oedipus complex was often unsuccessful with its apparent consequence: the inadequate internalization of maternal and paternal objects, i.e., the superego. As Freud stated,

The female sex, too, develops an Oedipus complex, a superego and a latency period. May we also attribute a phallic organization and a castration complex to it? The answer is in the affirmative; but these things cannot be the same as they are in boys. Here the feminist demand for equal rights for the sexes does not take us far, for the morphological distinction is bound to find expression in differences of physical development. Anatomy is Destiny, to vary a saying of Napoleon's. The little girl's clitoris behaves just like a penis to begin with; but, when she makes a comparison with a playfellow of the other sex, she perceives that she has 'come off badly' and she feels this as a wrong done to her and as a ground for inferiority. For a while still she consoles herself with the expectation that later on, when she grows older, she will acquire just as big an appendage as the boy's. Here the masculinity complex of women branches off. A female child, however, does not understand her lack of a penis as being a sex character; she explains it by assuming that at some earlier date she had possessed an equally large organ and had then lost it by castration. She seems not to extend this inference from herself to other adult females, but entirely on the lines of the phallic phase, to regard them as possessing large and complete—that is to say, male—genitals. The essential difference thus comes about that the girl accepts castration as an accomplished fact, whereas the boy fears the possibility of its occurrence.

The fear of castration being thus excluded in the little girl, a powerful motive also drops out for the setting-up of a super-ego and for the breaking-off of the infantile genital organization. In her, far more than in the boy, these changes seem to be the result of upbringing and of intimidation from outside which threatens her with a loss of love. The girl's Oedipus complex is much simpler than that of the small bearer of the penis; in my experience, it seldom goes *beyond* the taking of her mother's place and the adopting of a feminine attitude towards her father. Renunciation of the penis is not tolerated by the girl without some attempt at compensation. She slips—along the line of a symbolic equation, one might say—from the penis to a baby. Her Oedipus complex culminates in a desire, which is *long retained,* to receive a baby from her father as a gift—to bear him a child. One has an impression that the Oedipus complex is then gradually given up because this wish is never fulfilled. The two wishes—to possess a penis and a child—remain strongly cathected in the unconscious and help to prepare the female creature for her later sexual role. The comparatively lesser strength of the sadistic contribution to her sexual instinct, which we may not doubt connect with the stunted growth of her penis, makes it easier in her case for the direct sexual trends to be transformed into aiminhibited trends of an affectionate kind. It must be admitted, however, that in general our insight into these developmental processes in girls is unsatisfactory, incomplete and vague [pp. 177–179].

This line of reasoning is contained in the 1925 paper on the "Psychical Consequences of the Anatomical Distinction between the Sexes" where Freud stated:

In girls the motive for the demolition of the Oedipus complex is lacking. Castration has already had its effect, which was to force the child into the situation of the Oedipus complex. Thus the Oedipus complex escapes the fate which it meets within boys: it may be slowly abandoned or dealt with by repression, or its effects may persist far into women's normal mental life. I cannot evade the notion (though I hesitated to give it expression) that for women the level of what is ethically normal is different from what it is in men. Their super-ego is never so inexorable, so impersonal, so independent of its emotional origins as we require it to be in men. Character-traits which critics of every epoch have brought up against women—that they show less sense of justice than men, that they are less ready to submit to the great exigencies of life, that they are more often influenced in their judgements by feelings of affection or hostility—all these would be amply accounted for by the modification in the formation of their super-ego which we have inferred above. We must not allow ourselves to be deflected from such conclusions by the denials of the feminists, who are anxious to force us to regard the two sexes as completely equal in position and worth; but we shall, of course, willingly agree that the majority of men are also far behind the masculine ideal and that all human individuals, as a result of their bisexual disposition and of cross-inheritance, combine in themselves both masculine and feminine characteristics, so that pure masculinity and femininity remain theoretical constructions of uncertain content [pp. 257–259].

In the monograph *Inhibition, Symptoms and Anxiety,* Freud (1926a) discusses the dynamic and genetic aspects of animal phobias, obsessional neuroses and conversion hysteria in terms of the fear of castration. "The anxiety felt in animal phobias is the ego's fear of castration while the anxiety felt in agoraphobia (a subject that has been less thoroughly studied) seems to be its fear of sexual temptation—a fear which after all must be connected in its origins with the fear of castration" (p. 109). As he goes on to say later in this work, however, ". . . is it absolutely certain that fear of castration is the only motive force of repression (or defense)? If we think of neuroses in women we are bound to doubt it. For though we can with certainty establish in them the presence of a castration complex, we can hardly speak with propriety of castration anxiety where castration has already taken place" (p. 123). Thus the model of psychopathology and character formation at this stage in psychoanalytic theory still reflected, albeit unevenly, the concept of sameness between the sexes.

Hyman L. Muslin

In discussing the moral acquisition internalized in the superego in *The Ego and the Id*, Freud (1923a) said: "The male sex seems to have taken the lead in all these moral acquisitions; and they seem to have been transmitted to women by cross-inheritance" (p. 37). The cultural superego acquired as a result of the killing of the primal father and the subsequent father identification in the superego of the son seems to be a further example of cultural acquisitions to the exclusion of women. Thus this important facet of the superego Freud felt was diminuitive or lacking in females, i.e., the moral acquisition was "transmitted by cross-inheritance" from men.

Further elaboration of his thoughts on female sexuality, the Oedipus complex and the superego is contained in the 1931 paper on "Female Sexuality":

> Thus in women the Oedipus complex is the end-result of a fairly lengthy development. It is not destroyed, but created, by the influence of castration; it escapes the strongly hostile influences which, in the male, have a destructive effect on it, and indeed it is all too often not surmounted by the female at all. For this reason, too, the cultural consequence of its break-up are smaller and of less importance in her. We should probably not be wrong in saying that it is this difference in the reciprocal relation between the Oedipus and the castration complex which gives its special stamp to the character of females as social beings" [p. 230].

One of Freud's (1932) last statements about the superego in women is contained in Lecture XXXIII of "The New Introductory Lectures" where once again he stresses the lack of strength of the female superego and the length of the Oedipus complex:

> Girls remain in it for an indeterminate length of time; they demolish it late and, even so, incompletely. In these circumstances the formation of the superego must suffer; it cannot attain the strength and independence which give it its cultural significance, and feminists are not pleased when we point out to them the effects of this factor upon the average feminine character [p. 129].

In summarizing Freud's final positions on the superego in women it is apparent that he viewed the cathexis of the internal objects of mother and father in the female psyche as insufficiently complete to make for a so-called autonomous superego system. Thus, the usual superego signals of guilt and shame, the reflection of the autonomous superego systems are not as evident in the workings of the mental apparatus of the female. In its place there continues to be a wish for approval and love from parental objects in the environment, with its attendant displacements on objects serving the role of mother and father in the current environment. Thus, loss of love or esteem is as important or more important a set of signals in regulating the psychic economy of the female as is the fear of the autonomous superego, ordinarily made manifest by the signals of guilt and shame.

Over the several decades in which he worked, Freud's views of the superego in women underwent important changes, as did many other of his theoretical concepts. It was true of many of these constructs that there were substantial areas of unevenness, especially if, as one set of ideas were being worked out, complementary notions were yet to be integrated. Such was the case, I believe, in the construction of the theories of superego in women.

Freud's original notion of the superego was that this structure was identical in both sexes save that the father was substituted for the mother in the oedipal triangle. After Freud returned to his investigation of female psychology in 1915 and thereafter he described the biphasic development of the Oedipus complex. The resolution of the complex was often incomplete since the motive force was not castration anxiety but pressure from environmental objects, especially the threat of loss of love.

However, as has been indicated above, these notions were not integrated with other aspects of psychoanalytic theory so that the motive force for repression and symptom formation in itself was still, in 1926, described as castration anxiety without reference (save for a passing note) to the situation in females. The actual resolution of the oedipal struggle in females was not clear and often incomplete so that the girl's search for the penis-baby was not consummated. A stable crystallized system of introjects operating as a major restraint against instinctual derivatives could not obtain from this situation.

Freud's comment on the lack of cultural and moral achievement by women represented the special view on the subject of women ubiquitously held in the Victorian era. As an example of this view it will be remembered that in the "primal horde" theory it is only men who are left with a conscience after the killing of the primal parent.

Contributions of Other Psychoanalytic Authors

Freud remarked in the 1931 paper on female sexuality, "An examination of the analytic literature on the subject shows that everything that has been said by me here is already to be found in it" (p. 240). This was certainly not the case but there had been several other analytic workers who had begun investigation into female sexuality and the psychic apparatus in women starting with Abraham's (1929) description of the manifestations and consequences of the castration complex in women. However, he did not elaborate on the girl's original exclusive attachment to the mother and the subsequent phase, the entry into the so-called positive Oedipus complex with the father.

Deutsch, in a series of papers on the psychology of women starting in 1925 and thereafter, emphasized the girl's phallic activity and the intensity of the attachment to the mother, the so-called preoedipal phase of the girl.

In 1924 Karen Horney published her findings on the "Genesis of the Castration Complex in Women." Here she added an important set of data from analyses of women which made clear to her that the so-called "penis envy" which apparently became manifest at the inception of the positive Oedipus complex, along with the subsequent turning to father for the penis and child, was really not the deepest root of the little girl's expectations from her father. In her view, the more deeply repressed fantasy ascribed the loss of the male genital in a girl to a sexual act with the father partner. This to her was one of the roots of the castration complex in females.

Lampl-de Groot, in her 1927 paper, "Evolution of the Oedipus

Complex in Women," further elaborated on the intensity of the girl's preoedipal relation to the mother which she labeled the negative Oedipus situation. The castration complex, the awareness of the fact of castration and absence of the penis is the event that terminates what Lampl-de Groot called the negative Oedipus complex in female children and which she labeled a secondary formation in contradistinction to Freud. Thus, the positive Oedipus complex in women is made possible and ushered in by the castration complex which itself is a secondary formation, its precursor being the negative Oedipus situation.

Melanie Klein (1928) elaborated on her findings as a result of her analyses of children especially between the ages of three and six. Her notion was that the Oedipus complex comes into operation at about one year of age. Therefore, in her view, the superego as a structure was in effect at this early age and with it the sense of guilt as a result of the introjection of the Oedipus love objects. She made it quite clear that the sense of guilt attached itself to the oral- and anal-sadistic phases which predominated, ". . . and . . . the superego comes into being while these phases are in the ascendant which accounts for its sadistic severity" (p. 168).

Klein articulated the developmental sequence of superego formation starting with the early identification with the mother at about one year of age in which this anal-sadistic level predominated, the little girl derives "jealousy and hatred in forms of cruel superego after the maternal imago." However, there is a subsequent development of the superego based on an identification with mother on the genital basis, this set of identifications will be characterized by the devoted kindness of an indulgent mother-ideal. Thus, the final consolidation of the superego will depend on the extent to which the maternal mother-ideal bears a characteristic peculiar to the pregenital or the genital stage [p. 177].

Ernest Jones (1935) wrote along the same lines: "There is more femininity in the young girl than analysts generally admit; the masculine phase through which she may pass is more complex than is commonly thought" (p. 264). The girl enters into an early Oedipus complex ushered in by oral dissatisfactions. As he said in 1926, being unable to cope with the anger and reactive punishment, she temporarily takes flight in the 'phallic phase' and then later resumes her normal development, that is displaying femininity. This view seems to me more in accord with the ascertainable facts and also intrinsically more probable, than one which would regard her femininity to be the result of an external experience (viewing a penis). To my mind, on the contrary, her femininity develops progressively from the prompting of instinctual constitution. In short, I do not see a woman—in the way feminists do— as a permanently disappointed creature struggling to console herself with secondary substitutes alien to her true nature [p. 273].

In Jones' view the process that is initiated is a defense against the identification with the mother, that is, a defense against the already existing Oedipus complex and the identification with father, the so-called phallic phase, is not a question of the wish for a penis per se but a defense against the already existing Oedipus complex and its identification with the mother. This is in contradiction to Freud's view that the girl's wish for the child is mainly compensatory for her disappointment in not having a penis of her own. The girl's flight from femininity in Jones' view is essentially a reaction to the hatred and fear of the mother, that is, a defensive attitude towards her own wish for feminine identification. This is in agreement with Melanie Klein's views.

Here again, then, although no direct reference is made to the female superego, it seems clear that Jones' conclusion was that depending on the nature of the fixation of the little girl, she will develop either an anal-sadistic maternal superego born out of the so-called early Oedipus complex, or her superego will represent an identification with the more genital maternal superego thus allowing for an attitude of passivity and receptivity to the man.

Sachs (1929) noted what he felt to be the essential factor in the formation of the superego in women and the analogous process in men. "The man's superego has its origin in the threat of castration and therefore always has something of a menacing command about it ('thou shalt not be like the father or else')" (p. 45). The woman's superego, on the other hand, is based rather on the ideal of a renunciation. In Sachs' view no true female superego can be formed until the frustration at the hands of the father and the fantasied love relationship has been experienced and has resulted in the renunciation of the wish for the father. The woman does not obtain a superego at all unless the necessary renunciation of her claims to the penis leads to her accepting deprivation as a life-long ideal.

> From Robespierre to Lenin all the great revolutionary theorists and organizers of revolutions have been men. When the time has come for a revolution to be actually launched and for the masses to be convinced that the time of renunciation and self-denial is over, when the moment has arrived to strike the blow and break the bond, then a woman has always stood in the front ranks, thus it was in the French revolution. When Schiller with unconscious understanding of the oral factor says, "Da werden weiber zu hyanen" (women turn into hyenas); thus it was during the Commune in Paris with Louise Michelle, thus it was with the so-called Nihilists in Russia (Vera Figner) and thus it will be in all the revolutions of the future [p. 50].

Ruth Mack Brunswick (1940) contributed a paper on her collaboration with Freud, begun in 1930, entitled the "Pre-Oedipal Phase of the Libido Development." In her comments about the preoedipal development and subsequent developmental phases of the female, Brunswick stated that the preoedipal mother attachment in the girl develops into something surprisingly like the Oedipus complex of the boy with mother as the love object and father as rival. Upon the destruction of this "primitive Oedipus complex" there develops from its ruins, as it were, the positive or passive Oedipus complex of the little girl with the father as the new love object and mother as the rival. In her view the preoedipal phenomena may have even more importance in feminine development. Once in the Oedipus complex, she states, the normal woman tends to remain there in contrast to the male's development. In her view, it is the intense resistance of the female Oedipus complex to the powers of destruction which accounts for the differences in structure of the male and female superego.

In the literature on the female psyche and superego preceding the modern era of psychoanalysis, there is general agreement as to the major points that Freud posited in relation to the female Oedipus complex and its resolution or lack of resolution leading to the superego apparatus. Although several authors amplified the nature and importance of the preoedipal period (Lampl-de Groot, Brunswick, Deutsch), and others disagreed with the importance of penis envy as a motive force in the entry into the positive Oedipus complex (Horney, Jones), while still others placed the Oedipus complex at an earlier time in the developing child (Klein, Jones), it would seem that the major features of the theory elaborated by Freud have been accepted—to wit, the lack of "destruction" of the fantasies of the Oedipus complex, since castration anxiety is not a motive force, and the length of time (ofttimes permanently) the normal woman tends to remain involved in the fantasies of the Oedipus complex.

Of the modern writers, Greenacre (1952) stresses that the superego in the girl is imbued with feelings of wrongdoing emanating from past masturbation and the already present punishment of castration. This accounts for the aimless conscientiousness and worrying in females to be contrasted with the firmer, more condensed conscience in the male. Another concept she advances is that the higher and more vague ideals found in females may be tied in with the "unpalpable" area of which she is dimly aware, and perhaps bears some relation to the notion of deferment, i.e., that she will one day be mature and procreate.

Jacobson's (1964) comments about the development of the superego in women reveal a disagreement with Freud that the female superego is defective; she believes rather that it is different in nature from the male superego. In her view the girl develops a nucleus of a true maternal ego-ideal earlier than the boy. This, she relates, is due to the early onset of the castration conflict in girls. Directly as a result of the castration conflict, the girl suffers from intense castration fears but eventually her preoedipal disappointment and devaluation of her mother's and her own deficient genital lead to a rejection of her mother as a sexual love object in favor of the phallic father. This sometimes eventuates in the premature disenchantment with all genital activities and results in the early establishment of the maternal ego-ideal: the ideal of an unaggressive, clean, neat little girl, determined to renounce sexuality (in Jacobson's view, the female ego-ideal absorbs and forever replaces the "illusory penis" fantasy. These are the females who deny penis envy but unconsciously have as representation of their "inner penis," an uncommon pride in their inner values and their moral integrity).

> But the further maturation of the ego ideal and the setting up of more advanced superego standards in the little girl are frequently disrupted as her persistent wishes for recovery of her penis are turned toward her father. Because of its origin in her castration conflicts, the little girl's oedipal attachment to the father appears to activate regressive processes. They retransform to some extent those introjective mechanisms which constituted the precocious ego ideal into fantasies of oral and genital incorporation centered about the paternal phallus. Such regressive reactions inhibit and delay the establishment of an independent ego as the further internalization, depersonification, and abstraction of ethical codes in the little girl and lead to a reattachment of her wishful self image to an outside person: to the glamorous figure of her phallic father. Freud was certainly correct in stating that in woman the leading fear is not fear of castration but of loss of love; however, during this phase of her oedipal conflict, loss of her father's love represents also a narcissistic injury: the loss of her—i.e., her father's—penis.
>
> The experience of oedipal love and disappointment, supported by the biological increase of heterosexual strivings and of sexual rivalry with the mother, again influences the development of the little girl's identifications in a feminine direction. The final outcome of her conflict depends a great deal on the father's attitudes and on the mother's personality and love. On the whole, I believe that the eventual constitution of a self-reliant ego, and of a mature ego ideal and autonomous superego in women is all the more successful the better the little girl learns to accept her femininity and thus can find her way back to maternal ego and superego identifications [p. 114–115].

Thus Jacobson conceives of the outcome of the Oedipus complex in girls to be the autonomous superego, the superego proper which Freud ascribed only to boys. This would imply that the function of the autonomous superego, including the stimulation of repression by the ego, the holding out of ideals and prohibitions, in addition to the facilitation of instinctual gratification is carried out by the female in much the same way as it occurs in the male.

Hartmann and Loewenstein (1962) stress that the term super-ego should refer to the system which comes into being upon the resolution of the conflict of the oedipal phase with the following three functions: (1) the conscience, (2) self-criticism, (3) holding up ideals.

Their comments on the female superego point up that the female superego does have particular characteristics, among them that its origin is less climactic than is the case with boys, and that its formation extends over a longer period. However, they state that in the girl the ego-ideal tends to set in earlier, that is, at a time when integration and objectivation and their autonomous function are, comparatively speaking, less developed.

Piers' (1953) contribution to this area of theory stems from his views of shame and guilt. What he points to in his views of the superego and ego-ideal are not specifically referred to as either masculine or feminine. Thus, by implication Piers' understanding of these two institutions is that they function in a similar manner. He states:

> Accordingly we use here the term "Super-Ego" exclusively as stem-ming from internalization (introjection) of the punishing, restrictive aspects of the parental images—regardless of whether the original images corresponded to reality or were largely projections of the individual's own magical destructiveness. It may be stated here in an oversimplified fashion that no one develops a sense of guilt without a punitive parent image, the latter being based either on historical reality or projective imagination. For it has been shown that the projection of primitive destructive impulses and possibly fantasies into the parental images plays a large part in the formation of the Super-Ego. Since at an early developmental stage the primary narcissistic "belief" in the omnipotence of thought and wish prevail, the Super-Ego is automatically endowed with similar power.
>
> From this brief summary, it will be clear that we do not hold the formation of the Super-Ego contingent upon the "passing of the Oedipus complex." The development of an internalized conscience with its executive arm of guilt feeling occurs prior to and in large portions

independent of the Oedipal situation. E.g., the importance of oral aggressiveness and the role of the mother as punitive agent have been amply demonstrated in this connection [p. 6].

In a more recent paper, Hammerman (1965) once again notes the origin and development of the superego in women to be less climactic and extending over a longer period. He does, however, indicate that an internalized autonomous superego, a superego proper, does eventuate in the development of the female psyche (p. 330).

DISCUSSION

In *The Ego and the Id*, Freud (1923a) listed the activity of the superego to include two groups of functions. On the one hand, there were the functions that included self-judgment, prohibitions and injunctions, and a sense of guilt—those functions that served to prevent the expression of forbidden instinctual drives. On the other hand, there were a set of functions that had to do with social feelings—those functions that define the ideals and values of men. From this vantage point, one might now add as a superego function the gratifications of meeting standards and ideals, the loving part of the superego.

When one sets out to assign specific functions of the superego it soon becomes evident that "the superego is like a raw personage who can only function through his prime minister. The superego is a part of psychic structure that can be defined in terms of attitude, not in terms of action. Action is delegated to one other ego function" (p. 327). It seems clear, therefore, that in the complete understanding of the role and function of the superego, one is always speaking of interrelations between the executive agent of the psyche, the ego, and the superego. Thus we may view the superego as an agency which increases the ego's capacity to recognize specific kinds of danger situations apart from holding out ideals of behavior for the individual and for the social good. In the adult psyche, in both sexes, it seems reasonable to assume the impact of the superego in every psychic act, at once facilitating, inhibiting, or encouraging a certain channel of discharge. Thus, the superego functions become manifest only through some recognizable ego functions.

However, as has been documented above, the superego structure in women has been described as lacking in regard to some important attributes of this structure. The superego in women *is* a unique system in regard to the contents of this internalized system but not in terms of the function it serves within the psychic apparatus—specifically, to act as conscience, hold up ideals and to facilitate drive discharge. In these functions superegos are superegos but, in terms of the nature of the goals and ideas, the essence of the female destiny, this is unique to the woman.

The process of superego formation, the process of decathexis of objects replaced by internalization (identification, introjection) is a nonspecific feature of the human psyche, alike in male and female. As Kohut (1966) has pointed out: "If the psyche is deprived however of a source of instinctual gratification, it will not resign itself to the loss but will change the object image into an introject, i.e., into a structure of the psychic apparatus which takes over functions previously performed by the object. Internalization (although part of the autonomous equipment of the psyche and occurring spontaneously) is therefore enhanced by object loss" (p. 247). Kohut states further, ". . . during the preoedipal period there normally occurs a gradual loss of the idealized parent image and a concomitant accretion of the drive-regulating matrix of the ego, while massive loss during the oedipal period contributes to the formation of the superego" (p. 248).

Internalizations, ubiquitous aspects of the human psyche, dominate mental life in all aspects of intrapsychic and interpersonal reactivity. The superego as system may best be thought of as the total aggregate of "drive-regulating" structure, internalized from infancy and continuing through adulthood depending on the ego capacity to internalize, i.e., limited by cognitive ego capacity (perception, recall, etc.).

As such, these internalizations taking place throughout the entire long-lasting dependence of the human infant on parental figures provide for memory traces specific to drives emerging in a particular developmental sequence, e.g., an oral-sadistic drive struggling for expression stimulates memory traces of the original prohibitions emanating from the parent figure who symbolized prohibition in those times either in reality or as a projection of the infant's oral sadism. In this scheme each emerging drive carries with it in the struggle for expression the specific modifiers originally attached to it, with the addition of the ego function of neutralization. Freud's awareness of the *system,* superego coming into being at the end of the Oedipus complex makes clear that the complete system of prohibition and ideals is dependent on a major decathexis of objects to promote consolidation into a single system operational for most purposes in each mental act. This event, the termination of the Oedipus complex, rounds up, as it were, the so-called superego precursors into an aggregate structure. The notion of a stable, internalized structure operating with its own sources of energy derived from the instinctual reservoir with which it is in contact differentiates this system from the superego in the infants discussed by Klein. Pregenital drives do evoke drive regulators as a presuperego phenomenon but at these times in the infant's development, environmental regulators, the mother and father figures, as perceived objects are as important as the internalized memories and fantasies of the parental figures.

As the female continues in her drive development the object of her "biological aim of receptivity" becomes the father, mother's husband. The wish for exclusive contact with the father implies the loosening of libidinal ties with the mother as well as entry into competition with the mother. This special kind of separation stands for a loss of love which evokes fear and even panic, since the fear of loss of love is, as Freud (1931) said, the fear of aggression by the external authority: "This is, of course, what fear of the loss of love amounts to for love is a protection against this punitive aggression" (p. 128). In males the Oedipus complex comes to an end with the growing awareness of possible mutilation (castration) at the hands of the punitive father. Massive decathexis of the objects of the triangle occurs and internalization of authoritarian codes now is the result, included in this structure are restraints and modifiers from earlier developmental periods. In girls the barrier to the successful union with the father is not mutilation (nor is it in many cases a firm prohibition from mother and father to inhibit the romance between father and daughter or between son and daughter) but rather the growing awareness of the possibility of loss of love from the mother. This loss is not a minor stimulus as others have implied since it evokes memory traces of abandonment and destruction, the major anxiety of infancy. Dissolution of the female Oedipus complex is said to occur over a long period of time which is a reflection of the nature of the dangers causing the dissolution, i.e., the threat of castration is both more easily discerned and more articulated with boys than the more vague danger of abandonment and destruction experienced by girls since it is a part of the memory traces of infancy. The decathexis of the object representation in the female at this phase results in the internalization of authoritarian codes. This massive decathexis results in the consolidation of the superego system now including prohibitions from earlier periods. The special contents of the superego in women, the special memory traces evoked in relation to the goal of the oedipal quest are not the menacing prohibition of "thou shalt not have what I have," but rather, "I will abandon you; you will be destroyed." This special danger to the girl makes it difficult for the girl to enter into the so-called positive Oedipus complex since entry into the more intense, more exclusive relationship, albeit fantastic, implies the possibility of abandonment by the mother. Thus the fear of the superego later achieving representation as guilt is at the bottom the fear of abandonment and destruction in females as it is fear of mutilation (castration) in males.

Overcoming the demands of the childhood superego in women stands for overcoming the fear of abandonment by the mother image while involved in a heterosexual relationship—("I'm going home to Mother!").

Directly after consolidation of the superego as system, the function that we ascribe to the presence of the superego becomes manifest, i.e., the conscience and ideal functions occurring in both sexes. It is useful to conceive of the superego as involved in all mental activity when drives are pressing for discharge. Depending on the nature of the drive, superego and memory traces associated with it may either evoke ego decathexis and expulsion (repression) or actually facilitate drive discharge. The actual feeling of guilt probably amounts to an unsuccessful integration of superego tension with the ego's capacity for repression, ushering in the ego's awareness of guilt. If the ego has been able to respond effectively to the subliminal superego signals, the experience of guilt does not occur and the instinctual derivative is repressed. (The enforcing function of the superego is described by Hartmann and Loewenstein [1962].)

In all these *functions* of the superego there is no sexual differentiation, that is to say, the superego, once consolidated, functions to assist in the binding, neutralizing and discharging of drives by holding out standards and emitting signals to which specialized aspects of the ego respond in appropriate ways. Women typically experience symptoms, inhibition and anxiety as well as guilt with loss of esteem. Of course there are wide varieties of character types in females which resist stereotyping. Certainly ethical codes exist with wide degrees of rigidity or strength in women. The stability and impersonality of a woman's conscience is part of the same continuum existing in men; thus the capacity to see truth and fight for justice can be manifest in both sexes. Once formed, the superego processes may be seen as functioning similarly in both sexes in the service of maintaining repression, censoring, etc.—but the contents of the superego, which determine what instinctual derivatives are to be repressed or dissolved, are a particular of each individual as a reflection of herself or himself, and as a reflection of special values as befits a member of a group (or sex) that shares and transmits values.

The specialized socialization process of a girl involves "ought nots" that chart the course of expectations held out by authorities for the woman-to-be in her society. These values originally become manifest in infancy and are ordinarily unique for girls as distinct from boys. Such differences are especially marked in the area of aggressive activity permitted and encouraged in many societies for boys, contrasted with prohibition against aggressive activity for girls. This is similarly the case in the censorship and double standards surrounding sexual activity. Perhaps in the past this special kind of censorship internalized by females against aggressivity and sexuality has been misinterpreted as lack of drive, character, or moral standards in the female. This special kind of cultural fallacy with its roots in the ubiquitous anxiety of the omniscient, potentially devouring mother-figure finds expression in the restriction placed on females against the emergence of instinctuality and the ideal of the "sweet, kind, shy little girl" shared by countless generations of parents. Freud noted with some expression of surprise in the 1933 paper on femininity that: "Analysis of children's play has shown our women analysts that the aggressive impulses of little girls leave nothing to be desired in the way of abusiveness and violence. With their entry into the phallic phase the difference between the sexes are completely eclipsed by their agreements. We are obliged to recognize that the little girl is a little man" (p. 108). He had previously claimed in the same work, ". . . a little girl is less aggressive, defiant and self-sufficient" (p. 117). As is well known, the "new look" into the development of the woman's psyche came with knowledge of the preoedipal attachment of the girl to her mother, including the girl's wish to possess mother, with the father in this triangle being the competitor. As Freud (1931) said, "Our insight into this early, pre-Oedipal phase in girls comes to us like a surprise, like the discovery, in another field, of the Minoan-Mycenian civilization behind the civilization of Greece" (p. 226).

Another aspect of the superego in women which has often been discussed is the ego ideal, which Kohut (1966) refers to as "the phase-specific massive introjection of the idealized qualities of the object," the object that has been decathected and internalized (p. 248). This facet of the superego is the repository for the standards of the idealized parent, the carrier of the original narcissistic perfection of the infant, thus giving a unique importance to our standards and ideals. To meet one's standards enhances esteem, to fall short of our standards evokes the experience of inferiority or mortification in adults, a revival of the memory traces of failure to meet parental expectation. Shame arises, as Piers (1953) stated, ". . . out of a tension between the Ego and the Ego-Ideal," and at another point, ". . . shame occurs when a goal (presented by the

Ego-Ideal) is not being reached. It thus indicates a real "shortcoming" (p. 6).

Many authors have commented on the girl's internalizing ego-ideal standards at an early age (Greenacre, Hartmann, Jacobson) which in Hartmann's terms has to do with holding up of the "good." Jacobson speaks of the ideal of an unaggressive, clean, neat little girl.

On another level, Benedek (1956) describes what could be conceived of as the earliest ideal the girl is given: to be mother to her mother during the postpartum symbiosis. She writes: "To whom does the mother turn with her receptive needs, with her wish for care and love? Naturally, to her husband, her mother and other members of her immediate environment who are the sources of her physical and emotional security. But on a deeper level of her personality, her unconscious emotional needs are turned towards her infant for satisfaction" (p. 397). While this situation is alike for both boys and girls, the mother's identification with the daughter immediately becomes deeper, as Benedek indicates, since it ties in with the girl's future goal of her "maturation in motherliness." She points out that: "The dominant factor in the ego ideal in general is the one which, rooted in biological function and developed through identification with the mother, approaches its fulfillment through motherhood" (p. 413).

Thus an important facet of the contents of the ego-ideal is found in those internalizations the girl makes of her cherished object, the mother. The girl's wish to mother is further transmitted by other members of the family, the father and siblings, and held up as a standard in society in all cultures. From her early days, the girl is persistently lauded for so-called mothering attitudes. These mothering attitudes, however, to be lauded should not reveal destructive, devouring, omniscient traits ascribed and projected to the infantile version of "Mother." Investigations indicate that the reaction on the part of men in a wide range of cultures, during the female menstrual period, for example, vary from virtual imprisonment of the menstruating woman, to exclusion from the tribe, to elaborate cleaning rituals. While many of the fantasies of the men reacting to this phenomenon deal with castration anxiety, there are also clear fantasies of the possibility of women carrying the Mana, the power to destroy (Muslin and Pieper, 1961). The exclusion or restriction of women from tribal councils and priestly functions applies not only to the historical traditions of the Judeo-Christian civilization but of prior civilizations achieving psychic representation in the internalized ideal of the mothering woman. This is expressed in the latter-day expression of "the woman behind the man," "the little woman," "my little helper" and a "good woman," all manifestations of the cultural standard for the woman. Thus it *has* been the case historically that women show less "sense of justice" and further true that women have had fewer cultural acquisitions.

Freud (1923) pointed out:

> Religion, morality and a social sense—the chief elements in the higher side of man—were originally one and the same thing. According to a hypothesis which I put forward in "Totem and Taboo" they were acquired phylogenetically out of the father-complex: religion and moral restraint through the process of mastering the Oedipus complex itself, and social feeling through the necessity for overcoming the rivalry that then remained between the members of the younger generation. The male sex seems to have taken the lead in all these moral acquisitions; and they seem to have then been transmitted to women by cross-inheritance" [p. 37].

This observation by Freud describes a historical phenomenon and a segment of the standards held out to women, i.e., the standard of nonparticipation in the major institutions of society. It would represent a major development in our civilization if standards transmitted to and internalized by females would not be restrictive so as to begin to include the goal of motherhood and mothering with the goal of achievement in any areas.

The discussion of the ego-ideal to this point has centered on the contents of the ego-ideal in women; once the ego-ideal as substructure within the superego system begins to function it serves as the standard by which the self measures itself and feels loved or feels failure and shame. The memory traces revived are either of narcissistic bliss, the regaining of union with the idealized parental object or conversely the memory trace of being unloved. The interaction between the self and the ideal is similar in both sexes, thus once again the processes of functioning of the superego does not distinguish between male and female. The experience of shame, of mortification, the awareness of not living up to one's ideals is a human experience.

The previous remarks have been intended to describe the superego in women as a set of functions operating as a vital factor in the maintenance of intrapsychic equilibrium. It has been argued that there is no specifically female superego or masculine superego, but rather that there are ubiquitous processes of internalization and structure formation in men and women alike. These structures, once formed, exhibit specific functions as in the case of the superego. The superego in women does have specific contents, i.e., what becomes internalized is peculiar to their special instinctual needs and development, particularly to the cultural values held out for them. These superego contents frame for the individual woman the conscience standards, the measure by which the self experiences failure or victory.

However, although the contents of these structures are unique to women, the superego functioning is similar in both sexes.

The model of superego development and functioning in females has been outlined in a modal fashion, i.e., only outlining modal events in a girl's ontogeny. It is clear, of course, that given special circumstances and special parental objects for idealization and internalization, the superego would reflect these special contents. Thus a superego in females without ideals of motherhood, without the "indwelling qualities" common to the female psyche, would in many societies reflect either circumstances preventing phase-appropriate internalization of idealized parental objects (parent loss) or might accurately reflect the internalized prohibition against heterosexuality held out as a standard. The special configurations of the Oedipus complex necessarily eventuate in special configurations of the superego.

BIBLIOGRAPHY

Abraham, K. (1927), *Selected Papers on Psychoanalysis.* London: Hogarth Press, p. 483.

Benedek, T. (1956), Biology of depressive constellation. *J. Amer. Psychoanal. Assn.,* 4:389–427.

Beres, D. (1958), Vicissitudes of superego functions and superego precursors in childhood. *The Psychoanalytic Study of the Child,* 13:324–351.

Brunswick, R. M. (1940), The preoedipal phase of the libido development. In: *The Psychoanalytic Reader,* Vol. I, ed. R. Fliess. New York: International Universities Press, 1950, pp. 231–253.

Deutsch, H. (1925), The psychology of woman in relation to the functions of reproduction. In: *The Psychoanalytic Reader,* Vol. I, ed. R. Fliess. New York: International Universities Press, 1948, pp. 192–206.

Freud, S. (1900), The interpretation of dreams. *Standard Edition,* 4:241–278. London: Hogarth Press, 1953.

———— (1905), Three essays on the theory of sexuality. *Standard Edition,* 7:125–231. London: Hogarth Press, 1953.

———— (1916–1917), Introductory lectures on psycho-analysis. *Standard Edition,* 16:243–483. London: Hogarth Press, 1955.

———— (1921), Group psychology and the analysis of the ego. *Standard Edition,* 18:69–143. London: Hogarth Press, 1955.

———— (1923a), The ego and the id. *Standard Edition,* 19:3–63. London: Hogarth Press, 1961.

———— (1923b), The infantile genital organization: an interpolation into the theory of sexuality. *Standard Edition,* 19:141–149. London: Hogarth Press, 1961.

———— (1924), The dissolution of the oedipus complex. *Standard Edition,* 19:173–183. London: Hogarth Press, 1961.

———— (1925), Some psychical consequences of the anatomical distinction between the sexes. *Standard Edition,* 19:243–260. London: Hogarth Press, 1961.

———— (1926a), Inhibitions, symptoms and anxiety *Standard Edition,* 20:87–172. London: Hogarth Press, 1959.

———— (1926b), The question of lay analysis. *Standard Edition,* 20:183–250. London: Hogarth Press, 1959.

———— (1930 [1929]), Civilization and its discontents. *Standard Edition,* 21:59–145. London: Hogarth Press, 1961.

———— (1931), Female sexuality. *Standard Edition,* 21:223–243. London: Hogarth Press, 1961.

———— (1933 [1932]), New introductory lectures on psycho-analysis. *Standard Edition,* 22:3–158. London: Hogarth Press, 1964.

Greenacre, P. (1952), *Trauma, Growth and Personality.* New York: Norton.

Hammerman, S. (1965), Conceptions of superego development. *J. Amer. Psychoanal. Assn.,* 13:320–355.

Hartmann, H. and Loewenstein, R. M. (1962), Notes on the superego. *The Psychoanalytic Study of the Child,* 17:42–81.

Horney, K. (1953), On the genesis of the castration complex in women. *Internat. J. Psycho-Anal.,* 5:50–65.

Jacobson, E. (1964), *The Self and the Object World*. New York: International Universities Press.

Jones, E. (1955), *The Life and Work of Sigmund Freud*, Vol. I. New York: Basic Books.

—— (1926), The origin and structure of the super-ego. *Internat. J. Psycho-Anal.*, 7:303–311.

—— (1935), Early female sexuality. *Internat. J. Psycho-Anal.*, 16:263–273.

Kohut, H. (1966), Forms and transformation of narcissism. *J. Amer. Psychoanal. Assn.*, 14:243–272.

Klein, M. (1928), Early stages of the oedipus conflict. *Internat. J. Psycho-Anal.*, 9:167–180.

Lampl-de Groot, J. (1927), The evolution of the oedipus complex in women. In: *The Psychoanalytic Reader*, Vol. I, ed. R. Fliess. New York: International Universities Press, 1948, pp. 207–222.

Muslin, H. L. and Pieper, W. J. The death machine: A contribution to the study of menstrual taboos. Unpublished paper presented at the American Psychoanalytic Annual Meeting, 1961.

Piers, G. and Singer, M. B. (1953), *Shame and Guilt*. Springfield, Ill.: Charles C. Thomas.

Sachs, H. (1929), One of the motive factors in the formation on the super-ego in women. *Internat. J. Psycho-Anal.*, 10:39–50.

Sandler, J. (1960), On the concept of superego. *The Psychoanalytic Study of the Child*, 15:128–162. New York: International Universities Press.

6. Morality and Freud's Concept of the Superego

IRVING BIEBER, M.D.

M UCH has been written about the superego since Freud evolved his structural theory of the mind. The later writers either elaborated upon his views without making fundamental changes or, where significant theoretical alterations were attempted, the original conceptualizations lost their meaning despite adherence to the term itself.

Freud's view of morality and man's relation to society is most clearly reflected in his concepts of superego. The superego was conceived of as an agency of the mind which became a repository for internalized social strictures in the absence of parents and social authority. These authoritarian codes were represented in the superego as a kind of police agent whose function was to guard against the expression of pleasurable but antisocial id impulses. In the *Outline of Psychoanalysis* Freud (1938) wrote: "The superego may bring fresh needs to the fore but its main function remains the limitation of satisfactions" (p. 148). Freud's view of man's nature was strikingly similar to theological fundamentalist precepts. Man was selfish and sought pleasure. Indeed, one of Freud's central theses was that man's pleasures were in basic conflict with the needs of the larger society. Drives towards gratification, the egoistic urges, were located in and energized by an instinctual id, itself completely under the control of a hedonistic pleasure principle. Its aim was to achieve gratification at any cost, heedless of the needs of reality and society. "It almost seems as if the creation of a great human community would be most successful if no attention had to be paid to the happiness of the individual" (p. 140).

The instinctual id was depicted, not only as a seething cauldron brimming over with surging Dionysian pleasures, it was also represented as a repository of sociopathy. Antisocial acts resulted from a breakthrough of elements in the instinctual id from the controlling forces of the superego, while socially constructive acts were the evidence of a well functioning superego powerful enough to screen out immoral instinctual impulses. In superego theory, structure was emphasized over content and moral behavior was, by and large, handled in generalities; it was posed in simplistic opposition to immoral behavior. They are not, however, simple opposites along a conceptual continuum of good-bad. Socially constructive (moral) and antisocial (immoral) acts belong to entirely different sources and categories of behavior and personality, as shall be discussed later on.

The aggressive instincts, like the sexual, were also seen as pressing for expression and gratification and, unless controlled, presented an even greater threat to society than the sexual instincts. Unchecked, aggressive instincts would lead to the extinction of human kind. All men would be murderers. According to Freud's anthropological-fictional schema, they, in fact, once were. Did not the early brothers, like the later conspirators against Caesar, band together and murder the primal father? Murder, not sex, seemed to be man's original sin. Clearly, there had to be a powerful psychic agency such as the superego to protect society against the individual's unbridled aggression and his polymorphous perverse sexuality. Freud (1930) stated:

. . . aggressiveness is introjected, internalized; it is, in point of fact, sent back from where it came from—that is, it is directed towards . . . [one's] own ego. There it is taken over by a portion of the ego which sets itself over against the rest of the ego as superego which now in the form of conscience is ready to put into action against the ego the same harsh aggression that the ego would have liked to satisfy upon other extraneous individuals. The tension between the harsh superego and the ego that is subjected to it is called by us the sense of guilt; it expresses itself as a need for punishment. Civilization therefore obtains mastery over the individual's dangerous desire for aggression by weakening it and disarming it and by setting up an agency within him to watch over it like a garrison in a conquered city [p. 123].

Yet, Freud recognized man's need to be part of a group. He termed this need the altruistic urge but, again, it was seen to be in opposition to egoistic urges. "In the process of individual development, as we have said, the main accent falls mostly on the egoistic urge (or the urge to happiness), while the other urge (altruistic) which may be described as a cultural one, is usually content with the role of imposing restrictions" (p. 140).

The egoistic and altruistic urges find good fit within Freud's structural theory; the former appear to be synonymous with instinctual id impulses and the latter with superego. In many different ways Freud (1938) restated the same premise: society's function is to restrict man's hedonism while man tries to achieve gratifications. The superego as an agency of the mind internalized the interests of society and "its main function remains the limitation of satisfactions" (p. 148).

MORAL BEHAVIOR

I have observed in young children who were in the preoedipal era (and according to Freudian theory still uninfluenced by the superego which would not yet have developed) evidences of generosity, kindness and consideration. I believe such behaviors to be the product of innate, programmed, affectional potentials evoked by the appropriate stimuli. Between the ages of six and 12 weeks, the normal infant will respond with smiles and coos to the stimulus of adult smiling and head nodding. Affectional affects become part of a reciprocally interacting stimulus-response system between child and parent. The appropriate parental stimulus (head nodding and smiling) stimulates pleasure and smiling in the infant which stimulates pleasure and smiling in the parent, reinforcing the smiling and pleasurable stimulation in the infant. Biological maturational phases are species-specific and do not vary significantly from one normal child to another. Differences, then, depend upon how the parent initiates and manages this reverberating, reciprocal system of interaction. Where the parent-child affectional system develops satisfactorily, children develop the affectional behavior of humans; they become "humanized" as Robbins (1956) has emphasized (p. 289). Serious distortions in the developing affectional parent-child system produce disturbed children to whom we may refer as defectively humanized. They become the so-called affectionless characters whose moral behavior will be grossly impaired. Harlow's (1965) experiments demonstrated that monkeys brought up in isolation were incapable of object-related sexuality or of participating in social interaction with other monkeys. In humans as well, membership in a peer group, particularly in preschool and preadolescent eras, seems to be a prerequisite for the development of normal adult social behavior. Morality defined as humane and socially constructive attitudes and behavior can logically be associated with a system of affectional affects. A morality based on humanization articulates naturally with cooperative, socially constructive behavior. A morality based on sublimated behavior derived from the inhibition of instinctual urges and mediated through the conscience-stricken superego suggests a continuity between morality and original sin. Further, a morality which depends upon strength of inhibition, proposes a kind of motivational brinksmanship which maintains the personality at the uneasy edge of temptation. Morality powered by the superego can be compared to the use of ever greater repressive police action in civil disorders. If the police perform well and there are enough of them, there will be law and order; if not, chaos reigns. It is as if the civil disorders in large cities today are the consequences of judicial leniency and inadequate police protection, a notion maintained by many citizens. They do not accord causal primacy to the social, economic and political processes determining the disturbances. Similarly, if the variegated dynamic processes operant in determining sociopathy are not accorded primacy (and these processes involve anxiety, inhibition, perceptual and cognitive distortions among other variables) attention is directed instead to the primacy of the inadequate police functioning of the superego.

A society where man's biological and human needs can be

satisfied through equitable, democratic social arrangements has the material base for moral behavior. Where there is scarcity because of an inequitable distribution of wealth, where there is social stratification, where there are haves and have-nots, the social base for moral behavior is constricted and irregular. Such societies are characterized, at least in part, by the immorality of scarcity, where one man's gain is another man's loss and where conflicts exist between the social need for cooperative behavior, on the one hand, and competitive struggles for personal gratification, if not for survival, on the other.

In Freud's conception of man's relation to society, the gratification of instinctual needs came into conflict with society whose needs, in turn, were seen as running counter to that of individual, hedonistic urges which had to be repressed. According to this construct, the only kind of society that could be reconciled with the expression of egoistic urges would be a totally immoral society. In recent history, the Nazi leadership could gratify every instinctual wish; they could murder those whom they wished to; they could rob; they could and did engage in any type of sexual behavior, yet they still remained within the boundaries of their society as the power elite. Throughout history there has been a much closer concordance of wish fulfillment between the individual and society among the power elite whose prerogatives permitted gratification not accorded the common man. The conflict between egoistic and altruistic urges has much more theoretical relevance for the common man than for Man. The social revolutions we are witness to, i.e., the equal rights movement and the socially oriented youth movements, are struggles to reconstruct society in a way that will fulfill the needs of the masses so that egoistic needs will be concordant with a moral society and not antagonistic to altruistic urges.

IMMORAL BEHAVIOR

The terms "immorality" and "morality" are more at home in philosophy than in psychiatry. Immoral behavior stripped of value judgments by the psychoanalyst appear as neurotic, psychopathologic or sociopathic entities.

Psychoanalysts have been in the vanguard among those who would free sexuality and relegate the puritanical code to the past. Yet such terms as "perverse" and "perversion" continue in use though they have moralistic connotations. By and large the psychopathies and sociopathies are used to designate grossly antisocial behavior. The terms in themselves have no moralistic meaning but they carry a pejorative nuance, and, in this sense, have a moralistic overtone. In attempting to explicate these syndromes, classical psychoanalysis has directed its attention centrally to superego theory. Explanations for sociopathy remain oriented around the notion of superego defects; yet antisocial (immoral) behavior almost always turns out to be the aftermath of anxiety and inhibition rather than of untethered impulses that have escaped from the watchdogs of the superego. Psychoanalytic studies reveal that stealing, rape, prostitution, drug addiction and so forth, occur in individuals who are profoundly inhibited in sexual and work functions. A rapist is one whose sexual organization is so defective that he cannot fulfill romantic and sexual desires with women who would accept his advances. To consider rape an act motivated by a rush of sadistic sexual impulses that have overcome a defective superego like a prison breakout past a sleepy guard, is to locate psychopathology in a weakened, metapsychological abstraction rather then in the defective cognitive and psychosocial systems involved.

The idea that prostitutes are sexually inhibited usually evokes amusement, if not amazement, among psychoanalytic students; the prostitute is supposedly the personification of Erotica. Clinical examination reveals prostitutes to be sexually frigid; they are incapable of a monogamous love relationship for any length of time; many are homosexual (Greenwald, 1958). The psychodynamic underpinnings of their sexual inhibitions include profound early disturbances in their relationship with their mother, fears of a dominating, hostile, rejecting mother on whom there is often a pathologic dependency, and absent or inadequate paternal affection, protection and support. Disturbances in affectional affects are invariably present among the schizophrenic fraction of the prostitute population, and it is a sizeable fraction. Successful

Irving Bieber

treatment of prostitutes is rare, yet when it is achieved I believe it is through resolving the fears that determine and maintain sexual and other inhibitions, not by creating new ones.

Don Juanism, or male heterosexual promiscuity, is also usually viewed as an expression of great sexual freedom; it is less likely to be regarded as sociopathic when men seek numerous sexual partners than when women do. But as in prostitution, Don Juanism is associated with sexual inhibition. Should the Don Juan begin to love any one woman, he develops profound anxiety, frequently verging on panic. His anxiety requires flight which he may rationalize by claiming a loss of interest and by extolling the qualities of the new favorite. Within a socioethical frame of reference, sexual promiscuity is a time-honored symptom of immorality, a symptom that articulates with the dynamics of structural theory where a weakened, defective superego permits uncontrolled expression of sexual impulses. In operational terms, however, promiscuity and apparent immorality are the consequence of psychopathological syndromes of fear and inhibition.

Sexual deviations such as homosexuality are also the consequences of fear rather than defective moral values. Inversion is characterized by fear of heterosexuality that gives rise to sexual inhibition with the opposite sex. Narcotic addicts are often men who are intelligent and resourceful but who steal because they are so profoundly inhibited that they cannot use their abilities to earn a living legitimately. Their fears of success, so characteristic of addicts, cause them to renounce opportunities to work; instead, they fall back on stealing and addiction. The addict seems not to be satisfying hedonistic greed through stealing; he suffers from such overweening anxieties and inhibitions that effective work efforts are blocked.

The notion that sociopaths do not experience anxiety or guilt does not accord with my clinical observations. The absence of anxiety and guilt would not be inconsistent with the "sick superego" theory, though this does not appear to be the explanation. The sociopaths I have examined experience anxiety, guilt and depression which they may deny, repress or attempt to anesthetize through the use of drugs. The suicide rates among them, particu-

larly narcotic addicts, are significantly higher than among nonsoc-
iopaths in comparable age groups.

THE SUPEREGO AND EXPERIENTIAL INFLUENCES

Freud's statements about the effects of individual experiences
with parents and other authority figures on the evolution and
structure of the superego are often contradictory. They vary from
descriptions of the superego as a repository of highly specific parental introjects, i.e. parental tastes, class values, etc., to statements
suggesting that experience has essentially little influence on the
superego:

> A portion of the external world has, at least partially, been aban-
> doned as an object and has instead, by identification, been taken into
> the ego and thus become an integral part of the internal world. This
> new psychical agency continues to carry on the functions which have
> hitherto been performed by the people (the abandoned object) in the
> external world: it observes the ego, gives it orders, judges it, threatens
> it with punishment exactly like the parents whose place it has taken.
> We call this agency the *superego* and are aware of it in its judicial
> functions as our *conscience* [1938, p. 205].
>
> The superego is in fact the heir to the Oedipus complex and is only
> established after that complex has been disposed of. For that reason its
> excessive severity does not follow a real model but corresponds to the
> strength of the defence used against the temptation of the Oedipus
> complex. Some suspicion of this state of things lies, no doubt, at the
> bottom of the assertion made by philosophers and believers that the
> moral sense is not instilled into men by education or acquired by them
> in their social life but is implanted in them from a higher source
> [1938, pp. 205–206].

Yet, a few sentences later Freud states:

> . . . the superego continues to play the part of an external world for
> the ego although it has become a portion of the internal world.
> Throughout later life it represents the influence of a person's child-
> hood, of the care and education given him by his parents and of his
> dependence on them—a childhood which is prolonged so greatly in

human beings by a family life in common. And in all this it is not only
the personal qualities of these parents that is making itself felt, but
also everything that had a determining effect on them themselves, the
tastes and standards of the social class in which they lived and the
innate dispositions and traditions of the race from which they sprang
[p. 206].

Experience shows, however, that the severity of the superego which
a child develops in no way corresponds to the severity of the treatment which he has himself met with. The severity of the former seems
to be independent of that of the latter. A child who has been very le-
niently brought up can acquire a very strict conscience. But it would be
wrong to exaggerate this independence; it is not difficult to convince
oneself that the severity of upbringing does also exert a strong
influence on the formation of the child's superego. What it amounts to
is that in the formation of the superego and the emergence of a conscience innate constitutional factors and influences from the real environment act in combination [1930, p. 130].

Although Freud wrote extensively on the theory of parental introjection into the superego, one finds little in his writings which
distinguishes one superego from another except for a single parameter, the quantitative polarity of severity and leniency.
Throughout, the superego is referred to as though it were an organ like the liver; one is pretty much like another. The superego
model is severe and puritanical; in fact, the introjections often resemble not a parent so much as an angry, punitive deity whose
main function remains "its limitation of satisfactions." Indeed,
Freud (1930) depicted the superego to be quite an angry god—and
a paranoid one, as the following quotations reveal: "For the more
virtuous a man is, the more severe and distrustful is its behavior
(the superego) so that ultimately it is precisely those people who
have carried saintliness furthest who reproach themselves with the
worst sins" (p. 125). He stated that once the superego is constructed,
"Instinctual renunciation now no longer has a completely liberating effect; virtuous continence is no longer rewarded with the
assurances of love. A threatened external unhappiness—loss of love
and punishment on the part of external authority—has been exchanged for a permanent internal unhappiness, for the tension of

the sense of guilt" (1930, p. 127). And, "If civilization is a necessary course of development from the family to humanity as to a whole—then . . . there is inextricably bound up with it an increase of the sense of guilt, which will perhaps reach heights that the individual finds hard to tolerate" (1930, p. 133). With this dismal view of morality, it would have been appropriate for Freud to have added, "where superego was, there shall ego be."

Of the many complex and varied developmental influences, if any parameter of personality is experientially determined, it is one's moral and ethical values. Even those values that may have biological roots in the affectional system ultimately depend for its outcome on the attitudes and behavior of significant others, parents, peer group, reference group and so forth. Moral values differ from culture to culture and in a complex heterogeneous society as our own, from group to group. The Oedipus complex does not account for this diversity. In all societies with a nuclear family structure the Oedipus complex is essentially similar yet moral and ethical values may differ radically.

THE METAPSYCHOLOGICAL VERSUS THE ADAPTATIONAL APPROACH

"As long as things go well with a man his conscience is lenient and lets the ego do all sorts of things; but when misfortune befalls him he searches his soul, acknowledges his sinfulness, heightens the demands of his conscience and imposes abstinences on himself and punishes himself with penances" (1930 p. 126).

Some people respond to misfortune as Freud described but many do not. What determines the different ways which people cope with adversity? Does superego theory explain the differences most usefully? In the late 1950's a psychiatric research team at Memorial Hospital in New York City of which I was a member, was studying, among other things, psychological reactions to the diagnosis of malignancy (Orbach and Bieber, p. 301). Upon learning the diagnosis, each patient understandably experienced a reactive depression. In one group, however, there was an overlay of psychopathological depression with self-accusatory content. These patients held themselves accountable for becoming ill. Some had maintained the belief that if one ate the proper food, slept well, exercised regularly and did not carouse but led a sober life, illness, surely serious illness, would be avoided. Their security operations relative to maintaining good health had been based on vaguely formed, nonverbal beliefs about omnipotent control. When they became ill, it followed that they must have done something wrong; why else would their security system break down? Other patients whose security operations also involved omnipotent control assigned the omnipotence to a deity. These individuals felt that they had sinned. Attempts were then made to seek out of their past instances of wrongdoing which would justify their present punishment. Some patients who had been religious nevertheless did not regard themselves as sinners. "I have led a good life. If this could happen to me when there are so many people who are evil, maybe there is no God." These patients were prepared to give up their magical security system rather than distort reality for themselves. The patients who did not distort reality and did not rely upon magic, adapted to their misfortune most effectively; they expressed no self accusations nor needs to do penance. The notion of a punishing conscience in the face of adversity applied to but one segment of the group studied, but even in these cases, there is no explanatory gain in the idea that the superego becomes severe when things go badly for the ego.

THE SUPEREGO AND THE OEDIPUS COMPLEX

The Oedipus complex is not so much a theory as it is a constellation of observable data; it can be repeatedly observed—and not only psychoanalytically—in children and adults. Where Freud's inferences derived directly from observations of the family romance they were psychological, not metapsychological.

The Oedipus complex confronts the individual with at least three major moral issues; incest, stealing and murder. The Oedipus complex is predicated on the biological fact that heterosexual responsiveness begins at about the third year of life and that the nuclear family provides the setting in which this interpersonal conflict unfolds. Though a child's sexual responses are not confined to family members, the intimacy of family relations guarantees the inclusion of his cross-sex parent and siblings as objects stimulating sexual responses. The sexually determined competitive attitudes which accompany this new phase bring the child into conflict with a parent of the same sex around whom were organized affectional attitudes and security operations that began in the recent pre-oedipal past. The child must now attempt to extinguish both incestuous impulses and his sexual rivalry since he needs to preserve affectional and security ties. The precedence of family integrity required the invention of an incest tabu and the value to children of family integrity promotes the repression of incestuous and rivalrous impulses. The need then to control, repress or extinguish hostile feelings toward the same-sex parent does not derive entirely from external prohibitions and fears of retaliation, but also from a bio-social need to preserve positive affectional ties. The ways in which parental attitudes and behavior influence the resolution of the Oedipus complex (and other social aspects of childhood) help shape the ultimate course of moral and ethical values.

The Oedipus complex concerns a special type of murder—murder for gain. The law and ethical codes distinguish among various types of killing: self-defense, revenge and murder for gain or expediency, the last type being represented in the Oedipus complex. A son's patricidal wish is not inconsistent with love for his father in the ambivalent relationship with which we are familiar. The paid killer and the military mercenary do not necessarily hate their victims who are killed only for gain. Impulses to murder for gain are also present among rivalrous siblings. In these situations, however, murderous impulses are associated with rage and hatred, at least initially. In the adult the impulse to murder for gain has a tap root in the Oedipus complex.

Freud believed that the murderous impulses associated with the Oedipus complex determined the origin of the need for a superego. Although the Oedipus complex is a central determinant in personality development, it does not seem to be the prototype for all situations which evoke murderous impulses and defenses against it. Various species-specific behavioral patterns among social animals preclude intraspecies killing. These patterns have been well described by ethologists who have furnished convincing evidence that at least in some species such behaviors are likely to be innate. Similar species-protective mechanisms are probably operant in humans and may account for the revulsion experienced when, for example, one sees another human severely mangled. The hypothesis that revulsion under such circumstances is a reaction formation against an impulse to kill does not take into account species-specific, preservative, biological, defensive integrations. Built-in mechanisms, such as revulsion among humans under the threat described, are clearly not as effective in us as in other members of the animal kingdom, since only man with his vaunted conscience has exterminated countless millions of his own kind.

The development of normal affectional response systems probably constitutes the most important guarantees against intra-group murder. Socially based cooperative ties and mutual concerns strengthen affectional affects thus giving meaning and substance to moral codes against murder. The fear of murderous retaliation (legal as well as interpersonal) is also a potent deterrent.

Morality that derives from the Oedipus complex is essentially a family morality. Thou shalt not kill thy father or brother, thy sister or mother. How far this precept extends to community, state, nation and beyond, depends upon economic, political and social factors. The power elite may sometimes circumvent family morality. The history of royal families is replete with murder of close kin for the sake of power; later, the killers were accepted as rightful and lawful monarchs by the populace. In some primitive societies, intertribe murder is limited to token gestures; in others, a successful warrior is measured by the number of heads taken. Civilized societies score their successes in accordance with their technology, i.e., the number of planes shot down, and which side has the higher enemy body count at the end of a day's battle. The social killer experiences pride, not guilt, for he is fulfilling a societal ideal and his own ego-ideal. The warrior's superego rewards him with a feeling of pride for his predations, yet the main function of the superego is to prohibit murder for gain. During the Nazi occupation of western Europe, betrayers not infrequently exposed Jews to the Gestapo as a simple way of appropriating Jewish property;

they were neither punished nor excommunicated by their own group for participating in programmed murder. And later, when justice, retribution, and reparations were being considered by an international court of law, the concerns for minorities were uneven; the Nazi mass murder of gypsies, for instance, received comparatively little attention. In sum, the superego has been conceived of as an immutable structure which, if intact, remains as an established guardian of morality whereas, in fact, group and individual standards of morality and ethics change with time and circumstance in ways not provided for by the static concepts of superego function.

Stealing can be understood only in the social context in which it takes place. Where there is poverty in the midst of plenty, stealing from the rich to give to the poor may not be at all immoral. Robin Hood is a legendary hero, not a common thief. A parent who steals food from a rich man's kitchen to keep his family from starving need not believe his act is immoral and therefore should have no guilt about it. Parental guilt would reflect neurosis, not realistic, adaptive behavior. On the other hand, a starving prisoner, say in a concentration camp, who steals from another starving prisoner would be likely to feel guilt. Superego theory does not leave room for the behavioral dynamics which form part and parcel of complex changing, social realities. In general, stealing is a manifestation of psychopathology when it occurs among children or adults of means. The child of a middle-class family who steals almost always has psychiatric difficulties rooted in a disturbed and defective parent-child relationship. The complexity of the stealing syndrome cannot be accounted for simply by the failure of parents to instill adequate values of honesty. Whatever part the Oedipus complex plays in engendering impulses to steal, the ultimate fate of such impulses is determined by the totality of social experience.

GUILT AND THE SUPEREGO

Freud distinguished between two stages in the evolution of guilt. The first involved fear of loss of love for violating the wishes

Irving Bieber

and directives of power figures upon whom the helpless child was dependent. The second essential stage involved the internalization of authority with the development of the superego. Freud said (1930, p. 135): "A great change takes place when the authority is internalized through the establishment of a superego. The phenomenon of conscience then reached a higher stage. Actually, it is not until now that we should speak of conscience or a sense of guilt." The indiscriminate fear of violating directives of power figures may, of course, be differentiated from a cognitive, discriminating conviction that one is performing an antisocial act. In my view, however, the distinction does not rest upon the internalization of a fictitious superego as Freud postulated; rather, it depends upon conviction, that is, strong confidence in one's belief. Although convictions may evolve as the consequence of an automatic, submissive, uncritical acceptance of parental values, and may be compatible with the concept of internalization, they may also represent independent thought arrived at through the selection of alternatives. Choice is particularly relevant as a child grows into adolescence and adulthood and as he continues to form and revise ideas and convictions about questions of morality. The concept of automatic internalization of parental values does not account for human cognitive faculties in determining individual judgments nor does it leave room for changing moral convictions as social maturation proceeds.

Freud's concept of guilt as the punishment of the ego by the harsh superego for attempts at gaining unacceptable gratifications has several limitations. For one, it excludes guilt induced by guilt-provoking parents. Their children tend to manifest guilt reactions very easily even in situations where they are innocent of any wrong doing and where guilt is entirely inappropriate. Parents who inculcate guilt feelings as a technique of domination are usually egocentric, exploitative, perfectionistic and intolerant of shortcomings in their child whom they regard as personal property. A child's resistance against acting in accordance with his parents' neurotic demands may elicit from them guilt provocations such as, "you're killing me . . . you're making me sick . . . and so forth." He learns to respond in ways which will circumvent

140 ·

such parental behavior. In such families, the child experiences guilt for *not* doing what his parents wish, not just for *doing* some unacceptable instinctual act. Guilt associated with the lack of fulfillment of parental wishes may be unrelated to introjection. An adult may feel guilty if he does not phone his mother daily if this is what she expects, but his guilt reaction may disappear when she dies and he may not experience the same reaction with anyone else. Some such individuals may avoid relationships with guilt provocateurs. But those who remain vulnerable to guilt provocation by valued objects have developed the potential to react with guilt to cues or expressions of dissatisfaction, contempt or pain by others. One might say that under the circumstances discussed, a potential to react with guilt has been internalized, if one wishes to use a gastrointestinal metaphor.

Superego theory does not account for a type of commonly experienced guilt that accompanies self-destructive acts, as in masochistic self-sabotage where success or the fruits of success are destroyed. When a businessman destroys an established, successful enterprise, or when an athlete sabotages a well deserved victory, guilt is experienced for having destroyed something of value. In 1916 Freud described problems about achievement in his paper, "Those Wrecked by Success." He cited the case of a young woman who was finally in a position to marry the man she loved but could not accept her good fortune and soon broke down in a hopeless psychosis. In this instance, one might speculate theoretically that superego guilt stopped her from fulfilling her Oedipal strivings in marrying a valued love object identified with father. Superego theory does not provide for guilt experienced in destroying a valued relationship nor for the guilt about causing suffering to a rejected fiancé. This type of guilt might usefully be termed masochistic guilt. I have discussed the problem of masochism elsewhere and will not pursue it here (Bieber, 1956, p. 256). Others have referred to this type of guilt as existential guilt. The renunciation of fulfillment and pleasure may elicit masochistic guilt. This is the converse of superego guilt which explains but one category of guilt, that is, the guilt experienced when one fails to renounce forbidden pleasures.

Irving Bieber

In the range of affects associated with goodness and morality is the emotion we term compassion. According to Schopenhauer it represents the essential ingredient of the moral man. Where is compassion located in structural theory? Certainly not in the superego which is said to have no compassion for the ego. On the contrary, it uses the energies of the aggressive drives against the ego. Surely, compassion does not reside in the id. Then all that is left is the ego. Hence, compassion must be an ego function. If this is so, morality is only partially accounted for by the superego.

In conclusion superego, like id and ego concepts, presents the limitations and theoretical fallacies that characterize the structural and the libido theory (Bieber, 1953). Id, ego and superego are but metaphorical, fictitious constructs that have been reified by articulating them with reality structures in a way that creates an aura of realism. The energies of the id (a fictitious concept) are supposedly derived from somatic organs and processes (real structures) and the ego (a fictitious concept) has at its disposal all the resources of the organism—perceptual, motor, intellectual and so forth (all real organs and processes). The superego contains the introjects (a fictitious concept) of parents (real objects). Reification of metaphor is a serious logical fallacy and has no place in science. Not only does reification abound in metapsychology, but many constructs are anthorpomorphized, a poetic device that tends to obscure a clear presentation of human motivation and behavior; for example, "the superego treats the ego harshly." Whatever heuristic value it once may have had, this type of thinking is no longer acceptable. With the enormous development of psychoanalysis in the last 25 years, personality theory not only can be more consistently related to observational data but can also articulate more validly with biological and other social sciences. Metapsychology as a scientific methodology is today an anachronism that is hardly consonant with the sophistication of ideas in the present world.

BIBLIOGRAPHY

Bieber, I. (1966), Sadism and masochism. In: *American Handbook of Psychiatry,* ed. S. Arieti. New York: Basic Books, pp. 256–272.

Freud, S. (1916), Some characters met with in psychoanalytic work. *Standard Edition*, 14:309–336. London: Hogarth Press, 1957.

—— (1923), The ego and the id. *Standard Edition*, 19:3–63. London: Hogarth Press, 1961.

—— (1930 [1929]), Civilization and its discontents. *Standard Edition*, 21:59–145. London: Hogarth Press, 1961.

—— (1938), An outline of psychoanalysis. *Standard Edition*, 23:141–208. London: Hogarth Press, 1964.

Greenwald, H. (1958), *The Call Girl*. New York: Ballantine Books.

Harlow, H. and Harlow, M. K. (1965), *Behavior of Non-Human Primates*, ed. A. M. Schier, H. F. Harlow, and F. Stollwitz. New York: Academic Press, p. 323.

Orbach, C. E. and Bieber, I. (1952), Depressive and paranoid reactions. *A.M.A. Arch. Neurol. and Psychiat.*, 78:301–311.

Robbins, B. S. (1956), Sigmund Freud: 1865–1933. *Psychotherapy*, 1:289–295.

7. A Theoretical Note on the Ego in the Therapeutic Process

VICTOR CALEF, M.D.

PSYCHOANALYSTS take it as axiomatic that "the ego is made up of old abandoned object-ties," even though the phrase contains an apparent contradiction in terms. For reasons which are perhaps obvious, the studies which confirm that axiom have done a great deal to illustrate the introjections in ego development and identification, while the "abandonment" mechanism has not been sufficiently detailed. Consequently, we still know relatively little about how the ego abandons its objects. For example, there is little explicit knowledge about whether the ego passively experiences being abandoned or whether it actively renounces old objects, and if so, under what circumstances this is accomplished.

The emphasis on introjection as the main mechanism of identification has led to the belief that the therapeutic process can only proceed when, if, and after some identification takes place, or is alternately designed toward actively establishing it. Little is said about the conditions for instigating such a process and what must precede it.

Certain clinical experiences draw attention to that phase of the identification with the therapist which precedes the introjection. For example, in a case [1] only recently started in analysis it was observed that the patient was successful in avoiding an identification with his therapist. He had nevertheless formed a fairly firm identification and attachment to a previous therapist with whom he did not and could not express either his ambiva-

Read at the Society of Medical Psychoanalysts, Symposium on Moral Values and Superego Functioning, New York City, March 4, 1968.

[1] I am indebted to Dr. Samuel Hoch for this case report.

lence about his father or his therapist. In his present therapy he immediately embarked on an effort to get the analyst to seduce him into an attachment. When this was avoided and instead interpreted as a resistance, the patient immediately entered into a regressive moment of panic in which he threatened to leave treatment before he expressed the ambivalence toward his father. It seemed a correct view of the matter to consider that the frustrations imposed created a retreat to a narcissistic position which loosened the tie to the father, thereby permitting renunciation of him as an object. This set the stage for another and new identification with the second therapist, made immediately on the heels of the expression of the ambivalence. It is not clear whether the loosening of the object-tie to the father arises out of the beginning introjection and identification with the therapist or whether the loosening permits the identification to take place. The clinical sequence suggests that it is the retreat to the narcissistic position which permits the loosening of the object-tie. The renunciation process, as I would like to refer to the loosening of the object-tie, is of special interest in the therapeutic process and requires further study and clarification.

The following sketch might illustrate the most elemental form of renunciation which I believe to be necessary for analytic work. In the evening of the day on which a patient finally overcame her resistances to use the analytical couch for the first time, she dreamed that she was lying on her former analyst's couch. [2] (Since her first therapy had occurred during her adolescence, she had never used the analytic couch and had refused to do so in her second therapeutic effort.) In the dream she was stroking a "pussy" held in her arms. Her analyst seemed busy with many other patients. She was angry and anxious and remonstrated that if he was too busy with so many others it was of no value for her to try to work in analysis. However, she finally realized that her former analyst was her present one (she recognized both by name in the dream) and then experienced immediate relief. The many functions, meanings and wishes of the dream are not relevant here.

[2] The dream was recently reported in another context (Calef, 1967).

Victor Calef

The affect of relief reflects, I believe, something about the processes which occur in therapy. The second therapeutic situation, offering a new object for transference, placed the patient in a dilemma of loyalties which she did not resolve for a long period, simply rejecting the transference and precluding identification with the new therapist. The dream of her old analyst is a demonstration of her wish to be alone with him and her fear to relinquish the indenture to him. That in the end she gives him up with relief in favor of the new one is an important revelation of the dream. A set of complaints against the old therapist (and the new one too) hid her erotized attachment to him, while it permitted and justified giving him up (even if only by merging the two analysts). It was also the rationalization for relinquishing the resistance and lying down on the new analyst's couch on the previous day. The latter became the day residue for the dream. She was then able, in association to that dream, to produce the thoughts which were the connecting links to make sense out of her phobia. Rapid progress was made immediately thereafter—much of it a product of the work done with the previous therapist but which had not crystallized because of the remaining libidinized transference and identification.

It seems likely that the ambivalent relationship to the first therapist precluded losing him and simultaneously prevented progress in the analytical work. The dream and the progress which it heralded was brought about by relinquishing the tie to the old therapist, accomplished in overcoming the reluctance to using the couch. The dream was a testimonial to the giving up of old attitudes intimately connected to the first analyst. The renunciation of loyalty provided the basis for furthering the analytical process, at least momentarily.

The relationship to the new therapist, which was thus made potential when the initial object-tie was loosened, inevitably became the basis for a new resistance and in turn became difficult to surrender. The processes, more obscure when there is only one analyst, were made more clear in this instance because two therapists were involved.

Patients who have a powerful attachment to a pregenital, tran-

146 ·

sitional, or fetishistic object offer further evidence for the role of renunciation in therapy. Frequently during the course of analysis they call a halt (more or less) to the use of that pregenital object for sexual gratification. While they assure the analyst of progressive improvements and appear to relinquish the pregenital object, the improvement is more apparent than real, since only a substitution rather than a relinquishment has taken place. The analytic routine, its rules, the regularity of appointments, the paying of fees, the free associations, etc., substitute for the satisfaction previously derived from the pregenital object, thereby preventing "analytic" work for which "improvements" are offered to the analyst as sacrifices. During that period of substitution which cannot be properly understood as the product of an introjection, the patient does not experience any sense of loss. It is only after the interpretive work occurs that the analytical routine loses its substitutive value and the pregenital object is actively renounced and relinquished. That circumstance is attended by a sense of loss, of grief, as if something which was inside oneself has been drained. It is then that the analytical work takes place—or more correctly, that the analytical material flows in a free associative manner to confirm the previous interpretations of the resistances and to permit meaningful genetic reconstructions to take place.

It seems plausible to assume from such experiences that analytic progress is made only under the circumstance that some piece of the pregenital tie to the therapist (transferred from an old object-tie) is relinquished, very much in the way the patient (who dreamed of lying on her former analyst's couch) relinquished a part of her tie to the old therapist. The exact nature and sequence of these processes leading to identifications are relevant to the theory of the therapeutic process in analysis. [3] They have often been described as the splitting of the ego in the therapeutic process and the mechanism designated as an introjection or identification with the observing function of the analyst. It has not been clearly stated just what the differences are between the

[3] The above considerations also have implications for the conduct of second analyses and especially for those cases of resistances noted, for example, by Bibring (1936) and by Nunberg (1951).

so-called splitting of the ego in the therapeutic process and the splitting of the ego in the defensive process (as in the compulsive symptom, or in depression, or in the fetish). I believe that we have long known about those differences, though not all that is involved has been discussed under a single title, so far as I know.

The similarities and differences between the way the ego observes itself in the two processes have been extensively explored. They are both sometimes referred to as splits in the ego. However, the two processes are different and the events in the therapeutic situation can hardly be conceived as a splitting of the ego. On the contrary, it may be more accurately viewed as a consolidation of the ego, though "a differentiating grade," achieved by a particular mechanism, i.e., renunciation, with which we are familiar and which is, at minimum, implied in the exhortations to maintain the rule of abstinence and which is more clearly stated in the clinical discussions which make use of the concepts of desexualization, structuralization, superego formation, and sublimation. [Compare with Loewald (1962) and Lustman (1966).]

The question is frequently posed as to whether the function of observation should be ascribed to the ego or to the superego. Are the condemnations of a severe conscience a demonstration of an observing ego? What are the dynamic differences between the observing, condemning superego of the patient and another ego which is capable of observing itself and simultaneously able to experience itself as it is alleged to take place in the therapeutic process of analysis? It is not only Sterba (1934, 1940) who has addressed himself to these questions. There is by now in the psychoanalytic literature fairly extensive commentary on the observation function of the ego, on the development of the superego, and the events which take place in the therapeutic process of analysis. Fenichel, Anna Freud, Gill, Glover, Greenson, Hartmann, Kris, Lewin, Loewenstein, Loewald, Mahler and her associates, Rapaport, Sandler, Shafer, M. Stein, Stone, Strachey, Sterba and Zetzel are some of the best known psychoanalytic theoreticians who have provided definitive descriptions and important clarifications of the superego functions and their development. The many statements about the superego made by these authors and a large number of others not mentioned are too numerous to be reviewed here, though it should be made clear that what is stated in this paper owes its origin to those authors. All, following Freud (1923, 1927, 1940), recognize more or less explicitly the central role of the renunciation of the object in superego formation. (See for example Glover (1947), pp. 15–18).

The mechanism of renunciation has been repeatedly stated and understood; nevertheless, it might serve a purpose to recognize and emphasize once again that renunciation is the common factor in three types of structure building: superego formation, sublimation, and the therapeutic process. Sterba (1934, 1940) and others [4] explicitly said that the therapeutic process has as its prototype the formation of the superego. His statement of the analogy has been insufficiently emphasized, perhaps because of another oversight. To my knowledge there is no explicit discussion in the literature of the fact that Freud drew an analogy between the processes of sublimation and the dynamic processes which resulted in superego formation. The sequence in which he developed his thesis about the resolution of the Oedipus complex and the development of the superego suggested that the processes of sublimation were the same as those which permitted the development of the superego. In *The Ego and the Id* (1923) he speculated that perhaps every sublimation was achieved by a retreat from object love to narcissism, [5] followed by a change in the aim of the instinct. He thought

[4] For example Loewald in 1962 and again in 1966 emphasized that renunciation of objects was at the core of internalization and structuralization. He also made an analogy between these processes and those which occur in the terminal phase of analysis. The two papers by Loewald and the two by Sterba (1934, 1940) make this presentation superfluous, except for the circumstance that the role of incorporation and identification with the analyst as the central mechanism in analytic therapy is still too often emphasized, and therefore, seemingly, to the exclusion of other mechanisms. Stone (1961, pp. 86, 94, 95–105) in his recent book on the therapeutic situation stresses the early and middle phases of analytic treatment as characterized by transferences which are essentially of the latter variety. He seems to believe that these types of transference relationships carry the therapeutic process. His implication seems to be that only in the terminal phase of analysis (or after the analysis) is the renunciation of the object-tie important in the therapeutic work. Moreover, his implication seems to be that renunciation is the product and goal of the analytic work, rather than what is attempted to be stressed here—that the renunciation of the object-tie to the analyst is the mechanism which permits the analytic work to proceed beyond the limits inherent in an introjection and imitation of him.

[5] Freud also suggested that the mechanism of regression to a narcissistic identification might be the only way which the id had to give up its objects.

that perhaps all sublimations might be carried out by the transformation of object libido into narcissistic libido. In the very next paragraph he begins to describe the resolution of the Oedipus complex and the development of the superego. An important part of his theoretical description is that the superego is formed out of a *retreat* to identification, a retreat to a narcissistic position after the renunciation of an object.

The meaning and differentiation of identification and object relationship in that description in *The Ego and The Id* is not clear, since it describes the narcissistic retreat to identification both as renunciation of an identification and as a process which results in an identification. [6] The statements about the renunciation of an object of identification which results first in an identification with the self and then achieves in its next phase another and new identification is, however, only semantically confusing and only apparently contradictory. The triphasic process describes three different types of identification whose characteristics are dependent upon specific changes in the aims and in the objects of the drives. The abandonment of an object cathexis is the essence of the development of the superego. The latter is created out of a pregenital libidinal attachment which is given up in favor of what will become a new and different attachment. It is that new development which is called an identification as well as an object relationship. The process thus described is that of a decathexis. [7] The original cathexis to the object is conceived as a libidinal process, a pregenital one, an oral incorporative one (an identification) motivated by the narcissistic needs. In the formation of the superego, the specific dynamic of importance is that the pregenital libidinal cathexes are renounced; and those renunciations result in a retreat

---

[6] Similarly, a second level of unclarity arises out of designating the last identification which comes out of the development of the superego as an object relationship. There is an implied contrast between pregenital objects and genital ones which appears to disavow that pregenital objects possess the quality of object-relationships, though the former continue to be called objects. The contrast obviously implies that the aims of pregenital objects are different in the sense of arising from more archaic sources, while the objects are part objects, etc.

[7] It is my opinion that the decathexis described is what Freud conceptualized in the idea that the ego-ideal became the inheritor and recipient of the infantile narcissism.

to narcissism. In the recovery from the narcissistic state a new aim, or more correctly a new object, may be sought just because the old object has been given up and the tie between the object and the instinct is broken—a process which cannot be described simply as an experience passively received by the ego. The "self" may be passive in that process, but the ego is actively engaged. The desexualization thus described is to be contrasted with the processes of repression. When sexualization persists in the maintenance of an introjection it becomes necessary to revert to repression which insures an autoplastic identification. On the other hand, when the decathexis takes place as just described, a new alloplastic identification results, which is desexualized, and relatively free of its pregenital components. [8] The renunciation of an object of identification (Freud's regression to identification) culminates in the formation of the superego. That identification is not the same as the pregenital and libidinal identification arising out of the oral incorporative functions. It is a new, a "differentiating grade" in the ego which is the result of the process of renunciation, the accompaniment of a regression to narcissism and a form of desexualization accompanied by a change in the aim. The processes involved are identical to the economic changes which were said to occur in sublimation.

Obviously, the present effort is not the first time in the history of psychoanalysis, or the only way in which the importance of frustration for the development of structure has been pointed out. Every description of the development of the secondary process implies that frustrations (absence of gratifications) lead to secondary process thinking. Both Freud and Rapaport after him, as well as Hartmann, Kris, Loewenstein, and many others, have stressed that the development from memory-trace to hallucinatory wish fulfillment

[8] Frances Deri (1939) believes that only pregenital instincts are capable of sublimation or desexualization. Freud's theory of sublimation and superego formation states the pregenital impulses are desexualized by renunciation of the object. A genital aim cannot be renounced; it can only be deferred, at which point it may or may not become the victim of regression. The regression may revive pregenital impulses, but the genital aim will not become sublimated. The regression shifts focus to another instinct, with its subsequent change both in aim and object, which does not constitute a desexualization or sublimation of the genital impulse.

Victor Calef

and to the secondary process is a development which is dependent upon frustration. It is possible that this is the prototype which later will be repeated in the renunciation of the object in the development of the superego. However, in the latter renunciation *the frustration is imposed by the ego,* while in the development of the secondary process the frustration is imposed by reality.

To recapitulate, though he did not state the unity explicitly, Freud brought sublimation and the development of a special identification (called superego) into a psychological unit as analogous, if not identical, processes. Sublimation and the development of the superego are not just parallel processes, but are identical in at least the sense that they share the same psychological mechanism, i.e., a change in the aim of the instinct which occurs only after the *abandonment* of an object (a decathexis) in favor of a heightened narcissistic interest. Therefore, sublimation and the development of the superego (the resolution of the Oedipus complex) can best be viewed as two-stage processes. The first is incorporation, a libidinal pregenital activity which results in a sexualized identification; the second is the renunciation of this sexualized identification which prepares the ego for the tasks of making object relationships of a different quality. The retreat to narcissism results in a new identification, a desexualized one. It is the latter stage which is most characteristic of a superego identification and the sublimations, though obviously the second stage is dependent upon the successful outcome of the first. Ego identifications which arise only out of introjections contain pregenital libidinal components, while only the superego type of identification will show evidence of its origin in a desexualization by renunciation, though the latter will retain as its nucleus the mental representative of the pregenital object (now desexualized). Perhaps a better term for the superego identifications would be "sublimatory identifications."

The products of an oral incorporation, identifications, [9] differ

[9] This paper is concerned with those identifications which arise out of instinctual sources and with one form of identification, which becomes *relatively* free of its instinctual ties, i.e., superego identifications. The implication need not be drawn that identifications arise only out of instinctual sources and that there is only one method by which they free themselves from the drives.

from the superego identification which results from the resolution of the Oedipus complex. In the first, the instinctual impulses are gratified, while in the development of sublimation and conscience, gratification is renounced; or rather the instinctual gratification, perhaps because it is no longer satisfactory, is given up temporarily by renouncing the object of gratification in favor of a narcissistic regression (a regression to identification). While the object is renounced, the instinctual wish is held in suspended readiness for another object at a later moment, unless the impulse is discharged either somatically or in autoerotic activity.

The relationships of the instinctual drive to the object are the basis upon which the rule of abstinence in analytical work is justified. The neurotic symptom has as one of its hallmarks the fact that the instinctual impulse impels toward gratification and that indeed it achieves its aim (in a manner of speaking) in the very maintenance of the symptom. Or another and perhaps more correct way of expressing it is that the impulse is constantly seeking for objects in the external world upon which to discharge itself. If the object is not found, the available internal object cathexis will not be able to find a permanently suitable internal representation of the object or the self for discharge. The constant search for the suitable object in the external world absorbs a great deal of energy, insistent and imperative in the need for the drive to achieve its aim. And simultaneously, since the object cathexis is so busily engaged, there is a constant drain on the narcissistic cathexis. [10] There is a lack of mobility and flow in the conversion of object cathexis

[10] The way in which the term narcissistic cathexis is used here should be defined. I understand that during the phase of instinct theory in which Freud was still using the term ego libido, he equated "narcissism" and a part of ego libido. In that sense ego libido or narcissism was in opposition to object libido. It was a different energy, even though he described narcissistic libido as the ego's counterpart of the libido. However, when he gave up that duality (in *Beyond the Pleasure Principle*) for the new duality of libido and aggression, the concept of narcissism changed face. It was no longer a different energy—it was now identical to libido and the difference was purely in what the energy became invested. If it invested internal representations of the external world, it was libido (object cathexis), and if it invested self-representations, then it was narcissism (narcissistic cathexes). The term narcissism was reduced in stature from an energy concept to a clinical descriptive one of the objects invested by the energy. David Rapaport (1953) suggests that the concept of narcissism makes Freud's concept of the death instinct superfluous. It seems to me that it would

Victor Calef

to narcissistic cathexis and vice verse. The rule of abstinence is directed exactly toward that state of affairs. The analyst, by all he says and does, insists that the object cathexes for the pregenital drives need not be constantly sought in the outside world, nor alternatively, simply discharged every moment of the time, as it attempts to do by the neurotic compromise. When the analyst (by his techniques) insists on a moment of nongratification, he is demanding by implication that the patient do something which the neurotic does not usually do, namely, give up the instinctual gratification momentarily, i.e., renounce the external object. The demand becomes especially effective when the patient has reached a particular phase in the development of his transference. It is at that moment that the interpretive remarks or the behavior of the analyst implies that the transference object, which has previously been a source of gratification for the patient, has to be renounced.

What then is the internal state of affairs when the object is not sought? It is at that moment that the object cathexes become converted to narcissistic cathexes. The available energies cathect the internal images of the self (a narcissistic regression). Stated in those theoretical terms, the idea might have little merit and carry less conviction. However, it should not be difficult to make it more meaningful by translating it into clinical language to show that the moment of the conversion of the cathexis from object cathexis to narcissistic cathexis, the moment of giving up the search for the object, is that moment in which the patient permits himself to look at himself, his own associations, and his feelings for the first time and in a way in which he had not been capable previously, [11] and which he did not and could not do in seeking satisfaction of the pregenital impulse from the outside world.

---

be more correct to say that the concept of the dual instinct theory as expressed in *Beyond the Pleasure Principle* makes the concept of narcissism (as a primary energy) unnecessary and that it needs to be retained only as a clinical descriptive concept of value since it portrays certain clinical situations with clarity and economy, while it also implies that all libidinal energy has its source in what was once conceived as self-preservative sources and now conceived simply as somatic sources.

[11] The processes described here should be compared with Freud's statements (1915; pp. 134–135) and (1914; p. 77) about the relationship of narcissism to autoeroticism. It seems likely that frustration and renunciation eventually result in an attempt on the part of the

It would seem more correct to conceptualize the state of the ego as a split when the self seeks pregenital satisfaction in the outside world—and thus unconsciously treats its compromise formations as primary gratifications while dissatisfaction supervenes. In contrast, the moment when the ego turns upon itself for narcissistic gratification cannot be conceptualized as a split, even though the object is renounced and there is a momentary separation of instinct from its object. As the external object is rejected, it is no longer forced into identity with the internal representation of the object. Instead, some portion of the images of self become energized and differentiated from the reality objects previously used for gratification. It is perhaps at that moment that the ego can acknowledge the instinct as belonging to itself. It is of interest that there are several sources of gratification from this state of affairs. The patient at that moment obtains a narcissistic satisfaction by the libidinal regression that now envelops him and that he usually does not permit himself. It occurs at the very same time that he has renounced an instinctual impulse, which in itself probably satisfies some superego need. In addition, he is now more free to seek another avenue for his instinctual discharge, in the act of renouncing it and then reowning it. [12]

The psychic events described represent the achievement of a unit, a consolidation and/or an individualization [13] of the ego rather than, as has generally been stated, a split in the ego. The crucial element of psychoanalytic therapy is the renunciation of an identification with the therapist; it is not, as often stated, the identification with him or with his observing functions which provide the basis for the analytic process. Identifications of that type are pregenital in origin and do not necessarily precede analytic

---

human organism to satisfy itself not only by hallucinatory wish fulfillment but also by some autoerotic behavior, a result of a retreat to narcissism which is the basis for identification. The paper by Wulff (1946) and the one by Winnicott (1953) address themselves to the problems of decathexis of the pregenital instinct and the renunciation of the object, though slightly different conceptualizations of the matter are offered by each of those authors.

[12] Freud (1926, p. 97) suggested that the strength of the ego was dependent upon its maintenance of a bond with the instincts (id).

[13] Compare with the concept of individuation in a series of papers by Mahler and her associates.

Victor Calef

work, though they will always become hindrances [14] when they do occur.

If it is true that what occurs in the therapeutic process is dependent upon a renunciation as described, then it is similar to the process of sublimation and those processes involved in the development of conscience. The essence of all three processes is the renunciation of a love object by a decathectic process, in favor of a narcissistic retreat, ending in a new identification. It is not a split, but a consolidation of the ego. It is a high degree of differentiation out of which inner and outer reality are recognizably separated by a new agency whose chief function is to send signals to the ego about awakened derivatives from the instinctual drives (i.e., fantasy). Is it correct to ascribe observing functions to that new agency of conscience other than signals? It seems tenable to assume that it serves principally for signal functions to warn of feelings, sensations, and fantasies derived from the drives. The ego thus awakened by signal observes both the inner and outer realities and makes the necessary comparisons; whereas the splitting of the ego in the service of defense is a different mechanism which preserves the inner and out realities in isolation from each other without being able to call in the comparison function of the ego, perhaps just because of the failure of the signal function which warns of awakening dangers from within, especially of pregenital impulses.

When the fetishist insists with one part of his ego that a woman has a penis, he has taken a piece of childhood experience and converted it into a piece of inner reality. He has committed that distortion out of his castration fear. One might say that he has incorporated a distorted reality, internalized it; and in the process he

[14] Recent analytical writings have stressed the concept of the "therapeutic" or "working alliance" (following a statement made by Freud); and sometimes references are made to a mechanism of borrowing the analyst's ego and using it as an auxiliary for therapeutic purposes. I wonder whether such concepts do not overevaluate the pregenital aspects of transference and underestimate their power as hindrances to analysis, thereby overlooking the necessity for renunciation of object ties (abstinence) as a central and important factor for analytical work. Such conceptualizations may lead to the use of techniques which preclude the resolution of the transference neurosis. Where the "alliance" concept implies pregenital drives as motivational force, its value as resistance rather than as working force seems to me preponderant. However, where such concepts imply desexualization and perhaps autonomous drives as motivating toward analytical work, the concept gains greater validity even though no theoretical additions are needed to explain it.

has attempted to allay castration fears which now permit him the gratification of certain instinctual impulses. His oral incorporation of the penis is a perverse sexual gratification, a representative of his original pregenital instinctual wish used in the service of allaying his castration fear by possessing a part object from the external world. However, the castration fear has been converted into a derivative impulse by regression and incorporated into the ego by the secondary defensive process. The ego retains the pregenital instinct and the part object as a unity by splitting its function of reality testing—one part applicable for the conscious, and one part for the unconscious perception. In the unconscious the ego retains object and instinct tied together, rejecting the ego's conscious perception. Thus the part object is apparently rejected and divorced from the instinctual drive.

Something very similar happens to the compulsive patient whose apparent introspection makes one question why his introspections serve the purpose of his neurosis rather than those which lead to "insight." The compulsive introspection is a series of undoings. It is not an attempt to view the ego in its operation of achieving pleasures. It is an attempt on the part of the ego to guard its hidden pleasures. It is a false accusation against the ego which has already decided by a distortion that it has done something wrong. The undoing states that "it is not true that I want to hurt my beloved; it is not true that I have hurt my loved one." This form of negation does not in fact give up the pregenital instinctual gratification; indeed, it insures that a renunciation will not be necessary, that the ego may continue its course toward satisfaction and that it need not recognize that the instinctual impulse has not been surrendered. The instinctual impulse and the object of it remain tied together in the unconscious despite their having been split in consciousness. There is no renunciation. And again paradoxically, just because the instinct and object resist separation, the ego splits itself in a manner which will permit one of its functions to continue to operate.

It is specifically the capacity to renounce an instinctual impulse (or the object of it) which is the core difference between ego identification and a superego identification. Similarly it is the very

Victor Calef

same capacity to renounce an object which is the essence of sublimation; and we again describe the same process when we state that the ego splits into an experiencing and observing function in the therapeutic situation (and perhaps in other areas of ego functioning). However, for the purposes of this paper it seems a better distinction to say that the ego does not split. [15] Rather, the opposite occurs; it becomes unified. (We conceive of a split in the ego to occur only when one of its functions operates with one set of data from the unconscious and with another set of data from consciousness without communications between the two.) Restating in this way what we have always known forces the recognition that an oft-repeated analytic truism may nevertheless be false. Perhaps, after all, the analytic patient in achieving an analytic gain does not in fact identify with the analyst and his observing function. If he did, the patient would gratify an instinct via an incorporation and "split his ego," consequently preventing some part of reality

[15] At the December 1968 meetings of the American Psychoanalytic Association, sometime after this paper was written, Dr. Richard Sterba (1968) discussed a paper by Dr. Justin Simon et al on "Psychoanalytic Research and the Concept of Analytic Work." Dr. Sterba noted that in the literature on the analytic work one theme recurs with slight variations and that is the theme of oscillation between what the authors call two different sets of ego functions. One is the "cluster of functions which concern self-observation and which is supported and even *partly* (my italics) created by an identification with the analyst" (p. 2). The other set of functions relate to the experiencing ego. The thrust of Dr. Sterba's remarks was that he was much more concerned (in his paper on the therapeutic process) to describe the oscillation than the splitting of the ego. He says, ". . . almost all the authors quoted by the team point at the oscillations of the ego's attention center from the one set of ego functions to the other. In my paper, "The Fate of the Ego in Psychoanalytic Therapy" presented to the International Congress in Wiesbaden in July 1932, I described this oscillation and emphasized its significance in therapy. I was so impressed by this often very rapid shift from experience to observation and back that I used the term "ego-split" for this dual attitude—a term which is widely used nowadays for this phenomenon in therapy and which enjoys general acceptance. Parenthetically I would like to mention that the term "ego-split" as used in my paper presented in September 1932 aroused a storm of indignation and criticism in the Vienna Psychoanalytic Society. I was told that "ego-split" occurs only in psychosis and I had no business to apply it for a normal phenomenon in therapy (Federn, Helene Deutsch, Nunberg, Jekels). Only Anna Freud found it acceptable. However, when Freud's *New Introductory Lectures* appeared a few months later (in November 1932) my term "ego-split" did become acceptable. For Freud said in the chapter "Anatomy of the Mind": "The ego is the subject par excellence, how can it become the object? There is no doubt, however, that it can. The ego can take itself as object, it can treat itself like any other object, observe itself, criticise itself, and do heaven knows what besides with itself. In such a case one part of the ego stands over against the other. The ego can, then, be split; it splits when it performs many of its functions, at least for the time being. The parts can afterwards join up again" (pp. 3–4).

158 •

testing from adequately functioning. Instead, at a particular time the patient gives up his identification with the analyst, renounces his need to incorporate the analyst, and for the first time sees himself and the analyst as he has been unable to do before. He achieves an inner unity while the psychic energies now made more available can more easily scan the accessible and other internal object and self-representations as well as to be able to perceive external objects differently.

We have not come to the end of our questions by describing the renunciation of the object as the core event in the process of forming a new kind of identification. Why are some patients able and others unable to make such renunciations? The issues will not be resolved by generalizations—however useful—such as the stickiness of the libido and the relative strength of the resistances. We have only rediscovered and restated what is implicit in the axiom that a patient cannot be analyzed if he is incapable of suspending impulse gratification. It is not simply that he cannot form new object relationships, but, in addition and perhaps more importantly, that he cannot relinquish the old ones. And when the old object relationships are so retained, the quality of loving is affected in specific ways. Analysts have described those qualities as being pregenital, "narcissistic" (because the libidinal need seeks narcissistic objects and seems unable to find an adequate internal image of the self). Consequently such "love" lacks tenderness and consideration. It is only when the old object relationships are relinquished that it is possible for love to be a tender and considerate experience, insofar as the initial retreat to narcissism is experienced as a satisfaction. As we have always known, it is only through a satisfied selfishness that selflessness can be achieved.

The defensive situation as it exists in the depressions is of interest and particularly instructive. We have known at least since *Mourning and Melancholia* (Freud, 1917 [1915]) that in the depressions the ego peculiarly retains the object with a good deal of persistence and satisfies pregenital and aggressive drives. It keeps the object representation and the pregenital instinct cathexis tied together, thereby enforcing a split in itself, knowing consciously one thing about the object and acting out another piece of knowledge from the unconscious by merging the ego and the object. These statements recapitulate Freud's ideas and will be a reminder of the many ways in which he has discussed the ties between instinct and the object and the ego's relationship to the instincts in various neurotic illnesses. Some of our formulations about the concepts of the ego-alien and ego-syntonic impulses are based upon whether or not the instinct is acceptable to the ego and remains attached or detached from the object.

The limitations of experience preclude definitive statements about the relationships of instincts to their objects in the psychoses. However, it may be permissible to say that the splitting of the ego in depersonalization might profitably be studied from the point of view suggested by the comparison made here between the splitting of the ego in the defensive process and the unification of the ego in the therapeutic process. It will become most clear in the study of depersonalization that by paying attention to the fate of the object we are simply stating what we have long known. It is in the psychoses that analysis has made most explicit what happens to the object cathexis: namely that it is withdrawn more or less completely in a narcissistic regression. The object loss does not have the same quality of renunciation as it does in the neurotic compromise; in fact, it is not a renunciation of the object, perhaps because the relationship between instinct and object was tenuous and never established from the beginning, for obscure reasons. It is not clear whether in depersonalization the object cathexes are so completely abandoned and renounced that there is no longer the possibility of a fluid exchange between narcissistic and object libido. However, it may well be that what takes place in psychosis is an overwhelming pregenital instinctual discharge rather than a renunciation. Or, more likely, there occurs a particular simultaneous gratification and renunciation. Wherein is the renunciation? Wherein the gratification? It has been suggested that the instinct and its external object are split apart in the psychoses, and the object, along with the external world, is renounced or never existed in any established sense. The instinctual impulse is not diminished or renounced; at the same time, it is not held in suspended readiness. The instinctual gratification, pregenital in character, is absolute for the ego in a psychotic derealization in the sense that there is continuous discharge with the self as object. However, there is only an apparent relinquishment of the external object which does not have the function and significance of a renunciation. The instinctual cathexes remain tied to the self-representations as the object. Whether and in what way the object of an instinct is renounced has always been the basis of the psychoanalytic explanation for the various forms of depersonalizations, both in the psychoses and in the hysterias.

For purpose of clarity it seems necessary to restate what has been said before in so many different ways. The importance of the regression to narcissism and the renunciation of the object which the regression accomplishes is not always sufficiently and explicitly stated when such things as the resolution of the Oedipus complex, sublimation, desexualizations, and regressions in the service of the ego are discussed in the literature. [16] The attempt to follow the fate of the object in the clinical situation permits an answer to a technical question frequently raised: namely, whether—in any particular situation—the gratification of a patient's narcissistic wish is a contraindication to offering an interpretation. Some analysts believe that all satisfaction must be avoided at all costs. Some seem to believe it inevitable that every interpretation will gratify a narcissistic wish, that even attempts to frustrate the libidinal wishes end in the same way. Should the analyst avoid the gratification of the narcissistic wish or should he bow to the inevitable? What is it which will carry out the precepts of the fundamental rule and thus maintain the analysis? A theoretical answer suggests itself which might be considered an extension to the rule of abstinence: it is not the wishes which the analyst must frustrate—rather, he must not supply the object for gratification. It is the withholding of the objects which will allow for a regression to narcissism and which will permit the patient to find *narcissistic satisfaction only in the exploration of his own thoughts*. It is only the objects of the instincts which are attempted to be withheld by the analyst in the

[16] In all those situations regression to a narcissistic identification is not conceptualized as a pathological energy distribution, and any pejorative connotation which regression may have should be discounted.

sense that *he is not the agent which supplies them or suggests them,* while he chooses to interpret the defenses against and the achievement of such gratifications. What is characteristic of the analytic process is not the "falling-in-love-with-the-therapist" (i.e., the libidinal identification which patients have a habit of doing no matter what the persuasion of the therapist might be), but rather that the object of the analyst as the love object is renounced. Further, that renunciation or withholding is brought about by the interpretive sequences and staged by the refusal of the analyst to offer himself as the object for instinctual gratifications. This is, of course, not intended to say that the renunciation takes place at one moment, suddenly and completely. More likely, it is a gradual and piece-meal process, perhaps never completely accomplished. (However, the degree to which it is achieved will be a crucial index of the degree of the analytic cure.)

The intent of this paper to emphasize renunciation (arising out of narcissistic identification) as an active function of the ego in the formation of identifications and in the therapeutic process has been purposefully restated in several ways in order to illustrate how well known the concept is, even though we do not yet completely understand the exact nature of the process.

The discussion must now be brought to a close after a few remarks about one of the implications of this concept. It is tempting to reflect upon the differences between types of identification which have been outlined as the basis for differentiating between types of learning and between types of psychotherapy. Psychoanalytic theory has not yet provided an adequate conceptualization of the learning processes. Nevertheless, the theory does imply that there are at least three different methods by which learning takes place. The first method is probably instinctual. Perhaps much of the learning by repetition, exercise, habit formation and conditioning is accomplished through the biologic apparatus. The second method which encompasses the early imitative learning of the child is dependent primarily upon the sensory-perceptual experiences and their repetitions. It is a learning by identification, essentially through love (transference)—an erotization process which is dependent upon the tie between the one who learns and the teacher. The ambivalent aspect of that love must be minimal for maximal learning, while the erotic aspect must remain maximally unconscious. The third method may be designated as the superego type of learning, since it is dependent upon the capacity for a discriminating renunciation of old objects, as it is done in the formation of object relationships and sublimations. The capacity to permit an old and tightly retained gestalt to fall under scrutiny, dissection and dissolution may be the core of creative learning, while the rigid maintenance of the intact gestalt previously learned precludes progress in learning.

One could, for example, maintain that the superego type of learning is the principal method used by the mature student. Or one might attempt to say that the first two methods of learning are part of the processes of psychotherapy while psychoanalysis achieves its aims by the formation of a superego type of identification. Unfortunately, it is probably more correct to say that all three learning processes occur in most learning efforts, and that it is equally likely that all psychotherapies, including psychoanalysis, will be found to have admixtures of the three methods of learning. However, it is only psychoanalysis which specifically has as one of its goals the dissolution of the positive transference (the erotized, pregenital identification with the analyst). It is the only therapy which has specific techniques designed to dissolve the positive transference, the dissolution of which will permit a superego type of learning (learning through self-scrutiny). The latter statement must be corrected by the recognition that such a dissolution can only be relative and incomplete under the best of circumstances. Nevertheless, it seems correct to say that the psychoanalytic techniques are best designed to reach those specific goals which are connected to the dissolution of the transference.

It is, I believe, interesting to recognize that where therapy or learning takes place by imitation, by means of a libidinal identification, the ego is still dominated primarily by instinct, and has relatively little recognition of the process; whereas in the therapy and learning which is accomplished by a superego type of identification the ego actively participates (although not by conscious choice) in the process. In the latter case the ego is no longer driven by its own pregenital impulses. The processes which are involved are desexualizations. Such a description does not claim that the ego has achieved an absolute conscious and free choice of will, divorced from drives and determinism. Rather, the ego is now in a position to dictate and control according to the principles of function which govern the ego—no longer passively controlled according to those principles which govern the primary process.

I have failed to give adequate clinical material and sufficient theoretical exposition to support the claim made that the progress of analytical therapy is dependent upon the same renunciation of an object as occurs in the development of the superego. However, I have described only what I believe every analyst knows, and what many analytic authors have repeatedly stated in many publications, ever since Freud's (1923) description of sublimations. The theoretical considerations presented need no further data than that which we already have and can be either confirmed or invalidated on the basis of the clinical material that is available to every analyst. How then to justify the present repetition of that which has so frequently been said in so many ways by so many others? Perhaps little comfort will come from the reminder that explanatory statements of psychoanalysis encompass a variety of concepts which are subsumed under the titles genetic, economic and dynamic. A great diversity in the statements are permitted which then have many ramifications, combinations and permutations made possible by the coordinates which constitute metapsychology. At the same moment, structural and energic concepts are highly conjectural and insufficiently atomistic. While they have a limited descriptive and explanatory value, the analogies used to illustrate one or the other "point of view" of analytic theory might appear to contradict another analytic concept. Any single explanatory statement of analysis sometimes obscures for the psychoanalytic investigator the fact that he is exploring the same theoretical grounds that he and others have covered by previous investigations from other points of view. Sometimes we pose questions about clinical phenomena without recognizing that psychoanalytic theory has previously provided the answers which are finally again reached by way of the newer studies. To be sure, the original answers are at times implicitly rather than explicitly stated. Frequently we search for an answer to a question posed, and when we find that which we sought, we are left with a feeling of familiarity, as if the answer (as in the present instance on renunciation) was always preconsciously known, even though it was not always phrased in the identical way in which it now makes its appearance.

BIBLIOGRAPHY

Bibring-Lehner, G. (1936), A contribution to the subject of transference resistance. *Internat. J. Psycho-Anal.*, 17:181–189.

Calef, V. (1967), Alcoholism and ornithophobia in women. *Psychoanal. Quart.*, 36:584–587.

Deri, F. (1939), On sublimation. *Psychoanal. Quart.*, 8:325–334.

Fenichel, O. (1941), *Problems of Psychoanalytic Technique*. Albany: The Psychoanalytic Quarterly Inc.

_____ (1945), *The Psychoanalytic Theory of Neurosis*. New York: Norton.

Freud, S. (1914), On narcissism. *Standard Edition*, 14:69–102. London: Hogarth Press, 1957.

_____ (1915), Instincts and their vicissitudes. *Standard Edition*, 14:111–140. London: Hogarth Press, 1957.

_____ (1917 [1915]), Mourning and melancholia. *Standard Edition*, 14:237–260. London: Hogarth Press, 1957.

_____ (1923), The Ego and the id. *Standard Edition*, 19:3–66. London: Hogarth Press, 1961.

_____ (1926), Inhibitions, symptoms, and anxiety. *Standard Edition*, 20:77–124. London: Hogarth Press, 1959.

_____ (1927), Fetishism. *Standard Edition*, 21:149–157. London: Hogarth Press, 1961.

_____ (1940), Splitting of the ego in the process of defence. *Standard Edition*, 23:273–278. London: Hogarth Press, 1964.

Glover, E. (1947), *Basic Mental Concepts*. London: Imago Publishing Co., Ltd.

Loewald, H. (1962), Internalization, separation, mourning and the superego. *Psychoanal. Quart.*, 31:483–504.

_____ (1966), On internalization. Unpublished manuscript, read before the San Francisco Psychoanalytic Society in 1966.

Lustman, S. (1966), Impulse control, structure, and the synthetic function. In: *Psychoanalysis—A General Psychology*, ed. R. M. Loewenstein, L. M. Newman, M. Schur and A. J. Solnit. New York: International Universities Press, 1966, pp. 190–221.

Nunberg, H. (1951), Transference and reality. *Internat. J. Psycho-Anal.*, 32:1–9.

Rapaport, D. (1953), Some metapsychological considerations concerning activity and passivity. In: *The Collected Papers of David Rapaport*. New York-London: Basic Books, Inc., 1967, pp. 530–568.

Victor Calef

Sterba, R. (1934), The fate of the ego in analytic therapy. *Internat. J. Psycho-Anal.*, 15:117–126.

—— (1940), The dynamics of the dissolution of the transference resistance. *Psychoanal. Quart.*, 9:363–379.

—— (1968), Unpublished manuscript of discussion of a paper by Simon, J. et al.: "Psychoanalytic research and the concept of analytic Work."

Stone, L. (1961), *The Psychoanalytic Situation.* New York: International Universities Press.

Winnicott, D. W. (1953), Transitional objects and transitional phenomena. *Internat. J. Psycho-Anal.*, 34:89–97.

Wulff, M. (1946), Fetishism and object choice in early childhood. *Psycho-Anal. Quart.*, 15:450–471.

PART II

MORAL VALUES AND
THE PSYCHOANALYTIC SITUATION

8. Value Conflict and the Psychoanalyst's Role

NORMAN ZINBERG, M.D.

IT IS BECOMING increasingly clear that the future development of psychoanalysis will depend greatly upon a more precise understanding of values—not only those held by its individual practitioners and embedded in its theory, but the values incumbent upon the psychoanalyst's role as an urban middle-class professional. Freud himself, as Hartmann (1960) has pointed out, held an indifferent and essentially pragmatic attitude toward systems of cultural belief, and this may account for the failure of psychoanalysts, to date, to make any comprehensive study of the values implicit in psychoanalysis. Since those human value conflicts that arise out of socioeconomic differences involve such things as status, pride, success, even the size of material symbols, the psychoanalyst tends to regard them as relatively shallow when compared with the urge to rend, destroy, violate, or devour, with which he is more familiar.

The sociological efforts to describe human functions by grouping them structurally into roles or personae has been often viewed with trepidation by psychoanalysts. Somehow, it is as if this sort of theoretical attempt to explain human interaction diminishes not only the people so described—reducing them to masks, actors, players rather than persons—but, minimizing the emphasis on the unique experiencing, responsive, feeling quality of man, also diminishes psychoanalytic theory.

This is not to deny the emphasis that psychoanalytic theory in recent years has placed on social structure, while trying to avoid a dichotomy between social strivings and biological drives. Indeed, the variations on the major themes are infinite and specific to time, place, and person; the same fundamental conflict or motive can be expressed in ways determined exclusively by the society and the culture. To retain what makes psychoanalysis unique does not necessarily limit the scope of research into current social issues, and its theoretical elaboration. What may limit such investigation is the value system that adheres to the institutionalized role of psychoanalysis, not because the values themselves are good or bad, but because they are not considered as values. As man's capacity to alter both internal and external nature grows, the individual's essential problem becomes not so much a search for freedom, in the sense of permitting himself more choices, as it is a search for peace, in the sense of being able to make meaningful rejections. Though the two are not really separable, in the latter case there will be a greater emphasis on values than on inhibitions caused by basic drive conflicts.

In the course of this essay, I shall be arguing for a study, not making it, and though theory and practice will serve as examples, they will not be criticized. However unsatisfactory such a scheme may seem, it is justified by the swift pace of social change which is in fact part of the argument. In the course of the essay we shall consider (a) the pressures for social change in our society, and the role of psychoanalysis in such movements; (b) the problem of values in the one-to-one situation of psychoanalysis; (c) psychoanalysts as urban middle-class professionals; (d) the influence of their values on the pace of social change. To begin with, however, one must define the concept of value itself.

VALUES

In Webster, "value" is defined as "something, as a principle, quality, or entity, which is regarded as intrinsically valuable or desirable." Thus the concept of value depends on the person who "values" and on an objective something outside himself (Kluckhohn, 1951). It is not the concept itself which causes difficulty, but the semantics surrounding it. For example, in saying, "Joe Smith makes good (i.e., competent) speeches," one is placing a value. But, "I like what Joe Smith says," is merely a personal observation. One statement can lead to the other, just as the further step, "What Joe Smith says is good (i.e., right)" coordinates values by making a judgment. Thus value is a superordinate quality intrinsically related to attitudes and morals but not identical with either.

When, in a familiar analytic example, the analyst tells the patient, "you don't seem to be working well today," he means it to be an observation, but one which also conveys a value—working is important. When the patient responds by saying, "That's the whole trouble with me, I am always putting off working. You must think me a lousy patient," the value of work is subsumed in an attack on procrastination, and the result is a moral judgment based on this value. In making such distinctions, of course, one must pay attention to the speaker as well as to the word he is using, especially if the word conveys opinion, fact, hypothesis, ethics, symptom, belief, and ideology, as I have discussed elsewhere (1963, 1967a, 1967b).

All three factors—attitudes, values, morals—exert a dynamic and directive influence on behavior and perception. Our attitude toward an object influences what we notice, think, and feel about it, how we describe it to others, what linking concepts it is integrated with, and how it affects the action we will choose to take. The coordination of all this into what a person constructs as his value system is an intrinsic part of his identity as an adult, and though this value system is connected with earlier primitive desires, he assumes that the complex of motives governing his values is to some extent separate from them. People suffering from neurosis, or even psychosis, may exhibit a serious disturbance of value in some area, but at the same time most of their opinions, attitudes, and perceptions stem from their organized value system. The neurotic who cannot get along with authority figures nonetheless votes, chooses friends, dresses himself according to some fundamental scheme. By the same token, though a confirmed criminal misbehaves only a tiny fraction of the time, otherwise observing the laws and mores of his society, once he is caught, that fraction

Norman Zinberg

is what labels him a full-time deviant. In other words, to understand an individual, whether patient or analyst, one must notice
not just the specific value at issue, but the surrounding structure of
values, whose automatic acceptance and success are questioned
only when a conflict arises, either within the individual or because
of changes in the social definitions underlying his values. At present, the role position of the psychoanalyst is facing the second
form of conflict.

VALUES AND SOCIAL CHANGE

Organized psychoanalysis has dealt with value problems chiefly
through analysis itself, through scrutiny of the value system of the
individual analyst during his own analysis when, as patient, he
learns—emotionally and cognitively—about the relationship between unconscious conflict and everyday perceptions. Though his
values may seem relatively autonomous, they are not entirely separate from past choices determined by basic drives.

Since values as a subject received little formal intellectual attention in psychoanalytic institutes, the profession has relied heavily
on the training analysis for instruction in this area. During the
process, special emphasis is given to potential value conflicts
which might arise in a man's work as a therapist—the so-called
countertransference reactions. If his analysis went well, the psychoanalyst felt he could deal with individual patients whose personal values might question or threaten his own. In the case of
such potential or actual value conflict, he must be aware of his
own reaction in order not to impose his personal values on the situation. If, on the one hand, he is tempted to impose them, the
analyst is responding to the patient as if he were a significant
figure out of his past, resulting in a serious loss of analytic distance
and objectivity. A successful analysis, on the other hand, has informed him about himself, and explicated the infinite complications of human motive and behavior, including his own. His view
of people is relativistic, and he does not condemn them because
their values and his are different.

At this level of dealing with individual variations, psychoanaly-

sis worked well enough; the fact that only individual value systems were being considered, and not the values inherent in theory
and role, seemed unimportant. It was assumed that the second and
third groups of values became intelligible in the process of untan-
gling the values of the individual psychoanalyst.

In fact, such emphasis on the individual seemed entirely consistent with the larger value system of American culture, and it accounts in part for the comparatively great success of psychoanalysis in this country (Zinberg, 1965). The world of the pioneer
and the melting pot resisted the development of a rigid class structure, and fiercely supported the freedom of the individual to make
choices. In a society that considered "every man a king," free of
European class-bound hierarchies, opportunity was within every
man's reach. If the individual was indeed this important, individual
difficulties deserved long, arduous, time- and money-consuming
attention.

But now the focus in the United States has shifted from individual to *social* change. Kenniston (1969) explains this desire for
social change as being, in fact, two distinct revolutionary movements. One is economic, reaching for what, until the 1960's,
seemed the unlikely achievement of enough food and shelter, and
a decent existence for everyone. To the extent that the means of
achieving these aims may be available (Thernstrom, 1969), though
still not equally distributed, this revolution has been a success.
Hence the fury of the blacks, who feel they are being denied what
is potentially available, not something which can't be made to go
around. The second revolution, less tangible than the first, is social. Student activists find themselves being prepared to prosper in
a society that has achieved but still not fully accomplished the first
revolution. They question individual goals: "How can I make my
life worthwhile?" But they also question their own goals in relation to the relevance of institutional goals. "Will this effort do
anything worthwhile for society as a whole that has not *already*
been done?" goes beyond simply wondering where the student, as
an individual, might fit into the larger social scheme, and raises
questions about the validity of the goals of the social institutions
which dominate his life, particularly the school.

I believe that the students' questioning of values is valid and has been misunderstood by the universities. Erik H. Erikson once remarked, only half in jest, "Of course we should teach them how to be revolutionaries. Where else would they learn it?" Once the activists became skeptical about the rigorous, demanding, highly competitive race which had brought them to these superior universities in the first place, they turned to the university for guidance about the behavior, rationale, and underlying philosophy of these venerable social institutions. But the universities, threatened by the violence of the questioning, demanded that the students tell them what the behavior, rationale, and philosophies of the institutions ought to be. And since the students had not considered these matters in any organized fashion, they came up with inarticulate or impossible "demands."

This is, granted, a highly simplified example which cannot begin to explain the struggle between the New Left and the universities. But it does indicate how important it is for social groups to understand the fundamental value conflicts: the assault is being made not on individual members of the university but on the value structure of the social institution itself. Theoretically, someone in psychoanalytic treatment could at the same time be doing research that disproves psychoanalytic principles, just as some student activists would like to go on studying with certain professors while they also concentrate on destroying the university itself. Inevitably, when searching questions are raised about the goals and quality of urban middle-class life, psychoanalysis will come in for its share of scrutiny. For though it is not quite a social institution, it is an organized professional entity whose impact on our culture has been a great one, and it is urgent that these questions of value be raised now, when they can still be usefully related to what is going on elsewhere in our society.

Please keep in mind that when we think about the rapid rate of social change and its value implications for organized psychoanalysis as a social entity, we are not discussing the efficacy of an analysis of a patient by an analyst rooted as it is entirely in individual psychology and a one-to-one interpersonal relationship.

Neither is the desirability for psychoanalysis to maintain far-flung training institutes and organizations challenged.

We are considering psychoanalysis as the bastion of an intrapsychic introspective approach to individual psychology. As the focus of psychology in this country appears to be in the process of a rapid shift to a more generalized interest in social change and interpersonal organization—and the current popularity of group approaches indicates this—then if psychoanalysis is to function effectively during this period of social change it must know its own value system, potential conflicts, and how these lead to the development of institutions and particularly of institutionalized procedures and positions. The element of prediction as to where conflict will arise may be an important one; to be aware of potential conflicts one must be aware of the influence of current conflicting psychological precepts. The rejection of opposing intellectual positions is easy; the rejection of the subtle influence exerted by the broadening of value positions is much harder. Other schools of thought make their points. Kleinian, existential, and behavioral psychology, while not accepted by classical Freudians, have left their mark on our present theory and practice. They have forced psychoanalysts to broaden some theoretical positions such as the influences of early development, an emphasis on the present as a state of being, and the need to notice more consistently the operation of conditioning in and out of the therapeutic situation. How often do we accept more treatment "parameters" almost without noticing? It will be argued, probably correctly, that individual psychoanalysts can and do notice what they do in their practice. They withstand even subtle influences that affect their treatment activities, but the role of psychoanalyst and psychoanalysis as an organization are open to different threats. Organizations need to protect their own structure much more directly in the social arena than do individuals. To avoid subtle changes that cause positions not so much to change as to lose imperceptibly their sharpness and clarity is particularly hard when the rate of external value change is swift. Thus, prediction of where conflict may occur, based on a clear knowledge of the implicit and explicit value systems, may compensate for such a time lag by indicating what values need protection.

VALUES AND THE PSYCHOANALYTIC SITUATION

Most psychoanalysts today will admit that they are not blank reflecting screens in the psychoanalytic situation, but they are less clear about what they actually are. If one distinguishes between the patient's transference relationship to the analyst and the very different relationship between two human beings, it is assumed that the "transference neurosis" comes exclusively from the patient, and to that extent the analyst is indeed a blank screen. Nonetheless, analyst and patient are also two feeling human beings working closely together on a difficult and abstract task—a situation from which many values derive. To work on a problem is good; so is working *with* someone on the problem. The goals of their work are worthwhile. And beyond these values lies the psychoanalytic definition of a human being, which includes his potential for affect —in other words, his emotions have value, and so does his shared humanity.

All of these values are to some extent linked with class. The psychoanalytic belief in work, for example, is implicit in the work of Freud, all the way to Erikson (1964). Even Erikson with his emphasis on such virtues as fidelity and generativity, has all but ignored the values of a little-skilled, uneducated, illegitimate black male whose mother moved to a large city just a few years before he was born. A psychoanalyst working as a consultant for a social agency not only supports that agency by his presence but finds himself supporting the policies of that agency which seek to determine what is "better" for its clients. A black adolescent from a painful background with a psychotic mother and a semi-alcoholic father, who previously had shown some academic interest, becomes involved with a violence-oriented, politically active group older than himself. Within a few weeks he kicked in a window and struck a YMCA instructor with a ping-pong paddle. The agency personnel felt they could not continue to work with him and pleaded for the consultant to help arrange an institutionalized placement. The boy tells the consultant that the relationship with this political group provides him with close companionship and solid aspirations for the first time in his life. Obviously, these aspirations are anti-social as defined by agency policy and much of our society, and the consultant reluctantly agrees that the boy should not remain in his present atmosphere.

Psychoanalysis usually handles such differences by insisting that, in the one-to-one treatment situation, a psychoanalyst can, in part, make up the difference in values through his continuing efforts to understand what his patient has experienced. And this implies that the black patient shares in the mutual value system to some extent, or he wouldn't be there at all.

But here we are confronted with basic questions of potential value conflicts. Usually an analyst will work with a black patient, not as a private entrepreneur in professional practice, but in an institutional setting. What value conflicts are inherent in a psychoanalytic role when an analyst works in a hospital, court, government agency, clinic, school, and the like, and what is his commitment to his patients in these institutions (Szasz, 1965)?

Even in private practice, patients want to know about the limits of the analyst's tolerance—how he balances his ethical responsibilities to patients with his sense of duty to the community. When atrocities occur, like Charles Whitman's slaughter of the innocents from the Austin tower in 1966, not long after he had visited a psychiatrist, such questions take on special force, but such situations are usually hypothetical. Ordinarily, we simply ask the patient if he sees himself as such a threat to society, which is sound technique because it restores the treatment to proper focus—i.e., the patient's fantasy of himself—and eliminates irrelevant quibbling about the analyst's social responsibility.

But when the therapist is paid by a social institution, the situation changes. Leaving aside the matter of confidential revelations in the course of treatment, we assume that the analyst, by agreeing to work for the institution, therefore, approves of it whether or not he approves of most of its administrative policies. Yet the value the analyst places on the institution may clash so seriously with the patient's that there can be no trust between

· 177

Norman Zinberg

them. Can this mistrust be understood as resistance, or must the analyst, in fact, be aware of the significant message about social value he sends out simply by his presence in the institution?

The second question involves the value interchange that occurs merely in visiting a psychoanalyst—i.e., it is automatically assumed that the goal of such a visit is indeed worthwhile. In private practice, unlike institutional practice, a patient's motives may be rooted in a value system essentially different from the analyst's, but with seemingly similar aims. Take, for example, the patient who believes in magic—not just the remnant of an infantile conflict about omniscience, but a serious reliance on dream books and totems, sufficiently reinforced by the culture to render this belief autonomous. He accepts the analyst's ritual, but actually imagines an entirely different process at work. Analysts often deal with patients whose goals are distant from, even antagonistic toward, what can be expected of the psychoanalytic method. But is it possible for analysts living in a society dominated by Western scientific determinism with its almost total reliance on a reality governed by the five senses to understand a belief in magic which is relatively independent of primitive drive structures? How can an analyst, with his strong belief in causality, best challenge a patient's belief in magic? And once challenged, can such a basic clash of values be put aside while other "work" is done, if the patient's idea of magic is *the* force behind his visits to the analyst?

This kind of impasse leads to a third question, which can, in the physicist's language, be called the Heisenberg effect, the so-called uncertainty principle, whereby the accurate measurement of one of two related quantities produces uncertainties in the measurement of the other. Most of Freud's patients came to him with severe, even bizarre symptoms, but analysts today encounter few such neuroses. We speak instead of character disorders, meaning that patients seek help because some aspect of ordinary life has become exaggerated or distorted. They can't work, worry too much, can't love or be loved, can't decide who they are. Today even sexual symptoms are seen as secondary to this type of character problem, which expresses a person's values in terms of standards or norms. And except for borderline or psychotic patients,

178 ·

those afflicted with such character disorders are so only to a degree—they do work some, are not totally crippled by worry, interact with other people, and present a generally coherent idea of themselves. In fact, the standards these patients fail to meet, which force them to seek help, derive from the value system of psychoanalysis itself.

This is hardly a new idea, and enemies of psychoanalysis like Whitehorn (1951) have brayed that psychoanalysts "stuff the unconscious with all manner of things which to no one's surprise they then find there when they look." Even analysts, when they consider how psychoanalytic concepts can lead to uncompromising standards of behavior and feeling, have complained, as Erikson (1958) did in *Young Man Luther*, that "even as we were trying to devise with scientific determinism a therapy for the few, we were led to promote an ethical disease among the many [p. 19]. The historian, Robert Lee Wolff (1962) has perceptively noted the freedom of a writer like Harriet Martineau to present a thinly disguised autobiographical study as a novel, and remain anonymous, just as Ruskin, in his diaries, discusses his impotence as an illness inflicted on him, not something he participated in.

After Freud, such innocence vanished, and every writer since then has felt that bearded old man, head and torso thrust slightly forward, listening as he writes. Yet the analyst, though troubled by the impact of analytic thought on what it studies, argues that in the privacy of treatment one can separate culturally induced difficulties from basic drive-induced conflicts. Cannibalism, castration, incest, sadism, and other timeless matters need individual perspective despite shifting cultural values. In his work on suicide, Durkheim (1897) investigated the relationship of the individual to society in an attempt to discover how societies reach a consensus, especially a moral consensus, for regulating formal and informal social activities. But psychoanalytic theorists missed the full implications of Durkheim's thought when they stressed the flexible approach to an individual's conflicts about morality that can be found through the genetic developmental sequence.

Recent experiments of sociologists and psychologists with existing social situations, or with experimental ones, once more challenge psychoanalysis to delineate the limits of its Heisenberg effect on modern values. The research indicates that social situations have a greater impact on an individual than his individual personality, family attitudes, or social class, and impose more explicit strictures on his future. As Rosenthal (1968) discovered, school children's learning can be quite accurately predicted by knowing what the teacher expects of a child. A more ambitious British study (Himmelweit, in press), including a 10-year follow-up and sophisticated personality evaluation, shows that a child put in a secondary vocational school will adopt the values of that school after only one year no matter what intelligence, personality, family background and attitudes, and social class he begins with. Ten years later, he still adheres to the judgment that was made on him as a schoolboy by the authorities. And the reverse is equally true. A lower-class child of unexceptional intelligence and ambition, from a disruptive family little interested in furthering his education, placed almost by accident in a college preparatory school, will adopt its values in an astonishingly short time, though he may have to struggle academically and separate himself from his family. In 10 years, owing to his higher aspirations, he is economically and culturally far ahead of a matched group of his peers who did not go to the better school.

This is not meant to prove that nurture outweighs nature, but simply to assign relative importance to the operating factors. This becomes particularly important when analysts decide, as they must, what they mean by social deviation. Continuing Durkeim's work, Kai Erikson (1966) in *The Wayward Puritan*, shows that socially deviant behavior does not merely disrupt society, but aids it by testing boundaries and by constantly clarifying the limits tolerable to that society at a particular time. Psychoanalysts are familiar with this concept, for they must always consider how a patient's behavior or attitude is adaptive even when the scrutinized item seems disorderly. But when analysts shift from the individual to his social group, and back again, their thinking is not quite so clear.

When analysts refer the patient back to himself—"How do you feel about your work inhibitions?"—they seem to eschew normative standards, for the patient would not be there if he were not in conflict. But where does the conflict come from? Is success in a career an *inherent* value, or is it conferred by the social group? Obviously the latter, and hence the political rightist argues against the guaranteed annual wage because black males theoretically lack this work ethic. The analyst's question, of course, does not just reflect cultural values, but somehow he reinforces them, particularly when we consider class distinctions. Recently analysts have been seeing patients who use drugs for non-medical reasons. Would it be fair to say that they judge the user's improvement by his ability to do without the drug *and* whether or not he is working? This may reflect only the institution's or societies values, not the analyst's, but the distinction is debatable. In an influential psychoanalytic text (Glover, 1955), one of the criteria for "analyzability" was a stable work situation.

Standards that were foisted on society in the past can remain psychologically durable in the present. In Jamaica, 85 per cent of the live births are illegitimate, and logically the legitimate births should be considered deviant. Yet Jamaicans still feel stigmatized by the superimposed values of the British middle class, which until recently had the political, not social or numerical, upper hand. Coles (1967) points to a similar confusion in the United States, where socially coherent groups of blacks and poor whites are forced into social and psychological conflict by the attempted integration of their group norms with those of the dominant culture. Psychoanalysts may consider such matters as being outside their bailiwick, but this brings us back to Kai Erikson (1966) and Coles, (1967), and turns Erik Erikson's (1958) complaints about an ethical disease into an accusation.

How does a society impose its need for deviance upon its members? What social groups set the standards and the means of enforcing them? Moral police are as powerful as any other, but psychoanalysts persist in thinking of themselves as custodians of "mental health," instead of examining the values implied in their professional role. Questions of value are consigned to the flexible one-to-one treatment situation, where the impact of psychoanalytic theory on our culture is obscured. These may be sins of omis-

· 181

sion, but psychoanalysts are eminently capable of responsibility about such sins. Though psychoanalysts have shown little interest in value positions as a form of social communication, only careful scrutiny of the values inherent in all aspects of psychoanalysis—individual, group, theoretical—can reveal how much values influence the choice of social areas to be investigated, and the social labels that will be accepted.

MIDDLE CLASS STATUS AND VALUE CONFLICT

A cursory glance at the rolls of the American Psychoanalytic Association in 1968 showed that over 90 per cent of its members live within 30 miles of a large urban center (there are only 13 members practicing in 30 states). There is equally abundant proof that the profession is as middle-class as it is urban, if one judges by the value psychoanalysts place on money. It is almost as delicate a subject among them as it is among other doctors, but not quite, since analysts are open about their rates at the start, and insist that frank discussion of fees are part of the treatment. Many other professionals are more circumspect, reflecting the strong middle-class cultural connection between money and privacy. In one investigation by a market-research firm on American values (Yankelovish, 1967) money appeared as the most important middle-class American secret; a suburban housewife, after unhesitating frankness about birth control, parried a question about current income with, "Now, that's personal."

Among themselves, analysts are less frank about money than they are in the highly protected one-to-one intimacy of treatment. During my investigation of analytic values, I asked candidates from three cities how they learned what to charge their patients. To a man, they answered that although they had been taught formally about the technical and theoretical aspects of money in psychoanalysis, no course they took at an institute discussed fees (except for control cases), and almost no senior colleagues would ever discuss such matters frankly.

In fact, they had three chief sources of information about fees. One was discussion with their own analyst, who usually charged them less than his regular fee. This remained their standard for a time, but they planned to work up to his regular fee after they had gained experience and professional stature. Second, private patients were often referred to them by senior colleagues who had already discussed the fee with the patient. My informants were markedly ambivalent about this procedure, being grateful for the referrals, but also resenting the occasional exploitation when asked to take on an "unsatisfactory" patient for less than the senior colleague would charge. They also felt some coercion behind these referrals, in the senior's assumption that they should, as part of their apprenticeship, be paid less. If the candidate refused the case or demanded the senior's fee, he was judged too grasping or, worse, acting out his own competitive wishes.

The third channel, of course, is gossip. Analysts learned about senior colleagues who had charged "exorbitant" fees through patients who were hospitalized and whose histories became well known. Sometimes they just guessed this from the way a colleague lived, and he was either envied or censured as morally reprehensible. And in that very ambivalence one detects a role conflict for psychoanalysts. The method of referral described above is a model of the Puritan ethic: one must earn one's place in the ranks of the virtuous hierarchy. With this method, analysts show how thoroughly they guard their right to an appropriate middle-class income and a training system in value indoctrination. One need not go into the complex theoretical arguments behind the rule that a patient pay his way, but one aspect is worth discussing here: the patient is often asked to pay for the hours he misses even when he can't avoid being absent. Analysts frankly tell patients that without this rule they cannot afford to take him on, and the argument is economically valid and soundly based in the history and theory of psychoanalysis.

Freud (1913) recognized early that what he had to sell was time. "In regard to time, I adhere strictly to the principle of leasing a definite hour. Each patient is allotted a particular hour of my available working day. It belongs to him, and he is liable for it, even if he does not make any use of it" (p. 126). His frankness and honesty about the monetary relationship in psychoanalytic treatment has been discussed by Szasz (1968) who contends that in that contractual relationship, where one party leases time and the other pays money, lies the essential equality of analyst and patient. When Freud (1913) writes, "It seems to me more respectable and ethically less objectionable to acknowledge one's actual claims and needs rather than, as is still the practice among physicians, to act the part of the distinguished philanthropist—a position which one is not, in fact, able to fill" (p. 131), he renounces a higher status role for analyst than for patient. Whatever else one may get from reading Jones' biography of Freud, one could hardly imagine Freud a money-grubber. He had worked hard to achieve a certain security and he wished to live in a respectable manner. It is no different today; analysts feel entitled to this security, and it is a reasonable middle-class position. This essay intends no hint of criticism for this decision. The delicate subject of money is only introduced because it is so important in modern America; hence, the value ramifications of the analyst's reasonable decision to be middle class needs to be determined. A decent material life in the urban centers frequented by analysts requires between $25,000 and $50,000 a year, and most analysts value this life enough to organize their work methods around it. Some settle for less lucrative institutional work. But few try the ethical freedom of a private practice yielding $10,000 a year which would then enable them to treat patients unable to pay their "regular" fees. Refusing to practice psychoanalysis in the ghetto is *not* due to desire for money alone. Certainly, there are independently rich analysts who would be trying such a practice if monetary reward were the sole concern. It is that the process itself involving a contract between equals is required for analysis to function and that form of ethical interaction is middle-class protocol. To establish a $10,000 year practice would be to proclaim oneself a philanthropist, a role position that Freud indicated, specifically and reasonably, would undermine the basic psychoanalytic relationship of equality.

The issue about money is strikingly similar to those pointed to throughout this essay. The clinical legitimacy of the analyst's decision to receive a fee for service is unchallenged. Nonetheless, in continuing this valid practice, he finds secondary institutionalized procedures developing as a result, such as the indoctrination of candidates into the hierarchy, which make for potential value conflict. A contractual process intended to avoid according a lofty and benevolent status to one party in the treatment situation subtly becomes just that in relation to his junior colleagues—and not during the formal student-teacher interaction. A form of professional apprenticeship, enforced by unspoken sanctions, grows up as part of an informal procedure whose links to the American sensitivity about money makes it especially necessary to consider the resulting ambiguity to avoid value confusion. These secondary activities, resulting in large part from the popularity of psycho-analysis, supply the chinks in the role position of psychoanalyst that make for value conflict.

In point of fact, most analysts could earn more than they do, and many of them actually like to spend part of their time coun-seling, training, teaching, doing research outside their offices (Levin and Michaels, 1961) for less money. They do this not only because analysis is an arduous and surprisingly lonely occupation (Zinberg, 1963). Psychoanalysts are also decidedly ambivalent about their middle-class affluence, for they remember that at one time psychoanalysis was embattled against the established values of the day, in the cause of truth, scholarship, even the benefit of treating emotionally disturbed human beings. The very nature of their work enforces a strong humanitarian bent, and for many years this work was a sort of intellectual deviance aiming to re-define social boundaries by clarifying what it means to be human. The extent of their acceptance, as analytic concepts have been absorbed into the culture at large, still surprises them.

It is precisely their own ambivalence about their middle-class values and status that makes psychoanalysts peculiarly vulnerable at this moment of history. In the Joseph McCarthy days of the early 1950's, when academic and professional groups were being pressured into an anticommunist, gray-flannel suit conformity, the analytic position was eminently suited to defending the integrity of the individual. Given their professional loyalty to patients, they would of course refuse information about ideologies. Similarly, psychoanalysis made the individual aware of his struggle against a specific form of social coercion, though some people were already reflecting on psychoanalysis as a symbol of rigid social norms. Gill and Brenman (1959), and Rapaport (1960), particularly, stressed that the ego had to achieve a balance between social pressure and instinctive drives. Rapaport (1958) chose the example of George Orwell's *1984*, in which the instinctually derived emotion of love helped Winston reestablish a relative ego autonomy that had been consistently undermined by Big Brother's interminable meddling in memory, privacy, rationality, and the sequence of events, and by the constant external threat of punishment and war. Most psychoanalysts could find an analogy between Joseph McCarthy and Big Brother, while they heroically fought to protect individual freedom and autonomy.

But the 1950's seem exaggeratedly clear-cut compared to the chaotic multiplicity of patterns at the present time. Today patients say they speak for humanity and individual freedom, and the analyst for social restraint. Their passionate belief in civil rights, unobstructed self-investigation through drugs, new sexual mores, and anti-institutionalism—what they conceive to be individual liberty—sounds uncomfortably like the analyst's own position when it is linked to their questioning of life goals and traditional social solutions. But the analyst, believing as he does that human freedom is relative, disagrees not with their goals but with their methods. To him, the issue is not simply an awareness of what is in the unconscious, but an understanding of self-deception. Doubt alone is not enough; it is necessary to have the ability to tolerate doubt and still act with spontaneity and resolution. Relativism is a fine principle, but it depends not so much on fixed rules as on human conceptions of freedom, and how it can be preserved.

Older patients feel that essential qualities of the status quo are threatened by the young deviants, and the analyst, in doing his work, must help them distinguish between fears bred of their unconscious envy, and fears he can consider "rational." His problem is not that of making good clinical decisions, but of making them always on the side of restraint. If he opposed social restraints in the 1950's but supports them today, he may not only be trying to maintain his traditional balance. There could in fact be a conflict of value here, for the freedom he now tries to restrain may be very similar to the traditional values of psychoanalysis before analysts became so firmly entrenched in the middle class. They are still uncertain about the role of irrational commitment and ideology in social reform—like Freud's—and their participation in current social movements is uneasy.

Psychoanalysis has always been an unabashedly elitist procedure for both therapist and patient. In the past, the money and time and effort seemed justified because (1) analysts treated patients who could bring about social reform either through their influence on society, or by raising a "healthier" generation; (2) each case was a research project leading to further discoveries about the nature of man; (3) theoretical developments and research in psychoanalysis would influence other fields. It is still too early to balance the ledger of such wide-ranging hopes (my own guessing leads more to black than red), but there is an apprehensive mood within organized psychoanalysis, expressed by Gitelson (1963) in an address to the American Psychoanalytic Association. Just as an analyst is cautious about promising individual patients magically therapeutic results, so must the same restraint be applied to the larger ambition of psychoanalysis itself. This concern about both the success and the limitations of psychoanalysis might have led to a reassessment of its scientific and clinical possibilities, if all the disciplines of people working together had not been assaulted by the new politics, drugs, race, and the basic value changes they implied. The result has been apprehension, not re-evaluation.

In the 'thirties, radicals (Gitelson, 1963) attacked psychoanalysis as elitist, but the charge seemed to carry little weight when psychoanalysts were still considered deviants in academic institutions, and their work was still in a state of evolution. Now the situation is quite different: analysts are acceptable and economically comfortable, though they are uneasy about the stasis in psychoanalytic thinking. The radicals' demand for "participatory democracy" seems, ironically, closer to the social and psychological goals analysts have traditionally valued, and radical rhetoric—self-determination, individual integrity, personal relatedness, social consideration, love, peace—echoes psychoanalysis in its philosophical and ideological youth.

When the analyst's own ideas seem to be assaulting him, his role position requires explicit understanding of his dedication to social-class values. How does the middle-class ethos affect him? What does he indeed hold most valuable? These questions must be answered if he is to deal with a conflict about principles, not method; conflicts about method are invariably tendentious.

Psychoanalytic Values and the Pace of Social Change

We need a much more precise understanding of the way middle-class values influence psychoanalysis, not only to alleviate the analyst's conflict or to improve his clinical judgment, but because such understanding may make it possible for psychoanalysis to be of greater social value without sacrificing its present achievements. Clinical judgment continues to be satisfactory in part because patients tend to choose analysts whose values match their own (though this in itself does not mean the analyst will accept the patient). We can see this in the use of words. Analysts consistently show their patients how varyingly words can be used—as symbols, to show or to hide affect, magically, or rationally—and they are also instructed by nonverbal sources, such as tone of voice, posture, tears, bodily movements. But the ultimate consensual understanding is achieved through words, and both analyst and patient therefore value them greatly.

Yet we know, from research and from novels, that subcultures outside the middle class do not hold words to be sacred and in fact mistrust them. In a book by the black novelist Chester Himes (1969), a girl visits in prison a man she hardly knows, though they had shared a frightening experience. In an inarticulate exchange, she tells him she is pregnant by another man, and he asks her to marry him—an oddly touching scene, unthinkable in a novel about middle-class people, yet convincing because for people of this class, what counts is action, not words.

Of course, the line between acts and words is not always that clear-cut for analysts and their middle-class patients. In clarifying the fear of magic or the desire for omnipotence, analysts separate behavior and thoughts, fantasy and the acting out of fantasy. Psychoanalysis places important theoretical value on understanding the inner life, though there are exceptions based on the timing of interpretation and the significance of repression. But action based on such understanding is less clearly evaluated. When can one be sure that an insight isn't merely intellectual? If someone believes, magically, that his anger can actually destroy someone and he has therefore become oversuppressed, does he have to show his anger toward someone in order to test his analytic insight? Does an overactive patient need to refuse a dare—refrain from acting—to learn that passivity does not automatically represent castration? In these patients acts may be needed to verify the words. But in the Himes (1969) example, and in Coles' (1967) interviews, words are virtually irrelevant.

In considering words, physical well-being, and the nuclear family, it is hard to separate middle-class values from theory, but the distinction must be made. In some ethnic families, luxuries are preferred to dentists and doctors. Nor are they moved by talk about weakened bodies, self-destructive tendencies, or selfishness. All psychoanalytic thinking about deviance is based on the nuclear family, and it is precisely in this crucial area that the interweaving of theory and value can inhibit psychoanalysis from meeting the challenge of changing family structure; the father's absence would receive more attention than the mother's presence. For we will soon be living in a society that accepts one-parent families, group-communal living, and work-reversal patterns, and these will matter far more to the developing individual than an Oedipus complex. If they are to understand these diverse arrangements, analysts must work actively with people whose value structures are very different from each other's and the analyst's.

Efforts are being made, by individual psychoanalysts and by the organized profession, to study the connection between psychoanalytic theory and changing social values; the influence of peer groups and institutional socialization on social development; and changing standards of individual and family behavior. An increasing amount of time is being devoted to these issues at scientific meetings and in the Committee on Public Information. Although many factors have prompted these efforts, among them the desire of the informed public to know where psychoanalysis stands on social issues, the most pertinent to this paper is the need to redefine our values if we are to deal effectively with the problems of both older and younger patients who live in the present moment.

While the way such issues are presented by patients has a little to do with neurosis, it has much more to do with current value changes. However flexibly we try to connect behavior and motives, at a particular historical moment certain acts with far-reaching life consequences are chosen because they are socially determined. Whatever the individual motive a person may have for smoking marihuana, its omnipresence on the contemporary scene, unlike 10 years ago, makes only the generality of the action timeless, not the particular, which is the direct result of changing mores. The analyst needs to understand more than just his patient if he is to grasp what Weisman (1965) calls the existential core of psychoanalysis.

Although the analyst is remarkably flexible with each individual patient bothered as he is by the conviction that each patient must decide among alternatives for himself, the idea that the values of psychoanalysis are socially correct and, therefore, absolute may creep in. Elsewhere (1967a), in discussing psychoanalysts' relationship to their medical colleagues, I pointed out the extent to which many analysts unwittingly gave the impression of saying that it was better to understand each patient psychologically in order to treat him most effectively. Some surgeons, for example, indicated that they worked more comfortably with a routine that minimized individualization. To accept this discrepancy required a relative view of values. Neither was right or wrong, but each was illustrating a value position that governed and legitimatized a professional role and function. A psychoanalyst who did not differentiate and recognize the uniqueness of each patient could hardly be considered competent. But deciding about the extent to which humans are or are not similar, his professional function, differs intrinsically from a function which requires cutting up a fellow being and constantly facing death as a professional adversary.

Hence, many surgeons may do better with patients when they do not individualize them too thoroughly. The values of each work well in their separate contexts. But the discrepancy between them often leads to difficulties in communication about and collaboration in care of patients, particularly if both or either believe that their values are "better" and should prevail. This same preference for a relative rather than an absolute view of values extends into the historical context. That is, different historical periods, too, emphasize different conflicts which in turn create different crises and resolutions.

As Freud (1937) pointed out in *Analysis: Terminable and Interminable,* we can work only with what is presented, i.e., we are led by our patients. But at what rate? It would be unthinkable to abandon, in panic, what is basic to psychoanalysis, because of social fads or value changes. But neither should psychoanalysis harden into a professional role whose flexibility and ingenuity are hampered either because of values unnoticed for years or because repetition of them to patients has slowly made them seem right, i.e., absolute.

What changes in perceptual thresholds must automatically follow our understanding of the psychoanalyst as a middle-class role with a legitimatizing relative value system? Ego psychology teaches us that when an artist, a carpenter, a soldier, and an ecologist look at a tree, each of them perceives something different. Eventually they might agree on the objective reality, but initially each follows his value system. When the subject is more controversial than a tree, this tendency can block change, and a social group can influence the analyst only if he is aware of his potential inflexibility. This may seem like a truism—don't most psychoanalysts think of themselves as extraordinarily responsive men?—until one considers the history of psychoanalytic theory. In the past, psychoanalysts argued that once the individual achieved the utopia of genitality, he would be capable of almost infinite development. Erikson (1950) imposed a new dimension on this theoretical idea. In his attempt to bring the intrapsychic, interpersonal, and social factors together in a total developmental scheme, he characterized each phase of the life cycle as a specific developmental task to be solved. This solution is prepared for by previous phases and is carried further in subsequent ones. He assumed an inborn coordination with a predictable environment. This idea of mutuality specifies that crucial coordination occurs between the developing individual and his human (i.e., social) environment. The caretakers are coordinated with the developing individual by their specific inborn responsiveness to his needs, and by specific needs of their own. (A man can fulfill his generative desires when society recognizes him in the capacity of father.)

The caretakers are seen as representatives of their society who perpetuate the traditional institutional patterns. This focuses on the fact that society meets each phase of its members' development by institutions (parental care, school, occupations, etc.) specific to it; the sequence of epigenetic phases is universal, although solutions vary from one society to another. In contrast to the "culturist" theory of development, this does not assume that societal norms are grafted upon the genetically asocial individual by disciplines and "socialization," but that the society makes the individual a member of itself by influencing the manner in which he solves the tasks posed by each successive phase of his epigenetic development. Without being as explicit as Hartmann (1958), Erikson accepts the idea of relatively autonomous ego, independent of both instinctually derived drive structures and social institutions. Though keenly aware of the power of both, he respects the capacity of each to guarantee the relative autonomy of the other. Freud (1915), on the other hand, persistently assumed that there *are* specific drive-determined aims. Their libidinal or aggressive force may be diminished, their objects may change, their gratification may be temporarily or permanently delayed, or even modified, but there always remains some attempt to reduce the tension of the drives to the lowest level.

It is interesting to compare this psychoanalytic attitude with that of the sociologist Erving Goffman (1961), who argues that a man's attitude toward himself is formed by the particular social situation society has placed him in, and other people's response to it. In *Asylums*, his study of hospitalized mental patients, Goffman describes how friends, family, society at large see the individual as patient, and thus he becomes what he is labeled. It is a view diametrically opposite to Freud's. In this study of values a middle way is sought by illuminating the complex hierarchy of psychological structures within the psychic apparatus. They vary from simple automatic defense to more complex attitudes, values, ideological beliefs, and identities compatible with those accepted by society. These structures require social stimuli unique to that society not only to maintain themselves but to *develop*. Though Erikson accepts instinctual vicissitudes, he insists that simple psychological structures develop into complex values through current experience, and become a complementary series of experiences. The original organ modes of behavior develop into differentiated social behavior through the impact of traditions, institutions, values, and attitudes provided by the society in which the individual develops, and by the social places it makes available to him.

For an individual to grow up, in any society, it is assumed that the internal structures *and* the codetermined socially provided rituals must fall into a lawful sequence of differentiation. And it is in precisely this area that Erikson's theoretical explorations seriously challenge psychoanalysis today, both as a social organization and in individual practice. One must differentiate a complex sociopsychological response to a life situation from the rapidly changing social scene, which cannot remain static in order to accommodate the cultural changes necessary to this cog-wheeling process. Shifts in society that would formerly have been only quantitative now become, by their nature and their social potential, qualitative. The young person experimenting with cannabis or LSD knows that the general attitude of society toward the former, at least, is slowly changing. But given his kinship with his peer group, his use of the drug makes him deviant to the culture at large, and the result is a qualitatively different relationship to society. The change in attitude toward cannabis is not matched by the slow rate of change in public morality and the law—that is, there is no stable psychological regularity in the social organization's response to the individual.

In trying to consider changing behavior which clearly disrupts the social functioning of the individual and the society, the psychoanalyst can become hopelessly ensnared in trying to ascertain the psychological difficulty of a particular individual. How can one place the individual in this newly disruptive social context? This person is part of a social system whose pressures form attitudes and values. These are part of his accepted self, and not "neurotic," even though his life may be inhibited. Not only are psychoanalysts representative of a specific social role, and slow to define their attitudes toward social change, but they value psychological and social regularity. To use Erikson's touchstone, compatible social rituals must be legitimatized into a developmental scheme that accepts social change, so that individual and social needs can be coordinated.

This process must be studied if psychoanalysis is to be more than a method of treatment. The attitudes held by members of society toward that society end up by defining society, and the same holds true of psychoanalysis as a social organization. In a time of swiftly changing attitudes, psychoanalysis has to take this into account in its formulation of social and psychological regularity. The capacity of analysts to deal with these changes—in drug use, black activism, student rebellion—depends less on the individual's flexibility in recognizing his own values than it does on his grasp of the values inherent in the role position of psychoanalysis in our culture. Today the search is not so much for freedom from psychologically determined inhibitions as it is for meaningful rejection among all the choices available in an affluent society. Though drive structures may account for some people's trouble in making choices, Erikson's theory points clearly to the need for self-doubt. Standards for evaluating such commitments are more urgently needed in periods of psychological chaos, like adolescence, or of social disruption, like the 1960's.

Commitment in itself is no solution. Erikson (1964) solves this dilemma with the concept of totalism, which separates ideological commitment from the capacity to question it. But even commitment is inseparable from values, and therefore susceptible to doubt. Given a variety of possibilities, we must recognize the underlying value structure determining the boundaries of any social position or role, and this cannot be attained for psychoanalysis unless its basic value system and how it is currently derived are known. The fact that psychoanalysis has failed to do this for all this time does indicate that it has not been recognized as important which does not necessarily mean that psychoanalysts are totally unwilling to undertake this basic study. If they do not undertake it, however, others will who do not understand or appreciate either the effectiveness of psychoanalytic treatment with selected persons or the depth and complexity of its theoretical contributions. This paper raises harsh questions but not hostile or destructive ones. It asks that this needed value study be undertaken by those best equipped to tolerate the difficult conflicts that have inevitably developed as historical and social changes continue apace. Only then will its values be prepared to change as inexorably as conflict itself will develop.

BIBLIOGRAPHY

Coles, (1967), *Children in Crisis.* Boston, Mass.: Little, Brown.
Durkheim, E. (1897), *Suicide.* Glencoe, Ill.: Free Press.
Erikson, E. H. (1950), *Childhood and Society.* New York: Norton.
_____ (1958), *Young Man Luther.* New York: Norton.
_____ (1964), The first psycho-analyst. In: *Insight and Responsibility.* New York: Norton.
Erikson, K. (1966), *The Wayward Puritan.* New York: Wiley.
Freud, S. (1915), Instincts and their vicissitudes. *Standard Edition,* 14:117–140.
_____ (1937), Analysis terminable and interminable. *Standard Edition,* 23:209–253.
_____ (1958), On beginning the treatment. *Standard Edition,* 12:121–144.
Gill, M. M. and Brenman, M. (1959), *Hypnosis and Related States.* New York: International Universities Press.
Gitelson, M. (1963), On the present scientific and social position of psycho-analysis (Presidential Address, Twenty-third International Psycho-Analytical Congress). *Internat. J. Psycho-Anal.,* 44: Part 4.
Glover, E. (1955), *The Technique of Psychoanalysis.* New York: International Universities Press.
Goffman, E. (1961), *Asylums.* Garden City: Doubleday.
Hartmann, H. (1960), *Psychoanalysis and Moral Values.* New York: International Universities Press.
_____ (1958), *Ego Psychology and the Problem of Adaptation.* New York: International Universities Press.
Himes, (1969), *The Real Cool Killers.* New York: Putnam.
Himmelweit, H. et al., *Social Psychology, London School of Economics, British Education, A Follow-up Study.* In press.

Jones, E. (1955), *The Life and Work of Sigmund Freud,* Vol. II. New York: Basic Books.

Kenniston, K. (1969), You only know how tough it is if you grew up in Scarsdale. *New York Times Magazine Section.*

Kluckhohn, C. (1951), Values and value orientation in the theory of action: an exploration in definition and classification. In: *Towards a General Theory of Action,* ed. T. Parsons and E. A. Shils. Cambridge, Mass.: Harvard University Press.

Levin, S. and Michaels, J. J. (1961), The participation of psychoanalysts in the medical institutions of Boston. *Internat. J. Psycho-Anal.,* 42:271–277.

Orwell, G. (1949), *1984.* New York: Harcourt, Brace & World.

Rapaport, D. (1958), The theory of ego autonomy: a generalization. *Bull. Menninger Clin.,* 22:13–35.

_____ (1960), *The Structure of Psychoanalytic Theory: A Systematizing Attempt* [*Psychological Issues,* Monogr. 6]. New York: International Universities Press.

Rosenthal, R. and Jacobson, L. (1968), *Pygmalion in the Classroom: Teacher Expectation and Pupils' Intellectual Development.* New York: Holt, Rinehart, & Winston.

Szasz, T. S. (1965), *The Ethics of Psychoanalysis.* New York: Basic Books.

_____ (1968), Psychoanalysis and the rule of law. *Psychoanal. Rev.,* 55 (2), Summer.

Thernstrom, S. (1969), The myth of American affluence. *Commentary,* 48(4).

Webster's Third New International Dictionary, Unabridged.

Weisman, A. (1965), *The Existential Core of Psychoanalysis.* Boston, Mass.: Little, Brown.

Whitehorn, J. C. (1951), Lecture at Johns Hopkins Medical School.

Wolff, R. L. (1962), Neurosis and the novel—the case histories. Paper presented to a conference of the Psychiatric Service, Beth Israel Hospital, Boston, Mass.

Yankelovich, D. (1967), Personal Correspondence.

Zinberg, N. (1963), Psychiatry: a professional dilemma. *Daedalus,* 92:198–211.

_____ (1965), Psychoanalysis and the American scence: A reappraisal. *Diogenes,* 50:73–111.

_____ (1967a), The problem of values in teaching psychoanalytic psychiatry. *Bull. Menninger Clin.,* 31:236–248.

_____ (1967b), Psycho-analytic training and psycho-analytic values. *Internat. J. Psycho-Anal.,* 48:88–96.

9. The Impact
of Psychoanalysis on Values

PAUL ROAZEN, Ph.D.

I WOULD HAZARD the guess that a discussion of the relation between moral values and psychoanalysis would have made Sigmund Freud extremely uneasy. Freud never doubted that his
ideas were revolutionary, and therefore bound to have effects far
beyond the understanding and treatment of the neuroses. At times
Freud could even thunder as a modern prophet, challenging the
values and practices of western Christendom.

But he always feared that his empirical discoveries might get
swallowed up in mankind's search for ethical direction. As he
aged, his devotion to science grew increasingly pronounced; and
as his illness restricted his activities, he drew back somewhat from
therapy. After contracting cancer in 1923, Freud never again
wrote a case history. The writings of his last 16 years, as he gradually withdrew from the world, contain some of the most sustained
abstract restatements of his findings that can be encountered anywhere in his work (Roazen, 1970).

But even as Freud kept insisting more and more on the status of
psychoanalysis as a science, he found himself giving freer reign to
his own speculative impulses. In his later years he wrote about the
roots of religion, the future of civilization, and pondered other
such age-old quandries. He always hoped that some of his students
would be able to perceive the moral implications of psychoanalytic
principles, and that workers in other fields would be able to revo-
lutionize their disciplines as he had altered the shape of modern
psychology. With the tools that he had wrought, he expected almost unlimited developments in the future.

Paul Roazen

What were Freud's practices as a clinician? Far too little is known here, although more exists in the oral tradition of psychoanalysis than has ever made its way into print. [1] For all his genius, Freud was not exempt from many of the social prejudices of his day. By our current standards Freud, the therapist, was decidedly on the moralistic side. "Be better next time!" was the way one of Freud's patients once summarized the character of Freud's approach. Addicts, psychotics, delinquents, male perverts—those cases for whom the scope of psychoanalysis has been expanded since Freud's death—would have seemed more or less repugnant to him (Roazen, 1969). Though he wanted to understand as much of human behavior as possible, he was also a man of his time. Unless one can acknowledge how different Freud was from what would be acceptable in a therapist today, it is impossible to see just how great were the forces of social prejudice, both in the world at large as well as within his own soul, with which he had to contend.

Seeing Freud in proper historical perspective can in fact go far to illuminate many of the characteristic clinical shortcomings of our own day. For if Freud was more intolerant as a therapist than would now be considered usual, he was also much more boldly individualistic than many of those followers who pay him homage. The Central Europe of his time was far more cosmopolitan and less narrowly bourgeois than, for example, some contemporary practitioners of Freud's art. Standards of belief and value were more varied and less uniform than a modern mass society tends to produce.

In one case a middle-aged woman came to Freud because of her guilt over homosexual urges. Freud recommended her to a Viennese pupil for an analysis; as a result of a year of treatment the patient was free of her guilt feelings but actively homosexual. The analyst reported to Freud with some trepidation the outcome of the analysis. But Freud surprised his disciple by concluding that it was quite an appropriate point at which to terminate the analysis. The patient's children had grown up, her sexual affair was dis-

---

[1] For a study of the oral tradition in psychoanalysis, see Paul Roazen, *Professor Freud and His Circle* (forthcoming), Part I.

creet, and her husband was now interested in her mainly for social purposes. One wonders whether most candidates in training today would get off so easily were a similar outcome the final result of a supervised analysis.

Freud could be remarkably emancipated from some middle class values. In another case he actively intervened on behalf of a specific marriage choice, one that today might seem rather bizarre. This patient had had a long-standing sexual relationship with his brother's wife. As a result of an analysis with Freud, the man was freed from his incestuous bond, only to fall in love with his niece, the daughter of his former mistress. Freud thought that this new relationship represented a solid step forward for his patient. The girl, however, was recalcitrant and resisted the advances of her uncle. Freud thereupon recommended that she undergo an analysis. The girl's analyst was told by Freud (half-jokingly) that there was a secret in the case, and that when the analyst discovered it she should report it to Freud. Within a week or so the analyst returned with the news that not only was the secret uncovered, but there was a secret to the case that Freud himself did not know.

This case fits the archetype of the legendary Viennese love tangle. The young girl did indeed know about the long-standing liaison between her suitor and her mother, as Freud had wanted to find out; but he did not know that the girl had the fantasy that she herself was the child of the illicit union between her uncle and her mother, which fully explained her own hesitancy to get involved with him sexually. Once Freud was apprised of the girl's inner world, he dropped the idea of the match. When writing up this case for publication (for the sake of exploring a quite different problem, telepathy), Freud tried to suppress, no doubt out of discretion, the familial connection between the partners in this proposed union. [2] Yet the fact that he would countenance, even try to promote such a match should demonstrate what a world away

[2] At the very end of Freud's (1941 [1921]), account of this case, the familial connection—which he had tried to suppress—returned. The patient eventually "chose as his wife a respectable girl outside his family circle. . . ." Until this point in the narrative Freud had not hinted that any of the patient's loves had been within the "family circle" (see pp. 191–193).

from today's middle-class values was his own private therapeutic practice.

Freud's distance from the values of conventional society played a role in his individualistic conception of treatment. The analyst was not supposed to burden a patient with extraneous problems, either the analyst's or society's. Ideally the aim of an analysis was to help the patient, enriched from his inner resources, to become his own best self. Freud hoped and expected that in each patient the analyst could anticipate finding an ally, the struggling self weighted down by mistakes in upbringing and misconceptions of goals.

Freud took for granted what nowadays seems so rare in patients, a self that knows what it wants. The patients with whom Freud worked best were those who already had well-constituted egos. As Freud remarked to a patient at the end of a three-month analysis in 1908, "What I liked best about working with you was that as soon as I gave you something you were able to make use of it." Freud took for granted, at least in the early period of his practice, a well-functioning personality capable of integrating the insights he could offer.

Bold as he was as a practicing clinician, Freud remained shy about discussing the aims of analytic therapy. In his earlier years he had been far more outgoing and interventionist than later on, especially after he had contracted cancer; in those last years of his life he was a good deal more disillusioned about the prospects of therapeutic success, and altogether more preoccupied with the future of his findings as a scientific body. Yet almost nowhere did Freud seek to define the concept of psychic health. It was characteristic of him to have relegated a problem like freedom, for example, to a mere footnote. [3]

The healthy was not just the same as the worthy—on that point Freud was insistent. One might be healthy and still good-for-nothing; one might also be quite sick and yet, in Freud's mind, quite valuable as a human being. He did not want to have to give

[3] See p. 50 in: Freud, S. (1923), The ego and the id. *Standard Edition*, 19:3–68. London: Hogarth Press, 1961.

advice or preach to patients, for that would be to duplicate the techniques of hypnotic treatment and suggestion, as well as some of the mistaken tasks of traditional religions. Freud assumed in his patients the role of a well-integrated, even if overly severe, superego, which may in part explain his relative lateness in coming to discuss this concept. Even though people of fancy and imagination could hold a special place in his heart, Freud steadfastly admired the conscientious and the upright.

Freud could scarcely have foreseen the uses his concepts would be put to in the 30 or so years since his death. As much as Freud had not wanted psychoanalysis to become a mere "handmaid," as he liked to put it, to psychiatry, in America at any rate it would be hard to overestimate the impact his ideas have had on psychiatric theory and practice. Dr. Spock's child-raising manuals would be intellectually inconceivable without the backdrop of Freud's work.

Psychoanalysis has had its successes, and analysts are now hardly in the position of being an underpaid revolutionary band at odds with conventional wisdom. Analysts have direct as well as indirect influence not only on psychiatric departments but other institutions as well—schools, law courts, universities, professional training centers, business corporations, and so on. As long as Freud and his followers were themselves on the outside they could hardly be accused of advocating conformism. They could even afford to evade certain intellectual issues, thanks to the specific social situation they found themselves in. To the degree that today's analysts have become members of the establishment, however, Freud's ideas need to be clarified lest they be pressed willy-nilly into service in behalf of the status quo. A problem like that of moral values needs especially to be reexamined, in the very different historical conditions under which we now live.

For some time now psychoanalytic theory has been separated by a rather wide gulf from psychoanalytic practice. For those of a bookish cast of mind, it is disquieting that theoretical understanding is as little help in orienting one in a field as is the case, I believe, in psychoanalysis today. On theoretical grounds one may find little cause for worrying that psychoanalytic ideas will be used to promote conformism or mere adjustment. Yet due to the widespread influence of psychoanalysis today as well as the background and prior training of those who now become therapists, there is legitimate concern over the role certain types of values have come to play in clinical practice.

It is simply not possible to exclude from psychoanalytic thought the problem of moral values. To attempt to do so is only to encourage the uncritical acceptance of the prevailing standards of morality. No one of course can choose goals for other people; the task of good theory should be merely to make it as hard as possible for psychoanalysis to be used unthinkingly for a given political or social end.

Let me cite a few examples from my own experience. I remember seeing the case of a young Jewish girl presented at a psychiatric hospital. She came from the proverbial good middle-class family, but had run away, across the country, for the sake of adventure and "sleeping around." Her parents had finally retrieved her and put her in the hospital. She seemed to me a not especially intelligent young lady, and her rather standard manner of complying with the way some young people dress nowadays did not make her look any the more interesting.

To the clean-cut, hard-working resident who was treating her, however, she was schizophrenic, and with psychoanalytic theory in hand everyone in the room tried to examine the roots of her troubles. About two-thirds through the discussion the senior psychiatrist, an analyst, reacted with volcanic fury; he demanded to know on what grounds was there evidence for schizophrenia in the girl. Groping for justification, the resident finally had to admit that he did not like the way the girl dressed and wore her hair. By the end of the meeting the "diagnosis" of a hippie—or more seriously for the girl, perhaps a diagnosis of a pseudo-hippie—had been agreed upon.

From my participation in case conferences, two other illustrations come to mind of the role moral values can play in clinical practice. A depressed black man was having an affair with a white woman. As the psychiatrist explained his handling of the case, "I didn't exactly criticize the affair, but I tried to make him see that a white woman who has an affair with a black man must have a devaluated sense of herself." Perhaps this was so, and perhaps the hippie was also schizophrenic, but such pat ways of dismissing behavior that deviates from middle-class norms does seem humanly offensive and scientifically questionable.

At another meeting a Peace Corps psychiatrist described his work as largely focused on preventing young men from "going native" in the field. He regarded it as axiomatic that college educated white Americans who wanted to marry "barefoot girls with only a third-grade education" must be suffering from mental disturbance. In one case, the psychiatrist said, the young man in love had "shaky ego boundaries," which justified psychiatric intervention —as if any impending marriage were not an appropriate time for such an upheaval.

From many such instances one acquires the feeling that almost any prejudice can be defended by means of modern psychology. Since psychoanalytic concepts aim at being scientific, they should be capable of being used for very different political and social purposes, from the most conservative to the most radical. What is impermissible, however, is for someone to assume his values and beliefs in such a way that rather striking moral positions are taken via clinical categories without any awareness that the same categories might justify very different moral alternatives. Thanks to its successes, psychoanalysis has new intellectual responsibilities, one of which is facing the problem of moral values.

In one area of contemporary psychology the role of values has crept in rather notably, although quite surreptitiously, and that is in developmental models of personality growth. To what extent are these models (such as those of Erik Erikson) descriptions of how things do happen, and to what extent are they accounts of what we would like and approve? Have we in fact examined anything like all the possible human potentialities that it might be possible to try to foster? These are questions which on logical grounds alone psychoanalysis must try to answer. After all, to say that an act is immature or neurotic is to imply a standard of maturity or health. And yet how little attention is paid to what we could possibly mean by normality.

Paul Roazen

At his best Freud stood for the ideal of autonomy. It is a commonplace by now that the psychoanalytic revolution has contributed to the liberalizing trends in our time. It can never be enough, though, to call upon a heritage that values freedom of choice and labors against deceit and coercion. Hypocrisy arises precisely when, under the guise of certain glittering ideals, rather objectionable conformist values are permitted to flourish. The more psychoanalytic theory pays attention to problems of ethics and values, the harder it is going to be to make moral choices in undercover ways. Suggestion is still very much an element in treatment, even in the hands of well-trained analysts, and hidden ethical advice is all the more likely in those who think of themselves as morally aloof and neutral. New threats to human freedom are always arising, and psychoanalysis has to adapt to a changing social situation if it is not to become one more component in the social hierarchy at odds with the growth of human individualism.

BIBLIOGRAPHY

Freud, S. (1941 [1921]), Psycho-analysis and telepathy. *Standard Edition*, 18:175–193. London: Hogarth Press, 1955.
Roazen, P. (1969), *Brother Animal: The Story of Freud and Tausk*. New York: Knopf, pp. 175–195.
——— (1970), *Freud: Political and Social Thought*. New York: Vintage, pp. 101–110.

10. The Place of Values
in Psychoanalytic Theory,
Practice and Training

ISHAK RAMZY, PH.D.

T HE HUMAN MIND with all its remarkable achievements and admitted limitations is not a pure intellect. Not only do people perceive and remember or comprehend and reason, but they also like and dislike and prefer one thing to another, whether this is something they think of or something they recognize in the world around them. The most simple sensation bordering on the biological level of functioning, as much as the most abstract theory, is always coupled with a feeling of interest, pleasure and attraction, or of aversion, repulsion, and withdrawal. When such preferences are put in words, they take the form of statements about good and evil, beauty and ugliness, which are called judgments of value in contrast to judgments of fact, which are purportedly concerned with reality as such aside from individual or social preferences. In other words, whereas judgments of value are concerned with what is commendable or desirable, judgments of fact are concerned with what *is* (Goblot, 1927).

Within this frame of reference, one of the ways of classifying science is to divide it into the descriptive and the normative sciences. The term "normative" is derived from the Latin *norma*, the carpenter's square, or the mason's level. The normative sciences are those whose subject is judgments of value, such as ethics and esthetics. A "norm" does not mean an order or a commandment,

This is a revision of a paper previously appearing in the *International Journal of Psycho-Analysis*, 47:97–107, 1965.

as is wrongly understood at times, and normative sciences are not disciplines which end up by prescribing a certain way of conduct or putting down artistic rules or requirements (Lalande, 1929). Normative sciences study the different ways of appreciation, compare standards and levels, and may occasionally come out with certain recommendations based on observations and comparative investigations.

The word "value," as its origin suggests, is derived from the same root as the word "valor," since bravery, or courage, was considered to be the best quality of a man. But it has come, especially in modern usage, to refer not only to notions of worth, of ethical level, or of social rank, but also to the number or quantity represented by a figure or symbol in mathematics, the relative length or duration of a tone in music, and even to the relative effect or importance of a color in painting; and, needless to add, it is the main concern of those who work in the markets of shares and stocks.

It was Kant who reclaimed the word "value" for the moral and mental world, and contributed one of the most important treatises on human ethics in his book *Critique of Practical Reason,* comparable only to Aristotle's *Nichomachean Ethics* and Spinoza's *Ethics.* The German theologian Ritschl, in his famous defense of Christianity against the attacks of science, maintained that science deals with facts and laws, whereas religion deals with values which are not amenable to experimental or even deductive methods. One finds the same idea in the work of the Danish philosopher Hoffding on the *Philosophy of Religion,* where he defines the function of religion as that of the "conservation of values." Nietzsche, a second-rate philosopher but an eloquent writer, was the one who dealt most forcefully with the theory of values. In his writings about human nature, he propounded the will to power and the instinct of aggression against the Christian and Buddhist preaching of charity and peace; this was the "reversal of values," the *Umwertung,* for which he set himself as the spokesman. The use of "value" as a term and the work on the concept has since, and within or away from such a lineage, been taken up by a great number of philosophers, psychologists, and other scientists.

Of late the subject has been picked up again, especially in its bearing on psychoanalysis, by several authors from various disciplines, such as Feuer (1955), Reid (1955), Herbert Read (1951), Rieff (1959), Brinton (1959), Trilling (1955), and Julian Huxley (1960). Equipped with the erudition of their specialities, whether sociology, ethics, or epistemology, and unshackled by the weight of ordinary clinical facts, such authors have been able to publish in brief articles or extensive books several contributions worthy of study and critical inspection, contributions which the psychoanalysts themselves have not ventured to make. These papers and books scholarly and well documented as they are, suffer, though, from the lack in their authors of a firsthand knowledge of psychoanalysis as a concrete experience from which is derived a complex set of theoretical assumptions hardly comprehensible without reference to the data from which the theory was constructed. The contributions of behavioral scientists are, at their best, a modern version of the earlier speculative attempts of the philosophers. Thus, though these studies fill a gap which the psychoanalysts still leave vacant, and fill it in a more satisfactory way than the professional logicians do when they deal with the methodology of psychoanalysis, they cannot relieve psychoanalysis itself of the task of stating whether it has any set of values, and if so, what they are.

In spite of the fact that the psychoanalytic literature, theoretical and clinical, is replete with matters pertaining directly or indirectly to moral and other values, and although the analyst's everyday work involves him—whether he likes it or not as a scientist—in forming value judgments on the patient's way of life and on his dealings with himself or others, there have been only a few attempts to deal with the subject.

One of the books written a generation ago, and still occupying a unique place in psychoanalytic literature, is Flugel's (1945) book *Man, Morals and Society,* which was directly concerned with the influence of psychology in general and psychoanalysis in particular on the field of values—ethical, religious and esthetic. Gently, but firmly, Flugel asserted that since values are facts of mental life, psychoanalysis, whose task is the study of this mental life, is similarly concerned with the examination of values. In its applied aspects, psychological knowledge is also put to use in the service of certain values in modern life, such as those assumed in mental health, education, industry, criminology, and even politics and matters of war and peace.

At this point we have to recognize the difference between instrumental and intrinsic values, or simply between means and ends. Applied science is mainly concerned with instrumental values; the physician or the architect takes for granted that it is better to keep the body or the building in good condition, regardless of the purpose for which the body or the building is to be used. Ultimate purposes and values have been the concerns of the moral philosopher, not the scientist, who is concerned only with the means, and not the ends. Flugel did not deny, however, that in view of the relative position of intrinsic and instrumental values, it is hardly possible to say exactly at what point in the hierarchy of values the influence of psychology ceases. Still further, the factual change of attitudes, moral and legal, in the treatment not only of mental patients, but also of criminals and delinquents, is an undeniable proof that psychological understanding and scientific knowledge are gradually and steadily replacing moral outrage and emotional prejudice against those who disturb the established values of the society in which the offenders live.

Science may never give us ultimate values. Nevertheless, as it advances it may be of help in reaching ever higher levels in the hierarchy of values; and in this increasing usefulness of science, psychology will inevitably have its share. With this clear position, Flugel goes on to devote his whole book to the study of the moral implications of psychoanalysis and to the development and the essential functions of conscience in human life. However acclaimed and still held in high esteem as a source book for the study of the superego, such a book is well known not because of its emphasis on the role of values or their study, but because of the clinical discussions and the empirically grounded conclusions it contains.

During the last two or three decades, the new achievements in the field of fissionable materials and the possible catastrophic dangers to the continuation of human civilization, if not the very survival of mankind, have brought the topic of values within the concern of physicists and mathematicians. Thus the words of Bertrand Russell (1931) with which he concluded his book on *The Scientific Outlook* acquired more weight. Russell said:

> A world without delight and without affection is a world destitute of value . . . Men should not be so intoxicated by new power as to forget the truths that were familiar to every previous generation. Not all wisdom is new, nor is all folly out of date . . . A new moral outlook is called for in which submission to the powers of nature is replaced by respect for what is best in man [pp. 278–279].

The position of a Bertrand Russell and many others of his eminence in the fields of pure and applied science, their warnings and their actions, has led ultimately to the hopefully less precarious state of world affairs today. But more importantly, it led to a correction of the view about science and values. This was summed up in a paper delivered to the American Association for the Advancement of Science in 1960 by the scientist and writer C. P. Snow under the trenchant title of "The Moral Un-neutrality of Science," in which he affirmed that he cannot accept for an instant the doctrine of the ethical neutrality of science, and then announced:

> I believe that there is a spring of moral action in the scientific activity which is at least as strong as the search for truth. The name of this spring is *knowledge*. Unless we are abnormally weak or abnormally wicked men, this knowledge is bound to shape our actions" (1962).

Oddly enough, over the same period, psychoanalysts, who certainly are neither abnormally weak nor abnormally wicked, and who are better equipped than any other group of scientists to deal with value systems, since this is an integral part of their subject, have stayed away from expending any tangible effort to work on the topic. Except for an occasional symposium, such as that entitled "The Credo of the Psychoanalyst" arranged by the section on psychoanalysis of The American Psychiatric Association in 1955, or the panel of the Academy of Psychoanalysis on "Psychoanalysis and the Problem of Values" (Masserman, 1960), there have been but a few papers devoted to the subject, such as those of Brierley (1951), Nielsen (1960), Shor (1961), and two articles by Money-Kyrle (1952, 1961), none of which had enough echo nor attracted the attention which the topic deserves.

One of the most important recent contributions has been that of Hartmann (1960) on *Psychoanalysis and Moral Values*. Erudition, experience, and creativity made Hartmann's other contributions important landmarks in the history of psychoanalysis, but his essay on values is neither on a par with his other works nor an improvement on the traditional caution with which psychoanalysis looks at the subject from afar. With the candor of the careful scholar, Hartmann apologizes for the limitations of his essay. Nevertheless, it has to its credit that it brought anew the ticklish problem of values to the attention of psychoanalysts and pointed out its basic importance for theory and technique. On the other hand, Hartmann ultimately suggests that considerations of value should not be a source of great concern to the psychoanalyst, and that moral evaluations are beyond his competence as a scientist and his task as a therapist.

A significant addition to the psychoanalytic literature has been made by Erikson's (1964) book on *Insight and Responsibility* which rings a loud counterpoint to Hartmann's by its subtitle: "The Ethical Implications of Psychoanalytic Insight." In one of the papers collected in this book Erikson splendidly develops the theme of values in the life of men through his study of "Human Strength and the Cycle of Generations."

One of the main reasons for the chronic avoidance of the topic of values and for the generally upheld view among psychoanalysts that it is beyond their task as scientists, is their adherence, clearly demonstrated by Hartmann's position, to the opinion previously enunciated by Freud. In an often quoted passage from the 35th Introductory Lecture, Freud (1933) sums up his viewpoint as follows: "Psycho-analysis in my opinion is incapable of creating a *Weltanschauung* of its own. It does not need one; it is a part of science and can adhere to the scientific *Weltanschauung*" (p. 181).

Even if it were not erroneous to take such a statement out of context and to adopt it at the cost of neglecting several other thoughts which qualify its finality, it is neither essential nor fruitful to adhere to Freud in this respect. Such a view does not adequately represent the letter or the spirit of what empirical knowledge about values has accumulated through psychoanalysis; nor does it reflect the range and the depth of the work the psychoanalyst undertakes in spite of the confines of his ordinary therapeutic commitments to his patients and the scientific boundaries and regulations of his specialty. Freud did not utter the last word; nor has any science or scientist, for that matter. Better to put such a passage, and the note of caution and humility which it carries, in the context within which it was stated and in the light of the development of psychoanalysis itself in the history of human thought.

Freud was a product of the nineteenth century, when science, which had been advancing by leaps and bounds since the adoption of the methods of observation and experiment, was achieving still further conquests, especially in geology, biology and organic chemistry. The application of scientific findings, of new technologies and methods of production augured an era of unprecedented power over the physical world of man. Alongside this, a far-reaching revolt against the traditional ways of thinking about social and economic systems gave rise to strong attacks upon many beliefs and dogmas which were never seriously contested before. In that rationalist, positivist, liberal and humanitarian atmosphere, it was no wonder that a Sigmund Freud, the child of his age, urged by a keen curiosity about man's mental life, and familiar with the bankruptcy of prior philosophical attempts and their parallels in religious thought, was to seek the solution in the establishment of a science of psychology and to keep it away from the influence of any traditional prejudice handed down by any social, theological, or philosophical current which might contaminate its objectivity.

Having thus labored to achieve his goal, his trials and errors led him to discover many facts about the working of the human mind and to devise a way of treating its disturbances. It was thus that psychoanalysis, once it took shape, came to be known as a method for the scientific study of the human mind, a type of therapy and a body of knowledge. Contrary to what is assumed, psychoanalysis definitely has in each of its three aspects certain values which are highly upheld, however covert or implicit some of these values may still be.

VALUES IN PSYCHOANALYSIS AS A SCIENCE

The view that psychoanalysis does not have, or should not have, anything to do with value systems is based on the assertion that it is a science, and as such it has only to adhere to the rules and regulations of scientific method.

Even setting aside the fact that the subject matter of psychoanalysis imposes on it in a large measure considerations of value as such, psychoanalysis, since it follows scientific method, has to hold, like any other science, certain explicit values in high esteem. The following quotation, which crowns an outstanding book (Cohen and Nagel, 1934) on logic and scientific method, enumerates a few of the essential nonintellectual qualities of science:

> Scientific method is the only effective way of strengthening the love of truth. It settles differences without any external force, by appealing to our common rational nature. The way of science is open to all . . . Scientific procedure unites men in something nobly devoid of all pettiness. Because it requires detachment, disinterestedness, it is the finest flower and test of a liberal civilization [pp. 402–403].

For logicians to talk about such things as the love of truth, the unity of men, rising above pettiness, and the flower of liberal civilization is neither rare nor considered to be wandering away from the cut-and-dried field of scientific method. From Francis Bacon to J. S. Mill and Claude Bernard, and from Descartes to Poincaré, it is not uncommon to encounter similar descriptions of the scientific spirit and of those qualities which are essential for the scientist beyond curiosity, intelligence and hard work.

Scientific spirit presupposes the ability to question authority and to examine dogmas. In the study of facts, the scientist is called upon not to rely on what an Aristotle or a Freud has handed down, but to depend on his own investigations and the evidence which he derives from nature to sustain the hypothesis with which he might have started.

Since scientific spirit is positive, the causes which it seeks are neither supernatural nor mystic, and the order of nature is explained not as the doings of fools or devils, but as a result of the laws which science tries to know. Anything that cannot be referred to the facts and to the verifiable relations between facts is of no value to science.

In the study of the phenomena of nature, science tries to arrive at the constant relations which exist between these phenomena; namely, at laws. This amounts to a "belief" in determinism. This belief is admittedly an act of faith in the human mind, but without this, no scientific explanation is possible, and to accept the indeterminate is to accept the irrational and to abdicate reason (Ramzy, 1963).

As much as men of science believe in natural laws, they also know that these laws are intricate and not easy to discover. The scientist thus cannot fully trust his own ideas, his hypotheses, doctrines, or theories. Thus, though we stated just now that scientific spirit is a matter of faith or belief, we are stating here the reverse; namely, a matter of prudence and humility. To know one's own limits and to doubt one's conclusions has been a quality often mentioned since Descartes enunciated it as one of his four rules of method. However, it is necessary not to confound scientific doubt with skepticism. The skeptic is the one who does not believe in science, but rather in himself, whereas "the doubter is the true scientist; he only doubts of himself and his interpretations, but he believes in science . . ." (Bernard, 1927).

A further feature is what may be called disinterestedness; i.e., to guard against being inspired only by the search for the practical applications of science and the exploitation of knowledge. Though certainly new knowledge leads, in the short or the long run, to more security, comfort, or power, the supreme value of science in the light of the Greek heritage has been considered to be knowledge for its sake first. Henri Poincaré, the eminent mathematician, in his work on *La Valeur de la Science* (1904) praises the nobility

• 213

of the formula of science for science's sake, and opens up his book by affirming that "the search for truth should be the goal of our work, and it is the only end worthy of our efforts."

It is perhaps evident from what has just been said, that scientific method is not made up of only intellectual or rational components. Edmond Goblot (1925), in his extensive classic on logic, put it as follows: "Scientific spirit has extra intellectual qualities, notably moral qualities" (p. 377). He, together with several other authors, emphasizes such essential qualities as intellectual courage, sincerity, integrity, humility and tolerance.

Such prerequisites and qualities of scientific approach are not only taken for granted by psychoanalysis and adhered to in theory and practice as much as is humanly possible, but also the analytic systems of training, the rules of technique, and all that makes up the various psychoanalytic areas of observation or application are replete with those features that characterize scientific spirit. The terms may differ and the context may vary, but the study and the correction of magical ways of thinking, or of feelings of omnipotence and omniscience, the knowledge about transference or countertransference, or reality-testing or defense mechanisms are essentially an adoption, an elaboration, and an application of those intellectual and moral values which constitute scientific method.

In fact, psychoanalysis, with all its complexities and limitations, is in the unique position of being the tool which is designed to study just those factors which lead people away from objective, realistic, rational, creative and tolerant ways of thinking.

VALUES IN PSYCHOANALYTIC TRAINING

Psychoanalytic treatment, which has been and will always remain by far the main source of information upon which psychoanalysis as a science is anchored, is a venture which two people, the analyst and the analysand, undertake together to investigate the workings of the analysand's mind, with the explicit hope that this will lead to a better way of living. Since the analyst is a very important agent in this task for two people, as in any other trade or profession, or even more so, psychoanalysts consider that it is their task to pass on what knowledge or skill they may have acquired, from one generation to another. Once their discipline had achieved enough strength and its existence had started to attract students who wanted to learn it, formal systems of psychoanalytic education were set up in training centers and institutes.

From the very start, these systems of education have been guided by a few principles which characterize psychoanalytic training. Probably more than any other teacher, the educator in psychoanalysis realizes two things: one is his own limitation in judgment, and the other is that all men are born with an essential nature, certainly within a range that encompasses the differences between individuals. The psychoanalyst also believes that from cradle to grave no man is free of conflict, no one is a paragon of health or strength, nor is another all sickness and defect.

In addition, the fact that the potential psychoanalyst will be his own instrument in his day-to-day work made his personal analysis the axis of psychoanalytic training. In assessing the abilities and the liabilities of the student, and in following what desirable changes they would like to occur in the personalities of their students, the teaching staff of any psychoanalytic school are constantly evaluating a candidate from the moment they consider his application until his graduation. It is perhaps necessary to draw attention here to the fact that the very term "evaluation"—or any synonym—implies a set of values or criteria, some of which are certainly concerned with matters of intellectual ability, range of knowledge, capacity for psychological work; but some others are definitely concerned with the nonintellectual qualities which we consider to be a more specific equipment for the analyst. Our own views as to what character the analyst should have, or what qualities he should possess or develop, have, without any doubt, a great influence on our decisions in accepting a candidate, discontinuing his training, or seeing him through graduation.

A few concrete matters which justifiably occupy much of the time of many psychoanalytic educators and committees, on the local and national levels, may serve to illustrate this point. For instance, in spite of the fact that any form of mental illness or emotional disturbance is considered neither sinful nor shameful, and thus so-called health values are the only ones adopted in selection, certain troubles disqualify an applicant, such as psychosis, character disorder, or overt sexual deviation. That is not to mention the problem of the so-called "normal" applicant who smugly and beatifically reports that he is "contented and nonconflicted." It seems that what we take into account here are not only the personal liabilities which may grossly encroach upon the efficacy of the future analyst, but also the fact that it is hard for us to modify far enough, those basic nonintellectual features which we consider essential for the functioning of the psychoanalyst.

If the matter of what determines health or sickness is a moot point, and if it is argued that what we take into consideration are only those personal attributes which the prospective analyst should possess to equip him as a therapist or a scientist, there are over and above those attributes some clear-cut moral qualities which we look for. However tolerant or hopeful we may be about any pathological features and their cure, matters of honesty, integrity, and concern for others rarely fail to appear as indispensable assets in the reports of those who screen applicants. We certainly know of the many reasons and mechanisms which may lead a person to be dishonest or to be unable to care for anybody except himself, as we certainly know to a degree how to help him change his outlook or his ways. We neither condemn deviation from integrity nor claim that analysts themselves on all levels of their functioning are beyond all that may be called immoral; but it is because of our doubts that even a successful analysis will satisfactorily eradicate the factors that hamper the full exercise of such essential values in the potential psychoanalyst, that we consider such matters as integrity or human concern as important as, or more important than, brilliance, knowledge or skill. Whatever may be the criteria according to which psychoanalysts select their students, or the model image they strive to help them emulate, and whatever will be the outcome of the traditional controversy over what discipline or profession psychoanalysis should belong to, it is a specialty which has originated from medicine. Whether it continues to pertain to medicine or achieves an autonomous status, psychoanalysis is and will remain one of the healing arts, and as such will contine to share the age-old established values of the healers, ancient or modern; namely, to reduce pain or abolish it and postpone death until there is no way but to submit to it. By definition, then, for the psychoanalyst, life and its pleasures are good and desirable states to foster and maintain, whereas pain, suffering and death are states to avoid or reduce.

VALUES IN PSYCHOANALYSIS AS A THERAPY

Turning now to psychoanalytic therapy, we find that people, much as they may like to know about themselves, still seek psychoanalysis not to gain self-knowledge, but to suffer less than they do. And though, as Freud once put it, the analyst does not in fact promise any more than to replace their neurotic misery with common human misery, patients still seek his help when everything else has failed them. Whether their suffering is ultimately due to a physical manifestation, an incapacity to hold a job or get along with people, to enjoy sex or avoid getting into trouble with the law, there has accumulated enough evidence that they suffer because they are in conflict, conflict they know of and conflict they do not know of. This conflict is not mainly conflict with others, but mainly conflict within the patient himself—conflict between what he desires to do or to get and what he believes he should not do or get, conflict between the inborn needs and desires and the acquired conscience the individual has developed. Such conflicts in different forms and degrees are the factors which block man's capacity to adapt to the conditions he is in or to change them to fit his wishes.

There is nothing at all morbid or abnormal about having a conscience; in fact, our tendency to grow one, as Money-Kyrle (1961) once said about it, "must be as much a part of our innate endowment as the tendency to grow a beard or any other organ or function that emerges after birth." It is in the balance between this conscience and the instinctive urges that emotional health or sickness lies. The emergence, sources, development, and various forms and depths of this conscience, which came to be known as the "superego," make up one of the major subjects dealt with in clinical and theoretical contributions. Of no less importance, though much less written about, is the ego-ideal.

The analyst, even though he tries to stick to his neutral position between a man and his conscience or his ego-ideal, cannot help but take sides, however overtly or covertly, at one point or the other along the treatment of any case. From the very start, and though psychoanalysis neither encourages nor condemns one form of behavior more than the other, the fact that people are treated out of alcoholism, promiscuity, or feloniousness presupposes that sobriety, faithfulness, and honesty are more desirable according to some kind of value-scale, whether a health, moral, or social one.

The psychoanalyst is in constant contact with the moral feeling and moral judgment of his patient; and through his knowledge and understanding of the unconscious elements affecting the patient's conscience he may even be more in touch with it than is the patient himself. The development of the superego, its essential role in the integration of personality; its function in normal and abnormal forms of behavior; its effects in the genesis not only of the neurosis, but also of character disorders and psychoses; its relations, on the one hand, with the inborn drives and, on the other, with the ways, the conduct and the traditions of the community in which one grows up; its rigid authority or reasonable laxity in determining behavior—these are but a few of the areas which have become familiar to every analyst. No other branch of knowledge in the history of human thought, whether derived from faith or from speculation, has been in a position to study the rise and decay of the individual's morality as has psychoanalysis.

Psychoanalysts found from their own accumulated evidence not only that value systems and moral scales are necessary and present in every human being, that most people know very little, or almost nothing, about the basic motives for their conduct and attitudes, but also that man, as Freud once put it, is not only much more immoral than he thinks, but also much more moral than he knows.

Now, in the psychoanalytic situation the psychoanalyst, having learned, through precept and example, that "the urgency to reform, to correct, to make different, motivates the task of a re-

former or educator and the urgency to cure motivates the physician" (Sharpe, 1930), all that is left for him is to use "benevolent
curiosity," to suspend judgment and remain neutral. He listens
with that tolerance that he had acquired or increased from his
acquaintance with his own unconscious, and intervenes as little as
he can, so that the patient may arrive at the truth about himself,
form his own judgments, and make his own decisions.

That is what the analyst keeps in mind and genuinely follows.
But this is an ideal which, even if it were beneficial at all times
and for all patients, can hardly be attained in reality. First, the
subject matter of the analyst's work is a human being who is in
trouble, to a great extent because of a certain value system he has
been living by. To expect the analyst to perform his task with
that much professed neutrality is to expect a builder to build or
remodel a house without touching its beams, its mortar or bricks.
Neither can psychoanalysts, skilled and detached technicians as
they may be, handle their subjects like atomic technicians separated from their material behind insulating shields and with tools
they manipulate by remote control.

Secondly, the psychoanalyst works with his whole self. It is true
that through his knowledge of transference elements, countertransference influences, and all the odds and ends of theory, technique,
and experience he may have acquired, he strives to remain as neutral as can be; he neither praises nor blames, approves nor condemns. The analyst in his therapeutic work, as Hartmann (1960)
puts it, "will keep other values in abeyance and concentrate on
the realization of one category of values, only: health values."
Whatever these health values may be, whether they are new wine
in old bottles or old wine in new bottles, whether they overlap, supersede, or transcend what is more commonly referred to as moral
values, is not our concern at this point. Health values are still
values by definition, and in the analytic situation the doctor represents by function those values which he tries to help the patient
acquire. In this respect alone, he should not remain neutral, even
if he could. In any case, as Glover (1955) put it, "the idea of the
analyst's 'complete neutrality' under ordinary analytic conditions is
something of a myth."

Some analysts still claim, however, that they can keep their own value systems from getting through to the patient—at least to a very considerable degree, according to Hartmann. Several others, on the other hand, recognize that such a claim is not valid, useful, or humanly possible. Among these, for instance, was Zilboorg (1956), who once said:

> . . . a psychoanalyst, like any human being, must have a philosophy of life, or else he cannot function well as far as he himself or his patients are concerned. More than that, a psychoanalyst, more than any other professional man, must cultivate a philosophy of values, because the field that he is working in is always on the borderline of ontological and moral issues [pp. 709-710].

Redlich (1960) puts it this way: "Analytic therapy . . . is concerned with values and is influenced by values. It does not operate in a cultural vacuum" (p. 100). Gitelson (quoted by Menninger, 1958) relates that one of his patients told him: "You have helped me with your virtues and not hurt me with your defects. I can now be myself, my own man" (p. 94). Karl Menninger (1958) emphasizes that "what the psychoanalyst believes, what he lives for, what he loves, what he considers to be good and what he considers to be evil, become known to the patient and influence him enormously . . ." (p. 91).

Reflection upon what contribution the analyst makes to the analytic situation—his comments, his silences, his tone, his selections, his manner, his style, and a hundred other subtle and less subtle avenues—shows that the patient can have access to the analyst's values, however much he may strive for neutrality or reserve behind his analytic cloak.

VALUES IN PSYCHOANALYTIC THEORY

Familiar with the futility of the various attempts of the thinkers before them, and well versed in the methods of modern science, Freud and his earlier colleagues, once they discovered psychoanalysis, wisely vowed to protect the infant science from falling back into the arms of its speculative metaphysical origins. Nothing but the facts and the empirical findings were to be used as the source of this new knowledge about man. The new science became established; it survived and progressed.

The theories of psychoanalysis were thus built on the observation and description of the mental and emotional phenomena which enter into the formation of the different types of neuroses. Psychoanalysis concentrated on the study of the various factors which determine the individual's way of dealing with his own needs and drives, and of acting and reacting to the human environment in which he lives. These studies had perforce to investigate the hold which man's essential nature has on his behavior, and how he acquires the checks and controls which organize the natural and nurturant elements into a functioning whole which comes to be known as his "character."

Psychoanalysis never concerned itself with any one ethical judgment of man's behavior, and addressed itself only, as is expected from an empirical science, to the investigation of those components which determine the various forms of human behavior. The study remained always descriptive and explanatory. However, with increasing insights and knowledge, it led to the realization that people can be classified into types of character. Though the interest continued to be clinical and the approach empirical, the early attempts of Freud (1916) or Abraham (1925), up to the recent work on character disorders (Michaels, 1959), have led to a more or less recognizable hierarchy in classifying the psychological make-up of individuals according to a delineable schema. Every analyst knows that there is a gradation or a scale of personality organization on which we place a hysterical, a compulsive, a narcissistic, or an impulsive character. And however much they overlap, whatever dynamic, economic, or structural models we may use in our study, and whatever technical or nontechnical terms we use, the character of the individual manifests itself in such concrete qualities as egotism or altruism, peaceableness or aggression, truthfulness or lying, honesty, loyalty, and much that involves the pleasure, comfort, or joy of the person himself or those who come into contact with him. It is preposterous to deny that the accumulated evidence of psychoanalysis has already started to show that certain patterns of psychic organization are more conducive to a better way of life than others. Such patterns are not invented by psychoanalysis; neither are they imperatives handed down to people by psychoanalysts. Although the effect of such knowledge on mankind at large has been minimal, there has been a far-reaching impact of this new knowledge on education and art, especially in those parts of the world where psychoanalysis—and its wider ramifications—has been accepted.

By its method of investigation into what constitutes the values of the individual and by the findings which have accumulated over more than half a century, psychoanalysis has in fact and without design or plan taken over the study of values, while remaining, however, on purely empirical grounds.

This fortuitous and promising venture need not be disowned by psychoanalysis; neither should the progress of psychoanalysis be blocked by the warnings which were needed in its earlier phases. It may perhaps help psychoanalysis to know when it defensively denies that it does deal with values, that such a venture is not a breach of its codes as a science. Psychoanalysis has in fact started to undertake a task which was once proposed by some behavioral scientists who were well steeped in the rigors of methodology. Lévy-Bruhl (1900), inspired by the work of Durkheim (1893), more than half a century ago suggested the establishment of a "Science of Mores."

In their writings both Durkheim and Lévy-Bruhl advanced the view that it is possible to establish a science of ethics. This would not work at drawing conclusions from the premises borrowed from any one or more of the objective sciences, such as biology, psychology, or sociology, but at building up a completely separate discipline. Durkheim affirmed that moral facts are phenomena like any other facts; they are made of certain ways of behavior which have their particular features, and as such it is possible to observe them, describe them, classify them, and look for the laws which might explain them. In this way the moral scientist will not be "establishing" morals, since morality has always a factual existence similar to the reality of physics; he will only be attempting to analyze and explain the manifestations of morality, without passing judgments as to what is good or bad. This is what Lévy-Bruhl intended by a "Science of Mores" or "The Physics of Mores" as a new discipline which complements sociology.

It was further contended that this new science of mores could lead, like any other science, to practical applications in proportion to the theoretical advances and the conclusions it makes. It can help to differentiate with more clarity between what is normal and what is abnormal. Emphasizing that "there is a state of moral health only science can determine with competence," Durkheim attempted to define this "state of health" as the average social function of a group determined by the phase of its evolution. A science of mores would also help in prediction, where the observation of prior trends in the evolution of mores, about property, sexual behavior, or crime, for example, would point the way to what is to be expected in the future.

Such a proposal as the establishment of a "Science of Mores" remained only as a visionary plan of behavioral science, and the only discipline which has enough access to the data on which such a science can be soundly founded seems to be still reluctant to step into this area which is an integral part of its territory. Psychoanalysis is apparently the method most suited for the study of the ontogenesis of values. Hardly can any other method of investigation throw as much light on the elements which go into the structure of a man's character and determine his behavior as can the psychoanalytic method, which studies the past and the present, the conscious and the unconscious factors of man's morality. Neither is any other scientist—by the very assumptions of his specialty or the degree to which his personal equations have been corrected—equipped as the psychoanalyst is to look at man and his value systems as an integrated psychobiological unit functioning in a social environment.

It was the purpose of this paper to show how psychoanalysis is engaged in the consideration of value systems, and how such a broad subject does not transcend the technical, therapeutic, or theoretical work of the analyst. Nor can the analyst throw it all back into the fields of speculation and philosophy. Such ultimate riddles as the supreme good, the meaning of life, and human des-

Ishak Ramzy

tiny are not the concern of the analyst; but it *is* his immediate concern to deal with several other values which enter into the structure of personality. As long as the analyst adheres to the scientific and technical safeguards of his discipline, his concern about values will not make of him a moralist or a preacher, even when he is bold enough, like Erikson, to suggest a Schedule of Virtues or to speak about Hope, Competence, Fidelity, or Wisdom. The self-imposed moratorium against the study of values in psychoanalysis has been with difficulty enforced in practice and theory. To get over the artificial avoidance and to elucidate the findings of psychoanalysis in that area will be an important step towards rescuing value studies from the age-old speculative approaches and establish it as an empirical discipline and an integral part of human psychology. Psychoanalysis will thus become not a value-creating but a value-investigating science. Whether its findings will be similar to or different from those value systems built on evolutionary, utilitarian, rational, or humanitarian theories could be clarified when the study of values becomes a legitimate part of the professional training and tasks of the psychoanalyst. Whereas to continue clinging to the untenable pretense that it is ethically and morally neutral, psychoanalysis debars itself from contributing what no other science can contribute toward a better understanding of human values.

REFERENCES

Abraham, K. (1925), Psycho-analytical studies on character formation. In: *Selected Papers of Karl Abraham*. London: Hogarth Press, 1927.
Bernard, C. (1927), *An Introduction to the Study of Experimental Medicine* (English trans.). New York: Abelard-Schumann.
Brierley, M. (1951), *Trends in Psycho-Analysis*. London: Hogarth Press.
Brinton, C. (1959), *A History of Western Morals*. New York: Harcourt Brace.
Cohen, M. and Nagel, E. (1934), *An Introduction to Logic and Scientific Method*. New York: Harcourt Brace.
Durkheim, E. (1893), *De la Division du Travail Social*. Paris: Alcan.
Erikson, E. H. (1964), *Insight and Responsibility. Lectures on the Ethical Implications of Psychoanalytic Insight*. New York: Norton.
Feuer, L. S. (1955), *Psychoanalysis and Ethics*. Springfield: Charles C. Thomas.

Flugel, J. C. (1945), *Man, Morals and Society*. London: Duckworth.

Freud, S. (1916), Some character-types met with in psycho-analytic work. *Standard Edition*, 14:309–337. London: Hogarth Press, 1957.

―――― (1933), New introductory lectures on psycho-analysis. *Standard Edition*, 22:158–182. London: Hogarth Press, 1964.

Glover, E. (1955), *The Technique of Psycho-Analysis*. London: Baillière.

Goblot, E. (1925), *Traité de Logique* (4th ed.). Paris: Colin.

―――― (1927), *La Logique des Jugements de Valeur*. Paris: Colin.

Hartmann, H. (1960), *Psychoanalysis and Moral Values*. New York: International Universities Press.

Huxley, J. (1960), *Knowledge, Morality and Destiny*. New York: New American Library.

Lalande, A. (1929), *La Psychologie des Jugements de Valeur*. Cairo: Imprimerie Nationale.

Lévy-Bruhl. L. (1900), *La Morale et la Science de Moeurs*. Paris: Alcan.

Masserman, J. H. (1960) ed., *Psychoanalysis and Human Values*. New York: Grune & Stratton.

Menninger, K. (1958), *The Theory of Psychoanalytic Technique*. New York: Basic Books.

Michaels, J. (1959), Character structure and character disorders. In: *American Handbook of Psychiatry*, ed. S. Arieti. New York: Basic Books.

Money-Kyrle, R. E. (1952), Psycho-analysis and ethics. *Internat. J. Psycho-Anal.*, 33:225–234. Also in: *New Directions in Psycho-Analysis*, ed. M. Klein et al. London: Tavistock; New York: Basic Books, 1955.

―――― (1961), *Man's Picture of His World*. London: Duckworth; New York: International Universities Press.

Nielson, N. (1960), Value judgments in psycho-analysis. *Internat. J. Psycho-Anal.*, 41:425–429.

Poincaré, H. (1904), *La Valeur de la Science*. Paris: Flammarion.

Ramzy, I. (1963), The plurality of determinants in psycho-analysis. *Internat. J. Psycho-Anal.*, 44: 444–453.

Read, H. (1951), Psycho-analysis and the problem of aesthetic value. *Internat. J. Psycho-Anal.*, 32:73–82.

Redlich, F. C. (1960), Psychoanalysis and the problem of values. In: *Psychoanalysis and Human Values*, ed. J. Masserman. New York: Grune & Stratton.

Reid, J. (1955), The problem of values in psychoanalysis. *Amer. J. Psychoanal.*, 15:115–122.

Rieff, P. (1959), *Freud: the Mind of the Moralist*. New York: Viking.

Russell, B. (1931), *The Scientific Outlook*. London: Allen and Unwin.

Sharpe, E. (1930), The analyst. *Internat. J. Psycho-Anal.*, 11:257–263. Also in: *Collected Papers*. London: Hogarth Press, 1950.

Shor, J. (1961), The ethic of Freud's psychoanalysis. *Internat. J. Psycho-Anal.*, 42:116–122.

Snow, C. P. (1962), The moral un-neutrality of science. In: *The New Scientist: Essays on the Methods and Values of Modern Science*, ed. Obler and Estrind. New York: Doubleday.

Trilling, L. (1955), *Freud and the Crisis of Our Culture*. Boston: Beacon Press.

Zilboorg, G. (1956), Psychoanalytic borderlines. *Amer. J. Psychiat.*, 112:709–710.

11. A Clinical Illustration of a "Moral" Problem in Psychoanalysis

MARTIN H. STEIN, M.D.

T HE TASK of supplying a clinical illustration of the role of moral values and superego functions makes for a difficult choice. It would be valuable to present a case report in which the moral values of one particular patient are described and their role in the neurosis analyzed. This proves to be far more complicated than it sounds, since it requires extensive description and analysis of character, some careful attention to the context of the patient's life, and consideration of the moral attitudes which the analyst himself brings into the situation. Inevitably it introduces another complication: that a patient so well described is all too readily identifiable by any reader who happens to be acquainted with him.

Such a project seems beyond the scope of a relatively brief paper, but we do have an acceptable alternative. It is feasible to describe a typical conflict of the analyst himself as he functions within the special cultural milieu which includes patient and analyst, in a standardized setting with its own rules and customs.

Let me recount from my own experience an event which has occurred, I assume, in the work of all analysts who have been subject to anxiety, fatigue and the other usual human weaknesses. This is not a demonstration of technique, but rather, an idealized illustration of a very common conflict within the mind of an analyst.

Read on March 2, 1968 at the meeting of the Society of Medical Psychoanalysts Symposium on Moral Values and Superego Functioning.

My patient has been talking for some time, discussing important and rather difficult material. For reasons of my own, perhaps some private concern, my attention wanders for a moment, and suddenly I become aware that I have missed an important detail. For the present I will put aside my excuses for this lapse of alertness; the basic fact is that I am not listening, and fail to register a significant statement by the patient.

I am obliged to ask him to repeat his statement, and he replies with a question: "Didn't you hear me?"

How shall I answer? I have several choices, e.g., I may imply that he expressed himself unclearly; I may remain silent; or I may admit quite candidly that I suffered a lapse of attention.

It is this conflict to which I shall return later to illustrate moral values and superego functioning within the analytic situation.

In the context of this discussion, I shall denote as the central task of analysis the exploration of the *psychic* reality of the patient. This quest engages the energies and the observing functions of patient and analyst in a joint effort to discover and to describe as accurately as possible the mental processes and content of the former. Further, the attempt is made by both to trace these processes, including their weaknesses and distortions, to their origins in the patient's life experience.

As a corollary, we expect from the analysis the accomplishment of a second task: the achievement of an increased capacity for reality testing, in the sense of the ability to understand more precisely and quickly the source and meaning of external stimuli and events. This depends most simply upon a well-developed capacity to distinguish "inner" from "outer," i.e., for example, to tell whether a perceived image is an hallucination or not, or whether an opinion is based on projection or rather on an "objective" observation of a group of facts.

I shall leave aside the question of whether all knowledge of reality does not arise both from the outside, via perceptions of some kind and intensity, and from within, i.e., from memory traces and whatever is sensed of the operations of the mind itself. For the moment it is more useful to employ the point of view which regards an hallucination, or a similar "self-generated" phenomenon, and the perceptive recognition of an outside event as *not* the same, no matter what they may have in common on a more profound level of abstraction (Freud, 1917; Hartmann, 1956; Stein, 1966).

In most psychotherapies, particularly in those of an educational or supportive type, the improvement of reality testing, i.e., the determination of the accuracy of the patient's interpretation of events in his life, is likely to be the central task. In analysis, reality testing in this sense is a byproduct, admittedly an important one, but secondary to an increased power of those functions which observe, understand and control psychic reality. As these latter functions are rendered more effective, the distorting effects of intrapsychic conflict, anxiety and regression are minimized, and the capacity for spontaneous, self-impelled reality testing is correspondingly increased. Succinctly, it is the capacity "to face reality at all costs," [1] a statement about the ego, which carries at the same time the strongest moral implications and includes therefore some statement about the superego as well.

It was in *Psychoanalysis and Moral Values* that Hartmann (1960) focussed on this most interesting problem, the attempt to describe that aspect of the psychic apparatus which I shall call the "interface" between ego and superego functions. An essential aspect of characteristic behavior, which may be used to study this interface, is that which includes knowing and telling the truth. Here it is possible to demonstrate that an apparently simple activity, regarded as a prime example of ego functioning, must be described in terms of superego function as well. This is in accord with the principle of multiple function, described by Waelder in 1930 and restated in somewhat more general form in 1960.

In accordance with this principle we are to regard any psychic event as possessing meaning in terms of drives, ego and superego against the background of reality. The event may not be regarded as the product of one or another part of the psychic apparatus exclusively, although for purposes of exposition or interpretation we may choose to stress that aspect which predominates, or about

[1] Hartmann's (1960) tribute to Freud.

which we know the most. For example, when we describe an action as determined by the superego, we must be understood to mean only that this aspect of the psychic apparatus is most conspicuous in our analysis of the event. It may be so because this group of functions really does dominate the situation; for example, we regard the appearance of guilt as a manifestation of the superego's activity. Or it may be that our own vision is limited by the information available, or by bias—our own or the patient's.

Nevertheless, we retain, at least in the background of our theoretical understanding, the principle that *any* event is a manifestation of all major elements: id, ego, superego and the external impact of reality. According to this, the appearance of guilt implies activity not only of the superego, but of the ego as well, that regulatory apparatus which among other functions allows the experience to reach awareness. Similarly we postulate activity of the drives which evoked the response of guilt in the first place. And finally we take into account the reality which constitutes the background, which supplies stimuli, and which may in turn be affected by the behavior arising from the reaction of guilt.

Let us return now to the dilemma I stated at the beginning. I have not yet responded to my patient's question: "Didn't you hear me?"

It is tempting to protect myself, by replying: "Yes, but I didn't understand you"—a lie, to be sure, but at first thought a harmless one.

Or I might exert my privilege as an analyst to remain silent, allowing my patient to draw his own conclusions. The latter solution is even more tempting, because it does not require a direct lie. If the patient is inclined to idealize me, he will convince himself that he must have been at fault, that he mumbled or expressed himself obscurely. Or he may come to a similar conclusion out of compliance or masochistic need. If he is grandiose, or cannot tolerate the thought that he failed to hold me spellbound, he may still be inclined to blame himself for not being clear enough in his expression.

Of course, the patient might entertain the fantasy which corresponds to the truth, that I was not listening. If he goes on to accuse me of not listening, and I still remain silent, he will at least remain in some doubt. For me to fail to respond, therefore, would be for me still to avoid the truth. To be honest, therefore, I should have to admit frankly that I had not been listening.

But would it be so bad to withhold this embarrassing disclosure? Suppose my patient does go on believing that I was listening and that he was responsible for the lapse of meaningful exchange. Will he suffer any harm? I think he might.

If I say, or allow him to assume from my silence, that I was alert and he must have been mistaken in his impression that he had been expressing himself clearly, a fact which he must have registered on some level, I am urging him to change his "true" (i.e., accurate) view of reality for my "false" (inaccurate) statement of it; in other words, to deny perceived reality for the sake of preserving a fantasy about me. It should be obvious that this is, at least in theory, a direct contravention of the analytic purpose of exploring the psychic reality of the patient and of fostering his ability to bring his sense of reality into accord with experience. [2]

It will almost certainly constitute a reenactment of one of the potentially pathogenic experiences which figure so often in the histories of our patients. Let us say a five-year-old has seen his parents in intercourse. He asks what they were doing, and is told they were "only playing." It is an understandable enough response by the parents, maybe even a "normal" one, whatever that may be.

What happens to the child, who has acquired a pretty good idea that this was no usual playing, and that something sexual and highly exciting was going on? He may, of course, conclude that his parents are lying; but that would require a degree of bravery and independence given to very few children. It would, I suspect, be unusual in a five-year-old, although some, like Little Hans, have been capable of doubting more or less openly the statements of adults on sexual matters.

The child is much more likely, in the face of his own and his parents' anxiety, to attempt to dispose of the whole matter in

---

[2] See Greenson and Wexler (1969) whose advice, to "admit mistakes," would be in accord, ʋut whose reasons are different.

some other way. He may deny the experience altogether and eventually repress it; or he may distort the memory traces of what he has perceived, so as to bring the experience into accord with his parents' statement. He *will* try to regard the act he saw as "just playing," with whatever effects this may have on his sexual fantasies in the future. But he registers as well his parents' evasion of the truth, another observation which will have to be hidden from himself in the interest of maintaining his ideal images of them. The overall effect is regressive, in that denial, repression and isolation are fostered, while the child's capacity for reality testing is not at all advanced.

An event such as I have described is likely to occur of course in the best regulated families. Parents caught *flagrante delicto* are not in an ideal situation to tell the exact truth in language which can be understood by a five-year-old, and they are hardly to be blamed if they contribute to their child's confusion. The effects may be lasting but are not usually catastrophic or even serious.

Suppose, however, that such an event or, more probably, a series of such events occurs in the life of a previously traumatized child in a less well-regulated family, in which there is a severely disturbed marriage or a psychotic parent. Repeated distortions and outright lies are transmitted to a child whose ego functions, particularly those which contribute to reality testing, may have been impaired earlier by severe preoedipal traumatization. We should then anticipate much more serious damage to both ego and superego development. I need not elaborate further on the vicissitudes affecting the child's development of a sense of reality, his sure knowledge of that which is to be considered "truth."

When we deal with the transference of the neurotic patient, therefore, it becomes not merely a matter of general obligation, but an urgent necessity for us to be entirely scrupulous in our statements about the realities of the analytic situation. There is in fact no satisfactory excuse for concealing the truth. While we may be caught *flagrante delicto*, it is hardly a primal scene, except in the most abstract sense. We are not parents surprised in an emotionally charged private act; they have a better excuse, and we ought to be well enough analyzed to avoid acting as if our respective dilemmas were really comparable.

Still, it will not do to pretend that we are faced with an easy decision. The easy, evasive solutions are so tempting that our own devotion to the pleasure principle often enough traps us into making one of these choices. But we do know better, being aware that sooner or later both patient and analyst must pay for the error of having reenacted, perhaps carelessly, a pathogenic determinant in the former's experience.

In an actual analysis, of course, we may or may not choose to admit the fact of our inattention immediately. More often, we may prefer to allow the patient some time to associate, to develop and analyze his fantasies about the incident. These are potentially of great value, and in some patients an immediate confrontation with the analyst's lapse might deprive us of important material by shutting off the flow of associations.

Sooner or later, however, the patient must be left in no doubt about the actuality of the event which occurred within the analytic situation. Whatever he may have imagined, it was a fact that his remark went *unheard*. The timing of this confrontation is therefore a matter of choice—so long as the patient is not left with his misapprehension or uncertainty for too long.

Now we must take a further step, that of exploring those factors in the analysis which may have contributed to my lapse of attention. I refer here to the patient's own contribution to my state of inattention, a finding which is often of the greatest importance to the analysis, yet which can be explored fully only *after* the patient and I understand that the lapse really did occur.

We are then likely to find that the patient's role has been an essential one, inducing in me a less attentive state, in which I have become more susceptible to my own fantasies and less alert to the events of the analytic situation. The kind of "free-floating" attention which is so useful for the analyst is a very peculiar state combining a high degree of alertness with a degree of freedom and access to primary process thinking which may approach the hypnagogic state at times, and all too often requires one to fight a tendency to sleep. The analyst's state of consciousness varies a good deal, as does the patient's, with a varying correspondence between the two. Lewin (1955) has pointed out the role of the analyst as the dream inducer and the waker of the patient; the roles may be reversed, whereby the patient becomes the dream inducer and waker of the analyst. [3] This is not necessarily disastrous, but it may occasionally be embarrassing. It is not simply that the patient may be "boring;" not at all, for such influences may be exerted by patients who are very interesting indeed, but who from time to time induce by their material and presentation a state in the analyst which may be akin to dreaming. It may in fact be necessary for the analyst to share to some degree the patient's regression in thought processes to be able to follow the latter. And it is in such a state that the analyst may fall prey to some private concern of his own and thereby miss the patient's remark.

In a Faculty Meeting of the New York Psychoanalytic Institute, Isakower referred to the analyst's "analyzing instrument," a highly condensed term which includes among other things the analytic understanding of his own fantasies which have reached his consciousness in response to the patient's productions. The use of such an "instrument" implies, of course, the maintenance of a very delicate balance between wakeful hyperalertness and dreamy preoccupation on the part of the analyst.

None of this constitutes an "excuse" for the lapse of attention. But that first issue having been clarified, the patient may then be able to learn a good deal about his own role in attempting to influence the analyst's state of consciousness, a bit of knowledge which may become a major step in the analysis.

In any case it is "correct," i.e., realistic, to adhere to the dictum of knowing, facing and telling the truth to the patient. In this context, I have done no more than to restate the importance of the reality principle in analytic work. It would appear sufficient to note that this dictum is entirely in accord with that part of my analytic ego which is directed toward effective work; i.e., my own wish for mastery, my devotion to my own reality testing (which would also be threatened by deception, self- or outwardly directed) and my wish to avoid further trouble with my patient.

Why then is it necessary to introduce moral values? Have we

---

[3] See also Stein (1965).

not already been presented with sufficient reasons for following the rule of truth telling? It would seem so, and yet I cannot but feel that the description of this conflict is incomplete and inadequate to account entirely for my response, unless there is some reference to feelings of guilt. When I fail the test by yielding to the temptation to follow the path of least resistance, I find myself feeling quite guilty. And I assume that many analysts would respond in like fashion.

Since my response consists not only of regret for a technical error, but possesses a considerable share of guilt, I have good reason to believe that my superego functions are implicated. Further, even in this present attempt to discuss the conflict as objectively as possible, I cannot avoid experiencing within myself a sense of righteousness, as if I were claiming that this is *the* right way to solve the problem and that all other ways are wrong: not merely mistakes, but offenses. My response betrays every feature of a moral attitude, perhaps even a moralistic one.

Insofar as my superego functions have become a part of those forces which determine my feelings and behavior, I am influenced by a moral imperative which echoes certain parental and other voices of the past (especially analytic teachers—"model" analysts) which have been incorporated into my superego structure (Isakower, 1939). This influence is joined and reinforced by the "reality imperative," which is derived both from testing via experience and from identifications with those earlier figures recognized as "wise." It is in this latter respect an aspect of the ego, as well.

This synergistic phenomenon manifests what I describe as the "interface" between superego and ego, those elements of the psychic apparatus which here operate jointly in determining the subjective and behavioral manifestations of my decision to tell the truth. When I view the phenomenon from the aspect of ego function, I conclude that I must have decided that the price to be paid (in terms of analytic complications) for giving in to my instinctual impulse, to tell the easy lie, is too great. From the superego aspect, I avoid guilt by obeying the old dictum to tell the truth, to do the "right" thing. When I consider how to view this "correct" decision from the aspect of the drives, I find that one drive derivative may indeed have been frustrated by my virtuous and self-denying action; namely, that aggressive component which impels me to manipulate my patient's sense of reality in order to avoid immediate displeasure to myself. But another drive derivative may have been gratified, i.e., my positive feeling for the patient; and furthermore, my self-love is likely to be enhanced by my feeling rather noble about the whole thing—the id is gratified by resisting the devil, as well as by submitting to him!

We may view all of this as the coming together of a complex group of forces (or of multiple meanings—see Waelder, 1930, 1960) contributing to this apparently simple action of mine. Each of these plays a necessary part in the understanding of the final result, and each must be considered in a thorough analysis of it. Their confluence is in essence a manifestation of multiple function.

Of course the same could be said of any human action, or symptom, if it were painstakingly analyzed. What is noteworthy in this case is that ego and superego aspects of meaning correspond more closely than would be likely in most other human actions. The conflict need not be a very deep one, since there is no genuine choice of alternatives with which we could, as analysts, remain comfortable.

While the conduct of analysis may not be unique in this respect, the technique is unusual in that the demands of reality and those of conscience coincide with unusual precision. I have been reminded of this by certain patients who were particularly sensitive to their own conflicts in this area and to the advantages of my position as an analyst. One of them commented with some bitterness: "You are lucky to be doing work in which it always pays to tell the truth. You may be as moral as you please, and lose nothing by it. You are paid to be honest!" He was right, although he went too far in assuming that we can play this role with no serious conflict. It is only that the "correct" decision for us is likely to be fairly clear.

We do work in a setting in which honesty is the "best" policy, in the sense that it is the *only* policy, as the essential element in good technique. It is difficult to think of examples in which distortion of the truth is ever therapeutically or otherwise justified in the analysis of neurotic patients. Even the concealment of a major fact about the analytic situation is highly questionable. When such devices do become necessary, we ought to ask ourselves whether the analysis can go on, or whether it has been sufficiently established in the first place. And if we do consider the severity of the patient's pathology so great that we are afraid to tell him the truth, we must face the likelihood that we have given up hope of working with him analytically.

This discussion has introduced so many questions about technique that it becomes necessary to ask whether speaking the literal truth in this context may not carry the potential for undesirable as well as beneficial effects. [4]

Certainly an immediate, literally true statement by the analyst may be directed toward an analysand who is so absorbed by other, more urgent thoughts that he does not want a prompt answer in spite of his question, "Didn't you hear me?" The analyst's statement would then be mistimed and constitute an interference with the analysis. Obviously, it is essential that the analyst be sensitive to the state of the analytic situation, and not allow his own responses to be determined by a theoretical preconception.

There is the danger that guilt or self-righteousness in the analyst may lead him to use literal honesty as a dogmatic precept which could do considerable damage by fostering a similar attitude in the patient. The latter may then substitute literal verbal truth for the development through analysis of something much more important, the capacity to be truthful in the deepest sense. Such a patient might then tell his analyst "the truth" (in a superficial sense), but continue to be thoroughly dishonest with himself.

There remains the further possibility that literal truth telling may constitute a narcissistic demonstration by the analyst of his superiority to his patient and to the rest of the (dishonest) world. The potential for damage hardly needs to be pointed out.

It is evident therefore that even "the truth" can be misused to

---

[4] I am indebted to Dr. Marvin G. Brook of Celeveland for his discussion of this point.

conceal something quite different. It should be rather the *principle* of the "honest reply" which should rule. The burden of proof is on us if we withhold it; we should know our reasons and be sure that we are not deceiving ourselves.

I should add a perhaps unnecessary qualifying note here. When I talk of "the truth" or the avoidance of concealment, I do not imply that the patient must be made privy to all of the analyst's concerns and fantasies, or the facts of his personal life. But he is entitled to know what his analyst considers to be part of the analytic situation, and what he does not. And he is probably better off for having a reasonable explanation of whatever limitations are set by the latter.

In any case, precision in dealing with this problem serves as a necessary reinforcement of the patient's capacity for the understanding of his own mental processes; e.g., he can finally say to himself that he interpreted such an event correctly ("my analyst was really not listening"), rather than incorrectly ("he was listening, but I was obscure"). If the patient understands what he did to interfere with the analyst's attentiveness, all the better. An act of learning, perhaps of mastery, has been accomplished, and an important area of ego function has been reinforced.

I should like to return now to discuss some of the other effects of my decision to admit my lapse, e.g., on the functioning of the patient's superego. When I, the analyst, show myself capable of admitting an unpalatable truth, my patient is likely to identify with whatever is revealed about my standards of behavior. That part of his conscience and his ego-ideal which favors one mode of behavior over another is reinforced. This phenomenon supports Ramzy's (1965) statement (quoted by Furer) that there are values, either covert or implicit, in the *practice* of psychoanalysis (my italics). These values may be revealed not only in major exchanges between analyst and patient, but in such inconspicuous events as that which I have used as an example.

Insofar as the patient identifies with the analytic aspect of the analyst, i.e., with my behavior in the analytic situation, he must observe and to some extent incorporate the analytic practice of seeking the truth and of telling it as fairly and accurately as possible. This is a complex process including both ego and superego functions; descriptively, it may be classed as a moral value.

Even under ideal conditions there are very definite limits to my patient's incorporation of my attitudes and behavior, no matter how much they may be in accord with analytic goals. First, he may for a time at least reject his tendency to emulate me. My attempts to be honest with him are not always met with imitation, and may at times result in quite contrary swings of behavior. But we hope that such an analytic value as truth telling will eventually be accepted positively, after the more fundamental conflicts are analyzed.

If he has after all acquired a capacity to "face reality at all costs," does this mean then that he will never tell lies elsewhere? This is hardly to be expected, and it is by no means certain that it would be altogether desirable. We do hope that above all, he can tell the truth to himself. This accomplished, he may certainly *choose* not to do so in certain situations. A compulsion to tell the truth in every situation, without exception, is by no means a criterion of mental health. But the *capacity* to do so certainly is.

An interesting and somewhat controversial aspect of this problem deals with the degree to which my patient may feel compelled to adopt my personal morality in other respects, including that of my extra-analytic behavior. Or, to put it more correctly, to what extent should I, as analyst, give the patient the chance to do so?

Such a question introduces a multitude of difficulties. Am I required outside my work to be at all times rigidly honest in word and deed, invariably calm, rational and broadminded? This would be altogether too much of a strain, calling for a race of supermen to fill the ranks of the profession.

Most analysts are neither villains nor saints. The former group are likely to be weeded out by selection committees, or if they slip through, there is a good chance that they will be recognized by their teachers as unsatisfactory candidates and will consequently be persuaded to discontinue training.

Those individuals who do complete their training and still retain a very serious problem of fundamental dishonesty, or even psychopathy, must encounter severe difficulties in practicing analysis.

A "Moral" Problem in Psychoanalysis

One must have at least a well-developed capacity for honesty, reflecting sound ego-superego structure and integration, to be reasonably honest eight hours a day, often at the expense of one's self-esteem. It is difficult enough for well-analyzed people of reasonably good integrity to practice analysis. Individuals with serious defects in the sense of morality, and in whom this has not been resolved by analysis, must hardly be able to practice psychoanalysis at all.

As for saints, I don't think we come across them very often; and it is difficult to say much about this little known group, in which, as analysts, we are not likely to believe.

Certainly training analysis results in neither perfection nor saintliness. It should, however, permit the analyst to recognize his own frailties, to understand their unconscious sources and finally to control their manifestations surely and efficiently, so that they do not interfere with his self-assigned task of understanding and helping his patients. It is the least our patients can demand.

BIBLIOGRAPHY

Freud, S. (1917), A metapsychological supplement to the theory of dreams. *Standard Edition*, 14:222–235. London: Hogarth Press, 1957.
Greenson, R. R. and Wexler, M. (1969), The non-transference relationship in the psychoanalytic situation. *Internat. J. Psycho-Anal.*, 50:27–39.
Hartmann, H. (1956), Notes on the reality principle. *The Psychoanalytic Study of the Child*, 11:31–53. New York: International Universities Press.
—— (1960), *Psychoanalysis and Moral Values*. New York: International Universities Press.
Isakower, O. (1939), On the exceptional position of the auditory sphere. *Internat. J. Psycho-Anal.*, 20:340–348.
Lewin, B. D. (1955), Dream psychology and the analytic situation. *Psychoanal. Quart.*, 24:169–199.
Ramzy, I. (1965), The place of values in psycho-analysis. *Internat. J. Psycho-Anal.*, 46:97–106.
Stein, M. H. (1965), States of consciousness in the analytic situation. Including a note on the traumatic dream. In: *Drives, Affects, Behavior*, Vol. 2, ed. M. Schur. New York: International Universities Press, pp. 60–86.
—— (1966), Self-observation, reality, and the superego. In: *Psychoanalysis—A General Psychology*, ed. R. M. Loewenstein, L. M. Newman, M. Schur and A. J. Solnit. New York: International Universities Press, pp. 275–297.
Waelder, R. (1930), The principle of multiple function. *Psychoanal. Quart.*, 5:45–62, 1936.
—— (1960), *Basic Theory of Psychoanalysis*. New York: International Universities Press.

12. *Some Considerations on Moral Values and Psychoanalysis*

LILLY OTTENHEIMER, M.D.

P SYCHOANALYSIS is not the only discipline concerned with man's moral values. It shares this interest with other sciences like philosophy, ethics and sociology. What then are the specific contributions which psychoanalysis has made to the understanding of the human being's value systems?

Their existence has been known long before the advent of psychoanalysis; from the Hippocratic oath to the categorical imperative of Kant, enlightened people have elaborated, stressed and expanded them. But nothing was known before Freud about the phenomenon that only part of man's moral code was in conscious awareness. Today, of course, it is well known to every analyst that the hidden moral aspects of man influence his conduct and his interaction with his fellow men.

The second contribution which psychoanalysis made is its theories about the development of the value systems of the individual. It attempts to answer questions as to *how* biological man became moral man, how the newborn human animal becomes the moral adult (moral at no point should be confused with moralistic); how drive-gratifications can become renounced and replaced through satisfactions derived from the attainment of his moral goals. The morality of the adult is a part of his identity. It is outside the frame of reference of this paper to elaborate on the intricate and complex processes which go into the formation of this identity. Suffice it to say that psychoanalysis, by focusing on the prolonged dependency of the human young, arrived at conceptualizations

Read at the Society of Medical Psychoanalysts, Symposium on Moral Values and Superego Functioning, New York City, March 4, 1968.

like identification, introjection, incorporation, concepts which are helpful in understanding *how* environmental, sociocultural values can become part of the individual's self.

The third contribution was made by Freud through his structural theory, according to which he suggests a division of the mind into ego, id and superego. This conceptualization of the mind makes for organization and clarification of very confusing issues. This structural theory offers a vantage point from which it is possible to overlook the roads leading to inner conflicts whether they are only noticeable by the person's tensions within himself or whether they are projected on to the outside world. These conflicts arise from the juxtaposition of id tendencies and superego demands, or from contradictions between the two value systems: the self-interests or value system of the ego versus the ethical and moral quests of a person. Erik H. Erikson (1968) requests a differentiation between ethics and moral values, but this seems to me not necessary for the intent of this paper. Superego and moral values are not synonymous—to be sure—but I think we are entitled in the scheme of things to visualize all moral values of the individual as clustering around the nucleus of the superego, and the values of one's *self*-interests as revolving around the core of the ego. A harmonious coexistence of these two systems is the condition sine-qua-non for goal-directed activity and peace of mind.

Our society is a precipitate of the moral values of many cultures, but for the most part it falls under the influence of the Judaic-Christian principles. Within the broad frame of the sociocultural values there are value modalities which are specific for one group and not for any other sector of the population, i.e., the Hippocratic oath expresses the moral values specific for and lived by the "healers." The moral values of the individual arrange themselves in a hierarchy. Some hierarchies are more rigid than others; the possibility of a regrouping reflects an individual's flexibility.

Now a word about the influence of psychoanalysis on the value systems of the analysand. Every analysis is bound to change, expand or restrict the value systems of the individual under analysis. It does so by dint of the insights at which the person arrives, which in turn replace irrationality with rationality; it does so by exposing "false" values mostly derived from distorted convictions. The arbiter who decides what is false and what is genuine, what rational and what irrational, is doubtless the analyst. Inadvertently, the question arises: what about the analyst's own value systems; don't they intrude themselves into the analysis and exert a molding influence upon the analysand? Certainly, there are transient identifications during an analysis of the patient with his analyst. Some of those are even a prerequisite for the analysis, i.e., for the formation of the "working-alliance" as Greenson (1967) terms it, by which is meant that a part of the patient's ego identifies with the exploring truth-seeking analyst; other identifications will be regrouped and dropped altogether after the termination of the analysis. The analyst himself does not introject his own values into the analysis; nor does he attempt to inflict his own moral values upon the patient. What enables him not to do so has been expressed by Hartmann (1959) in his paper on "Psycho-analysis and Moral Values":

> In the therapeutic situation something appears that we can account for only if we decide to make a distinction between the therapist's general moral codes and the one he is guided by in his therapeutic work which could be called his "professional code." In his therapeutic work he will keep other values in abeyance and concentrate on the realization of one category of values only: health-values [p. 55].

Hartmann goes on to point out that in the analyst's personal code values of health may not necessarily assume primary importance as they do in his professional role. It seems to me that this concentration on health values forms the best protection of the patient and the analyst from the influence of moral values. I should like to suggest two more factors which keep the analyst from introjecting his own codes into the analysis: one is the respect which the analyst has for the individuality of his patients as human beings. Voltaire's conviction that even if he did not agree with what one said, he should defend to the last one's right to say it applies to this issue inasmuch as the analysand, after his analysis (having shed what hampered his growth), has the right of choice, the right to his own set of values, even if they differ from those of his analyst as a part of his individuality.

Moreover, mental health is the goal of analytic therapy; freedom of choice is a part of mental health and restricting the mental freedom of his patients is contradictory to the analyst's goal.

There is one more factor which will keep the analyst from imposing his values upon patients. As an analyst he belongs to a group which have the truth as their greatest professional value. The search for the truth is not only a value in itself, but it is also a valid therapeutic means. From the use of free associations, which means "tell me the truth of what you are thinking about," to the interpretation of dreams—"let us see the truth behind the disguise," the quest is for the truth. Therefore, the value of the truth in the hierarchy of the analyst's values exceeds all other values of his own personal code. The truth in itself is, of course, neither good nor bad—*it is*. The so-called permissiveness of the analyst refers to his permission, even requests, to express the truth. The value placed upon truth makes it possible for the analyst to be nonjudgmental and accepting, even if those truths reflect values which are normally not in the analyst's value system.

People, before entering analysis, are sometimes beset with the fear of losing all moral values through their analysis. It is almost unnecessary before this audience to state that this fear is unfounded. If this were so, analysis would simply change a neurotic into a psychopath, i.e., exchange one mental illness for another one. The mentally healthy person is not amoral; normal man is moral man.

BIBLIOGRAPHY

Erikson, E. H. (1968), *Identity, Youth and Crisis*. New York: Norton.
Freud, S. (1923), The ego and the id. *Standard Edition*, 19:3–68. London: Hogarth Press, 1961.
_____ (1930 [1929]), Civilization and its discontents. *Standard Edition*, 21:59–45. London: Hogarth Press, 1961.
Greenson, R. (1967), *The Technique and Practice of Psychoanalysis*. New York: International Universities Press.
Hartmann, H. (1959), *Psychoanalysis and Moral Values*. New York: International Universities Press.

13. Psychoanalysis and Moral Values

IRVING BIEBER, M.D.

ORAL VALUES constitute an order of beliefs associated with the ethical aspects of behavior as expressed in interpersonal transactions and, more broadly, social acts that society may deem to be right or wrong, good or bad, virtuous or evil. In every culture, at any given time, prevailing mores affect and are affected by societal values and standards of morality. At first, moral values are learned through the agency of the family where behavioral modes and affective experience are initially patterned and directed. Later, through a continuity of the reinforcing influences of social institutions, many come to accept the moral values of one's time as the givens of social reality. One's moral values are then felt to be right, socially constructive, inviolate and inexorable. Personal motives and behaviors that threaten to violate established moral standards precipitate feelings of guilt, diminish self-esteem and evoke expectations of rejection.

Philosophers, of course, and in more recent decades, sociologists, have lavished much thought and ink on the nature and role of moral values. In my brief discussion I shall touch upon three aspects that seem to me most germane to our discipline: (1) the psychoanalyst and moral values; (2) the psychoanalyst and moral judgment; and (3) psychoanalysis as a scientific tool for evolving a rationally based ethical system.

THE PSYCHOANALYST AND MORAL VALUES

People move into their work orbit with a developed system of moral values. The psychoanalyst enters his profession no differently. In general, his beliefs conform to popularly held ethi-

---

Read at the Society of Medical Psychoanalysts, Symposium on Moral Values and Superego Functioning, New York City, March 4, 1968.

cal values but since analysts as a group tend to be philosophical and since they are likely to have given thought to the more abstract subjects, such as moral values, it is usual that at least in certain particulars, some of an analyst's moral values will have been modified through having contemplated upon personal experiences and observations including personal psychoanalysis. Operationally, the psychoanalyst is inevitably more deeply involved with value systems than are his colleagues in the more purely medical specialties. As a behavioral scientist, the analyst delineates the motivational components of behavior and evaluates the behavior itself, using for the most part a medical model to do so. Gross dichotomies such as normal and healthy or sick and pathological are refined and placed into categories such as nonneurotic and normal versus neurotic or psychotic, as assertive versus hostile-aggressive, and so forth. Some workers, notably Thomas Szasz, have sharply criticized the use of the medical model in psychiatry and psychoanalysis. It is asserted that in essence psychoanalysts use a medical model as a cover-up for translating culturally bound value systems of good and bad into scientific-sounding language. I do not believe that the central issue is whether a medical model is useful or whether it conceals naive, moralistic notions, but rather that psychoanalysts direct themselves to two basic questions: A. Do one's moral values influence diagnostic judgment; and B. If this is so, does it then follow that such judgments are necessarily based upon unscientific, prejudicial criteria, the derivative of a submissive conformity to cultural mores?

A particularly interesting example of moral bias is a statement by Freud (1917) which appears in the *Introductory Lectures:* "We actually describe a sexual activity as perverse if it has given up the aim of reproduction and pursued the attainment of pleasure as an aim independent of it" (p. 316). This view is completely consonant with the ethical tenets of several religions but as a supportable statement of science *and* a moral value, I think it is not acceptable. It is my feeling that the term "perverse" is rarely used precisely today, because it has such moralistic implications. The word "perverse" has been replaced by the more neutral term "sexual deviation." In our era of sexual emancipation and "The Pill," pleasure-motivated sexuality is considered to be neither perverse nor deviant. Masturbation provides another example which seems to trigger moral bias. In the past, psychoanalytic attitudes toward masturbation articulated with the prevailing mores. It was undesirable. Though to a far lesser extent, one, however, still observes psychoanalytic bias regarding masturbation that reflects moral values and judgments based upon the therapist's own personal attitudes.

THE PSYCHOANALYST AND MORAL JUDGMENT

Psychoanalysis began as a therapeutic innovation and psychoanalytic therapy remains its major orientation. Moral values are an implicit part of all professions concerned with therapeutics. The healing professions have traditionally been directed to people's welfare and betterment—to fostering development and improvement in the physical, mental, and more recently, economic and social spheres. The therapist's goal, that of benefiting his patient, is the expression of a positive moral value and direction. One of the directives of the Hippocratic Oath enjoins the physician to suspend all moral judgment in the treatment of patients, whether they be sinner or saint. Now moral judgment must be differentiated from moral evaluation. If I am confronted by a thief, my defensive, aggressive reaction will evoke a moral judgment that may lead to his arrest. However, in a therapeutic context, say as prison psychiatrist, I would evaluate this man's predatory acts as antisocial, but in my role of therapist I should be able to free myself of antipathic, hostile responses, aggressive and other. My fundamental orientation should be to treat the patient, which would also involve determining the motivation and meaning of his socially destructive behavior.

Within the framework of therapeutics, to the extent that one cannot dissociate oneself from moral judgment, to that extent countertransference becomes a determining and contaminating variable. In the presence of a kleptomaniac one might see to it that the family silver is locked away but this is not countertransference; rather, it is a legitimate right to protect oneself from the acting out by a patient. Self-protection need not stimulate countertransferences. The enjoinder to suspend moral judgment and to adhere to the role of healer can sometimes present difficult challenges and perhaps insurmountable problems. An analyst might find that treating a confirmed and active Nazi evokes irrepressible counterreactions of hatred and moral judgment which would interfere with the legitimate course of treatment. But, as in other instances, psychoanalytic principles governing the resolution of countertransference must prevail and if moral judgment cannot be successfully suspended, if countertransference cannot be resolved, then the analysis must be terminated as it would be in the instance of an unresolved *positive* countertransference.

PSYCHOANALYSIS AND ETHICAL AND MORAL SYSTEMS

In my view, the goal of moral and ethical systems should be that of providing standards for developing and maintaining optimal development and cooperation in human relationships. Based upon this hypothesis, psychoanalysis can provide a scientific reference for evolving new, sophisticated ethical systems and for testing old ones. Psychoanalysis has the know-how for evaluating the human condition in all its stages through its study of the effects of familial and extrafamilial influences and pressures upon the individual. By studying patients who have decompensated on a continuum of mild to severe, we can determine the commonality and range of stress points within class and caste. In this sense, the psychoanalyst is a social microscopist who is therefore in a position to make broadscale contributions to sociology and political science in its thrust toward a better society. Thus, psychoanalysis can furnish essential information as to the types of sociopolitical arrangements most suitable to human groups in various societies. Certainly, if data were pooled, it would be no insurmountable task to demonstrate scientifically which aspects of social structure and process promote feelings of rejection, anxiety and low self-esteem and which influence the ability to pursue happiness. It is a commonplace that differential social acceptance and status stratification are not commensurate with the moral values espoused by a democratic society; and further, that a highly disparate distribution of products and advantages induce a competitiveness discordant with the tenets of brotherly love. To demonstrate its psychiatric effects on populations and its effects on the moral fabric of society is perhaps the moral responsibility and challenge of psychoanalysis today.

Psychoanalysis has evolved in a historical era during which a sexual revolution has been in progress, a change that has radically altered sexual moral values. The revolution is not yet over. New guidelines remain to be established and society looks to psychoanalysis for help in formulating a rationally based sexual ethic. There are many questions that need to be answered, such as, what is the psychoanalytic view on the subject of premarital and extramarital sexual relations and on what bases do such views rest? We must look to systematic methodologies for the gathering of reliable data on which to base moral precepts. One could, for example, compare a population who have had premarital sexual relations with a similar population who have not, and then contrast the two groups in areas such as sexual effectiveness, capability of forming a stable, heterosexual love relationship, work effectiveness, level of social relatedness, and so forth. I have found that young married people, under the age of about 35, who had not engaged in premarital intercourse, tend much more often to suffer from neurotic difficulties than those who had premarital intercourse. I have also found that individuals of either sex who have had the advantage of higher education and are still virginal at the age of 22 or 23 are also more likely to have neurotic problems than are educated young people who have started intercourse by their early twenties. Thus, those who are unable to avail themselves of the advantages of a more liberal sexual ethic, for whatever reason, are more likely to have psychiatric problems. One could say then that it is moral for men and women of about the age of 22 to have had sexual intercourse whether or not they are married. But how about ages 18 or 16 or 14? At the present time, one must individualize with each patient and evaluate a concatenation of data. Standards of sexual behavior for the very young await the needed studies which must be done, as I have emphasized, in order to formulate knowledgeable guidelines.

When we approach the question of extramarital relations, we find ourselves in the middle of the lake, surrounded by the shores of stern morality and virtue. Yet, psychoanalytic experience articulates in certain ways with the traditional views about monogamy. The psychoanalytic contribution to a new morality in marriage may rest, at least in part, upon the conclusion that if a spouse is physically and psychologically capable of good sexual and affective relatedness, then extramarital activity is almost always neurotically determined.

To conclude, if we grant the proposition that a psychoanalyst's viewpoint will be shaped by his own beliefs and value systems, that moral values are part of his "mind set" and hence are playing a determining role in what he observes and how he orders his data, then clearly the analyst's beliefs and moral values must be based upon the best available scientific information and not upon traditional mores, mythology and folkways. As analysts we are trained to be cognitively aware of countertransference and of the psychodynamic processes operant in our patients. So must we be consciously aware of the assumptions on which our moral values are based as well as how they have been derived.

BIBLIOGRAPHY

Freud, S. (1917 [1916–1917]), Introductory lectures on psycho-analysis. *Standard Edition*, 16:243–463. London: Hogarth Press, 1963.

PART III

CLINICAL PAPERS

14. The Need for "Real" Experience: A Note on Acting Out

SEYMOUR C. POST, M.D.

I T HAS PROVEN fruitful to apply the structural concept of psychic functioning in studying the question of choice of neurosis (Arlow, 1959; Wangh, 1959). In recent years analysts have been attempting to understand why, with similar conflicts or unconscious fantasies, certain patients act out rather than develop inhibitions, symptoms or anxiety.

There are many factors which influence certain individuals to resolve their conflicts predominantly in terms of action. My intention is to describe one such constellation.

I have observed two patients whose behavior is characterized by a pattern of Don Juan activity. Analysis of these patients demonstrates that this pattern can be understood in terms of acting out a fantasy of identification with the mother. The motive for the identification was to combat the danger of separation from the mother, according to the formula "To be equals to have" (Freud, 1914).

An unconscious feminine identification in a man can lead to a variety of psychological responses—e.g., symptom formation, perversion, inhibition, etc. Was there some characteristic peculiar to these patients which might shed light on why they were given to

The author gratefully acknowledges the critical and editorial advice of Dr. Jacob A. Arlow in the preparation of this paper.

An earlier version of this paper was delivered before the American Psychoanalytic Association, Fall 1965 Meeting.

the acting out of fantasies of identification with the mother through the Don Juan activity? My material suggests an answer. It became apparent after repeated observation that there was a compulsive quality to the Don Juan activity. On almost every occasion, just before the patients began this activity, they complained of feelings of "phoniness." In other words, they felt they were imposters. Whatever freedom from anxiety had been secured by the unconscious identification with the mother seemed, under the circumstances, in danger of being undone. A further step was required to buttress the effects achieved by the mechanism of identification. In these instances, acting out served to consolidate the effects of the defensive identification with the mother.

The situation may be compared with the dynamics of certain types of pseudologia fantastica as described by Fenichel (1939). He points out that certain liars operate according to the following principle: "It frightens me when I realize, as I must, that so and so is true (usually the reality of the female genital). I cannot lie to myself. I cannot believe my own lie. However, if I can get someone else to believe my lie, maybe I will not have to be frightened." It is an example of denial by proxy. Something similar happens in transvestism. Deceiving others may have the reassuring quality usually connected with deceiving oneself (Fenichel, 1930).

REVIEW OF THE LITERATURE

Kanzer (1957) has made the point that acting out was originally described in terms of resistance but the emphasis today is more on ego functioning, generally. It is in the latter context that I shall speak of acting out in this paper. An extensive bibliography of the literature on acting out exists (Greenacre, 1963), and I will merely point to several of the antecedent writings on this subject which are particularly pertinent.

Freud (1914b) in speaking of acting out, states, "the patient reproduces instead of remembering." Fenichel (1954) described disturbances of orality in the early months of life as giving an important etiological background to the future actor. Altman (1957) stressed the oral basis of acting out, noting a "peculiar reverberating circuit"—a type of mutual identification between the patient and his mother. He found that the augmentation of the instinct makes defense impossible—"the only course open as in the case of the traumatic dream, which repeats an overwhelming experience in order to find a way to dispel and overcome it, is for repeated acting out." He also noted the similarity of these patients to the addict. The facility of these patients for fleeting and indiscriminate relationships has been noted by many authors, and has been considered a correlate of a tendency to multiple and transient identifications.

Johnson and Szurek (1949, 1952) showed renewed interest in superego aspects of the problem. They stressed that in individuals with superego lacunae, these lacunae were based on a specific relationship with one or both parents, namely that these patients acted out the unconscious conflicts of the parent. Bird (1957) found symbiotic relationships between mother and child, as well as incomplete differentiation between the child's ego and that of the mother. Deutsch (1955) stated that acting out may represent accumulation of anxiety and aggressiveness, mobilized by transference, creating in these patients increased tension which has to be discharged in periodic attacks, analogously to what occurs in addicts. Kanzer emphasized (1957) the significance of successful identifications to strengthen internalizing and sublimating tendencies, rather than acting out. Spiegel (1954) stressed the prominence of a sense of humiliation which is being warded off by acting out. Wangh and Beres (1959) have noted that there is a reciprocal relation between phobia and acting out—as long as the patient acted out his impulses, he did not have the phobia. The authors have also mentioned actual seduction in early life as often playing a role in both kinds of phenomena.

Greenacre (1950, 1958, 1963), noting these factors, speaks also of those situations where speech has been deformed or devalued as being a possible additional element in certain cases of acting out. In discussing a type of patient similar to those I will discuss, who acts out in the transference, she profiles them as having had a peculiar relationship with the parents, characterized by a narcissistic love which leaves their needs unmet. These patients have also frequently been involved in primal scene experiences with resulting intense visual and motor stimulation, and a humiliating sense of having been abandoned by the parents afterwards. Greenacre related the scoptophilia and exhibitionism seen in such patients to imitativeness, which serves the child's need to quickly sense the mood and responsiveness of those around him.

In summary, the literature makes it clear that these persons suffer damage in the phase of separation-individuation, during which there are formed the essential ego capacities to tolerate delay of gratification, to achieve detour of discharge through thought and verbalization, and to synthesize the disparate elements of the personality.

The crucial dynamics in these patients take the form on the one hand of excessive erotic stimulation by parents who use their children either as sources of libidinal gratification or as narcissistic extensions of themselves, or on the other hand, of failure to encourage age-appropriate toleration of frustration by parents who project their own unresolved oral difficulties onto thereby overindulged children. In both cases, there is interference in the process of individuation. In more severe, chronic cases, there is prolonged and massive deprivation or traumatization, occurring as Greenacre suggests, at or before the onset of communicative speech. Thus overwhelmed by stimuli they cannot contend with through verbal discharge, or autoplastic modification, these children achieve tension reduction and return to homeostasis through activity.

This review of the literature, highlighting the factors which predispose to acting out, corresponds to my patients' experiences. An examination of the data, however, suggested an additional factor which has not been commented on previously in the literature —a factor which contributed to these patients' need for real experiences, and it is to this factor that I would like to call attention. This element impressed itself on me in connection with subjective feelings common to both patients. In the course of their defensive endeavors to ward off anxiety, it became apparent to the patients themselves, that the system of defense that they had erected was not operating effectively. This system of defense relied heavily upon identification with an aggrandized ego-ideal, the failure of which was indicated by feelings of imposture. The sense of being an impostor would be followed by acting out. Successful acting out served to negate in these patients their nagging sense of doubt about the stability of their identifications. They required realistic confirmation from other people in order to convince themselves of the stability of their identifications. The episode of acting out confirmed this, and in this way acted as a secondary system of defense to buttress the other mechanisms of warding off anxiety.

CASE REPORTS

Case 1

The patient, Paul L, was the youngest of four children, born to a Greek father and French mother. A successful and responsible young man, married and the father of a child, he entered analysis at 30, suffering from depression intensified by the birth of his son, and his marriage on the verge of divorce.

Within three months after marriage, he began the first of what were to be numerous and continual extramarital adventures. His wife's sexual frigidity served as a rationalization for these excursions, but it became clear that they were essentially unrelated to her sexual problems. The relationship with the "other woman" was primarily a narcissistic one for the patient. He was proud of his sexual performance, proud especially of his phallus, and eager to have it admired by the woman. He had no concern for her beyond his immediate sexual interest. The feeling of being "close to the brink"—of coming close to the edge of danger, but surviving despite all odds—was an important feature of the adventure for him. There was always a feeling of intense excitement and curious "aliveness" in these encounters—more so than in everyday life.

The patient's father was a hard-working and extremely successful man, large, personable and influential in his community and church. He had risen from the ranks, succeeding in a predominantly Jewish business field although he was not Jewish. The family lived in Jewish neighborhoods throughout the patient's childhood, and he identified himself with Jewish boys, feeling that he "looked Jewish." He wished that he had been circumcised.

When the patient was two years of age, his father became ill with a heart condition, and from then until his death when the patient was 10, this illness was a most significant feature of the boy's life. His father's "weak heart" was continually referred to with alarm. The illness kept the father preoccupied and perpetually removed from the patient. It was Paul's feeling that the illness served as an excuse for his father to ignore him, inasmuch as he did continue many other activities, and from the patient's point of view, did not appear ill. When the father died, the patient consciously felt angry about being deserted. He experienced no grief.

Paul's mother was an ineffectual, disorganized and indecisive woman, who had emotionally deserted Paul in his childhood. Her husband's illness served to remove her attention from the patient, even more than had been the case prior to that when she passed him off to be cared for by his sister, A., and by hired nurses. She left for Florida when he was three, because of depression resulting from her husband's illness, and stayed a number of months, leaving him to be cared for by a nurse. In later childhood, she neglected and disappointed him frequently, for example, invariably failing to show up for school functions.

The narcissistic nature of his value for his mother was clear. He recalls in adolescence being told by her that she had observed him masturbating, and that she thought he "had a nice penis." A screen memory was further indicative of his exhibitionistic value for her: he recalled that she compelled him to wear a costume for a school play that exposed his genitals, and became furious with him because he expressed feelings of humiliation. She was noticeably seductive with him: on several occasions before his father's death he was allowed by her to come into her bed, and as late as age nine, she would put his feet between her naked thighs "to warm them." Despite her neglect of him, he was aware that he was her favorite, in preference to his sisters. Family legend had it that he was "mother's baby." In adult life, she took excessive pride in exhibiting his professional status to her friends.

Always indulging him, she failed particularly to set a moral climate in the home. The patient recalls that she readily falsified absence notes if he wanted to play hookey from school, and that she permitted his sisters sexual license in the home, to the point of not discouraging sexual intercourse in the unlighted parlor while the family was home.

The patient's castration anxiety was intense: there was transvestism in childhood. To the family's delight Paul would dress up as a little girl at family parties and do a "striptease." After marriage he had a homosexual relationship with a weak, ineffectual man of whom he was contemptuous. Fantasies in this experience related to incorporation of the phallus. The homosexual acts were carried out under circumstances where disastrous exposure was a likelihood. With his wife, sexuality represented worshipful acceptance of his phallus by her—or alternately, rejection of it, which constituted a narcissistic humiliation, and led to feelings of depression.

The patient's career was unfailingly successful, and characterized by diligent hard work. This notwithstanding, he was plagued by feelings of inadequacy. Intermittently, he would become dissatisfied with his progress and achievement, and feel "like an impostor." He was extremely competitive with rivals. With his superiors he had a characteristic relationship: he attempted to get close to them, but clearly this was designed for the purpose of usurping their position.

Analysis

Let us focus first on Paul L.'s relationship with his father. The strong father of Paul's early childhood was suddenly cut down by illness and became unavailable as a figure of male strength with whom he could safely identify. The death of his father when Paul was 10 put to a close a long history of cardiac invalidism that began when Paul was two, but which left him with an intensified castration anxiety.

It is clear from various fantasies produced in analysis that the patient originally had feeling of awe about father's phallus, as well as an intense feeling of inferiority in comparison to him. Derivatives of his feelings of awe towards the inflated phallus-father persisted

in later life, manifested among other symptoms in passive homosexual trends. Character attitudes derivative of this phase of early
life were a sullen submission to men who could be viewed as being
stronger than he, coupled with fantasies or actual attempts to
undermine them and steal their strength. Initially expecting too
much from his idols, he would quickly find their feet of clay.

This archaic image of the phallus of the father was supplanted
by one of an inferior, deprecated phallus—stemming from the image
of the invalid father of later days.

The feeling of imposture, of attempting to supersede his father,
appeared consistently in fantasy, dream and acting out. In a dream
at the time of his son's birth

> . . . there was a case of mistaken identity. I was being evaluated as an
> All-American, although I hadn't played football in years, and was really
> not a good player at all. I hoped to be mistaken for a star player.
> Throughout I had the anxious feeling I would be found out. We were
> in a single line that led to three portals. Those who had excellent
> records were directed to door 9.

This is a dream of rebirth, in which the patient is identified with
the grandiose, phallic father, but fears he will be discovered to be
an impostor.

The transference contained numerous expressions of the impos-
turish identification with the powerful father. He would place his
coat over the analyst's desk chair, and after speaking of what he
considered to be the analyst's huge income, he substituted his
name for the analyst's in paying his bill.

The identification with the inflated image of the father could
not be persistently maintained however. Fantasies and dreams
showed that he attacked the possessor of the large penis or breast,
destroyed or minimized it, and feared retaliatory attack. The
memory that the respected father of a friend had been discovered
to be an abortionist resulted in the patient's developing feelings of
unreality on the couch. It would appear that the attack upon the
archaic ego-ideal annihilated the object. However, since there
was magical identification (fusion) with the phallus-father, destruc-

tion of him was equivalent to destruction of himself, and that annihilation appeared clinically as a feeling of unreality.

The patient underwent shifting oscillating transformations of his self-image and object-image. Identification with the inflated phallic father was accompanied by feelings of grandiosity, while the destruction of this image, and identification as the castrated father, or mother, was equivalent to feelings of the most intense worthlessness.

In order to maintain intact the reparative identification with father's omnipotent phallus, this patient resorted to reinforcing experiences in the real world. Sexual acting out served the purpose of attempting to undo the painful feelings of imposture resulting from his inability to sustain his identification with the phallic father:

> I stop feeling like a little boy when I act out—I have the sudden feeling of being a man, and in control. I work towards manipulating the girl. I'm living an episode of being a man. To the girl I'm a man, and not a boy. You know my approach to the girl is not sexual, it's fatherly and protective. I'm being strong, someone that they'll adore. Maybe it's acting out the feeling I had at father's death. Mother was totally inadequate.

The requirement for reality was also related to a tendency towards fusion, which was a concomitant of his identification with the archaic ego-ideal.

Let me first establish the nature of the patient's tendency to fusion. A nightmare stemming from age five reveals aspects of this in the childhood neurosis:

> There was a colored disc, on a plunger. As it turned around it looked like a circle going into the center. It's a vortex. In the dream, the whole dream area, like a movie screen, was taken up by a man's face. He was death, or the devil, and was going to harm me. I awakened and was taken into mother's bed.

Connected to this nightmare, which took place at the time of his tonsillectomy, were thoughts of being buried, swallowed up, and anaesthetized to have his tonsils taken out. He was guilty at being in mother's bed after surgery, and had the thought, "I'm father."

He had the conscious fantasy "If I fuse with another person, he's inside me and can't be outside to attack me." On certain occasions in the analysis, when he entertained fantasies of the analyst as an omnipotent and idealized phallic figure, he began to have feelings of vertigo, described as "spinning like a top." These came on when he was making comparisons between himself and the analyst, at a point when his image of the analyst shifted from his being inferior and worthless, to his being grandiose and powerful, and were connected with thoughts of seeing the analyst's phallus. These feelings of unreality represented fusion with the grandiose ego-ideal (the phallic father) and consequent loss of a sense of self.

A variant of this was what has been called the "pleasant surprise" phenomenon. At times, he would have the feeling that the analyst was not present. Upon arising from the couch, he would be "surprised" to see the analyst. Here the patient was defending himself against his wish to destroy and supersede the analyst-father, and was "pleasantly surprised" to see that he had not been annihilated.

Because of this tendency towards fusion, and the concomitant disturbance in the sense of reality, this patient required *actual* experience for purposes of defense. Sexual acting out represented one such type of actual experience. It was also demonstrated in the transference:

> . . . before I leave a session I like to look at you face to face—to make some trenchant comment. You suddenly become very real. I could touch you. You are not just a voice.

The patient's relationship with his narcissistic mother represented the other major area of disturbance. Already unable to provide for Paul's needs, she was pulled even further from him after his father was stricken, and intensified Paul's attachment to her by her very lack of responsiveness to his needs. This danger—lack of maternal response—was the forerunner of subsequent reactions of intense feelings of humiliation in similar situations. He was wholly intolerant of such narcissistic injury, and it contributed significantly to the disturbance of his sense of an independent self.

The mother's intense castration anxiety led her to set upon the patient the requirement that he serve as the embodiment of her missing phallus. In a dream he is

> . . . trying to seduce someone who was a virgin, attempting to have intercourse with her in a bathroom. Another male was present. I tried to do it standing up. The bathroom was like where I saw my brother's penis. I saw the glans and he said he couldn't tell me why it didn't look like mine.
>
> I wanted her to put one leg up on the toilet and I'd penetrate her. She was dressed. I undressed her. She had no breasts, it was like a man's chest—slighter than mine. She had a flat abdomen, but a female escutcheon and genitals. I was shocked! I said "NO!"

The feeling of unreality at visualization of the female genital is demonstrated, as well as his fantasy of restoring the phallus by intercourse. It is significant that the dream followed a typical incident of sexual acting out. The castration anxiety implicit in this female identification with the mother was handled either by endowing her in fantasy with the phallus, or by acting out his intuitively sensed awareness that mother wished him to be her phallus.

It was clear that in acting out, this patient was living out an exhibitionistic fantasy. He exposed himself in an extremely injudicious manner in the course of his sexual escapades, while at the same time behaving as though "he could not be seen." This expressed both the fantasy that the unacceptable female genital that he had observed was "unreal" as well as his need to deny that "unreal" genital by his exhibitionistic demonstration of himself as the "real phallus" in his acting out. The feeling of unreality stemming from identification with the mother's phallus required the defense of "being believed in by others."

The mother's indulgence and exhibitionism ultimately destroyed her effectiveness as a model for superego as well as ego identifications. Prohibitions and the means of control necessary for an in-

Seymour C. Post

ternalized resolution of instinctual demands were markedly absent.

Case 2

Sam W. was a 24-year-old professional man, who came for treatment with complaints of intense anxiety and various phobias —fear of travelling, elevators, social meetings, tunnels, and psychosis.

The phenomenon under investigation was briefly alluded to in a description of a related phenomenon (Post, 1964). The reader is referred to this earlier paper for details of the developmental history and psychodynamics of this patient. I will restrict myself here to a brief summary of that data, and to delimiting aspects of the case material which pertain to the problem at hand.

The symptom of promiscuous escapades began shortly after the patient's marriage. These were characterized by the patient's arranging to meet a woman with whom he had some glancing contact—in the subway, on the street, or in the course of his work. There was always intense apprehension prior to the tryst, which itself was characterized by lack of warmth and relatedness. There was only a sexual interchange—but that was most often of a nongenital nature. It was of special importance for him to *touch* the woman, even if it was only a fleeting gesture. On occasion he would passively submit to fellatio. Whenever possible he avoided intercourse, which frightened him in these encounters as it did with his wife. There was considerable guilt after each such incident, following which the patient would soon repeat the entire experience, and usually with another woman, since he rarely saw this kind of partner more than once. There was a heightened excitement and feeling of being more intensely alive than usual during the escapade.

The developmental history revealed the patient's mother to be an intensely narcissistic woman, whose fear of castration was expressed in an identification with the patient. The symbiotic relationship with him was illustrated by her requirement for him at the time of her mental hospitalization when he was three, and also by her hypochondriacal concern about him. She considered him her phallus, which she had lost at his birth. The father was de-

264 ·

valued and denigrated by the mother, and the patient put in his place. She spent long hours talking to him in childhood, and in the course of this described to him her fantasies of promiscuity and prostitution. The mother was given to explosive outbursts, often as a defense against her guilt feelings, and would storm out of the house, threatening to become a prostitute, saying that she would never return; the terrified patient would pursue her, begging her to return. There was a frightening tonsillectomy at age three, with terror of the anaesthesia; this fear remained with him as a symptom into adult life. There was also an early traumatic viewing of the mother's genital. The patient suffered a severe fear of success, and had intense feelings of being an impostor. An aspect of his fear of success was his relationship with his partner, which closely paralleled his symbiotic relationship with his mother: he supported the partner, who got a feeling of illusory strength and power from the alliance, and tried to pass off the patient's brilliant work as his own. A similar symbiotic relationship existed with his wife: he had attempted to become dependent upon her, but she became increasingly dependent, demanding and hypochondriacal. A marked tendency to identify characterized the patient. This was expressed in many ways: he identified with his mother through the affect of anxiety, through a fear of sleep, and loss of control; he also identified with her through prostitution, which she had openly expressed as a wish and threatened to act out. Concerning the latter, he had the fantasy that if he walked in the street he would meet a man wearing a wig—a man masquerading as a prostitute. (It is of some interest that the mother was bald and wore a wig.)

The mother's narcissistic preoccupation with the patient intensified an already existing fear of loss of the mother. A feeling of oneness with her was strong. The patient defended against the danger of loss of the mother by the aforesaid identification—notably by the affect of anxiety and prostitution fantasies.

The following dream is significant.:

There was a woman I see periodically. As I come to meet her she's affable. Suddenly she pulls out a knife. I'm stunned. The police and detectives are there.

There is one segment of an island here, and one segment there. A strip of land connects them. As I make a trip over the strip of land, I meet Carol, my friend's wife. I'm surprised. She's deceiving my friend—committing adultery. She discards her wedding ring.

Associations: I keep aloof. I have no emotional involvement with the women I meet. Carol almost ran off with a tennis pro. She's been promiscuous. I feel sexually frustrated. I think I'll go to a prostitute. I lost my wedding ring.

This is a caput medusa dream—in which the patient reveals his "stunned" reaction to first observing mother's absence of a penis. His defense is to endow her with the phallus in the dream. The first dream reveals the original trauma and the resulting castration anxiety—the second makes clear the fantasy established in defense, which emerged as the symptom of acting out: "mother is going out as a prostitute to get a penis." The patient is identified with her, indicated by the lost wedding ring, and the link of promiscuity. He believed that women thrived on sex, that they "suck a man dry," and that prostitutes become strong from intercourse. In these fantasies, as in the wig fantasy, he showed his unconscious wish to give the phallus back to mother, by which he strove to insure himself against castration anxiety. The "prostitute-mother" fantasy served both his mother's and his own requirement for the acquisition of a penis. The female genital is denied—seen as "unreal" in this dream, and in other contexts. The contribution of this element in the patient's mental life to acting out will be discussed later.

There was an intensification of infantile narcissism, attributable not only to his symbiotic relationship with his mother, but also to the *carte blanche* he was given to supersede his father:

I think of my father's castrated manner. He had nothing. I was his replacement. She used me instead of him. I replaced him *really!* And because of that I feared revenge. She wanted more of me than I could give. She needed this bloated image of me. I was supposed to be Superman, and redeem her. I became the All-American boy as a result. Every time she bragged about me I shut her up. I was idealized in her mind. She could identify me as a conqueror. I was very anxious as a kid, with the feeling that I was too big for my britches. I was saying too much, doing too much—and my father couldn't even write! Mother loved me achieving any kind of success, more than anything in the world, but I find that whatever I get becomes worthless. If I want a suit, and get it, it becomes worthless instantly.

I was better than my father, therefore I could be of use to her. I could arrange a symbiotic situation with her. I could bargain with her because I had something to offer. If not, she would have destroyed me too!

The patient's mother fostered an identification as her grandiose phallus. The supersedence of the father also contributed to the patient's narcissism, and further served to undermine his sense of reality while predisposing him to real experience to defend both against castration anxiety and the fear of being devoured. Feelings of worthlessness were dealt with by identification with this inflated archaic ego-ideal as mother's phallus. However, the feeling of *being* the magnificent phallic-mother would periodically break down, and the fusion turned into its opposite, as the uncontrollable aggression destroyed the glorified object. There was a characteristic oscillation between phallic grandiosity and hypochondriacal anxieties and depression. Thus, the patient's identification with the inflated archaic mother-phallus could be threatened at times, and required reality for substantiation:

When I go out after a strange woman, I have to have a "brief touch." Figuratively and literally I have to have a real touch. I get a feeling of renewing contact with my mother when I do this. I also give my mother contact with me. That is some way reassures me. I feel that even though I solicit the contact, the woman derives the benefit. It reminds me of my responsibilities for mother. That way I could preserve her. I strengthened her—and often it happened on the street. The street figured prominently. Often she would lament to me about her fate, on the street, and I would have to reassure her. I was to be her sustenance, her provider, her great friend. By giving myself to mother I kept her from running away.

The patient required real experience, as reassurance both for himself and mother, that the mutual identification as the inflated phallic-ideal still existed. This could be achieved by sharing a real affect with her, such as anxiety, or by the real experience of sexual acting out.

The fear of fusion implicit in this identification however, served as another factor leading the patient towards real experience, in order to avoid feelings of unreality. The attempt to fulfill oedipal wishes and restore mother's phallus are expressed in the wish to enter mother. However, insofar as this reactivates the wish to fuse with her regressively, conflicts against being devoured are instituted —in this instance taking the form of a need for real experience to avoid feelings of unreality.

DISCUSSION

In the narcissistic neuroses, in contrast to the symptom neuroses where the conflict is dealt with in fantasy, i.e., intrapsychically, there is a general tendency for real experience. The environment has to be brought in by the patient in his attempt to deal with his anxiety. These patients require narcissistic supplies from the environment, consequently they are notoriously vulnerable, since the environment cannot be controlled. Because the sense of self is fragile, there is often the need for contact with another person —as Deutsch has pointed out in her description of the "as if" patient. In particular, feelings of worthlessness require continual testing of the environment. Only brilliant men and beautiful women (and as Deutsch (1955) notes, saints and psychotics) can meet the demands of the archaic ego-ideal—but even in these instances there is a tendency for the level of aspiration to be raised, so that the patient continues to feel a gap between ego-ideal and aspiration.

Reich (1960), elaborating some of Jacobson's (1954) ideas in the area of narcissism, has described a pattern of defense against feelings of worthlessness which is characteristic of one type of narcissistic neurosis. Briefly stated, in these patients defense occurs by identification with the archaic ego-ideal. The two patients I have presented are instances of this type of narcissistic neurosis—

one, Paul, a character neurotic, who might have become a case of perversion under unfavorable conditions, and the other, Sam, a borderline case. What I am describing in my patients is the temporary failure of that identification with the archaic ego-ideal to provide relief against feelings of worthlessness, and the attempt to buttress the identification by real experience. The fact that the identification is at best transitory results in a characteristic feeling of imposture.

I have described in both of my patients a tendency to regress to states of fusion. It is my belief that the clinical data demonstrate that as a consequence, the need for real objects to avoid feelings of unreality is increased, and there occurs a tendency to action in "the real world." [1] In this respect, the need for an actual experience to ward off the danger of castration and/or separation, and of being devoured, can be compared to the comments which Lewin (1950) has made concerning the need of the fetishist for an actual experience which serves to deny the danger of castration—and the desperate need of the hypomanic for any kind of object ties, no matter how tenuous, in order to ward off the danger of loss of the object.

Reich points out that early traumatization of the ego results in a predisposition to react in an infantile way to later danger situations. The imagined danger is taken for reality—something that has already happened. The only defense is to use methods available to the infantile ego, especially magic denial. This regressive return to compensatory narcissistic fantasy is based on primitive identifications with idealized infantile objects, which are actually primitive ego-ideals, and may occur as isolated lacunae in otherwise well-functioning personalities.

[1] This portion of the present paper, the concept of acting out as a defense against feelings of unreality, based on a fear of fusion, was orginally described in a paper entitled "Anxiety Because of the Absence of Anxiety," which was read in December 1963 before the American Psychoanalytic Association Mid-Winter Meeting.

The published version of that paper (Post, 1964) was limited to the phenomenon of re-evocation of anxiety as a defense against loss and castration of the object. It was left to the present paper to include the concept of acting out as a defense against fear of fusion in a wider discussion of the requirement for reality in such patients.

In the interim, a corroborative account of the relationship between acting out and fear of fusion has appeared (Angel (1965), Loss of Identity and Acting Out, *J. Amer. Psa. Assn.*, Vol. 13).

Drives toward oral or anal incorporation of the admired object prevail, resulting in feelings of *being* the object temporarily. With growing ego differentiation, the child becomes increasingly aware of his smallness, as well as his separateness from objects, hence the still completely sexualized and glorified object is set up as a primitive ego-ideal. Under unfavorable circumstances, the boundaries between this ideal and the self-image blur again. Repair is achieved again by magic fusion—the patient feels as if he *were* his own ego-ideal, the magnificent phallic parent. Feelings of powerlessness necessitate continuous reparative measures, and a turning away from objects to an overvaluation of the body or particular organs. An important example of this is the body-phallus equation, which clearly represents fusion between self and object image. The grandiosity previously attributed to the object now belongs to the self.

It is at this point in the process that the phenomenon that I am describing occurs: these patients now require real experience, rather than symptom formation, in their attempts to defend themselves against the effects of intense castration or separation anxiety, or fear of being devoured.

Both patients exhibited a type of Don Juanism—sexual love conquest—the purpose of which was to cope with feelings of worthlessness by buttressing an identification with an idealized phallic object.

The first patient, Paul, intensely attached to the mother because of her symbiotic interest in him, and the absence of the father through illness and then death, developed an intensification of infantile narcissism, and loss of a sense of separate self. Identification with the devalued, castrated mother, or the sick, castrated father —and the castration anxiety and failing sense of reality implicit in that identification—was defended against by a reparative identification with the inflated phallic-father, an identification which was unstable, and at times required substantiation by reality, which occurred in incidents of sexual love conquest. The tendency towards fusion, a concomitant of the identification with the archaic phallic father, lent weight to the requirement for reality, as a defense against feelings of unreality.

A somewhat similar mechanism operated in Sam W. This patient had a primitive tie to mother, by identification. The maintenance of that tie was essential, but could not be persistently effected. When he felt that tie to be threatened, he needed some actual experience which either denied the rupture with mother or attempted to make up the loss. This could be accomplished by the re-evocation of the affect of anxiety or by real experience, as in sexual acting out, which similarly represented the buttressing of his identification with the inflated archaic ego-ideal, the phallic mother. Intensification of infantile narcissism, fostered by mother's interest in him, favoring fantasy, and the identification with the phallus of the mother, undermined the sense of reality, thereby predisposing him to real experience, which expressed in action the wish to acquire a phallus for mother as a prostitute.

The exhibitionistic defense suggested by mother was another factor in the overdetermined necessity towards acting out. Sam W. was required by his mother to be a living demonstration of her illusory phallus. The feeling of "being believed in by others," in addition to gratifying the exhibionistic demonstration of oneself as "a real phallus," served to heighten these patient's failing sense of reality. This accounts for the excitement of the escapade, and the associated feeling of being more than usually "alive." It might be recalled that both patients perceived the female genital as "unreal"—remember those dreams in each patient where he is "stunned" by the sight of that genital. As a comment on their need to act out, the suggestion can be made that this is so additionally because of their need for real sensory experience to negate the impression of the "unreal" female genital.

In passing, I must make allusion to those other obvious factors which contributed to a tendency of these patients to act out: lack of a proper matrix for the development of stable ego identifications, with the formation of primitive magical identifications; the development of omnipotent fantasy and a defective sense of reality; maternal rejection, requiring these patients to seek actual response from the environment; and the requirement set upon this kind of patient by defects in the maternal superego, for him to establish for himself actual prohibitions in the outer world. All of these factors have been described previously in the literature, and I mention them only for the sake of completeness.

It will be noted that these patients show in encapsulated and occult fashion, features markedly similar to those that have been described as being characteristic for cases of pathological imposture (Greenacre, 1959). The question arises as to what differences, if any, exist between these patients and cases of overt imposture. My observations suggest that the difference between these patients who have a strong *feeling* of imposture, and the *actual* impostor, is largely a function of the nature of the identification with the archaic ego-ideal; i.e., in the former, it is only a transitory one.

Like the overt impostor, these patients "endeavor to eliminate the friction between the exaggerated ego-ideal and the other devalued, inferior guilt-laden part of the ego in a manner which is characteristic for them: they behave as if the ego-ideal is identical with the self, and the patient needs everyone to acknowledge his status. Even though the inner voice of his devalued ego on the one hand, and the reactions of the outside world on the other remind him of the unreality of his ego ideal, the patient still clings to this narcissistic position. He desperately tries through pretending and under cover of someone else's name, to maintain his ego-ideal, and force it upon the world" (Deutsch, 1955, p. 503). Unlike the impostor, however, these patients are unable to succeed at this maneuver. One might say that they attempt unsuccessfully what the impostor succeeds at: whatever the impostor is trying to ward off is successfully defended against by the imposture, i.e., by the identification with the archaic ego-ideal. My patients however, who have a *feeling* of imposture, are also trying to ward off a danger by identification with the archaic ego-ideal, but never quite feel they achieve it.

SUMMARY

Two patients were analyzed who had a clinical pattern of repeated Don Juan experiences. Closer examination of the data revealed this to be related to the need to fend off certain anxieties, namely, castration anxiety, the fear of separation, and the fear of fusion.

The question as to why these conflicts led to this characteristic type of acting out as opposed to symptom formation was raised. An examination of the data suggested a factor not previously commented on in the literature, which contributed to the need for real experiences. In the course of their defensive endeavors to ward off anxiety, it became apparent to the patients themselves, that the system of defense they had erected was not operating effectively. This system of defense relied heavily upon identification with an aggrandized ego-ideal, and failure of this defense was indicated by feelings of imposture. This sense of being an impostor was followed by acting out. Successful acting out served to negate in these patients their nagging sense of doubt about the stability of their identifications. They required *realistic* confirmation from other people in order to convince themselves of the stability of their identifications. The episode of acting out confirmed this, and in this way acted as a secondary system of defense to buttress the other mechanisms of warding off anxiety.

In addition, the undermining of the sense of self, and the tendency to regress to a state of fusion, a concomitant of identification with the archaic ego-ideal, also led to the need for real experience to restore a sense of reality.

BIBLIOGRAPHY

Altman, L. (1957), On the oral nature of acting out. *J. Amer. Psychoanal. Assn.*, 5:648-663.
Arlow, J. A. (1959), The structure of the *déjà vu* experience. *J. Amer. Psychoanal. Assn.*, 7:611–632.
Bird, B. (1957), A specific peculiarity of acting out. *J. Amer. Psychoanal. Assn.*, 5:630–648.
Deutsch, H. (1955), The impostor. Contributions to ego psychology of a type of psychopath. *Psychoanal. Quart.*, 24:483–506.
Fenichel, O. (1930), The psychology of transvestism. In: *The Collected Papers of Otto Fenichel* 2:167–181. New York: Norton, 1954.
—— (1939), The economics of pseudologia phantastica. In: *The Collected Papers of Otto Fenichel*, 2:129–141. New York: Norton, 1954.

Seymour C. Post

_____ (1945), Neurotic acting out. In: *The Collected Papers of Otto Fenichel*, 2:296–304. New York: Norton, 1954.

Freud, S. (1914a) On narcissism. *Standard Edition*, 14:73–102. London: Hogarth Press, 1957.

_____ (1914b), Remembering, repeating and working through. *Standard Edition*, 12:145–156 London: Hogarth Press, 1958.

Greenacre, P. (1950), General problems of acting out. *Psychoanal. Quart.*, 19:455–467.

_____ (1958), The impostor. *Psychoanal. Quart.*, 27:359–383.

_____ (1963), Problems of acting out in the transference relationship. *J. Amer. Acad. Child. Psychiat.*, 2:144–175.

Jacobson, E. (1954), The self and the object world. *The Psychoanalytic Study of the Child*, 19:75–127. New York: International Universities Press.

Johnson, A. M. (1949), Sanctions for sugerego lacunae for adolescents. In: *Searchlights on Delinquency*, ed. K. R. Eissler. New York: International Universities Press, pp. 225–236.

_____ and Szurek, S. (1952), The genesis of antisocial acting out in children and adults. *Psychoanal. Quart.*, 21:323–342.

Kanzer, M. (1957), Acting out, sublimation and reality testing. *J. Amer. Psychoanal. Assn.*, 5:663–685.

Lewin, B. (1950), *The Psychoanalysis of Elation*. New York: Norton.

Post, S. C. (1964), The re-evocation of anxiety by its absence. *Psychoanal. Quart.*, 23:526–536.

Reich, A. (1960), Pathologic forms of self-esteem regulation. *The Psychoanalytic Study of the Child*, 15:215–235. New York: International Universities Press.

Spiegel, L. (1954), Acting out and instinctual gratification. *J. Amer. Psychoanal. Assn.*, 2:107–119.

Wangh, M. (1960), The structural determinants of phobia. *J. Amer. Psychoanal. Assn.*, 7:675–696.

_____ and Beres. Phobia and acting out. Unpublished.

15. Volition and Value:

A Study Based on Catatonic Schizophrenia

SILVANO ARIETI, M.D.

IN THE FIRST part of this paper I shall illustrate some of the terminal phases of that great evolutionary process which first gave autonomous movement to the animal organism, then coordinated motion, finally resulting in voluntary acts and moral deeds. I shall discuss these phases also in relation to their ontogenetic counterparts. In the second part of this paper I shall make an attempt to show how catatonic schizophrenia represents the most dramatic disintegration of this developmental process. This will be illustrated with a case report.

Lest I am misunderstood, my references to phylogenetic mechanisms are not attempts to explain, in Jungian fashion, the dynamics of psychopathological conditions occurring in our time. Phylogenetic and ontogenetic studies are important in studying the structural or formal mechanisms, or the similarities between the various patterns of development, but not for the analysis of content or motivation.

The first movements that we must study in relation to motor actions are no longer the reflexes, as we did until a few years ago, but the so-called autorhythmic movements (Lorenz, 1954; von-Holst, 1936), spontaneous movements of the organism from which

Portions of this paper appeared originally in *Comprehensive Psychiatry*, Vol. 2, April 1961.

eventually reflexes or fixed patterns of responses emerge in evolution. But neither autorhythmic movements nor reflexes can be regarded as real volitional acts.

The first real volitional act is an inhibition, or at least an inhibition of a reflex response. For instance, during toilet training, the baby has the impulse to defecate when the rectum is distended by the passage of feces. The child, however, learns not to yield to the impulse and to postpone defecation in spite of the fact that it would be more pleasant to do so. He learns to control his sphincters because his ability to do so will affect his relation with mother. Obviously he has the neurophysiologic potentiality for sphincter control, but such control, inasmuch as it affects the people in his environment, is not purely a physiological act; it is also a social one. Furthermore, in order to control himself, he must inhibit the still available simpler and more pleasant physiological mechanisms of immediate defecation.

His first act of will is thus at the same time an inhibition and a compliance to the will ᶜᶠ others. It seems almost a paradoxical contradiction, just as paradoxical as negativism is a little later, an assertion of the emerging will (Arieti, 1955). But will is a very complicated and portentous function, and like many other complicated functions appears to originate from what at first seems its opposite, just as logical thought originates from what at first seems its opposite: irrational thought. But somebody could object: are acts of inhibition and compliance, as they occur, for instance, in toilet training, really the first voluntary acts? What about those actions of the baby, who toward the fifth or sixth month of life grabs rattles and other objects? Certainly these acts of the baby, like grabbing a rattle, must be included under the large category of conative acts, but actually they are not volitional in a mature sense; they are protovolitional. The baby responds to the stimulus rattle and enjoys the pleasure of the response which later on he seeks again. But there is no choice, not even a minimum of conflict, as there is between pleasing mother and defecating. If the action is a reflex response or, though conative, has the purpose only of maintaining the homeostasis or of producing immediate pleasure, without alternative possibilities, we do not yet have volition, but protovolition.

Inasmuch as these alternative possibilities are at first created by the exposure to the interpersonal situation, the act of will becomes, so to say, socialized. The action loses its primitive characteristic of a purely motor or physiologic mechanism because its outcome is anticipated in relation to the interpersonal world. As Parson (1951) writes, action is concerned not only with the internal structure or processes of the organism, but with the organism as it exists in a sort of relationship. Action has additional dimensions, which may be called at the same time the social and the moral dimensions.

At this early ontogenetic level, volition is not only inhibition but also, as I said before, extreme submission. It is more than submission: it is enormous receptivity to the interpersonal world, necessary for the development of the social self, or, as Erikson (1959) would say, for the epigenesis of the ego. Volition at this stage has some hypnotic qualities and may be related to the phenomenon of hypnosis. It is possible that hypnosis is a more acute artificial reproduction of this stage of life when the child is extremely receptive to the will of others and does not remember who gave the instructions or suggestions. Later on he may rationalize his unconsciously introjected attitudes. The transference is also a repetition of attitudes generally acquired during this period of high receptivity. The origin of the transference is repressed and the phenomenon is rationalized. We have thus that triad of characteristics that Spiegel (1959) considers inherent in the hypnotic situation.

This transient period of suggestibility has more manifest sequels in primitive cultures, where mass hypnosis, voodoo phenomena, and latah are relatively common (Arieti and Meth, 1959). It is perhaps not too difficult to understand the importance of suggestibility in primitive society. As Kelsen (1943) has described, in primitive societies *to do* and *to be guilty* are approximately the same thing. To do is at least potentially to be guilty because often one does not know the event that will follow one's action. The event might even have an effect on the whole tribe, such as an epidemic or drought. When the prevailing way of thinking is ruled not by deterministic or scientific causality, but by what is considered the will of animate things, the will becomes a portentous and frightening weapon. Its possession is liable to make one feel very guilty. But one will not feel very guilty if one accepts the will of others, of the gods, of the collective will of the tribe in a form of almost automatic obedience.

Automatic obedience is not the only way primitive men free themselves from guilt and fear. They also refrain from acting freely; they perform only those acts which are sanctioned by the tribe. For any desired effect, the tribe teaches the individual what act to perform. The life of primitive man is completely regulated by a tremendous number of norms and restrictions. The individual has to follow the ritual for practically everything he does. By performing the act according to the ritual, the primitive believes that he will avoid guilt for the act. These rituals are found again at an ontogenetic level as compulsive acts. The individual, who has not been able to develop his potentiality of acting freely without anxiety or guilt may resort to obsessive-compulsive mechanisms to obviate this anxiety and guilt.

In normal development we find a minimal quantity of compulsive behavior, just as we find traces of autism and of automatic obedience, etc. But in persons whose development was accompanied by excessive anxiety, obsessive-compulsive behavior may remain more pronounced than is normal, and later on, when the individual is confronted by difficulties, obsessive-compulsive patterns may be resorted to again.

Conversely, the psychopathic person does not resort to obsessive behavior. His attempt to remove anxiety will consist in allowing his actions to follow his desires without consideration of the interpersonal world, or of the rightness or wrongness of the act.

The patient who is to become catatonic is generally a person given to fits of overpowering anxiety, especially anxiety connected with the carrying out of some action. He generally does not resort to hypnotic or autohypnotic mechanisms, nor to psychopathic denial of responsibility. When in his life he is confronted with an important challenge or decision which causes him excessive anxiety, he fabricates many obsessive-compulsive mechanisms. But the anxiety may overpower him acutely, and he may not have time to manufacture compulsions. The anxiety will then be experienced as fear and guilt connected with any action and will be generalized to every action, to every movement determined by the will. He has a last resort to avoid these feelings: to fall into catatonic immobility. In stupor the immobility is complete, but in other less pronounced catatonic conditions it is not. The patient follows orders given by others not because he is in a state of automatic obedience of hypnosis, but because these orders are willed by others, and therefore he does not have the responsibility for them. In the state called waxy flexibility he retains the positions imposed by others, even if uncomfortable, because he cannot will to change position.

Insofar as most of these acute catatonic episodes are forgotten by the patient when he recovers, there is a scarcity of reports in the literature about these experiences and their interpretation. I have been able to collect a few rare cases in which full memory was retained, and have reported some of them elsewhere (Arieti, 1955).

I am now going to report the case of John, which bears striking similarities to others I have reported, but which also bears some important differences that, in my opinion, may increase our understanding somewhat of the pathology of volition and value.

Case Report

John is an intelligent professional man in his thirties, Catholic, who was referred to me because of his rapidly increasing anxiety— anxiety which reminded him of the kind he experienced about 10 years previously, when he developed a full catatonic episode. Wanting to prevent a recurrence of the event, he sought treatment.

The following is not a complete report but only a brief history of the patient and a description and interpretation of his catatonic episode as it was reconstructed and analyzed during the treatment.

The patient is one of four children. The father is described as a bad husband, an adventurer who, although a good provider, always caused trouble and home instability. The mother is a somewhat inadequate person, distant from the patient. John was raised more or less by a maternal aunt who lived in the family and acted as a housekeeper.

Early childhood memories are mostly unpleasant for John. He recollects attacks of anxiety going back to his early childhood. He also remembers how he needed to cling to his aunt and how painful it always was to separate from her. The aunt had the habit of undressing in his presence, which provoked in him mixed feelings of sexual excitement and guilt. Between the ages of nine and 10 there was an attempted homosexual relation with his best friend. During his prepuberal period he remembers his desire to look at pictures of naked women, and how occasionally he would surreptitiously borrow some pornographic books or magazines from his father's collection and look at them. Fleeting homosexual desires would also occur occasionally. He masturbated with fantasies of women, but had to stimulate his rectum with his fingers in order to experience, he says, "a greater pleasure." Among the things that he remembers from his early life are also obsessive preoccupations with feces of animals and excretions in general of human beings. He had a special admiration for horses because, "They excreted such beautiful feces coming from such statuesque bodies."

In spite of all these circumstances, John managed to grow more or less adequately, was not too disturbed by the death of his aunt, and did well in school. There were practically no dates with girls until much later in life. After puberty he became very interested in religion, especially in that it provided a method whereby he could control his sexual impulses. Anything connected with sex was considered evil and had to be eliminated. This attitude was in a certain way the opposite of that maintained by one of his sisters, who was leading a very promiscuous life. Several times John considered the possibility of becoming a monk; however, he was discouraged from doing so by a priest he had consulted. When he finished college at the age of 20, he decided to make a complete attempt to remove sex from his life. He also decided to go for a rest and summer vacation at a farm for young men where he would cut trees, enjoy the country, and be far away from the temptations of the city. On this farm, however, he soon became anxious and depressed. He found out that he resented the other fellows more and more. They were rough guys given to the use of profane language. He felt as if he were going to pieces progressively. He remembers that one night he was saying to himself, "I cannot stand it any more. Why am I in this way, so anxious for no reason? I have done no wrong in my whole life. Perhaps I should become a priest or get married." When he was feeling very badly he would console himself by thinking that perhaps what he was experiencing was in accordance with the will of God.

Obsessions and compulsions acquired more and more prominence. The campers had to go chopping wood. This practice became an ordeal for John because he was possessed by doubts. He would think, for instance: "Maybe I should not cut this tree because it is too small. Next year it will be bigger. But if I don't cut this tree another fellow will. Maybe it is better if he cuts it, or maybe that I do so." As he expressed himself, he found himself "doubting and doubting his doubts, and doubting the doubting of his doubts." It was an overwhelming, spreading anxiety. The anxiety gradually extended to every act he had to perform. He was literally possessed by intense terror. One day, while he was in this predicament, he observed another phenomenon which he could not understand. There was a discrepancy between the act he wanted to perform and the action that he really carried out. For instance, when he was undressing he wanted to drop a shoe, and instead he dropped a big log; he wanted to put something in a drawer and instead he threw a stone away. However, there was a similarity between the act that he had wanted and anticipated and the act he actually performed. The same phenomenon appeared in talking. He would utter words, which were not the ones he meant to say, but related to them. Later, however, his actions became more and more disconnected. He was mentally lucid and able to perceive what was happening but he realized he had no control over his actions. Given these circumstances, he worried that he might commit crimes, even kill somebody, and became even more afraid. He was saying to himself: "I don't want to be damned in this world as well as in the other. I am trying to be good and I can't. It is not fair. I may kill somebody when I want a piece of bread." At other times he had different feelings. He felt as if some movement or action he would make could produce disaster not only to himself but to the whole camp. By not acting or moving he was protecting the whole group. He felt that he had become his brother's keeper.

Fear soon became connected with any possible movement. It was so intense as to actually inhibit any movement. He was almost literally petrified. To use his own words, he "saw himself solidifying, assuming statuesque positions." However, he was not always in this condition. As a matter of fact, the following day he could move again and go to chop wood. He had one purpose in mind: to kill himself. He remembers that he was very capable of observing himself, and of deciding that it would be better for him to die than to commit crimes. Accordingly, he climbed a big tree from which he jumped, but received only minor contusions. The other men, who ran to help him, realized that he was mentally ill, and he was soon sent to a psychiatric hospital. He remembers understanding that he was taken to the hospital and being happy about it; at least he was considered sick and not a criminal. But in the hospital he found that he could not move at all. He was like a statue of stone.

There were some actions, however, which could escape this otherwise complete immobility—the actions needed for the purpose of committing suicide. In fact he was sure that he had to die to avoid the terror of becoming a murderer. He had to kill himself before that could happen.

During his hospitalization, John made 71 suicidal attempts. Although he was generally in a state of catatonia he would occasionally perform impulsive acts, such as tearing his strait jacket to pieces and making a rope of it to hang himself. Another time he broke a dish in order to cut the veins of his wrist. At other times he swallowed stones. He was always put under restraint after a suicidal attempt. He remembers, however, understanding everything that was going on. As a matter of fact, his acuity in devising methods for committing suicide seemed sharpened as a result.

When I questioned him further about this long series of suicidal attempts, John added that the most drastic attempts were actually the first 10 or 12. Only these could really have killed him. Later, the suicidal attempts were not very dangerous, consisting of such acts as swallowing a small object or inflicting a small injury on himself with a sharp object. When I asked him whether he knew why he had to repeat these token suicidal attempts, he gave me two reasons. The first was to relieve his feeling of guilt and fulfill his duty of preventing himself from committing crimes. But the second reason, which he discovered during the present treatment, was even stranger. To commit suicide was the only act which he could perform, the only act which would go beyond the barrier of immobility. Thus, to commit suicide was to live; the only act of life left to him.

The patient was given a course of electric shock treatment, the exact number of which could not be ascertained. He improved for about two weeks, but then he relapsed into catatonic stupor interrupted only by additional suicidal attempts. While he was in stupor he remembered a young psychiatrist saying to a nurse, "Poor fellow, so young and so sick. He will continue to deteriorate for the rest of his life." After five or six months of hospitalization his catatonic state became somewhat less rigid and he was able to walk and to utter a few words. At this time he had noticed that a new doctor seemed to take some interest in him. One day this doctor told him, "You want to kill yourself. Isn't there anything at all in life that you want?" With great effort the patient mumbled, "Eat, to eat." In fact, he really was hungry as his immobility prevented him from eating properly, and he was inefficiently spoon-fed. The doctor took him to the patients' cafeteria and told him, "You may eat anything you want." John immediately grabbed a large quantity of food and ate in a ravenous manner. The doctor noticed that John liked soup and told him to take even more soup. From that day on John lived only for the sake of eating. He gained about sixty pounds in a few weeks. When I asked him if he ate so much because he was really hungry, he said, "No, that was only at the beginning. The pleasure in eating consisted partially in grabbing food and putting it into my mouth." Later it was discovered by the attendants that John would not only eat a lot but he would also hoard food in his drawers and under his mattress.

I cannot go into detail about many other interesting episodes which occurred in the course of his illness. John continued to improve and in a few months he was ready to leave the hospital. He was able to make a satisfactory adjustment, to work, and later to go to a professional school where he obtained his Ph.D. On the whole he has managed fairly well until shortly before he decided to come for psychoanalytic treatment.

I shall now attempt an interpretation of these phenomena. It is obvious that John underwent an overpowering increase in anxiety when he went to the camp and was exposed to close homosexual stimulation. His early interpersonal relations had subjected him to great instability and insecurity and had made him very vulnerable to many sources of anxiety. This anxiety, however, retained a propensity to be aroused by or channeled in the pattern of sexual stimulation and inhibition. His personality defenses and cultural background made the situation worse. John was not a psychopath, he was not deprived of that part of the self called social self, conscience or superego; nor could he go against his cultural-religious background as did his philandering father and promiscuous sister. Sex, for him, was evil, and homosexuality much more so. As a matter of fact, homosexual desires were not even permitted to become fully conscious.

When he was about to be overwhelmed by the anxiety, he at first resorted to some of the defenses commonly found in precatatonics. He found refuge in religious feelings. God or religion gave him the order of eliminating sex from his life and of becoming a monk. This may be considered a form of autohypnosis, but as was already mentioned at the beginning of this paper, hypnosis and autohypnosis are not used by catatonics. He resorted, then, to obsessive-compulsive mechanisms. The anxiety, which presumably was at first connected with any action that had something to do with sexual feelings, generalized to practically every action. Incidentally, Ferenczi (1950) has reported similar feelings in one patient. Every action became loaded with a sense of responsibility.

Every willed movement came to be seen not as a function but as a moral issue. Every motion was not considered as a fact but as a value. This primitive generalization of his responsibility extended to ideas of damaging the whole community. By moving he could produce havoc not only to himself but to the whole camp. His feelings were reminiscent of the feelings of cosmic power or negative omnipotence experienced by other catatonics who believe that by acting they may cause the destruction of the universe (Arieti, 1955).

To protect himself at first, John resorted to obsessive thinking and compulsions, as, for instance, when he was cutting trees. But even this defense was not sufficient to dam his anxiety; as a matter of fact, it made the situation worse and gave rise to other symptoms. The first one was the unrelatedness between the act, as anticipated and willed, and the action which followed. But, and this is a point of great importance, at first the actions were not completely unrelated from their anticipation. They were analogic. In other words, two actions, like dropping a shoe and dropping a log, had become psychologically equivalent, i.e., they were identified just because they were similar or had something in common. This fact is, in my opinion, of theoretical importance because it extends to the area of volition or of willed mobility, those characteristics which have already been described in paleologic or analogic thinking of schizophrenics (Arieti, 1955). It would seem to indicate that the same basic formal psychopathological mechanisms apply to every area of the psyche. It may also be connected with neurological studies of motor integration, as recently outlined by Denny-Brown (1960). The analogic movement may be viewed as a "release" or "dedifferentiation or loss of restriction to specific attributes of adequate stimulus."

The reason why the phenomenon of generalized analogic movement escapes notice, and has not to my knowledge been reported in the literature, is to be found in the fact that it is of very transient occurrence. In most patients the symptomatology proceeds rapidly to following stages, e.g., the stage where the actions are completely unrelated to the will, as in catatonic excitement, or the stage in which the actions are all eliminated, as in catatonic

Silvano Arieti

stupor. The catatonic excitement may be the result of two facts. In some cases the patient senses that he is sinking into stupor because he is afraid to act and tries to prevent this occurrence by becoming overactive and submerging himself in a rapid sequence of aimless acts. In other instances the opposite is true and the patient acts, but his actions are so unrelated to the conceived or willed actions as to result in a real "movement-salad," the motor equivalent of word-salad. The patient then has no other resort but to sink into the immobility of the stupor.

In many cases the barrier of immobility is not completely closed. In a very selective way it may allow passage to actions of obedience to the will of others or to some special actions of the patient himself.

In the case of John the actions necessary for the suicidal attempts were allowed to go through. Incidentally, these suicidal attempts in catatonics, accompanied by religious feelings and eventually by stupor, have often led to the wrong diagnosis of the depressed form of manic-depressive psychosis. Kraepelin (1925) himself described suicidal attempts and ideas of sin in catatonics, but did not give to them any psychodynamic significance. What is of particular interest to our case is the fact that the suicidal act eventually became for John the only act of living. It is not possible here to examine in greater detail the therapeutic effect of the encounter of John with the doctor in the hospital. Important is the fact that the doctor gave John permission to eat as much as he wanted. Thus the only previously possible act (of killing oneself) was replaced with one of the most primitive acts of life, nourishing oneself. I have described the placing-into-mouth habit (Arieti, 1945a) in very regressed schizophrenics. In slightly less regressed patients we find the hoarding habit (Arieti, 1945b), a stage John went through in his progress toward recovery. In acute cases of catatonia we often find, in very acute form, symptoms appearing in other types of schizophrenia after many years of regression.

Many other aspects of the interesting case of John cannot be examined for lack of space. However, I feel that by adding what we have learned from John to what has been reported about other cases (Arieti, 1955) some conclusions may be drawn:

(1) Catatonia is predominantly a disorder of the will. It is not a disorder of the motor apparatus.

(2) Contrary to appearance, the state of catatonia is not that of an ivory tower. It is a state where volition is connected with a pathologically intensified sense of value, so that torturing responsibility spreads like fire to every possible act. Such pathological sense of responsibility reaches the acme of intensity when a little movement of the patient is considered capable of destroying the world. Alas! This conception of the psychotic mind reminds us of its possible actuality today, when the pushing of a button may have such cosmic effects! Only the oceanic responsibility of the catatonic could include this heretofore unconceived possibility.

(3) The passivity to the suggestion of others found in some catatonics is not an acceptance of power from others, as in hypnosis, but a relief from responsibility.

(4) Only those actions may go through the catatonic barrier which may compensate or atone for the intensified responsibility. This selectivity is dramatically exemplified in our case report, where only the movements necessary for self-inflicted death penalty could be carried out, but even more than that—where self-inflicted death penalty became the only voluntary movement, thus life itself.

(5) Catatonia appears to present certain phenomena such as the analogic movement which may be related to the general pathological funtioning of the psyche as well as to principles of neurological disorganizations.

(6) The recognition that the catatonic patient is not an ivory tower but, on the contrary, a volcano of not at all petrified feelings, lends itself to possible therapeutic maneuvers, already being implemented in other cases, which will be reported elsewhere.

REFERENCES

Arieti, S. (1945), The placing-into-mouth and coprophagic habits. *J. Nerv. & Ment. Dis.*, 99:959–964.

—— (1945b), Primitive habits in the preterminal stage of schizophrenia. *J. Nerv. & Ment. Dis.*, 102:367–375.

Silvano Arieti

_____ (1955), *Interpretation of Schizophrenia.* New York: Brunner, pp. 109–129.

_____ and Meth, J. (1959), Rare, unclassifiable, collective and exotic psychotic syndromes. In: *American Handbook of Psychiatry,* Vol. 1, ed. S. Arieti. New York: Basic Books, Ch. 7.

Denny-Brown, D. (1960), Motor mechanisms-introduction: the general principles of motor integration. In: *Handbook of Physiology,* Vol. 2, ed. J. Field. Washington: American Physiological Society, p. 781.

Erikson, E. H. (1959) *Identity and the life cycle.* [*Psychological Issues,* Monogr. 1]. New York: International Universities Press.

Ferenczi, S. (1950), Some clinical observations on paranoia and paraphrenia. In: *Sex in Psychoanalysis.* New York: Basic Books.

Kelsen, H. (1943), *Society and Nature—A Sociological Inquiry.* Chicago: University of Chicago Press.

Kraepelin, E. (1925), *Dementia Praecox and Paraphrenia.* Edinburgh: Livingston.

Lorenz, K. Z. (1954), Comparative behaviorology. In: *Discussions on Child Development,* Vol. 1, ed. J. M. Tanner and B. Inhelder. New York: International Universities Press.

Parson, I. (1951), *The Social System.* Glencoe: The Free Press.

_____ and Shies, E. A. (1951), *Toward a General Theory of Action.* Cambridge: Harvard University Press.

Spiegel, H. (1959), Hypnosis and transference: a theoretical formulation. *Arch. Gen. Psychiat.,* 1:634.

Von Holst, E. (1936), Von Dualismus der motorischen und der automatisch-rhythmischen Funktion im Ruckenmark und von Wesen des automatischen Rhythmus Pflug. *Arch. ges. Physiol.,* 237:356.

16. Moral Considerations in the Psychotherapy of an Adolescent Who Attempted Murder

PATRICIA CARRINGTON, Ph.D. and
HARMON S. EPHRON, M.D.

T HE MOST MORALLY repugnant of man's acts, murder of a fellow human being, is probably one which is least understood. The reason for this appears to be that persons incarcerated for homicide or attempted homicide rarely, if ever, receive long-term intensive psychotherapy which could afford a study in depth of their personalities, motives, and the total milieu from which the antisocial behavior sprung. Most studies of such individuals are based on only a few psychiatric interviews, at the most they may be based on several months of psychotherapeutic treatment.

The information to be presented in the present article is the result of the authors' unique experience in administering intensive psychotherapy for seven consecutive years to an adolescent who had attempted murder. These years of work gave us the opportunity to explore with a highly intelligent youngster his own motivations and emotional conflicts in depth. It also afforded an opportunity to assess the manner in which psychotherapy administered in this intensive fashion might contribute to the growth of such an individual on a personal, social and moral level. We will, accordingly, attempt to delineate in the present paper both the psychodynamics of the criminal act and the general moral atmosphere surrounding and supporting this act. In addition, we will evaluate

Read at the Society of Medical Psychoanalysts, Symposium on Moral Values and Superego Functioning, New York City, March 4, 1968.

the moral growth achieved by this patient in the course of psychotherapy.

The patient, when first we met him, was a young boy of 14 years, who had attempted the murder of a 13-year-old girl by stabbing her nearly fatally with two ice picks. Following the homicidal act, the boy had attempted suicide. Subsequently he had been committed to a state mental hospital where we initially became acquainted with him when he was presented before a staff seminar conducted by one of us (Dr. Ephron).

As a result of our expressed interest in the case, arrangements were made with the hospital for us to conduct psychotherapy with the patient during his stay there. This psychotherapy (consisting of an average of six hours per week) was continued for the duration of the patient's two-year stay in the hospital, and for five years following his discharge. The seven years of psychotherapeutic interviews were collected on tape and from this case material we have abstracted the data for the present paper.

CLINICAL BACKGROUND

Danny was 14 years old when he attempted homicide. The only child of middle-class parents, he was a boy of superior intelligence who had led an isolated life filled with lonely activities such as building with architectural blocks and drawing comic strips. While he was generally unable to mix with schoolmates, Danny had several close friends who shared some of his intellectual interests, although his parents often discouraged his seeing them.

During Danny's formative years his immediate household included his aunt and uncle (the uncle was also the father's business partner), his maternal grandmother, and the two children of his uncle's first marriage, a boy and a girl. Danny was the youngest and seemingly the least significant member of this household. Somewhat later, when we interviewed Danny's male cousin who had lived in the home with him, this cousin referred to the home as "a house of hate" with Danny being "the whipping boy for all of us . . . no one paid any attention to him unless they were yelling at him."

The household did indeed seem to hold frustration for Danny on every level. Mr. R., Danny's intelligent, but cold, detached and ineffectual father, had failed at one business after another and in the year of Danny's breakdown was fighting bitterly with his partner, Danny's uncle by marriage. This uncle was a ruthless and unscrupulous man, cruel to both family members and business associates alike. Shortly before the patient's homicide attempt, the father's manufacturing plant burned to the ground—the second time in Danny's lifetime that a business of his father's had gone up in flames.

Danny's mother, a cold, tense, harsh woman, was generally hostile to both husband and son, berating them for their lack of masculinity while at the same time sneering at any evidence of assertiveness or independence on their parts. A veritable "tomboy" in her youth, able to play ball "as well as my brothers if not better," Mrs. R. had nagged Danny since early childhood to participate in sports. Her nagging was so aggressive in nature that he reacted by refusal to participate in them at all. She would then scoff at his "weakness and flabbiness."

Obsessed with cleanliness, Mrs. R. regularly indulged in fanatic cleaning of the house. She would, for example, insist that the family scrub the Brillo pad after each use and then dry it with towels, as well as patting dry every corner of the sink after each use. While at times she seemed an attractive and even flirtatious woman with a rather childlike charm, she would turn on her family with harsh shouts reminiscent of a drill sergeant, and carried on a continuous battle with her son over his "messiness."

The only member of the family with whom Danny had a continuing, close, meaningful relationship was his female cousin, Collette, who was six-and-a-half years older than himself. For many years Collette had lived in the same household and even slept in the same room with Danny. From the first moment Collette appeared, when Danny was about six years of age, she had showered hugs and kisses upon the little boy, treating him with exaggerated warmth which he hungrily accepted.

In many respects, however, Danny was like a teddy bear or toy to Collette. She seemed to pick him up and toss him down at will, often using him as an excuse to gain entrance to ice cream parlors where boys were congregating whom she wanted to meet. Such a ruse was necessary because the household forbade dating to Collette, even in her middle teens, and condemned her for being "wild" because she was interested in boys.

When Collette began dating (secretly of course), she also began to neglect Danny, considering him a nuisance much to his bewilderment, rage and despair. While she had always been sexually tantalizing to him, there had been no overt sex play between the two, although Collette regularly took him to bathe in the shower with her. One time he had reached out to touch her breast while in the shower, to which she responded with screams of anger and a recounting of the incident to her parents. This betrayal left Danny embittered and withdrawn. The final blow came when Danny was 11 years old. At this time Collette eloped with her latest boy friend. Her abrupt departure was traumatizing for Danny who was left in a cold, indifferent, unfriendly world.

Collette's elopement was but one in a series of painful separations which Danny experienced during his lifetime. When he was three months old his mother had left for California, not returning to her infant son for a number of months. In infancy and early childhood he had been cared for by some warm, devoted Negro maids, but each one of these maids had left abruptly after not too long a period, causing great distress to the child. No relationship seemed to be a stable or dependable one for him.

Not surprisingly, as a child, Danny was beset with allergies and other psychosomatic symptoms such as frequent stomach aches. He often was bedridden for extended stretches of time. While obviously of superior intelligence, he could never learn to enunciate clearly; rather, he appeared to swallow his words in continuous excessive salivation. This speech defect was still apparent when the authors commenced work with the boy but faded during the course of psychotherapy to a point where today it has become scarcely noticeable.

A symptom evident in Danny from an early age was involuntary defecation. Following Collette's elopement when he was 11 years old, Danny's soiling became an almost daily occurrence causing much distress to the family. While the incontinence usually occurred at home when Danny was with his parents, it also occurred at school, frequently enough to elicit derogatory nicknames and contempt from his peers. This name calling served to increase Danny's isolation from the others.

Danny took no part in the regular activities of his peer group. When his mother forced him to go to dancing school at age 13, he ran away and hid day after day on the way to class, thereby avoiding exposure to the terrifying experience of having to contact others, especially members of the opposite sex, in a social situation.

The year in which he was to commit the crime, Danny entered a large high school where he found himself not only alienated from peers, but also without the contact and support of interested teachers he had experienced in previous years. In addition, his one very close friend, Jeff, developed a new group of friends in high school and, in effect, seemed to have deserted Danny. This was highly disturbing to this boy who was so sensitive to separations from significant others.

High school also presented Danny with a challenge to make a heterosexual adjustment for which he was totally unprepared and to the idea of which he reacted with terror. He was abnormally uninformed about sex, having managed to repress any knowledge of it. He even claims to have been unaware of the anatomical difference between the sexes, and states that he never consciously knew that he was a boy in any clear-cut sense. As he was growing up he felt that he was "just sort of a *thing*—actually sexless."

Vivid, although somewhat confused sexual fantasies became increasingly prevalent, however, in Danny's first year in high school. These fantasies were greeted by him as alien impulses which made him feel monstrous and abnormal, particularly since he was totally unable to share them in a social setting. Because even the mildest swearing was not permitted in Danny's family, there was no opportunity to exchange sexual allusions with comrades in the form of off-color jokes or stories. When Danny first entered therapy, he was unable to use the word "damn," and his first enlightenment on sexual matters was obtained after his admission to the state hospital in a lecture on sex delivered by a psychiatrist to adolescent patients.

In addition to the increasing social isolation of his first year in high school, his emerging sexual problems, the desertion by his friend Jeff, and the humiliation of a highly competitive school situation where he was no longer either outstanding in his school work or in close contact with teachers, Danny's first year at high school was further clouded by the growing tension at home. Mr. R. was continually in a state of rage and despair over the treatment he was receiving from his partner in business but, at the same time, was totally unable to stand up for himself and put an end to the unpleasant situation. The home was the scene of daily battles with the partner, Danny's uncle by marriage, who took much of his frustration out on Danny through harsh criticism.

About four months prior to the homicide attempt, Danny commenced to immerse himself in the reading of morbid science fiction and subsequently began to write his own murder mysteries with distinctly Hitchcockian "tricky" plots. He turned in some of these murder stories to his teacher as English compositions, but the shocked teacher publicly denounced them and forbade him to submit them anymore. The teacher's actions seemed to shut still another door to Danny who, despite his inability to engage in adequate peer-group relationships, tended to be a "teacher's pet."

Following this rejection of his murder stories by the teacher, Danny withdrew into a totally unshared fantasy world. He began to engage in increasingly lonely rumination, a fact which no one in this troubled household noted at the time, but which was all too apparent to them in retrospect. He spent more and more time alone in his room and, during the summer prior to the crime an incident occurred which presaged the homicide attempt a year hence. On this occasion, Danny struck the mentally deficient son of his parents' best friend over the head with a toy gun, causing some bleeding. This incident was glossed over by his parents as an "accident" at the time, but it was actually the beginning of the acting out of a fantasy which was attaining increasing power over Danny—a fantasy of destroying himself or others.

In obedience to his growing preoccupation, Danny began research on every known means of suicide, classifying each in a methodical manner. He entered this information in a special notebook, assigning each weapon of death a final "rating" which he determined. In the booklet, which he entitled "How to Commit Suicide—39 Main Ideas" he analyzed an exhaustive number of suicide methods. Among the weapons analyzed were knives, "both of the sharp-pointed variety and of the kitchen variety," sleeping pills, hammers, ice picks, electric saws, axes, guns, and a multitude of poisons. About the object he later chose as a murder weapon, he had this to say

> *Ice pick:* this form of suicide is better than average. You must fall on pick or plunge it into your body. It doesn't hurt too much. Instead of an ice pick you may use a paper holder that is sharply pointed. Advantages: Picks clean and easy to get. Hurts for about five seconds. It's not too bloody. Easier to do than knifing. Harder for doctors to help you. Pick is sharper than pointed knife. Disadvantages: You need to drive it into the heart, possibly through stomach, for it to be successful. There is always the chance of not killing yourself. It is not bloody but very nerve wracking. I rate this method of suicide good to excellent.

In mid-winter, Danny's mother left for California for a month's vacation. She went with her best friend, the mother of the boy whom Danny had struck over the head. After his mother's departure Danny's rumination increased sharply, resulting in an eventual truancy from school which went undetected at the time. Entirely alone in the house during the day, since his father was at work and his mother away, Danny's thoughts turned increasingly to the idea of murder. The victim whom he selected was the 13 year-old daughter of his mother's best friend. She was the younger sister of the boy he had struck on the head the previous summer. The girl, whom we shall call Emily, lived across the street from Danny. Danny and his father had been dining at her house each evening while Mrs. R. was away. The murder weapons were to be two ice picks, one which he was to hold in each hand. The entire procedure was contemplated in an unnatural state of increasing excitement which kept Danny absorbed in fantasies of destruction and oblivious to all else for days. Finally the rumination culminated in an explosion, the criminal act.

On the evening before the homicide attempt, Danny telephoned Emily and told her that a "surprise" would be arriving in the mail for her; when he received it he would call her so she could come over to his house and pick it up. The next afternoon Emily received a call from Danny telling her that the "surprise" had come. When she entered Danny's home, he locked the front door and led her down to the basement playroom where he told her to turn on the TV set as loud as it would go. She complied, whereupon Danny ordered her to sit down while he put a blindfold on her so that she "couldn't see the surprise." He then placed a flower pot in her lap, apparently for the purpose of keeping her hands occupied, and as she sat there he proceeded to stab her in the gallbladder, kidneys, one lung, and at the edge of the heart. In that ice pick stabs are not immediately painful, Emily at first thought Danny was punching her in the breast and stomach and put up her hands to protect herself. When she felt one of her hands knicked she pulled off the blindfold. Later she recalled that Danny had looked "awfully strange; his eyes were awfully glassy" at this time.

On seeing that her hand was bleeding slightly, Emily told Danny to get her a bandaid and he complied. He brought her a single bandaid, then left the room abruptly and ran upstairs. Emily, becoming aware of a burning sensation in her stomach, and noticing blood oozing through her sweater, had the presence of mind to go to the telephone and call home for help. Subsequently she was rushed to the hospital by her father.

Almost an hour later, Danny's father, who had been alerted, discovered his son in his own bedroom closet, crouched on the floor, his knees drawn up under his chin in a fetal position. He was in a coma which had been induced by drinking a bottle of carbon tetrachloride. Mr. R. rushed his son to the hospital where his stomach was pumped out before fatal liver damage could occur.

Emily, having been successfully operated on, subsequently made a complete recovery. Although she inquired about Danny's condition upon regaining consciousness, Danny on his part did not once ask about Emily, nor did he exhibit any particular emotion or express regret about what he had done. He was placed under technical arrest while in the hospital and arraigned in juvenile court directly upon termination of his hospitalization. Subsequently he was remanded to the custody of a state mental hospital.

CLINICAL IMPRESSIONS

When we first interviewed Danny, we were struck by a quality of frailty which he presented. A dark boy with a long face, strikingly narrow head and tiny ears, Danny's gray eyes were misted over with a dreamified expression, while at the same time he seemed to have the perpetually startled "on guard" quality of a forest animal. Quick to sense "danger" anywhere, from anyone, when he sensed it his eyes became hard and fighting, his face paled and became drawn. If challenged or pressured by questions, he would inadvertently jab pens or pencils into the table, or jab pins or unwound paper clips against his own trousers, or against wood, books or paper. These movements were explosive, swift and sudden.

Danny's mood varied greatly with the emotional climate of the interview. When put at ease he would smile and chat in a friendly fashion, appearing more like a warm, relaxed puppy or a small child in need of being petted. Indeed, a baby-like quality made Danny often seem like a suckling babe or awkward wriggling puppy. This quality even extended to the movement of his hands. These hands seemed like clumsy extensions of his arms, lacking the fine apposition of thumb and forefinger or the precision of finger movements characteristic of the adult. The hands seemed instead to form a spade-like unit somewhat like an animal's paw. Initially the family reported that Danny was "no good with his hands," but during the course of psychotherapy Danny became increasingly able to use his hands with precision and eventually was able to execute beautiful and delicate art work.

During the initial psychotherapeutic interviews, Danny seemed to reach with his whole body toward the interviewer. Often he inadvertently kicked against the interviewer beneath the table, his head bent forward, his whole body curling and seemingly begging for contact. When standing, he would sometimes reel toward the interviewer as a drunken person might reel. At such times he looked as though he were going to knock into or fall against the person he wanted to approach, and it was particularly evident that Danny suffered at the end of each session from having to part from the interviewers.

Danny appeared a helpless prey, not only to his sudden surges of rage, but equally to his strong needs for love. He would respond instantly to gestures of warmth by a delighted, almost pathetic smile and his face would suddenly become suffused with color. He seemed to lack the ordinary defenses or delays in responding to others. One might surmise that Danny had had to build up his peculiar cunning, his plotting and trickiness because he was in terror of his vulnerability in human relationships. His high intelligence and inventiveness seemed to have been used to develop techniques of desperation.

Danny had been given a diagnosis of *schizophrenic reaction: chronic undifferentiated type* by the hospital. A consultant to the hospital had suggested that the crime had been committed in a state of catatonic excitement. Clearly the boy was not a psychopath, and although the clinical picture was not typical of a schizophrenic reaction, clinical interviews revealed that Danny's view of the world and of himself was badly distorted despite a surface appearance of adequate reality adjustment.

Childhood fantasies that he was Superman, by his own description, represented a borderline delusional state. He had once corrected his therapist when she referred to "your fantasy of being Superman" by saying, "It wasn't a fantasy—it was much stronger. At those times I really thought I *was* Superman." This borderline delusional state did not occur only in very early childhood during the period when children indulge in imaginative games, but persisted throughout the latency period.

What is more, Danny many times repeated the assertion that when growing up he actually did not "know" what a boy or a girl was, or even that *he* was a *boy*. This confusion involves a severe distortion of the body image, implying ties with reality which are

298 ·

so thin as to strongly suggest an underlying schizophrenic process.

The glazed expression on Danny's face, which the victim described as occurring during the homicide attempt, and a wild, confused and glassy-eyed look seen on occasion during the clinical interviews when the patient came up against material which created in him strong, unmanageable rage, offered evidence of the disorienting effect of strong emotion on this boy. It seemed that he could decompensate under emotional pressure.

PROGNOSTIC INDICATIONS

Only gradually, as therapy progressed over the first year, was Danny willing to reveal his rich observations of other people, but as he did so it became evident that he caught almost every nuance of behavior and mood of those about him. He did not initially sense others empathically, however, but with the painful astuteness of one who must watch every step he takes lest he offend someone and bring about retribution.

What crippled his innate creativity was obsessional concern about taking any step without first having a guarantee that all would work out perfectly. He could not, for example, buy a table game of baseball without writing letter after letter to people all over the country to obtain testimonials that it was *worth* purchasing. It would thus appear that he was overwhelmed with the fear of being less than perfect.

From the first, Danny was reluctant to discuss the homicide attempt and did not do so spontaneously until his third year of psychotherapy. When required to discuss the incident in the diagnostic interviews he showed no remorse, however, and little awareness of the import of what he had done in any true moral sense. He was not glib about the crime, however, in the manner of a psychopath who might boast to his peers of his deed or distort it when talking to authorities. It was striking to note that when either the crime or any other personal or embarrassing matter was mentioned, Danny inadvertently, and quite unconsciously, shielded his face from the seminar group. He would raise one hand at such times to cover the side of his face, much like the blinders of a horse, and twist in his chair in an apparent attempt to hide himself from the view of all, often raising his whole arm to blot out his head from view. While he showed no mature remorse over the criminal act, he thus seemed to be experiencing some form of intense shame concerning it on an infantile or early childhood level.

This shame reaction seemed to us to be evidence of a rudimentary moral sense operating in connection with the criminal act which might be utilizable in therapy. Also prognostically important was Danny's emotionality which, while it left him helpless in the wake of its ebb and flow, nevertheless represented an emotional aliveness which could be used in the therapeutic relationship. Danny seemed to be reaching with appropriate affect for contact, warmth and understanding, and from the first he responded eagerly to the therapists' interest in him. He was a vivid and colorful person whom we soon found to be lovable despite the illness which was so evident. Our warm response to him prompted us to feel that we could be useful to him as therapists. It was decided that one of the authors (Dr. Carrington) should work with him on a regular basis, with the other (Dr. Ephron) conducting interviews from time to time, since it was deemed that the patient's early childhood nurturing needs might more satisfactorily be met by a woman therapist. This modified form of dual therapy turned out to be most advantageous since it afforded the patient two parent-surrogate figures with whom to identify at a crucial point in his adolescence.

Before discussing the actual psychotherapy, however, let us consider the moral climate of the patient's family and the family's reactions to the crime.

FAMILY ATTITUDES

Danny's father never reprimanded his son for the homicide attempt, nor questioned him at any length about why he did it. Mr. R. seemed largely concerned with the newspaper coverage of the story and with the legal aspects of the crime. Years later, after he had undergone a considerable amount of psychotherapy, the patient commented on this by saying, "I kept waiting for Dad to get mad at me, but he didn't. He had no reaction at all. It was as if I hadn't done anything." Mr. R. even failed to notify his wife in California about what had happened, and she arrived home several days later quite unaware of what had taken place. On hearing the news, Mrs. R. showed no sign of emotion, and when it was suggested to her by a friend that she go to the hospital to see her son she said, "No, let it go until tomorrow." She asked no questions about what happened to her son, said very little, and the next day went to his room at the hospital composed and smiling. She made no comment to Danny about his situation but talked to him about her trip to California.

Another inappropriate reaction to the crime was that of Danny's aunt. This aunt had lived in the house with him for many years and professed a great affection for her nephew. When she was shown the list of suicide weapons and their ratings, which Danny had prepared, she exclaimed: "Just like a doctor! Can you imagine that *mind?*" In line with this reasoning, she insisted to the hospital staff that her nephew was a "genius."

Not the least curious reaction was that of the victim's own mother. She was one of the first people to visit Danny in his hospital room. While, in itself, this might be understandable since she had been very close to the boy as well as to his parents, she also wrote affectionate letters to Danny for the entire duration of his stay in the mental hospital, and would frequently send him candy. When he was eventually allowed home on weekends she would slip him five-dollar bills whenever she saw him, in her words, "just as a gift." When the therapist sent word to Emily's mother that it would be helpful for the boy's therapy if she stopped giving Danny the money, she became enraged at the therapist and asked, "What does she [the therapist] want me to do? Let the boy murder *me* too?" When Danny was released from the state hospital, Emily's mother suggested to Danny's parents that Danny and Emily be brought together for a meeting so that she could see "what will happen when they meet." It was only due to the therapist's intervention that the parties involved did not carry out this bizarre confrontation.

In evaluating Emily's mother's reaction, it is of interest to note that this woman suffered from a postpartum psychosis at the time of Emily's birth, in which her presenting symptom was a fear that she would murder her infant daughter. While this occurrence was entirely unknown to Danny, we cannot overlook the possibility that some form of subtle communication took place whereby Emily's mother's unconscious hostility toward her daughter was transmitted to Danny. While it is doubtful if this could have provided sufficient motivation for a crime of this sort, it is not inconceivable that Emily's mother's attitude toward her daughter influenced Danny's choice of the murder victim. It is also possible that Emily, conditioned by a basically hostile mother, may have in some manner been an unconsciously willing victim.

The reactions of the two families involved appear, then, to have been atypical in many ways. Danny's family showed extreme denial with regard to the criminal act and an absence of an appropriate sense of horror. While the victim's family displayed initial shock and concern, the placating behavior of Emily's mother toward Danny served to compound the psychopathology of the family-community milieu which surrounded, and in some subtle sense seemed almost to support, the crime. These people's reaction to the murder attempt suggests that Danny's act may have expressed unconscious fantasies of those around him, as well as his own. It is possible, for example, that the mother of the victim may have unwittingly engineered Danny's choice of victim by communicating to Danny her unconscious hostile fantasies toward her daughter. It is also possible that Danny's violence may have served in his mind to vindicate his father's obviously failing masculinity by demonstrating to the world and himself that he, his father's son, was a superman—not a weakling to be scoffed at and dominated. Individual and family sessions conducted with Danny's relatives following the crime, tended to support the assumption that the homicidal act expressed the emotional illness of the nuclear and extended family.

In this light, we might note the general atmosphere of moral hypocrisy which characterized these people. The affective response to others which forms the basis upon which a genuine, flexible, mature moral sense can be built seemed particularly lacking in this family. In its place they showed what might best be characterized as a child's tyrannical superego, where emphasis was placed in a highly arbitrary fashion on the "blacks and whites," the "do's and don'ts" of life.

During his formative years, Danny's parents insisted that he "respect" his elders and conform to rigid requirements for social behavior, emphasizing money as a supreme value. Interestingly, in the course of therapy, it was against his family's materialistic outlook that Danny first directed an articulate rebellion. In questioning the materialistic orientation of his family he made his first steps toward the formation of a system of genuine ideals.

PSYCHODYNAMIC FORMULATIONS

Homicide vs. Suicide as Motivation

In investigating the motives for the crime, one might commence by questioning whether the primary motive was homicidal or suicidal, since the attempt to take his own life was an integral part of Danny's ritual.

In our opinion, suicide was not the prime motivation for this aberrant behavior, despite the manual of methods for committing suicide which he had prepared prior to the crime. Our reasons for referring to Danny primarily as an attempted homicide, rather than an attempted suicide, are several.

When the patient mentioned the homicide-suicide incident during the course of his psychotherapy he always referred to it as "that incident with *Emily*" and spoke of his "destructive" murderous fantasies toward other people as motivating the act. He talked little, if at all, about self-destructiveness, and even more importantly, his reaction to frustration was, in our observation, not depressive or suicidal, but rather took the form of a recurrence of his murderous fantasies. When this happened, it would trouble him greatly.

In the course of his therapy Danny spontaneously told about his complex sexual motivation for the homicidal act by describing himself as obsessed with thoughts of *murder* before the crime. When asked why he had tried to kill himself afterwards, he simply replied, "I had to. That's all I *could* do then." The suicidal act appears to have been an immediate means of satisfying a punitive superego with regard to a totally forbidden act.

We do not know why Danny entitled his treatise on methods of killing as a manual on *suicide*. The very method which he chose as an attack upon Emily, that is, death by stabbing with ice picks, was described in the manual, but termed a means of suicide. We never questioned Danny about this because he never mentioned this manual; our knowledge of it was second-hand, through the hospital which, in turn, had obtained it from the police. We followed a strict procedure of not introducing factual material into psychotherapy sessions unless it was introduced by the patient himself.

We can speculate, however, on the basis of our knowledge of Danny, on why the manual was titled this way. At the time we first knew him, Danny prized a quality in himself which he termed "trickiness." He was extremely manipulative in his dealings with others and his murder story plots were diabolical and ingenious in their ability to cast suspicion away from the individual who was actually planning a murder. It seems entirely possible that Danny intentionally called his booklet "How to Commit Suicide" rather than "How to Commit Murder," in order to insure that had the book been accidentally discovered by his family, in advance of the planned act, they would not have been able to guess his actual intentions.

Affectional Deprivation as Motivation

Turning to a consideration of the motives for the crime, we see that, as in any other complex act, Danny's homicide-suicide attempt was highly overdetermined. First in importance was the patient's history of severe affectional deprivation. While the female members of his family, in particular his aunt, grandmother, and cousin Collette, all professed great "love" for Danny, they alternatingly smothered then rejected him. They were seductive at one moment and hostile or else coldly indifferent and remote the next.

Basically, Danny was a child whom everyone used and for whom no one was really concerned. In his early years he had experienced repeated separations from the nursemaids who had represented his only genuine nurturing figures, while his own mother had been unyielding, critical and often even physically dangerous to the little boy who felt her handling of him as rough and often frightening. She would scrub him so harshly in the bathtub, for example, that he later described his reaction to the painfulness of it as the response of a child afraid for its life. The little boy lived within a family where everyone seemed to seek nurturance *from* him, but where no one gave any *to* him in return. He was an object of the oral hunger of deprived, hating, bitter, noncohesive familial figures who inevitably ended up rejecting him because he was unable to supply the fulfillment that each longed for.

One can view the homicidal act as being, on one level, an unconscious maneuver in which the patient tore into the body of a love object as though with primitive fang and claw (in this case the "claws" being two ice picks). In doing this he seemed to tear at a female figure much as females had symbolically clawed at and devoured him. The homicidal act was, in this sense, an act of desperation in which a deprived individual tried to wrench from the love object sustenance he despaired of obtaining in any other manner. The ferocity of the act seems commensurate with the intensity of the emotional frustration behind it. Nevertheless, even as the patient reached desperately to the mothering figure, he did *not* reach her. The impersonal ice picks were like non-touching hands, and the act was remote and unreal. Danny could not break through to warmth and genuine contact with the mother.

It seems no coincidence that the criminal act occurred after Danny's mother had left for California, causing another abandonment in addition to the one brought about by his best friend's desertion at school and his teacher's rejection of his murder mystery stories. If viewed as the act of an abandoned and frustrated infant furiously biting at the denying breast, the homicidal attempt can be considered compulsive and premoral in nature—that is, to arise from a level of development where morality is not yet a meaningful concept. The infant knows only his overwhelming need for mother contact and mother protection. Sensitivity to mature social and moral values grows only when basic needs have been at least minimally met and an incentive for identification with moral values established. Because this requirement had not been fulfilled in the case of Danny, he perceived the criminal act as a necessity, perhaps even a reasonable one, since it was a symbolic attempt to tear out of the living flesh that which should have come easily, naturally and tenderly to the boy in his early years. "Need" thus appears to have become equated with justification, and to have replaced moral considerations.

Sexual Frustration as Motivation

The homicide attempt also had sexual overtones. During psychotherapy, the patient revealed that the fantasy surrounding the act was that of exploring the inside of a woman's body and satisfying his curiosity about it in the only manner in which he had conceived such a thing to be possible—that is, if the love object were dead and could not reprimand or thwart him. Danny had fantasied having sexual activity of a confused sort with the corpse and this was deeply troubling to him. Because bodies, especially his own, seemed fecally tainted and therefore loathesome to him, he was terrified lest his degrading sexual wishes in connection with the crime be discovered. When attempting homicide, Danny, with untouching symbolic hands—two cold steel ice picks—had both contacted and simultaneously counteracted and denied his wish for contact with a female body. In a family where touching was equated with messing and contamination, the murder ritual represented a bloody embrace and an intimacy which eventually had to be accompanied by punishment—his own death. The act of suicide also seems to have aimed at accomplishing absolute denial of this mechanical sexual embrace. By means of his flight, his retreat into the closet, and his drinking of poison, Danny was able to blot out any awareness of the love object's response in pain and death and thus to negate his attempted intimacy with her. He even appears to have dissociated himself from his own actions during the homicide attempt when, as the victim reported, his eyes had a "strange, glassy look."

In evaluating the patient's crushing shame reactions in connection with the crime, we can see the operation of an early childhood tyrannical superego with its uncompromising condemnation of the life impulse. Danny was conditioned to deny his body and his manhood, even to the point of having to deny to himself that he was a boy or that he knew what a boy or a girl was. Seeing himself as neither male nor female, but essentially as fecal, Danny could only loathe himself, which in turn led to the stunting of his moral growth, since genuine, flexible moral values had no room in which to flourish; all was crushing condemnation and resulting terror. The patient appears to have been destroyed by his overriding superego to a point where only an explosion, an act of violence, offered promise of breaking the prison walls.

Revenge as Motivation

Another motivation for the homicidal act was profound revenge. Through the homicide, Danny had attempted to turn the tables on the women who had used him emotionally, and at the same time humiliated him throughout the years. Through violence he sought unconsciously to prove to himself that in spite of all their belittling, in spite of their use of him as a toy, a symbolic "rag doll," he really was a man capable of strength, even violence, a man with a penis to be reckoned with by the world. On this level, the ice picks represented the phallus, and the act constituted an attempt to deny his own feminine, submissive traits which were becoming all too obvious to him. Having had no support from his weak father in building a masculine self-image, Danny embraced the supreme power inherent in the taking of a life. This was a grandiose gesture by which a frightened, submissive boy became in his own eyes a heroic superbeing. The homicidal act seems to have represented the continuation of the childhood fantasy, where, as a little boy, Danny used to walk down the street imagining that he was Superman. So convincing was this fantasy, it could be regarded as bordering on delusion in that at times he truly believed he *was* Superman. This preoccupation with the attainment of superhuman powers is reminiscent of the Superman fantasies which played such an important part in the Leopold-Loeb crime of a similar nature.

From a moral standpoint, one might say that the homicidal attempt was significant precisely in that it attempted to overthrow all morality. Like Atlas toppling the world, the murderer sought to emerge in his own eyes as supreme victor with the insistent whisperings of self-doubting silenced forever. Instead of experiencing fear, he would then be the one who created fear. Instead of the victim, he would be the powerful aggressor. Conformity to a moral code could only at this point have been equated with weakness and unmanliness.

Such fallacious reasoning was dispelled only gradually during psychotherapy as the patient came to sense his own genuine strengths and learned to substitute constructive ways of asserting himself for pathological and destructive ones. In the course of therapy, destructive murderous fantasies were discovered to reoccur at times when Danny had been particularly submissive in some life situation, and were quickly dispelled once he could vent his rage at others and himself, in *words,* thereby finding a constructive means of standing up for his rights.

Anal Sadism and the Criminal Act

The homicidal attempt should also be viewed in the context of Danny's previous malignant symptom of incontinence. The soiling was in its own way an explosive and antisocial act. Through it the boy who as a child had been scrubbed clean until his skin felt raw, soiled himself openly and blatantly, befouling the family living room. In the course of therapy, he described the soiling as having been in some sense strangely pleasurable. It appears to have represented to him a symbolic freedom as conceived by a small child, a freedom to move his bowels wherever and whenever he pleased, even to force his bowel movements upon others, a freedom to be accepted not only in spite of, but actually *because* of the bodily processes which he was trained to view as repugnant. Conformity to social values seemed oddly reversed in that he now made an unconscious demand on others to conform to *his* pleasure values. In this manner he fought for self-acceptance in a pathologically distorted fashion.

The homicidal act took on an anal-sadistic quality in that Danny attempted to reduce his victim, and later himself, to a corpse, presenting it like lifeless feces for all the world to see. In his descriptive evaluation of the murder weapons he had been careful to weigh each weapon in terms of the degree to which it was "messy," rating highly only those methods which were clean and not too bloody or unpleasant for spectators to see afterwards. Through this preoccupation with finding a "clean" method of murder, the patient betrayed both his anal-sadistic preoccupations and his defense against them. Submissive to an early childhood superego prohibition against soiling, he attempted to be clean even at the moment of supreme soiling, in the act of violent assault. An ambivalence of role with respect to the act was further evidenced in his readiness to respond, during the murder attempt itself, to the victim's request for a bandaid. Had Danny been merely intent on a savage attempt to kill at all costs, no such interruption of the act would have been possible, for he would not have been motivated to be his mother's "good" boy and comply with her request. That he did cease stabbing her, fetch her the bandaid, and then run off to drink poison, attests to the ritualistic and symbolic nature of the act and the deep conflict of roles involved in it. It also suggests the operation of a simple, childlike, rudimentary moral sense with regard to his own actions at this moment.

MORAL GROWTH IN PSYCHOTHERAPY

While it would certainly be of interest to describe in considerable detail the moral growth of this patient in psychotherapy, such an endeavor is not feasible within the scope of the present paper. We shall therefore summarize the manner in which such growth was achieved.

The therapeutic approach consisted of several different strategies. The first was an attempt to ameliorate the patient's severely punitive superego by encouraging him to experience himself in a spontaneous manner, to achieve freedom to be *imperfect*, rather than rigidly clean, and to break from the compulsion to be what we jokingly came to term "your mother's model boy." We thus sought to loosen the bonds of an immature pseudomorality in order to encourage spontaneity, warmth and a life-affirming quality. It was felt that only in such an atmosphere of spontaneity could a genuine sense of morality and social values flourish. We wanted to soften the patient's crushing superego and replace it by flexible and realistic standards of conduct.

One of the primary methods used to achieve this goal was our support of the patient's efforts to assert himself, particularly his attempts to express anger in an appropriate and constructive manner instead of bottling it up until it burst forth in an explosion.

Danny was initially highly resistant to the concept that the world of other persons could in any way be influenced or dealt with on a level of compromise, by talk and by reason. He was deeply cynical about people, feeling that they were all "indifferent" (his word), an assessment which was applied particularly to his parents. His sense of futility with regard to reaching an understanding with his family, or with regard to obtaining any concession from them which might reflect his own needs, was profound.

It was with genuine surprise that he greeted the fact that the therapist's interviews with the family over the first six months of treatment began to have positive results in terms of his parent's relationship to him. The first time his parents agreed to alter a family routine, even though it was on such a simple matter as granting him a fixed allowance, Danny made a noticeably stronger commitment to the therapeutic process. He began to accept the possibility that the psychotherapist was "on his side," in that she was attempting (and to some degree succeeding) to make his environment a more flexible one. He appeared to sense that his needs were understood, reflected upon, and responded to, and this instituted an important change in his attitude. Constructiveness and an ability to struggle to achieve that which was meaningful to him seemed unleashed in him at this point.

Soon thereafter Danny began to discuss the profound disturbances in human relationships which characterized his troubled family. With a glimmer of hope that it would not always remain so dim a picture, he could now face the despair which he had known. By seeing that the therapist could deal with the parents in an effective manner, Danny also began to try to deal effectively with his parents. He was learning he had avenues of recourse open to him other than repression, followed by explosion and violence.

Among the techniques used to effect softening of the punitive superego were finger-painting sessions through which Danny had the opportunity to accept a form of "messiness" which could be enjoyed as a shared experience with another person. This strategy proved far more effective than had been anticipated. Danny literally threw himself into the finger painting with an abandon which was truly moving to watch. He reveled in the paint, the color and the lush possibilities of combining color and texture to form powerful abstract designs.

At first Danny's finger-painting experiences were striking in their portrayal of intense and violent emotions. During the first two sessions, for example, he used only vivid red paint, splashing it about the page, over the table, and even onto the floor. The impression which this slushing of crimson finger paint gave was similar to that which one might have experienced on watching blood poured profusely over paper, and then contacted with primitive relish.

At one point during these initial finger-painting sessions, Danny picked up a doll's baby bottle and filled it with the red paint. He then squeezed the nipple in such a manner that the red dribbled out of the bottle onto the blank finger-painting paper, making lively designs of dots and splashes. This bottle, forced to exude symbolic blood, suggested to us that for Danny the infantile oral phase had been severely traumatizing, so that now, rather than a need to nurse *milk* from the breast, this youngster seemed to have what might best be described as "a placental hunger,"[1] that is, a

[1] We are indebted to our colleague, Bradford J. Wilson, for suggesting this expressive term.

need for a direct infusion of blood from the mother's body into his own, in order to live.

While we cannot here describe in detail the development which took place over a large number of finger-painting sessions, one could summarize the experience by saying that Danny quite obviously experienced a powerful release of energy during these sessions. As he worked with the paints, his sallow face would become suffused with color, the usual tension lines about the mouth would relax into a soft and easy smile, and at times as he threw his whole body into the movement of color and design across the page, he would make involuntary, relishing grunts as an animal might do when abandoning itself to a feast. In this sublimated release of energy, he seemed to find freedom in color and contact, and to experience both hunger and its satisfaction, both violence and its acceptance. As we were to discover, this was probably Danny's first successful sublimation of anal aggressive drives. That his therapist was able to go along with him, encouraging him in this activity, was, we believe, of prime importance.

As the finger-painting sessions continued, the color red took its rightful place amidst striking combinations of many colors, and to the surprise of all (no less to Danny) his sense of design turned out to be a powerful one, winning him considerable acceptance from others. Danny for the first time found himself significant *because of* a "mess" which he made, rather than because of irrational *avoidance* of a mess.

He soon began to paint in his spare time and developed an interest in various types of poetry as well. Danny's poems, quite in contrast to his former science fiction stories, now reached consistently toward emotion and human values, extolling the ability to feel, to love, and to have fun, as the essential values of life.

One of Danny's poems, written approximately two-and-a-half years after the commencement of his psychotherapy, appears to reflect the struggle between destructiveness and compassion, between callousness and humanity, which was raging within him at this time. It reads as follows:

Moral Considerations in Attempted Murder

Tribute to a Child

You walk through meadows;
Meadows filled with weeds;
Beautiful steep grass;
Insects you crush;
Vines you break.

You walk through meadows;
A bird child flutters;
Flutters beneath your feet;
A black unknown bird;
An unsuspecting, frightened bird.

You walk through meadows;
A child picks up the angel;
A child, a human child;
You feel pity, he does not;
Child brings child to children.

You walk through meadows;
As children greet child you hope;
Hope for children's compassion;
Some have, others do not; you have;
You, American, do not rebel against group.

You walk through meadows;
Children fight, they always do;
Fight, argue, over other child;
Sympathetic children have their wish;
Permission is theirs for child.

You walk through meadows;
Adult thinking children;
Shown is bird to others;
Finally fun is had, ant is freed;
Freed by the anteater.

You walk through meadows;
Mother calls father, father calls brother;
Fly over, mourn loudly;
Nothing else can be done;
They just pray.

You walk through meadows;
    to your destination;
Sympathetic are you;
But human, forgets and does business;
Momentarily mourns.

You walk through meadows;
Business is through;
Upon a figure you come;
A figure, a dead figure;
A figure of a winged child.

You walk through meadows;
Ugly meadows, mournful meadows;
No sound, just silent tribute;
Tribute to a child;
A forgiving, loving, trusting child—
You mourn too.

Danny's impulses toward brutality are clearly manifested in the imagery of crushing insects, breaking vines, and in the children who harm the little winged bird which is the tender essence of life. The antithesis of this destructive, callous, and impersonal attitude manifests itself in the main character of the poem, the author himself, who feels compassion and tenderness for the little bird. Thus the poem is filled with a mournful plea for understanding and for life.

In a sense the little bird typifies Danny himself, the child who was not nurtured, the child who was not allowed to grow up in a meaningful way, or to sense his own sexuality and masculinity. The phallic symbol, the bird, is not allowed to function in the poem. Its life is snuffed out, as life and sexuality had been stifled in Danny by crushing moral strictures. Within Danny, a "once forgiving and trusting child" had long ago been turned into a cold and hating human being by the condemning superego. In this poem he seems for the first time to articulate this loss, and to commence a fight to regain his humanity.

When Danny eventually entered college (two years after his discharge from the hospital) his writing skills had evolved to the point where, as editor of a college newspaper, he was able to write fiery editorials denouncing war, racial discrimination and other imperfections of our society, and defending the individual's right to sexual freedom. In these journalistic tirades, Danny's residue of destructiveness was pressed into the service of newly developing ideals.

Another psychotherapeutic strategy of importance in the present case was fostering ego-building activities. This effort involved the therapist's participation, over time, in a number of creative projects (e.g., stamp collecting, photography, reportage) in which Danny was interested. As psychotherapy progressed, however, the extent of the therapist's participation with the patient in such ego-building activities diminished, and utilization of insight therapy markedly increased. During the final three years of his psychotherapy, Danny was able to handle his sessions in a modified analytic fashion, lying down on the couch and searching with honesty and directness for answers to his problems.

Family sessions were maintained as a continuing therapeutic strategy, and, while they were only occasional, were sufficient to alter family attitudes so that Danny could play a new role in his own family, one where he was accorded as much respect as these emotionally damaged people could give to one another. After many years of turbulent and painful strife with them, Danny, today a young man in his early twenties, has finally achieved a modicum of genuine respect for his parents. His occasional contacts with them lead him to feel that they have "grown into people who are more real."

As his therapy progressed, Danny developed a value system of his own. It was not, and still is not, the value system subscribed to by the "establishment." It is closer to the Hippie ideal, with its emphasis on love as a major value, and de-emphasis on material possessions. However, insofar as Danny eschews the use of all drugs, he differs from many of his peers. While at present he advocates a form of total sexual freedom which is of a polymorphous-perverse type (seeming to reflect the continuing presence of unresolved longings for infantile bodily contact), he nevertheless lives his life deeply concerned with those persons to whom he gives allegiance and love.

Today, two years after completing individual psychotherapy, Danny's is a restless existence. His unconventional life style shows persistent evidence of the damage wrought by his early environment, yet he distinctly holds to ideals of a humanistic, meaningful sort. Currently he is devoting himself to founding a Utopian community where people can live and work together. Of this he writes:

> Each of us will agree on one thing: we will intensely and honestly work to discover our repressed and buried selves. . . . It will take more supreme work and honesty than perhaps anything we have ever done . . . and all these words are but words until one day we can, unromantically, unintellectually, without acting or games or fantasy, but with great compassion and passion, with deep love, touch one another.

We believe that the growth of Danny's social and moral sense was effected largely through his identification with his therapists, both of whom were deeply interested in and genuinely fond of this patient. These therapists seem to have served as parent surrogates to the boy, enabling him to establish a belief in humanity, and to develop a wish to emulate people whom he felt to be genuinely good.

Danny's actions clearly show introjection of the therapists' value systems. For a number of years, he has spent time helping friends who are in emotional difficulty, often talking to them through the course of a whole night, if necessary, to ease their troubles. He has recently assisted a close friend in overcoming a semidelinquent background by teaching him to be an accomplished photographer. He has encouraged the boy to believe in his own gifts, and to express himself freely, even as he himself was encouraged during the first years of his therapy to develop his own creative abilities and emotional freedom. Quite frequently, Danny is instrumental in obtaining psychotherapy for others whom he believes can benefit by it. His delight in seeing a friend achieve emotional growth is no less than our pleasure as we watch him become a person with warmth and sensitivity.

Despite the fact that Danny still shows a sense of alienation from his own body and its spontaneous capacity for joy, and the fact that he has as yet not achieved a satisfying sexual adjustment, he *has* evolved from a frightened, suspicious, maneuvering, and cynical youngster to a richly endowed, sincere and loyal human being. That Danny rates his own moral growth a personal triumph was evident in a recent visit when he came into the office to report excitedly that he had discovered for the first time that he could still love a friend even when that friend seemed to have deserted him temporarily. He was able to overcome his own vicious, vengeful fantasies and be happy *for* his friend despite frustration of his own needs. This represented to him an emancipation from an infantile self-centered orientation which he felt had degraded him and left him less of a person.

Perhaps a statement of Danny's expresses his feelings about his own growth through psychotherapy better than our words can. One of the authors (Dr. Ephron) met him in the waiting room and greeted him with the remark: "Well, Danny—we've known each other a long time, haven't we?"

Danny's answer was "Yes . . . a lifetime."

PART IV

PSYCHOANALYSIS, MORAL

VALUES, AND CULTURE

17. Religion and Morality: A Psychoanalytic View

MORTIMER OSTOW, M.D.

IN THE FIRST flush of psychoanalytic enthusiasm, Freud and his colleagues tried to work out the dynamics of many different forms of human endeavor, among them, religion. On the basis of the evident modus operandi of religion and what had been learned about the Oedipus complex and other aspects of early family relations, Freud reconstructed an idealized "prehistory" of religion. He pointed out the similarity of religious behavior to the symptoms of obsessive-compulsive neurosis and religion's use of magic and illusion in offering comfort. These he considered maladaptive and unrealistic. Ultimately he tried to relate some of the cultural attitudes held by the Jews to the prehistory of the Jewish people.

Most of the psychoanalytic writers on religion have followed Freud's example. They have tried to uncover the psychodynamics of religious behavior by reference to traditional texts and practices. More recently, actual case studies of individuals who lived in a religious ambience have been presented. For example, Margaretta Bowers (1963) in her book, *Conflicts of the Clergy,* presented case histories of clergymen who are conflicted about religion, and of religious individuals generally who have similar conflicts. In its most recent report, the Committee on Psychiatry and Religion of the Group for the Advancement of Psychiatry has tried to demonstrate with a case history how religion provides idealized images with which young children can identify.

Assuredly many difficulties present themselves in the study of religious influence. What is meant by religion varies from time to

time and from place to place. For example, one would not expect
to find the Western monotheistic religions exerting exactly the
same influence as Oriental religions. Mystical sects create a religious ambience which differs from that created by more pragmatic groups. Celibate orders impose abstinences and restrictions
which exert primary shaping influences even on their already
highly selected membership. Therefore we must recognize that
our clinical observations pertain to a specific kind of religious influence and not to religion in general.

The influence of even a specific religious institution depends
upon the role of that institution within the broader society. In a
relatively irreligious society, the individual can resist the influence
of religious institutions to a greater degree than he can in a religious society. While our clinical experience may inform us of the
circumstances which prevail in our community, and more specifically, our individual practices, we must begin somewhere, bearing in mind that our data can tell us nothing about relative inci-
dence.

An additional problem appears when one tries to focus on the
relation of religion to morality. Moral teachings and imperatives
pervade our whole society to the point where they affect even
those untouched by religion. Those who live a thoroughly religious
life do not escape the influence of the morality of the general society. We must recognize the implications of this secular source of
moral influence in evaluating the morality of our patients.

When we review our cases, it becomes immediately apparent
that we are dealing with at least two distinct groups: those patients whose entry into religious life follows from their accepting
the orientation of the family into which they were born; and those
whose religious interest appeared as an innovation, in response to
a specific event, external or intrapsychic, or as part of the symptomatology of an illness.

Let us consider first the patient who is religious because his
family is religious. The patients of this group do not differ in any
consistent way from patients with similar symptomatology who
are not religious. No particular diagnostic category is especially
well represented here, and none is underrepresented. In these in-

stances, one sees ambivalence toward religion manifested overtly
or covertly, consciously or unconsciously. It is clear however that
the ambivalence toward religion was originally directed toward
the parents and is displaced from them onto the religious institution. In most cases it is the father who is the principal target of
the ambivalence.

Morality is seldom an issue with such patients. Typically, the
morality which is required by the religious life does not conflict
seriously with the prevailing morality of the culture, though it
may not conform to it in every detail. While the ambivalence
finds representation in intensification of, or rejection of religious
behavior, it seldom goes so far as to affect morality. Ambivalence
toward the religious system within the religious group may find
expression in reaction formation, that is, being excessively meticu-
lous in observance, or in projection, accusing others of being irreligious. One seldom finds gross repudiation of moral standards
within the religious group because there is an automatic selection
process. Those who do repudiate morality also repudiate the religious system and so do not number among the religious. In general, given a perverse disposition, the religious patient will make a
greater voluntary effort to overcome it. For example, seminarians
with homosexual tendencies are more likely to abstain from overt,
unsublimated homosexual activity than would a nonreligious contemporary. This difference in behavior does not represent a real
difference in psychodynamics or diagnosis. Since each symptom of
mental illness represents a compromise between the expression of
inadmissible instinctual impulses and the suppression of them, the
extent to which the compromise is weighted in one direction or
the other is strongly influenced by social pressures. Individuals
who accept religious discipline are influenced to give greater
weight to restraint than to gratification in the formulation of their
symptoms of mental illness.

As a rule, the decision about whether to adhere to the family
religious position or depart from it is made for the first time
during adolescence. In a homogeneous society this is a more
significant decision than it is in a culture such as ours. Opting out
of the common religion in the former case means opting out of the

community. In a pluralistic society, as it exists in our present metropolitan community, the adolescent can choose to adhere to any of a large number of groups. He will select one which deviates from his parent's position by any degree which he chooses: it may be diametrically opposed, exactly the same, or neither one nor the other. For example, there exists now a group of young radicals who are trying to set up a new society or at least a new form of religious community within the orbit of traditional Judaism. Thus its members can adhere and reject at the same time.

There is of course a consistent tendency to swing back toward the parental position, which becomes manifest especially when the individual becomes a parent himself or upon the death of the parents, especially the father. This phenomenon represents the influence of the tendency to identify with the parents as well as the tendency to deferred obedience. Between the ages of 35 and 60, out of a sense of depression and a need to become reconciled with images of the parents, the tendency becomes even stronger. The swing back toward religion is usually accompanied by an elevation of moral and ethical standards, although there may be some slippage. Thus, the individual may satisfy his superego by adhering to outward forms of religious observance while indulging himself in forms of behavior which do not conform to religious standards.

To summarize, for those who are born into a religious family, religion offers a framework within which the individual may interact with family and community. Adherence to the religion implies no special dynamic and no special vulnerability. Rather it involves a choice to maintain residence in one of several social milieus into which the patient was born.

The situation becomes more interesting when we consider the individual who orients himself to religion in response to the distress of mental illness. Of the various forms of neurosis, obsessive-compulsive neurosis most readily looks to religion for assistance in resolving ambivalence. As Freud pointed out, there is a kinship between the mechanism of religion and that of obsessive-compulsive neurosis. The defensive mechanisms common to each include isolation, displacement, reaction formation, and ritualization. In contradistinction to hysteria and anxiety hysteria in which the individual comes to terms with sensual needs for a specific partner, in obsessive-compulsive neurosis the major issue is subordination, that is, accepting one's subordinate place, originally with respect to one's father within the family, and subsequently to one's superiors within the community. Accordingly, we find obsessive-compulsive neurotics fixated at the anal phase wherein they first accept self-control in deference to authority. Most obsessive-compulsives, if they are not explicitly committed to a religious life, maintain one or more fragments of behavior which are religious in essence or in form. It may be a recitation of simple daily prayers, usually with the formula "God bless my parents, my wife, and my children." It may be kissing or touching a ritual object. These things are generally done privately because the patient is ashamed of them. He usually recognizes their idiosyncratic nature but still protests that they have religious significance. The concern to avoid soiling, which occurs universally in obsessive-compulsive neurosis, fixes especially upon the "sacred" objects.

Obessive-compulsives tend to be conservative, adhering to the familiar and avoiding the novel. This tendency applies to political and social attitudes, as well as to their interest in religion. There is a preference for the conventional as opposed to the radical and at times the conventional is overdone to the point of conspicuously eccentric hyperconventionality.

The morality of the obsessive-compulsive is paradoxical. He professes to the highest standards of ethical and moral behavior, generally behaving in a manner consistent with these professions. Analysis, however, usually reveals one or more areas of dishonesty which he has concealed and minimized. There are generally struggles over decisions, and while he ultimately decides to comply with moral expectations, the compliance is frequently carried out in such a way that its force is vitiated. The moral posture is consistent with religious interest and yet it is seldom related to it overtly, that is, it is consistent for a person who professes to be religious to wish also to be moral. However the patient seldom says that he must make the moral decision because that is a religious commandment. His morality is in fact primitive. The obsessive-compulsive behaves correctly not out of any commitment to correct behavior nor out of concern for the other individual, but rather out of fear of being found guilty or even blamed. There are three kinds of offense which tempt the individual at any of several levels of consciousness. First is insubordination to authority, specifically to the father, with an accompanying tendency to degrade him and to violate sexual taboos. Second is the killing of rivals, especially siblings and children. Third is stealing and hoarding.

Obsessive-compulsive neurosis may be seen as a disorder of the process of accepting one's relative position as a maturing individual within the family structure. The developing child must accept authority; he must refrain from murdering his siblings; he must not take more than his share; he must keep himself and his quarters clean; his sexual appetites must be satisfied outside the family. [1] We say he must accept the discipline of the superego. From one point of view, religion may be seen as a social structure which by placing constraints on its members, enables them to function cooperatively. It may therefore also be seen as a device wherein the superego is concretized. It supplements a fairly flexible inner control with a more rigid external constraint. Like obsessive-compulsive neurosis, religion makes use of some primitive techniques for overcoming tendencies toward insubordination, namely, isolation, displacement, ritualization and reaction formation. Morality could be defined as a set of propositions, explicit and implicit, which describe the required relation of the individual to his society. Ethics may be defined as the required relation of each individual to every other.

Why does one tend to comply with superego expectations? We have two explanations. First, there is an automatic superego control which the ego may combat, evade, overcome or obey, but which it cannot ignore. Superego demands acquire the force of instinct. The superego achieves its power because the individual has a need to be a member of a family and of society. Some of these automatic controls seem to prevail under the most distressing circumstances. No matter how angry a person may become,

[1] Between the ages of four and 10 he must gradually give up expectation of sensual gratification at the hands of his parents; and when, at puberty, genital sexual drive evolves, it must be directed only toward extrafamily partners.

unless he feels that he is under attack, he will resist the impulse to murder. So strong is this resistance that he may turn the impulse upon himself, become depressed or psychotic, or ultimately destroy himself.

The second explanation is that the individual complies with the superego just as the child needs to retain the love of his parents and avoid being punished. I prefer to regard the first formulation as the effective force of the superego and the second as the motivation for learning the requirements of the superego. The difference is comparable to different aspects of motivation for learning. Although children learn out of a need to sublimate and out of a kind of instinctual curiosity, the original motivation is a desire to please the parent. I believe that a similar distinction may be made in considering the individual's need to comply with religious demands. In western religion as we know it, individuals are thought to comply out of fear of God or love of God or both. While this may be true in some instances and especially in the case of children, I suspect that in most instances the individual adult merely complies with an instinctual tendency to obey which has replaced the need for parental protection as the primary motivation for religious devotion. Since most of us are not aware of our instinctual tendencies, it is not surprising that practitioners of religion ascribe their adherence to the specific promises or threats of the official doctrine. However as analysts we need not be taken in by manifest content or rationalization. It is true that in analysis of religious patients we do encounter these primitive motivations, for example, the wish to retain the parent's love, or fear of being castrated by the father. But we are witnessing such phenomena in neurotic or otherwise mentally ill individuals. These cases tell us about the patient's relation to society in his regressed state. The same motivations need not be assumed to prevail in the individuals who adhere to religion simply because they were born into and have grown up in a religious ambiance, and who are sufficiently well integrated that they do not come under analytic scrutiny.

I believe that most of the changes in attitude toward religion are to be ascribed to a change in the "depressive status" of the individual. I use the term "depressive status" to refer to the condition of the individual with respect to his being free from a depressive tendency, being threatened by depression, or having succumbed to it. The forces conducive to depression exert effects before the depressive syndrome actually appears. The changes to which I am referring are actually related to depressive illness because they appear in a regularly repeated sequence before and after the definitive form of the depression, and because they can be influenced by the same drugs which influence depression.

Many people respond to the first, unconscious threat of depression with a craving for stimulation, for excitement and thrills. For example, they may engage in unusual sexual activities, they may become unfaithful or promiscuous; they may indulge in perversion or take up gambling. Or they may look for exciting and dangerous avocations. The antidepressant effect of stimulation and excitement motivates much of the adolescent unrest today. The more threatened "predepressive" individuals feel, the more desperately they search. In this state of mind they ignore religion but seldom find it necessary to make an issue of repudiating it. Similarly they ignore conventional standards of morality but they are usually too busy seeking thrills to become involved in flouting them. Yet they do seem to have the impression, at least unconsciously, that they are defying fate. It is not that they are interested in repudiating morality, they just do not feel that it applies to them. It used to be said, for example, that adolescent psychopaths had no superego. The superego in such individuals appears to have been put out of commission, ignored. Yet, unacknowledged, it frequently seems to loom overhead represented as a fate waiting to retaliate. If this form of behavior is to be interpreted as a regression, then it must be a regression to a time before the superego existed or before it exerted an effect. While these stimulating activities may involve other individuals, their concern is essentially narcissistic. They have only one aim, to secure maximal sensual pleasure, or more generally, maximal excitement.

A gulf separates this type of sensual activity from religion at least with respect to western tradition. We know that in ancient times, religions existed which prescribed the very same type of activity as a form of worship. These religiously sponsored stimulating activities included group sports, orgiastic sexual activity, and public sadism, including human sacrifice. It seems reasonable to infer that these activities were utilized to protect the populace against threatening depression which was probably no less prevalent then than now. It would be incorrect to assume that the indulgence in these activities indicated an absence of morality. The restraints placed on the individual in these early, tightly organized civilizations were as severe as was true of later civilizations influenced by western types of religion. To the extent that morality consists of conformity to prescribed and definite roles in the community, it existed in these civilizations too. The sensual indulgence was itself circumscribed and ritualized, usually being restricted to certain categories of individuals on certain occasions. Most of the population merely looked on and derived its gratification vicariously. Much of the mythology associated with these activities dealt with the adverse consequences of universal licentiousness. Looked at in one way, the society purchased the loyalty and compliance of its citizens by offering them this powerful and recurrent prophylaxis against depression. In such a culture, the superego was concerned with one's role in society, the acceptance of restrictions, doing one's duty, limiting exciting behavior to the occasions, forms and limits described. Hubris, presuming to privileges and liberties beyond those appropriate to one's role, was inevitably punished by the gods.

The contemporary individual who is trying to combat depressive pressures by engaging in stimulating activities differs from the pagan in that he does not consciously acknowledge a social context in which he acts. Yet he resembles the pagan in that he does not feel entirely free to ignore all social and cultural norms, at least on an unconscious level.

There is another method of combatting depression which is likely to be invoked when and if the first method fails. It is more characteristic of older people, while the first method is more characteristic of adolescents and young adults. However, it should be noted that these are relative rather than absolute frequencies. It consists of clinging to a parent or a parent surrogate for sustenance and protection. The clinical picture is that of a patient who s attached himself to another individual; he cannot be alone, requiring constant expressions of affection and concern; nor can he tolerate criticism or any expressions of indifference. Ultimately, he regresses to an oral-dependent phase of development. In this modality of behavior the individual is apt to show an interest in religion which may be an intensification of an existing religious commitment, a return to a previously abandoned religious position, or a new interest.

The attitude toward morality in this situation is complex. On the one hand there is a strong tendency to recommend one's self to authority by professing and adhering to current moral codes. On the other hand the principle of compliance with social expectations is only a means to an end, while the individual's protection is primary. Consequently, where there is a conflict, the individual may be hard put to choose between personal indulgence and self-restraint. For example, there are religious young people who are constantly tormented by a desire for homosexual comfort, but will not indulge their desire because of their religious commitment.

The commitment may be intense if the need for protection is intense. It is likely to endure so long as the need endures, which may be for years. It is not likely to survive, however, after the need passes.

This kind of situation occurs fairly commonly. One patient, in the course of a schizophrenic depressive breakdown, suddenly became interested in religion and vowed to become and remain observant after she recovered. She did recover and promptly forgot her vow. A patient who is struggling with depression may commit himself to a religious life and remain religious for years if the depressive threat persists. A religious individual may protect himself against impending depression by becoming more religious. In most instances when the need passes the interest in religion also passes. Typically, the interest is in religion rather than in morality, and ritual is emphasized rather than behavior control. The emphasis is more likely to be on morality when the individual has just brought to a close a phase of excessive indulgence such as that described above.

The shift from excessive indulgence to conformity and abstinence frequently takes the form of religious conversion. It is usually accompanied by moral conversion but the religious aspect predominates. Morality appears in these situations only as an aspect of religious behavior.

The attitude of anaclitic dependence lends itself to the attitude of our western religions in the same sense that the attitude of excitement lends itself to the attitude of pagan religions. The form of morality which it encourages resembles the morality of the small child who obeys and behaves himself out of a need to retain the love and protection of his parents. Since it is based specifically on the need to hold onto parents it is a contingent morality in which absolute principles are less important than obtaining and retaining favor. It is a presuperego morality. The feeling of guilt is especially prominent in this phase. Readiness to accuse oneself and to accept blame is a feature of the clinging attitude. The patient says to the parent, "I was naughty. I will be good. Love me!" In this sense, the feeling of guilt represents the wish for reconciliation and it is often accompanied by the need for punishment which is the result of a persisting hostility toward the love object. This hostility is now deflected against the self.

Eventually there may come a point at which both defenses against depression fail and the individual succumbs. If he falls ill slowly, he may spend some time in a phase of angry repudiation. Here he rejects all commitments he had made, makes a desperate attempt at independence, and becomes very angry. He may reject religion too, especially if the religious commitment was made during the phase of clinging. A commitment to morality which accompanied the turn to religion will be withdrawn though immorality will not necessarily follow.

In the phase of definitive depression, there is no concern other than narcissistic hypochondria. Religion may be affirmed or rejected but the words are not accompanied by action. There are frequently loud protestations of guilt, many of which are delusional, and they are associated with the anguish of self-castigation. This attitude seems to be a residue of the guilt-ridden attitude of the earlier clinging phase. However, whereas the guilt of the clinging phase may lead to realistic steps toward reconciliation, the guilt of definitive depression leads to no action at all. The phase of definitive depression seems to be one in which the individual has abandoned society and has no use for morality.

Yet if we step back and view depressive illness against the social context in which it appears, we may reach a different conclusion. It is my contention that the depressive process is initiated by the situation of being trapped. We call the condition "reactive depression" when the trap is truly an external one. But in most cases of depression, even when the trigger appears to be external, the trap consists of the irreconcilable coexistence of love and hate for the same individual. The decision, unconscious though it is, to deflect hostility against oneself by making oneself ill—in its extreme form by suicide—may be regarded as a primitive form of morality, or more accurately, a precursor of morality. Since the child cannot survive without his parents, the dependent individual must not kill the parent unless he is himself prepared to die immediately thereafter.

Finally, let us turn our attention to the phenomenon of "otherworldliness." I use this term to refer to the attitude toward reality which is shared by schizophrenics, mystics, and antinomians. These three groups of individuals also hold a psychodynamic mechanism in common, i.e., confronted with what the subject considers an intolerable reality, he puts it out of his mind and thereby figuratively destroys it. Unable to tolerate the desolation of having lost his world, he then proceeds to construct, in fantasy, a new one. The process involves mental changes which create for the individual the illusion that the world is being destroyed and that it will then be reborn. In schizophrenia the detachment from actual reality is complemented by a delusional system and by the attempt to achieve sensual pleasure. In mysticism the detachment from reality is accomplished by a willed mental set; by special circumstances, for example, sensory isolation or instinctual frustration; and by encouragement of a fraternal, mystically oriented group. If we use the term "antinomianism" in its general rather than strictly religious sense, it refers to a repudiation of the traditionally established social order justified by an articulated hope for a new one. It may take the form of social or philosophic reorientation, social action, or actual revolution.

Let us start with a consideration of schizophrenia. From the social point of view, the moral issue here seems clear. Basically the schizophrenic wishes to destroy, to kill. By expending most or all of his fury in making himself mentally ill he spares those elements of society which he cannot tolerate. Self-destruction in the interest of society we described above as a primitive form of morality or a precursor of morality. But we must also consider that the patient himself has to assume responsibility for his repudiation of society and for his hostility to it. Here the moral issue is not so clear because we recognize that individual idiosyncrasy or weakness may make a person unable to conform to social expectations.

The schizophrenic, especially the paranoid schizophrenic, will frequently cultivate a set of religious ideas to support his rejection of a society which he accuses of being immoral. He is apt to denounce existing religious institutions, accusing them of hypocrisy, and frequently announcing that he is a new prophet or a new savior. The material usually suggests that he in fact identifies with God. The Schreber case illustrates this point.

Religion appeals to the schizophrenic because it sanctions rejection of reality and a belief in things other than the immediately perceptible. This it does in the interest of optimism and hope but the schizophrenic uses this sanction to justify his rejection of society although unconsciously he knows that it is fundamentally immoral to do so.

The mystic cannot tolerate society either, though the reasons may be less personal and more social than in the case of the schizophrenic. The religious mystic will outwardly adhere to the religious institution in which he resides but, appealing to a higher standard, he challenges existing attitudes and espouses changes which may be revolutionary. The mystic professes to new knowledge, to illumination, which he says gives him authority to demand and to make changes. In his visions he sees himself first experiencing God in some literal way and then merging with Him. By becoming one with God he derogates those outside his mystical fraternity.

Mortimer Ostow

Since morality is a function of the individual's relation to his society, when an individual withdraws from his society he automatically abrogates the morality which prevails in his relation to it. Religion lends itself to mysticism because both depend on other-worldliness. The mystic disarms his critic by professing a "higher morality" though his adversaries in the established religion generally take a different, more realistic view. Some mystical sects, for example, the Frankists of eighteenth-century Poland, cultivate forms of behavior which violate the most elementary moral principles of the society in which they reside.

Antinomianism differs from schizophrenia in that it is less a matter of changing one's attitude than making an attempt to change society. The mystic usually does both: he adopts an unusual attitude and he tries to change society. The antinomian addresses himself primarily to changing society, and in repudiating society he also repudiates morality. He justifies his attack on society and his departure from morality by denouncing society and promising to build a better one.

I do not know what the motives of antinomians have been in the historical past. Current antinomianism in the younger generation I attribute to disappointment with a society which fails to provide the supplementary stimulation which many of these young people require in order to facilitate their maturation into the adult world. [2] While many, perhaps most young people can make the transition from childhood dependence via adolescent turmoil to adult maturity, primarily driven by their own motivation and with a minimum of supporting encouragement, there is a large minority who require the external stimulation of social encouragement and demand. In its absence they become angry and development is likely to be arrested at a narcissistic level. They then form an antinomian fraternity which dedicates itself to securing for each of its members protection against depression by offering

[2] Maturation in adolescence is facilitated by challenge and responsibility. The need to contribute to the economic support of one's family and oneself and the obligation to defend one's community or one's country against hostile attack, encourage maturation. The conditions of life characteristic of the frontier society make for a wholesome, vigorous and constructive adolescent generation. The conditions of life which prevail in our affluent society retard adolescent maturation.

the affectionate support of the other members within an underprivileged subsociety. The latter requires active defense, and defending it provides and sanctions exciting methods of stimulation. Among the latter we find orgiastic sexuality, intense sensation and defiance of fate where fate is seen in the role of authority and of objective danger. These antinomian fraternities attack the existing social order which, by failing to provide the needed encouragement, has become the enemy of the young people. Therefore these fraternities are dedicated to probing the weaknesses of society, denouncing it for these weaknesses and attempting to bring it down.

Let me clarify, parenthetically, my notion of the interaction between society and the young individual which tends to generate an antinomian attitude. It is not that I subscribe to the accusations which the young people themselves make, that society is hypocritical, that adults are indifferent, that human relations have been deprived of affect and been replaced by computerized programs. These accusations, while undoubtedly true of some people and places, must be understood as projections of the young people's own problem. It is they who feel alienated, uninvolved and hypocritical. Those feelings arise in the course of the difficulty of their emancipation from childhood dependence to mature independence and the assumption of responsibility for others.

This emancipation is facilitated by a society which requires the services of these young people, which impatiently integrates them into adult society and which depends upon them for vital functions. Adolescents mature rapidly and with least impediment when their society is in clear and present danger so that its survival depends upon their efforts. Contrariwise when the young person finds himself in a society which not only has no real need for him, but which resists his maturation by providing all of his material needs for the present and the future, his emancipation becomes more difficult, and in some cases, impossible. It is true that society fails to help these individuals and, in fact, by failing to assist their maturation, it is virtually creating difficulties for them. But the failing is not in terms of remoteness, indifference and hypocrisy; on the contrary, it lies in the affection, concern, generosity, and often possessiveness, all of which seduce the adolescent into remaining dependent, thereby obstructing his progress. If I may generalize, I suspect that affluence and security constitute an unwholesome environment for maturing youth, while hardship and danger facilitate their growth.

In the sense that religion is conservative and antinomianism is revolutionary, one would expect the two to clash openly. Yet the antinomians are able to find an ally in religion as well. Many clergymen, viewing themselves as defenders of the individual against excessive pressure by society, are influenced to support antinomians in the face of their complaints that they are persecuted. They are further influenced by the truth that the disaffection of the young stems from the failings of society, even though the clergymen may not know what the real failing is. The other-worldliness of the clergymen offers grounds for common cause with the other-worldliness of the antinomians. Both share an idealistic expectation of a utopian society. Both share a preoccupation with bizarre sensory experiences, mystical ruminations, illusions and hallucinations which in some instances are facilitated by the use of drugs that can impair psychic function. The antinomian then may exploit this support by sectors of the religious institution as sanction for his attack upon temporal authority.

The antinomian demands a revolution in moral standards too. The repudiation of existing society which is the essence of immorality, as immorality is defined from a social point of view, he declares to be a moral imperative. He challenges and violates existing standards of sexual behavior. The stability of society depends upon a restriction of violence by the individual. Each individual accepts his role and refrains from challenging those above or hurting those below. The antinomian declares that all attack from below upward is meritorious, and any resistance, even in the interest of defense from above, downward, is immoral. For example, students may provoke police but police may not respond. Negroes may attack Jews, but Jews must not criticize Negroes. Arabs may murder Israelis, but it is immoral for Israelis to retaliate. The larger society must not defend itself against its enemies. Our young antinomians oppose the military posture needed to present the appearance of strength to enemies. Obviously, carried to its logical extreme, their position would require that our government make itself vulnerable to external attack, and this, we may infer, is the actual goal of the antinomian.

The antinomian celebrates the freedom of the individual from social restraint but refuses to acknowledge that a society lacking in the working support of its members becomes weakened to the point where it cannot defend them. He also refuses to acknowledge that the complex society which is needed to provide a maximum of support, protection and gratification to its members requires a high degree of organization and reliability. If the antinomian is successful, he destroys his society, leaves it open to conquest by external enemies, and leaves its members vulnerable to the consequences of both internal disorganization and external conquest. His program must be seen as both murderous toward others and suicidal, reminding us of the schizophrenic or the severely depressed patient who first murders and then commits suicide in rapid succession.

The psychodynamics of other-worldliness is not entirely clear. The hostility which is implicit in it appears in reaction to frustration. The latter in turn comes about as a result of the individual's own inhibitions or as a result of society's obstructing his maturation, or at least its failure to facilitate it. The withdrawal from the world of reality with reinvestment of cathexis in inner sensation may be seen as a regression to infantile narcissism, to a state of mind which prevailed before the time when the infant first took cognizance of the external world. In this state of mind the individual is unable to sustain an affectionate relation with another individual. In their mystical fantasies, these "other-worldly" individuals approach the parent or God. They derive voluptuous sensations from the proximity; they become terrified at the prospect of close approach or contact; but ultimately they feel united with Him—or Her. For example, one young man told me of a fantasy which he experienced while under the influence of LSD. He saw himself approaching his father. As he did, sparks flashed between the extremities of his body and his father's extremities. These were overwhelmingly frightening and the fantasy then changed to an image of his parents dying and their house collapsing. Even in fantasy this young man could not tolerate the acknowledgement of his overwhelming love for his father. However, in the case of the more controlled mystic, the exciting approach is followed by a *unio mystica*. The mystic identifies with the parent as does the infant, i.e., by withdrawing secondary process cognizance that the two are individual and separate. While this is essentially a preoedipal form of identification, primarily oral with some anal and phallic elements, the pressure of an identification with a sexually potent and mature parent suggests an oedipal component as well. The fact that the subjective experience resembles that characteristic of functional temporal lobe disturbance suggests that the regression is actually to a point before temporal lobe function had matured. I speak of temporal lobe disturbance because the latter is characterized by many of the same features that characterize the mystical vision, namely, illusions of familiarity and reality, disturbances of perceptual intensity, perceptual clarity and judgment of distance, and a preoccupation with light.

The other-worldliness of the antinomian betrays a return of the repressed. The mystical orientation of the antinomian signifies a desired reunion with the parents. Adolescent hippies and their fellow travelers often exhibit a surprising sentimentality in their attitude toward religion. The young man referred to above was especially angry with his father who, offended by his son's strikingly unconventional appearance, refused to let him accompany him to the synagogue. One young woman who had come into conflict with her parents because she insisted on living with her boy friend, assured me that she intended to go home for the Jewish holidays because she would not under any circumstances miss *Kol Nidre.*

If religion functions basically as a system to stabilize society, why does it encourage other-worldliness? (I refer here to a belief in invisible deities, commitment to a mythical history and concern with transcendental ideas.) My feeling is that the other-worldliness serves to establish an ideal image of a social order which is unaffected by the individual men and the fortuitous events of the real and current world. It permits the individual to achieve perspective, to avoid being diverted from his proper social role by events which are personally inimical and discouraging. Other-worldliness is basically the encouragement of denial and illusion and in that sense it may be considered an "opiate of the people." But in so far as it functions to preserve the social order it ulti-mately serves the interests of the members of society. It can be pushed to a point of withdrawal from society and can be sub-verted to sanction attack on the existing social order. For example, while religion encourages idealism and a commitment to the transcendental, it is not served by the solitary anchorite mystic and it frequently finds itself under attack by the mystical fraterni-ties within its own ranks. The attack upon organized religion by religious mystics is represented in the drama of the recurrent conflict between mystical prophets and the priests of the establish-ment. The prophet, like the schizophrenic and the antinomian, is generally angry and depressed, frustrated and full of death wishes. He justifies his attack by visions of a social rebirth, an ultimate utopia. To the extent that his attack is intended to eliminate ac-tual corruption and inequity in society, it is constructive. To the extent, however, that it merely expresses his personal bitterness and his desire to destroy society, it is dangerous. What-is confusing to most of us is that attacks which express personal bitterness and fury may locate and expose actual evils in society which require correction; but the correctness of the attacks should not blind us to the destructive aim of the mystical prophet.

BIBLIOGRAPHY

Bowers, M. (1963), *Conflicts of the Clergy*. New York: Nelson.
Group for the Advancement of Psychiatry (1968), The psychic function of religion in mental illness and health, *Report No. 67*, Vol. VI.
Ostow, M. (1970), *The Psychology of Melancholy*. New York: Harper & Row

18. The Young and the Old:

Notes on a New History

ROBERT JAY LIFTON, M.D.

W HAT IS a New History? And why do the young seek one? I raise these questions to introduce the idea of a particular New History—ours—and to suggest certain ways in which we can begin to understand it.

Let us define a New History as a radical and widely shared re-creation of the forms of human culture—biological, experiential, institutional, technological, aesthetic, and interpretive. The newness of these cultural forms derives not from their spontaneous generation, but from extensions and transformations of existing psychic and physical components; that is, from previously unknown (or inadequately known) combinations. This is not to say that there is nothing new under the sun. Rather, what is most genuinely revolutionary makes psychological use of the past for its thrust into the future. A New History, to the extent that it takes shape, reasserts a collective sense of connection, integrity, and movement. It provides new combinations for the symbolic sense of immortality which man requires as he struggles to perpetuate himself biologically, communally, through his works, in his tie to nature, and via transcendent forms of psychic experience.

The shapers of a New History—political revolutionaries, revolutionary thinkers, extreme holocausts, and technological break-

This paper has appeared in *History and Human Survival. Essays on the Young and Old, Survivors and the Dead, Peace and War, and on Contemporary Psychohistory.* New York: Random House, 1969.

Ed. note: Insofar as Dr. Lifton's presentation is more informal than the other works in this volume, the usual bibliographic citations have for the most part been omitted.

throughs—also express the death of the old. This has been true of the American, French, Russian, and Chinese revolutions; the ideas of Copernicus, Darwin, and Freud; the mutilations of the two world wars; and, most pertinent to us, the technological revolution which produced Auschwitz and Hiroshima, as well as the postmodern automated and electronic society. Each of these has been associated with "the end of an era," with the devitalization, or symbolic death, of forms and images defining the worldview and life patterns of large numbers of people over long periods of time.

Great events thus, in different ways, cause, reflect, and symbolize historical shifts. The combination of Nazi genocide and the American atomic bombings of two Japanese cities terminated man's sense of limits concerning his self-destructive potential, thereby inaugurating an era in which he is devoid of assurance that he will live on eternally as a species. It has taken almost 25 years for beginning formulations of the significance of these events to emerge—formulations which cannot be separated from the technological developments of this same quarter-century, or from the increasing sense of a universal world society that has accompanied them.

The New History, then, is built upon the ultimate paradox of two competing, and closely related, images: that of technologically induced historical extinction, and that of man's increasingly profound awareness of himself as a single species. It may be more correct to speak of just one image, extraordinarily divided. And whatever the difficulties in evaluating the human consequences of this image, psychologists and historians who ignore it cease to relate themselves to contemporary experience.

I think we should take seriously the assertion by the young framers (or framer) of the celebrated "Port Huron Statement" of the Students for a Democratic Society, in 1962, still something of a manifesto for the American New Left: "Our work is guided by the sense that we may be the last generation in the experiment with living." Just as many of us took seriously Albert Camus' declaration that, in contrast with every generation's tendency to see itself as "charged with remaking the world," his own had a task "perhaps even greater, for it consists in keeping the world from destroying itself." What I wish to stress is the overriding significance for every post-Hiroshima generation (and one must remind oneself that the S.D.S. leaders, though 25 years younger than Camus, made their statement just five years after his) of precisely this threat of historical extinction. The end of the next era becomes associated, psychologically speaking, with the end of everything.

Do the young feel this most strongly? They themselves often say just the opposite. When I discuss Hiroshima with students, they often make a generational distinction between my sense of profound and specific concern about nuclear weapons and their feeling that these weapons are just another among the horrors of the world bequeathed to them. Our two "histories" contrast significantly: my (over 40) generation's shocked "survival" of Hiroshima and continuing sense of revolutionary distinction between the pre-Hiroshima world we knew and the world of nuclear weapons in which we now live; their (under 25) generation's growing up in a world in which nuclear weapons have always been part of the landscape. This gradual adaptation, as opposed to original shock, is of great importance. Man's unique psychic flexibility permits him to come to terms with almost anything, so long as it is presented to him as an ordained element of his environment.

But such adaptation is achieved at a price, and achieved only partially at that. I believe that the inner knowledge on the part of the young that their world has always been capable of exterminating itself creates a significant undercurrent of death anxiety, against which they must constantly defend themselves—anxiety related to man's fundamental terror of premature death and unfulfilled life, and to high uncertainty about all forms of human continuity. Their frequent insistence that nuclear weapons are "nothing special" is their form of psychic numbing (as opposed to other forms called forth by their elders). What I am suggesting is that the young must perform a great amount of continuous psychological work to maintain their nuclear "cool." And this in turn may make them unusually responsive to possibilities for breaking out of such numbing, and for altering the world which has imposed it upon them.

All perceptions of threatening historical developments must occur through what Ernst Cassirer (1944) called the "symbolic net"—that special area of psychic re-creation so characteristic of man, the only creature who "instead of dealing with . . . things themselves . . . constantly converses . . . with himself." In these internal dialogues, every kind of symbolic death becomes merged with anxieties about technological annihilation. Hiroshima and Auschwitz become psychologically associated with the advanced worldwide disintegration of traditional cultural forms, partly replaced by new institutions (governmental, occupational, and academic) with power and standing which belie the absence of nourishing communal bonds. They become associated also with the confusions of the knowledge revolution, and the unprecedented dissemination of half knowledge through media whose psychological impact has barely begun to be discerned. There is a very real sense in which the world itself has become a "total environment"—a closed psychic chamber with continuous reverberations, bouncing about chaotically and dangerously. The symbolic death perceived, then, is this sense of *formless totality*. And the young are exquisitely sensitive to this kind of "historical death," whatever their capacity (which we shall return to later) for resisting an awareness of the biological kind.

They are struck by the fact that most of mankind simply goes about its business, as if these extreme dislocations did not exist—as if there were no such thing as ultimate technological violence or existence rendered absurd. The war in Vietnam did not create these murderous incongruities, but it does exemplify them, and it consumes the American youth in them. No wonder, then, that in their "conversations with themselves," the young everywhere ask: "How can we bring the world—and ourselves—back to life? How can we move beyond formless totality? How can we create a New History?"

II

Students of revolution and rebellion have recognized the close relationship of both to death symbolism, and to visions of transcending death by achieving an eternal historical imprint. Hannah Arendt (1963) speaks of revolution as containing an "all-pervasive preoccupation with permanence, with a 'perpetual state' . . . for . . . posterity.' " And Albert Camus (1954) refers to insurrection, "in its exalted and tragic forms," as "a prolonged protest against death, a violent accusation against the universal death penalty," and as "the desire for immortality and for clarity." But Camus also stressed the rebel's "appeal to the essence of being," his quest "not . . . for life, but for reasons for living." And this brings us to an all-important question concerning the psychic forms of revolution: that of ideology versus image and idea, and the place of self in relationship to all three.

Men have always pursued immortalizing visions. But most of the revolutionary ideologies of the past two centuries have been notable in providing elaborate blueprints for individual and collective immortality—specifications of ultimate cause and ultimate effect, theological in tone and scientific in claim. For present-day revolutionaries to reject these Cartesian litanies is to take seriously some of the important psychological and historical insights of the last few decades. For one is rejecting the oppressive constellation of ideological totalism—with its demand for milieu control, its imposed guilt and cult of purity and confession, its loading of the language, and its principles of doctrine over person and even of the dispensing of existence itself. This refusal, at its best, represents a quest for a new kind of revolution—one perhaps no less enduring in historical impact, but devoid of the claim to omniscience, and of the catastrophic chain of human manipulations stemming from that claim.

It is of course quite possible that the anti-ideological stance of today's young will turn out to be a transitory phenomenon, a version of the anti-dogmatic euphoria that has so frequently appeared during the early moments of revolution, only to be overwhelmed by absolutist doctrine and suffocating organization in the name of revolutionary discipline. Yet there is reason for believing that the present antipathy to total ideology is something more, that it is an expression of a powerful and highly appropriate contemporary style. The shift we are witnessing from fixed and total forms of ideology to more fluid *ideological fragments* approaches Camus' inspiring vision of continuously decongealing rebellion, as opposed to dogmatically fixed, all-or-none revolution. I would also see it as the emergence of contemporary or *protean man as rebel*—the effort to remain open, while in rebellion, to the extraordinarily rich, confusing, liberating, and threatening array of contemporary historical possibilities, and to retain in the process a continuing capacity for shape-shifting.

Fluidity and shape-shifting are specific talents of protean man, and they greatly enhance his tactical leverage. For instance, Daniel Cohn-Bendit, the leader of the recent French student uprisings, in an interesting dialogue with Jean-Paul Sartre, insisted that the classical Marxist-Leninist principle of the omniscient revolutionary vanguard (the working class, as represented by the Communist Party) be replaced with "a much simpler and more honorable one: the theory of an active minority acting, you might say, as a permanent ferment, pushing forward without trying to control events." Cohn-Bendit went on to characterize this process as "uncontrollable spontaneity," and as "disorder which allows people to speak freely and will later result in some form of 'self-organization.'" He rejected as "the wrong solution" an alternative approach (urged upon him by many among the Old Left) of formulating an attainable program and drawing up realizable demands. While this was "bound to happen at some point," he was convinced it would "have a crippling effect." In the same spirit are the warnings of Tom Hayden, a key figure in the American New Left, to his S.D.S. colleagues and followers, against "fixed leaders"; and his insistence upon "participatory democracy," as well as upon ideology of a kind that is secondary to, and largely achieved through, revolutionary action. So widespread has this approach been that Kenneth Keniston has characterized the American New Left as more a process than a program.

I would suggest that the general principle of "uncontrollable spontaneity" represents a meeting-ground between tactic and deeper psychological inclination. The underlying inclination consists precisely of the protean style of multiple identifications, shifting beliefs, and constant search for new combinations. Whatever

Robert J. Lifton

its pitfalls, this style of revolutionary behavior is an attempt to mobilize twentieth-century fluidity as a weapon against two kinds of perceived stasis—that of old, unresponsive institutions, and that of newly emerging but fixed technological assumptions (concerning, for instance, a "technetronic society"). A central feature is the stress upon community formation. And here too we observe another back-and-forth movement of the protean style—an alternation between conservative images of stable and intimate group ties, and images of transforming society itself in order to make such ties possible.

The process and the psychological substrate are, moreover, universal. Observing the nearly simultaneous student uprisings in America, France, Japan, Germany, Italy, South Africa, Czechoslovakia, Yugoslavia, and Spain, one can only view them all as parts of a large single tendency, within a single worldwide human-technical nexus. Here the planet's instant communications network is of enormous importance, as is the process of psychological contagion. One need not deny the differences in, say, Czech students rebelling against Stalinism, Spanish students against Fascism, and American, French, and Italian students against the Vietnam War, the consumer society, and academic injustices, to recognize the striking congruence in these rebellions. In every case the young seek active involvement in the institutional decisions governing their lives, new paths of significance as alternatives to consuming and being consumed, and liberated rhythms of individual and community existence. Nonspecific and ephemeral as these goals may seem, they are early expressions of a quest for historical rebirth, for reattachment to the Great Chain of Being, for reassertion of a viable sense of immortality.

The French example is again revealing (though not unique), especially in its extraordinary flowering of Graffiti. Here one must take note of the prominence of the genre—of the informal slogan-on-the-wall virtually replacing formal revolutionary doctrine—no less than the content. But one is struck by the enormous stress of the slogans (sometimes to the point of intentional absurdity) upon enlarging the life-space, mostly by means of expanded ethical affirmation. Characteristic were "Think of your desires as realities,"

346 ·

"Prohibiting is forbidden" (a play on words in which the ubiquitous "Defense d'afficher" is converted to "Defense d'interdire"), and, of course, the two most famous: "Imagination in power" and "Imagination is revolution." Sartre was referring to the overall spirit of these Graffiti, but perhaps most to the revolutionary acts themselves, when he commented (in the same dialogue mentioned before): "I would like to describe what you have done as extending the field of possibilities." He spoke not only as a predictably sympathetic fellow revolutionary but also as a protean man of long standing who is able to recognize worthy successors. Precisely such "extending [of] the fields of possibilities" is at the heart of the worldwide youth rebellion—for hippies no less than political radicals —and at the heart of the protean insistence upon continuous psychic re-creation of the self. The extension and the re-creation, projected continuously into an imagined future, become in themselves suggestive bases for a new mode of revolutionary immortality.

III

Of enormous importance for these rebellions is another basic component of the protean style, the spirit of mockery. While young rebels are by no means immune from the most pedantic and humorless discourse, they come alive to others and themselves only when giving way to—or seizing upon—their very strong inclination toward mockery. The mocking political rebel merges with the hippie and with a variety of exponents of pop culture to "put down" his uncomprehending cohorts, and especially his elders. (There has always been a fundamental unity in the rebellions of hippies and young radicals, which is perhaps just now becoming fully manifest.) In dress, hair-beard-sideburn arrangement, and general social and sexual style, the mocking rebel is not only extending the field of possibilities, but making telling commentary—teasing, ironic, contemptuous—on the absurd folk-ways of "the others." The mockery can be gentle and even loving, or it can be bitter and provocative in the extreme.

Here the Columbia rebellion is illuminating. What it lacked in Graffiti it more than made up for in its already classical slogan,

Robert J. Lifton

"Up against the wall, motherfucker!" I make no claim to full understanding of the complete psychological and cultural journey
this phrase has undergone—indeed, a truly comprehensive account
of that journey would teach us a very great deal about contemporary America, about the psychological and revolutionary condition
of the world at large, and much more. But let me at least sketch
in a few steps along the way:

(1) The emergence of the word "motherfucker" (increasingly
un-hyphenated) to designate (let us say now) a form of extreme
transgression. The word might well have originated within the
black American subculture, and certainly has been given fullest
expression there (though an equivalent can probably be found in
virtually every culture); and has been used with great nuance to
express not only contempt but also awe or even admiration.

(2) The attachment of the word to a contemptuous command by
white policemen when ordering black (and perhaps other) suspects
to take their place in the police line-up, thereby creating the full
phrase, "Up against the wall, motherfucker!" The mockery here
was that of dehumanization, and use of the phrase was at times
accompanied by beatings and other forms of humiliation.

(3) LeRoi Jones' reclaiming of the phrase for black victims—and
in the process, achieving a classic victimizer-victim turnabout—by
means of the simple expedient of adding to it, in a poem, the line,
"This is a stick-up."

(4) The appearance of a far-out East Village Yippie (Youth International Party)—style group which embraced Jones' reversal to
the point of naming themselves the "Up-Against-The-Wall-
Motherfuckers."

(5) The attraction of Columbia S.D.S. leaders to this East Village
group ("mostly because we liked their style," Mark Rudd said on
one occasion); and the use of part of the phrase ("Up Against the
Wall!") for the title of a pre-uprising one-issue newspaper, and all
of the phrase to express contempt for Grayson Kirk in Mark Rudd's
open letter to him published in that same newspaper. The threatening chant, "To the wall!" or "Up against the wall!", adopted
by young American radicals from the Cuban Revolution might also
be a factor in this sequence.)

(6) The slogan's full flowering during the course of the Columbia strike, both in abbreviated and complete form, in shouted student chorus, for confronting just about all representatives of what was considered negative authority—police, city officials, administrators, and faculty. Rudd has claimed that his group adopted the slogan "in order to demonstrate our solidarity with the blacks and our understanding of the oppression they have been subjected to." But other student-strikers told me this was "a public explanation." They attributed the slogan's popularity to the students' general mood and feelings about their adversaries; and also to the presence of a few members of the East Village group. One, known as "John Motherfucker," was constantly in view, wearing his "club jacket" with the organizations' name lettered on it, and advocating indiscriminate violence. He became an object of both humor (other students thought his ideas "crazy") and affection.

(7) The arrested students' renewed encounter with the police version of the shorter phrase ("Up against the wall!") when *they* were called to the police line-up ("I can't get over how they really do use the term," wrote "Simon James" in his *New York Magazine* article).

(8) The by now well-known pun of Lionel Trilling, in characterizing the striking students (not without affection) as "Alma-Mater-fuckers"—a witty example of an important principle: the continuous mocking of the mockery.

In evaluating the significance of the phrase and its vicissitudes, the classical psychoanalytic approach would, immediately and definitively, stress the Oedipus complex. After all, who but *fathers* are mother-fuckers? And who but sons yearn to replace them in this activity? Moreover, the authorities at whom the Columbia students aimed the phrase could certainly qualify, in one way or another, as father-substitutes. And there was much additional evidence throughout the student rebellions of a Totem-and-Taboo-like attack upon the father—as exemplified, mockingly and playfully, by another bit of French Graffiti, "Daddy stinks" (Papa pue); and, mockingly and nastily, by Columbia students reported to have shouted at their faculty elders, "Why don't you go and die!"

But one does well to move beyond this kind of psychoanalytic explanation—to take it as a beginning of rather than an end to understanding. For if we assume that the mother in question is, so to speak, the fucker's own, we are dealing with an image of the ultimate violation of the ultimate incest taboo. Now it has been said recently that this taboo is society's last inviolate principle— the only psychomoral barricade which contemporary experiential rebels have not yet stormed. Whether or not this is true, there is no doubt that sexual prohibitions between mother and son are fundamental to the ordering of all societies. The bandying about of the phrase "Up against the wall, motherfuckers," then, is a way of playing with an image of ultimate violation, and of retribution for that violation. The tone could be menacing and hateful, but on the whole (at least among the students) less one of irreconcilable rage than of taunting ridicule and mimicry. And the continuous reversals characterizing the whole sequence—the switches between victimizer and victim, accuser and accused— ultimately mock not only the whole social order and its linguistic and sexual taboos; like the Trilling pun, they mock the mocking phrase itself.

Midst such reversals of stance, the tone of mockery can be a source of great unifying power. One could argue, for instance, that mockery provided the necessary continuity in the evolution (metaphorically speaking) from hippie to Yippie—from socially withdrawn experiments in feeling-states to activist assault upon social institutions. I have said that hippie and political-activist rebellions are psychologically of a piece, but their functional coexistence in the same mind (and I refer not only to Yippies but to student radicals in general) is a function of the ordering principle of mockery. In the Columbia rebellion this principle was able to unite, if not in political action at least in a measure of shared feeling, such disparate groups as blacks, hippies, Yippies, student radicals, and perhaps Cuban revolutionaries (the police could also be included, but from across the barricades). And one can add to the list the distinguished professor whose pun I quoted, many of his faculty colleagues, a large number of Columbia students not involved in the strike, the writer of this essay, and probably most of its readers. For what protean men share—and I assume that all of us are in some degree protean men—is precisely what mockery confronts: a sense of absurd incongruity in the relationship of self to society, and of death to life. There are moments when this incongruity can be dealt with only by the combinations of humor, taunt, mimicry, derision, and ridicule contained within the style of mockery. For when historical dislocation is sufficiently profound, mockery can become the only inwardly authentic tone for expressing what people feel about their relationships to the institutions of their world. And in this sense young rebels express what everyone —from conservative Wall Street broker to liberal college professor to black militant to anti-black Wallaceite—in one way or another inwardly experiences.

At the more affirmative border of mockery are such slogans of the French students as "We are all undesirables!" and the much more powerful, "We are all German Jews!" The slogans refer directly to the origins of Cohn-Bendit, the student leader, but their significance extends much further. They mock not only anti-Semitism and national-racial chauvinism, but the overall process of victimization itself, and the Old History for harboring such victimization. The method by which this was done is worth noting: a vast open-air charade with thousands of students who, by shouting in unison, "We are all German Jews!," momentarily became classical European victims, and thereby rendered ridiculous the very categories of victim and victimizer. At this affirmative border of mockery, then, and in the far reaches of proteanism, is a call for man to cease his folly in dividing himself into what Erik Erikson has called pseudospecies, and to respond to the ethical and technological mandate to realize himself as the single species he is.

One can also observe the protean impulse toward inclusiveness, though in much more confusing ways, in the diversity of ideological fragments embraced. Thus hippies, for their experiments with the self, draw upon Eastern and Western mysticism, chemically induced ecstasy, and various traditions, new and old, of polymorphous sexuality. Young radicals may incorporate any of these aspects of hippie culture, and combine them with ideas and images drawn from all revolutionary experience (pre-Marxist utopians, anarchists, Marx, Trotsky, Lenin, Rosa Luremburg, Mao, Castro, Guevara, Debray, Ho, Gandhi, Fanon, Malcolm X, Martin Luther King, Stokely Carmichael, and H. Rap Brown); from recent psychological and social theorists (Sartre, Camus, C. Wright Mills, Herbert Marcuse, Norman Brown, Erik Erikson, Abraham Maslow, and Paul Goodman); and from just about any kind of evolving cultural style (derived from jazz or black power or "soul," from the small-group movement including Esalen-type stress upon "Joy," or from camp-mockery of Victorian or other retrospectively amusing periods), including all of the revolutionary and intellectual traditions just mentioned.

Moreover, the emphasis upon the experiential—upon the way a man and his ideas *feel* to one right now, rather than upon precise theoretical constructs—encourages inclusiveness and fits in with the focus upon images and fragments. Detailed intellectual legacies tend to be neglected, and even revered figures are often greatly misunderstood. But the overall process can be seen as a revolutionary equivalent to the artist's inclination to borrow freely, selectively, impressionistically and distortingly from predecessors and contemporaries as a means of finding his own way.

Of enormous importance as models are heroic images of men whose lives can themselves be viewed as continuously revolutionary. The extraordinary accomplishments of Mao, Castro, and especially Guevara, can combine with romantic mythology of many kinds, including that of perpetual revolution. In a sense Castro and Guevara are transitional figures between the total ideologies of the Old History and the more fragmentary and experiential ones of the New History. (I shall comment later upon the particular dilemmas Mao presents for the new rebels.) But heroes and models tend to be easily discarded and replaced, or else retained with a looseness and flexibility that permits the strangest of revolutionary bedfellows. In lives as in ideologies, the young seek not the whole package but those fragments which contribute to their own struggle to formulate and change their world, to their own sense of revolutionary process. Their constant search for new forms becomes a form in itself.

To dismiss all this as a "style revolution" is to miss the

point—unless one is aware of the sense in which style is everything. One does better to speak of a *revolution of forms,* of a quest for images of rebirth which reassert connectedness and reestablish the sense of immortality; and of a *process revolution,* consistent with the principles of action painting and kinetic sculpture, in which active rebelling both expresses and creates the basic images of rebellion. Donald Barthelme's principle, "Fragments are the only form I trust," has ramifications far beyond the literary. Whatever the pitfalls of this principle for social and especially political revolution, we deceive ourselves unless we learn to focus upon these shifting forms—that is, to adopt an increasingly formative (rather than classically analytic) perspective. Indeed we require a little revolutionizing of our psychological assumptions, so that both the young and the old can be understood, not as bound by static behavior categories, but as in continuous historical motion.

IV

Let us, for instance, turn to the extremely important symbolism surrounding fathers and sons. A thematic key is that of fatherlessness—but not in the sense of a search for a "substitute father."

In addition to his biological and familial relationship to his children, we may speak of the *formative father* as a human nerve-center, mediating between prevailing social images on the one hand, and the developmental thrusts of his children (biological or symbolic) on the other. Because the father is clearly not a simple conduit, and imposes a strong personal imprint (his "personality") upon the child, we tend to fall into the lazy psychoanalytic habit of seeing every authoritative man or group coming into subsequent contact with the child from the larger social arena as a "substitute" for the father, as a "father figure." Yet considering the enormous part played by general historical forces in shaping what the father transmits (or fails to transmit), one might just as well say that he himself is a "substitute" for history, a "history figure." The analogy is admittedly a bit absurd—a flesh-and-blood father, and not "history," conceives the child, teaches him things, and tells him off—but so is the tendency toward indiscriminate labeling of one person as a "substitute" for another. We do better, especially during periods of rapid change, to see fathers and sons as bound up in a shifting psychological equilibrium, each influencing the other, both enmeshed in forms specific to their family and their historical epoch. (Mother and daughters are of course very much part of all this. But the mother's "mediation," for biological and cultural reasons, tends to be more heavily infused with nurturing; her way of representing forms of social authority tends to be more indirect, complex, and organically rooted. And revolutionary daughters, like their mothers, deserve an evaluation of their own, quite beyond the scope of this essay.) A son's developing image (or images) of the world should not be attributed to a single cause, nor considered a replacement for an earlier imprint, but should be seen as an evolving inner combination that is both idiosyncratic and collectively shaped.

Nor is the father by any means a pure representative of the Old History. Rather he is a molder of compromise between the history he has known and the newer one in which the life of his family is immersed. During periods like the present he is, psychologically speaking, by no means a clear spokesmen for stability and "order." He is more a troubled negotiator, caught between the relatively orderly images he can retain (or reach back for) from the Old History, and the relatively disorderly ones anticipating the New History. While likely to be more on the side of the former than the latter, in the midst of a revolution of forms his allegiances may not be too clear. He finds himself suspended in symbolic time, weakened by the diminishing power of old forms, and by his inability to relate himself significantly to (or even comprehend) the new.

During earlier revolutions (the French Revolution or the social revolution of the Renaissance) the Old History under attack, however vulnerable, was still part of a coherent formulation of the world—theological, political, and social. One suspects that this formulation provided the fathers of the time with psychic ammunition sufficient at least to confront, and oppose directly, their rebellious sons. But the Old History now being attacked, reflecting as it does more than 200 years of erosion of traditional forms of every kind, permits fathers no such symbolic strength, no such capacity for confrontation. Instead we find a characteristic father-son paradigm emerging in families everywhere—of young American radicals (as reported by Kenneth Keniston), middle-class Germans (described by Alexander Mitscherlich), Japanese *Zengakuren* student-activists (whom I interviewed), and, very likely, of many young French student-rebels. The paradigm is this: The son, fortified and recurrently exhilarated by his radical convictions, and by his sense of being ethically and historically *right*, pities rather than hates his father for the latter's "sellout" to evil social forces. Whether kindly or contemptuous in this judgment, he views his father as one who has erred and been misled, as a man in need of patient re-education (if he is to be salvaged at all) rather than total denunciation. Inwardly, the father, himself, cannot help but share many of these judgments, however he may try to attribute them to his son's immaturity and youthful excess. This is the sense in which fathers no longer exercise ethical authority over their sons. What they have lost is what may be termed their *formative hegemony*, their capacity to guide their offspring (rather than be guided by them) through the shifting forms of their common world.

This loss of formative hegemony is what we generally call "the absence of male authority." Its large-scale occurrence reflects the *historical* absence of a meaningful set of inner images of what one should value, how one should live. But it is experienced by the individual as a profound sense of fatherlessness. Sons perceive the world as devoid of strong men who know how things are and how they should be. The young feel abandoned by their fathers, feel a sense of separation rather than connection, stasis rather than development, and disintegration rather than integrity or meaning. They experience the hunger for forms—and especially imagery of rebirth—which I have described as characteristic of protean man.

But precisely this kind of symbolic fatherlessness, as I have also suggested, makes possible every variety of experiment and innovation. Just as the young lack the nurturing comfort of fixed social forms, so are they free of the restricting demands of these forms. Since nothing is psychologically certain, everything is possible. Thus there emerges an *unencumbered generation* (if we may give it still one more name), in politics as well as in experimental life styles.

Unencumbered rebellion can include every variety of tactical and ideological foray—as expressed in this country's "new politics" (the young radicals' politics of confrontation, the Yippies "politics of ecstasy," and the more staid but still politically unconventional and youth-influenced campaigns of Eugene McCarthy and Robert Kennedy); and especially in contemporary novels (such as the nightmare version depicted by Sol Yurick in *The Bag*). This innovative potential is perhaps the least understood dimension of the new rebels. It particularly confuses members of the Old Left, provoking them to assert judgments derived from the Old History about how radicals should behave, or else to attempt (often with considerable sympathy) to subsume the new rebellion under a traditional ideological label. (Anarchism is the most tempting, because of its stress upon human relations in autonomous communities and opposition to centralized power, and because of what George Woodcock has referred to as "its cult of the spontaneous . . . [and] striking protean fluidity in adapting its approach and methods to special historical circumstances." But even Woodcock speaks of "a new manifestation of the idea"; and the young themselves tend to alternate between accepting the anarchist label as one of their ideological fragments, and expressing wariness toward it as still another potential ideological trap.) Perhaps Sartre was wiser in his characterization of the phenomenon to Cohn-Bendit: "You have many more ideas than your fathers had. . . . Your imagination is far richer."

The formative fathers of the young rebels are the middle-aged members of the intellectual Left. (I recently heard one articulate young rebel say as much to an audience made up mostly of university professors: "We are your children. You taught us what American society is like.") And the encounter between formative fathers and their sons takes on special importance. On the one hand the young rebels seize upon their innovative freedom and seek to live out both the classical revolutionary myth of making all things new, and the contemporary protean myth (if I may call it that) of infinite shape-shifting to the point of rendering the Old

History totally "irrelevant." They may thus view their formative fathers as no more than rickety impediments. But on the other hand, they give the impression of constantly seeking *something* from this group of their elders: confirmation in radicalism, adult-dispensed legitimation (psychological and ethical), authoritative support and at times even guidance (but never direction) concerning theory and tactics. (One must keep in mind the origins of many of the ideological fragments of the young rebels in older-generation thought—the writings of Herbert Marcuse and C. Wright Mills—without viewing these origins as totally determinative.) The young, then, do seek connection, but without suffocation and with a minimum of restriction. The connection may be essentially negative —the young focusing upon the distinctions between their activism, flexibility, and moral intensity, and their elders' passivity, fixity, and shameful compromise—but even this can be a form of connection.

The "fathers" involved also crave connection. As longstanding advocates of liberal or radical programs, now puzzled or even terrified by their intellectual offspring, they too ask themselves where they can link up with the Great Chain of historical-revolutionary Being. But nothing for these formative fathers is clear-cut. They do not live in a time (Confucian or Biblical) in which sons are expected to honor, and seek to become like, their fathers. Nor do the young bring to them the kind of total negation expressed in a three-sentence commentary by a member of Hell's Angels: "I don't like nothin'. I don't like nobody. Fuck everything." Either of these extremes could call forth fairly standard responses—the first an assertion of continuing intellectual and social authority, the second condemnation or reforming zeal toward wayward youth. Instead the middle-aged Left-intellectual finds the encounter to be replete with ambiguities. It takes place, moreover, while he is in the midst of his own crisis of forms. He is likely to be alternately attracted, repulsed, impressed, bedazzled, jarred, and bemused by young rebels and their behavior—his historical sense and paternal impulse combining to tell him he should *do* something, he knows not what.

He at times responds with a reactivation of his own radicalism

Robert J. Lifton

—possibly an awakening from a long political sleep—which can in turn take the form of either a profound re-examination of his world, or of an uncritical psychological identification with the young to the point of near total self-surrender. Or he may have the opposite response of angry and unyielding dissociation from the young, sometimes with searching criticism of their programs, but all too often with a petulant and willfully uncomprehending declaration of generational warfare. A third response, a favorite of postmodern intellectuals in times of crisis, is that of escape into technical and professionalized preoccupations—though the allergy of the young to this stance is making it more and more difficult to maintain. There are of course other kinds of responses, as I shall soon suggest. But here I want to stress the very real psychological—actually psychohistorical—problems faced by these members of the "older generation."

For instance, they experience severe self-condemnation (feelings of guilt) over reminders of never-quite-abandoned ideals and never-quite-confortable accommodations, over not doing more to embrace the young and their movement; or if they do embrace them, over the possibility of repeating their own past political mistakes in response to a new call to revolution. They feel rage toward the young because of the severe formative threat they represent (sometimes accompanied by envy of the strength and conviction behind that threat), as well as rage toward themselves because of their own sense of impotence. Most of all, they sense a fundamental threat to overall integrity, to whatever degree of wholeness they have been able to achieve in their blend of individual struggles and historical forms—in their decent liberalism, ordered radicalism, professional autonomy, and personal privacy —that is, a threat to the entire formative structure of their lives. And even those who, like Sartre, wish to acknowledge the imaginative hegemony of their "sons," must sense that they themselves, as older models, are likely to be rather quickly "used up," and either discarded or retained condescendingly (as is to some extent already the case with Marcuse), in order to make way for new imaginative forays. (It could be argued that the young have by-passed fathers for formative grandfathers, such as the 70-year

358 ·

old Marcuse and the 75-year old Mao, a pattern frequently resorted to when rapid historical change weakens the former and renders the latter in various ways more heroic. But I would see this as only one among protean patterns, and point to younger models such as Guevara and Castro, as well as to "old" young radicals such as Tom Hayden.) In any case, formative fathers risk inner agreement with the young's accusatory chant of "irrelevance" until they themselves can discover just where their genuine "relevance"—their authentic personal and historical connection—lies.

V

Formative fathers and sons meet at the university. There has been much discussion about young rebels' selection of the university as a primary target for recent upheavals. Many distinguished commentators (David Riesman, Christopher Lasch, Steven Spender, Herbert Marcuse, Lionel Trilling, and Noam Chomsky, among others) have cautioned students about the dangers of confusing the vulnerable centers of learning they attack, and for periods of time "bring down," with society at large. Spender stated the matter eloquently when he said that "however much the university needs a revolution, and the society needs a revolution, it would be disastrous . . . not to keep the two revolutions apart." He went on to point out, as have others also, that the university is "an arsenal from which [student-rebels] can draw the arms from which they can change society"; and that "To say, 'I won't have a university until society has a revolution,' is as though Karl Marx were to say 'I won't go to the reading room of the British Museum until it has a revolution.'" Yet wise as these cautionary thoughts undoubtedly are, one also has to consider the ways in which the university's special symbolic significance makes it all too logical (if unfortunate) a target for would-be revolutionaries.

What makes the university unique as a formative area is the extent to which the prevailing concepts of a society are—simultaneously, and with varying weightings—presented, imposed, examined, and criticized. The university is indeed a training ground for available occupational slots in society, as young rebels are

Robert J. Lifton

quick to point out, and can at its worst approach a technical instrument in the hands of the military-industrial complex. But it can also be precisely the opposite, a training ground for undermining social institutions, as Spender suggests, and as the young rebels themselves attest to by the extent to which they are campus products. In most cases the university is a great many things in between. It provides for students four years of crucial personal transition—a *rite de passage* from relatively unformed adolescence to a relatively formed adulthood. And the fact that many are likely to move through continuing protean explorations during the postuniversity years renders especially important whatever initial adult "formation" the university makes possible. For these reasons, and because both groups are *there*, the university is the best place for the rebellious young to confront their ostensible mentors, and thereby both define themselves and make a statement about society at large.

The statement they make has to do not only with social inequities and outmoded institutions, but with the general historical dislocations of *everyone*. And in this sense the target of the young is not so much the university, or the older generation, as the continuing commitment of both to the Old History. But the university provides unique opportunities for the young to reverse the father-son mentorship—and, moreover, to do so *in action;* in a manner that has special importance for them in their quest for personal and historical revitalization. The reversal may be confused and temporary, with student and teacher moving back and forth in protean-style shifts in leadership and followership, but in the process the young can assert their advanced position in the shaping of the New History. Though the "generation gap" seems at times to be increasing beyond redemption, there is also a sense in which the gap narrows as the young engage their elders as they never have before, and the university becomes a place of unprecedented intellectual and emotional contact between the generations. What happens at one university can be repeated, with many variations, at any other university throughout the world. Universities everywhere share a central position in the generalized anticipation of the New History, and tend also to present students with

360 ·

very real grievances; the global communications network provides not only the necessary contagion but instant instructions in the art of university rebellion. Protean principles extend across the whole field of stimulation and response, as the last (the American university) becomes the first, sleepers awake, positions are exchanged and re-exchanged, and specific actions and reactions give way to a generalized historical process.

We can learn more about the university in the midst of militant social disorder by turning to the greatest of recent national upheavals, the Chinese Cultural Revolution. More than is generally realized, universities were the focus of much that took place during that extraordinary movement. Not only were they a major source of activist Red Guard revitalizers, but within them a series of public denunciations of senior professors and administrators by students and young faculty members preceded—and in a sense set off—the Cultural Revolution as a whole. These denunciations originated at Peking University, which has been the scene of many such upheavals over the decades prior to the Communist victory in China, and during the subsequent series of extraordinary campaigns of "thought reform" that have become a trademark of the Chinese Communist regime. The Cultural Revolution was the most extreme of these campaigns, and contrasted with more recent student rebellions elsewhere in one very important respect: the young were called forth by their elders (Mao and the Maoists) to fight the latter's old revolutionary battles, and to combat the newly threatening impurities associated with revisionism. But from the beginning there was probably a considerable amount of self-assertion and spontaneity among Red Guard leaders and followers. And throughout the Cultural Revolution, overzealous Red Guard groups became more and more difficult for anyone to control, especially as they split into contending factions, each claiming to be the most authentically revolutionary and Maoist. And during the summer of 1968, reports of jousts, fights, and pitched battles among them, also taking place at Peking University, revealed how within two years that institution had shifted in its function from provider of the spark to receptacle for the ashes of the Cultural Revolution. Significantly, members of the Red Guard were then demoted to the status of "intellectuals" who required the tutelage of workers and peasants (and the control of the Army). But Peking and other universities continued to preoccupy the regime as places in need of fundamental reform.

Indeed the remolding of educational institutions has been greatly stressed over the course of the Cultural Revolution. And the extraordinary step of closing all schools throughout China for more than a year was both a means of mobilizing students for militant political struggles beyond the campuses, and revamping (however chaotically) the nation's educational process. I have described the Cultural Revolution as a quest for symbolic immortality, a means of eternalizing Mao's revolutionary works in the face of his anticipated biological death and the feared "death of the revolution." The university was perceived throughout as both an arena of fearful dangers (revisionist ideas), and as what might be called an immortalizing agent (for the promulgation at the highest cultural levels of the most complete Maoist thought).

In its own fashion, the Cultural Revolution was a response to the New History, which in China's case includes not only Russian and Eastern European revisionism but early manifestations of proteanism. Chinese universities, however, have been forced to flee from contemporary confusions into what is most simple and pure in that country's Old Revolutionary History, in contrast to the more open-ended plunge into a threatening but multifaceted future being taken by universities throughout the rest of the world. Yet these issues are far from decided. Universities everywhere, China included, are likely to experience powerful pressures for "restructuring" along lines consistent with a protean revolutionary ethos. While this hardly guarantees equivalent restructuring of national governments, it may well be a prelude to fundamental changes in every aspect of human experience.

VI

One can hardly speak of definitive conclusions about something just beginning, and at that an emerging process rather than a well-defined entity. Nor would I claim a position of omniscient detachment from the events of the New History—I have in no way been immune from the combinations of feelings they have evoked for my generation of Left-intellectuals, and have here and there contributed to dialogues on them. But having earlier in this essay affirmed the significance of the New History, I wish now to suggest some of its pitfalls, and finally, present some present-day potentialities for avoiding them.

From the standpoint of the young, these pitfalls are related to what is best called romantic totalism. I refer to a post-Cartesian absolutism which is primarily experiential, a new quest for old feelings. Its controlling image, at whatever level of consciousness, is that of *replacing history with experience.*

This is, to a considerable extent, the classical romanticism of the "youth movement." I have heard a number of thoughtful European-born intellectuals tell, with some anxiety, how the tone and atmosphere now emanating from young American rebels is reminiscent of that of the German youth movement of the late Weimar Republic (and the Hitler Youth into which it was so readily converted). What they find common to both is a cult of feeling and a disdain for restraint and reason. While I would emphasize the differences between the two groups much more than any similarities, there is a current in the New History that is more Nietzschean than Marxist-Leninist. It consists of a stress upon experiential transcendence, the cultivation of feeling-states so intense and so absorbing that time and death cease to exist. The pattern becomes totalistic when it begins to tamper with history to the extent of victimizing opponents in order to reinforce its own feeling-states; a genuine danger signal is the absolute denial of the general principle of historical continuity.

The replacement of history with experience—with totally liberated feeling—is by no means a new idea, and has long found expression in classical forms of mysticism and ecstasy. But it has reappeared with considerable force in the present-day drug revolution, and in the writings of a number of articulate contemporary spokesmen such as Norman O. Brown. This universally increasing stress upon experiential forms of transcendence would seem to be related to the impairment of alternative modes of symbolic immortality (whether biological, or through man's works) brought about by the threat of nuclear weapons, and to the as yet unappreciated impairment to our death symbolism to which these weapons contribute. This impairment is probably central to the New History's *unique degree of blending of experiential transcendence with social and political revolution.*

We have already noted that political revolution has its own transformationist myth of making all things new. When this combines with the experiential myth (of eliminating time and death) two extreme positions can result. One of these is the condemnation and negation of an entire historical tradition: the attempt by some of the young to sever totally their relationship to the West by means of an impossibly absolute identity replacement, whether related to immersion in Oriental mysticism, or to "becoming" an Asian or African victim of colonialism or slavery. A second consequence of this dismissal of history could manifest itself in the emergence of a single judgmental criterion: *what feels revolutionary is good, what does not is counterrevolutionary.*

A related, equally romantic pitfall is that of *generational totalism.* The problem is not so much the slogan, "Don't trust anybody over thirty," as the unconscious assumption that can be behind it: that "youth power" knows no limits because *youth equals immortality.* To be sure, it is part of being young to believe that one will never die, that such things only happen to other people, old people. But this conviction ordinarily lives side-by-side with a realization—at first preconscious, but over the years increasingly a matter of awareness—that life is, after all, finite. And a more symbolic sense of immortality, through works and connections outlasting one's individual life span, takes hold and permits one to depend a little less upon the fantasy that one will live forever. Under extreme historical conditions, however, certain groups—in this case, youth groups—feel the need to cling to the omnipotence provided by a more literal image of immortality, which is in turn contrasted with the death-taint of others. When this happens we encounter a version of the victimizing process: the young "victimize" the old (or older) by equating age with death; and the "victim," under duress, may indeed feel himself to be "as if dead," and

collude in his victimization. Conversely, because the older generation has its victimizing needs, sometimes (but not always) in the
form of counterattack, it may feel compelled to view every innovative action of the young as destructive or "deadly." Indeed the
larger significance and greatest potential danger of what we call
the "generation gap" reside in these questions of broken historical
connection and impaired sense of immortality.

The recent slogan of French students, "The young make love,
the old make obscene gestures," is patronizing rather than totalistic, and its mocking blend of truth and absurdity permits a
chuckle all around. But when the same students refer to older critics as "people who do not exist," or when young American radicals label everyone and everything either "relevant" ("revolutionary") or "irrelevant" ("counterrevolutionary") on the basis of
whether or not the person, idea, or event is consistent or inconsistent with their own point of view—then we are dealing
with something more potentially malignant. We approach the totalistic tendency I referred to before as the dispensing of existence, the drawing of a sharp line between people and nonpeople,
between those whose right to exist can be recognized and those
who possess no such right. Perhaps the ultimate expression of generational totalism was that of an early group of Russian revolutionaries who advocated the suppression and even annihilation of
everyone over the age of 25 because they were felt to be too con-
taminated with the Old History of that time to be able to absorb
the correct principles of the New. I have heard no recent political
suggestions of this kind; but there have certainly been indications
(beyond the Hollywood version of youth suppressing age in the
film "Wild in the Streets") that young radicals at times have felt a
similar impulse; and that some of their antagonists in the older
generations have felt a related urge to eliminate or incarcerate
everyone *under* 25.

I have stressed the promiscuous use of the word "relevant" as
an indicator of totalism. Beyond its dictionary meanings—applicable, germane, apposite, appropriate, suitable, fitting—its Latin
origin, *relevare*, to raise up, is suggestive of its current meaning.
What is considered relevant is that which "raises up" a particular

version of the New History—whether that of the young rebels or
of the slightly older technocrats (such as Zbigniew Brzezinski) who
are also fond of the word. Correspondingly, everything else must
be "put down"—not only criticized and defeated but existentially
negated.

Such existential negation is of course an old story: one need
only recall Trotsky's famous reference to the "dustbin of history."
But the New History, more paradoxically, calls it 'forth in relationship to the very images and fragments we spoke of before as protean alternatives to totalism. An example of such *image-focused
totalism* is the all-encompassing concept of the "Establishment":
taken over from British rebels, it has come to mean everything
from the American (or Russian, or just about any other) political
and bureaucratic leadership, to American businessmen (from influential tycoons to salaried executives to storekeepers), to university administrators (whether reactionary or liberal presidents or
simple organization men), and even to many of the student and
youth leaders who are themselves very much at odds with people
in these other categories. And just as Establishment becomes a
devil-image, so do other terms—such as (in different ways) "confrontation" and "youth"—become god-images. It is true that these
god- and devil-images can illuminate many situations, as did such
analogous Old-History (or Old-Left) expressions as "the proletarian
standpoint," "the exploiting classes," and "bourgeois remnants,"
these last three in association with a more structured ideology.
What is at issue, however, is the degree to which a particular
image is given a transcendent status and is then uncritically applied to the most complex situations in a way that makes it the
start and finish of any ethical judgment or conceptual analysis.

This image-focused totalism enters into the ultimate romantici-
zation, that of death and immortality. While the *sense* of immortality—of unending historical continuity—is central to ordinary psychological experience, *romantic totalism tends to confuse
death with immortality, and even to equate them.* Here one recalls
Robespierre's famous dictum, "Death is the beginning of immortality," which Hannah Arendt has called "the briefest and most
grandiose definition . . . [of] the specifically modern emphasis on

politics, evidenced in the revolutions." Robespierre's phrase still resonates for us, partly because it captures an elusive truth about individual death as a *rite de passage* for the community, a transition between a man's biological life and the continuing life of his works. But within the phrase there also lurks the romantic temptation to court death in the service of immortality—to view dying, and in some cases even killing, as the only true avenues to immortality.

The great majority of today's radical young embrace no such imagery—they are in fact intent upon exploring the furthest outreach of the life process. But they can at times be prone to a glorification of life-and-death stances, so that all-or-none "revolutionary tactics" can be applied to pretty disputes hardly worthy of these cosmic images. In such situations their sense of mockery, and especially self-mockery, deserts them. For these and the related sense of absurdity can, at least at their most creative, deflate claims to omniscience and provide a contemporary equivalent to the classical mode of tragedy. Like tragedy, mockery conveys man's sense of limitation before death and before the natural universe, but it does so now in a world divested of more "straight" ways to cope with mortality. Only those young rebels who reject this dimension, and insist instead upon unwavering militant rectitude, move toward romanticized death and the more destructive quests for immortality.

The theme of militant rectitude brings us back once more to the Chinese experience—and to Maoism as the quintessential expression of romantic totalism. Mao himself possesses in abundance the most impressive qualifications for heroic revolutionary standing among today's young. On the basis of the life he has led and his unparalleled accompishments, he could well be considered the greatest revolutionary of them all. And he has done everything with a hero's insistence upon continuous all-or-none confrontation with death—always with a tone of transcendence, and with an extraordinary capacity for revitalizing his people, so much so that I have described him as "a death-conquering hero who became the embodiment of Chinese immortality." Young rebels throughout the world can perceive something of this aura, however limited

Robert J. Lifton

their knowledge of the concrete details of Mao's life. Moreover, the embrace of a *Chinese* revolutionary can reinforce their condemnation of, and sense of severance from, Western cultural tradition. Further, Mao can be perceived as the greatest individual representative of what some now call "the external proletariat," meaning the people of the Third World, now seen (according to post-Marxist doctrine) as possessing a vanguard revolutionary role which makes them the contemporary international equivalent of the working class.

Whether or not young rebels see Mao in such terms, they are likely to respond to his stance of militant opposition to both the American and Soviet "Establishments," and in a sense to the shared American-Soviet—and therefore Western-dominated—"World Establishment." What clinches the matter for many is Mao's longstanding distrust of bureaucracies, culminating in his remarkable assault during the Cultural Revolution upon the organizational structure of his own Party and Regime. Young rebels often view this assault as an assertion of vibrant spirit over static organizational machinery. Several whom I asked about Mao gave as their first reason for admiring him: "He's against institutions." Add to this Mao's specifically romantic attributes—his brilliant record as a guerrilla leader, his affinity for the great Chinese outlaws, and his sentimental but often moving poetry with its stress upon revolutionary immortality—and it is no wonder that even Chinese Communist spokesmen have referred to him as a "romantic revolutionary." (Only an earlier death—in battle, or prior to carrying out his revolutionary vision—could have rendered him more romantic.)

Yet Mao's style of romanticism—his glorification of the revolutionary spirit—has given rise to what is perhaps the most intense form of external and internal control of the individual—and certainly the most extensive program of psychological manipulation—known to history. For the past two Cultural-Revolution years, Mao's celebrated Thought has become the basis for an immortalization of words on a scale unprecedented in China or anywhere else, and for a deification of Mao himself so blatant as to offend even admirers of long standing. Young rebels who embrace from

368 ·

afar Mao's stress on "permanent revolution" may too easily over-look the consequences of the recent program expressing this prin-ciple: irreparable national dissension, the most convoluted and meaningless forms of violence, and extreme confusion and disil-lusionment among Chinese youth (as well as their elders), especially among those who responded most enthusiastically to the Cultural Revolution's initial call for national transformation. Nor are young rebels in the West aware of the extent to which the Maoist vision has already been modified and in some ways abandoned, in response to the deep-seated opposition it encountered throughout China, however the image of the leader-hero is retained.

Intrinsic to Mao's romantic-totalistic conduct of the Cultural Revolution is a pattern I call "psychism"—a confusion between mind and its material products, an attempt to control the external world and achieve strongly desired technological goals by means of intrapsychic exercises and assertions of revolutionary will. Now the radical young in more affluent societies have a very different relationship to technology; rather than desperately seeking it, they feel trapped and suffocated by it (though they may also feel its attraction). But they too can fall into a kind of psychism, which in their case takes the form of confusing a rewarding inner sense of group solidarity with mastery of the larger human and technologi-cal world "outside." The recent Maoist vicious circle of psychism, socioeconomic catastrophe, and compensatory (more exaggerated) psychism can find its counterpart in an experiential sequence of young rebels in the West: deep inner satisfaction accompanying bold collective action, disillusionment with the limited effects achieved, and more reckless and ineffective action with even greater group solidarity. This is not to say that all or most behav-ior of young rebels falls into this category—to the contrary, their political confrontations have achieved a number of striking suc-cesses largely because they were *not* psychistic and could mobilize a wide radius of opposition to outmoded and destructive academic and national policies. But the enormous impact of high technology in the postmodern world, and the universal tendency to surround it with vast impersonal organizations, present an ever-increasing temptation to transcend the whole system (or "bag") by means of romantic worship of the will as such, and especially the revolutionary will.

Whatever their admiration of Mao, the majority of young rebels find themselves in tactical conflict with pure Maoists of the kind who make up the Progressive Labor Party in America, and who were depicted in their French version by Godard in his film "La Chinoise." Such pure Maoists worship every phrase in the little red book of quotations as a transcendent truth, and insist upon apocalyptic violence as the only form of authentic revolutionary action. As advocates of Maoism from a distance, who lack their mentor's pragmatism and flexibility, they are somewhat reminiscent of the non-Russian Stalinists of the '30's. But for most young rebels, Mao and Maoism are perceived less as a clearly demarcated historical person and program than as a constellation of revolutionary images with heroic, and above all antibureaucratic, contours. The problem for these young rebels is to recover the historical Mao in all of his complexity—which means confronting the tragic transition from great revolutionary leader to despot. To come to terms with their own Maoism they must sort out the various dimensions of the original—on the one hand its call for continuous militant action on behalf of the deprived and its opposition to stagnant institutions, exhilarating principles which are consistent with evolving forms of the New History; on the other, its apocalyptic totalism, psychism, and desperate rear-guard assault upon the openness of contemporary or protean man.

VII

Yet precisely the protean qualities of the young, of both their inner and outer world, can help them to avoid definitive commitments to these self-defeating patterns. They need not be bound by the excesses of either Cartesian rationalism or the contemporary experientialism which feeds romantic totalism. Indeed, though the latter is a response to and ostensibly a replacement for the former, there is a sense in which both are one-dimensional mirror-images. But today's young have available for their formulations of self and world the great twentieth-century insights which liberate man from the senseless exclusion of the experiential versus rational bind. I refer to the principles of symbolic thought, as expressed in the work of such people as Cassirer and Langer, and of Freud and Erikson. One can never determine the exact effect of great insights upon the historical process, but it is quite possible that, with the decline of the total ideologies of the Old History, ideas as such will become more important than ever in the shaping of the New. Having available an unprecedented variety of ideas and idea-images, the young are likely to attempt more than did previous generations and perhaps make more mistakes, but also to show greater capacity to extricate themselves from a particular course and revise tactics, beliefs, and styles—all in the service of contributing to embryonic social forms.

These forms are likely to be highly fluid, but need not by any means consist exclusively of shape-shifting. Rather, they can come to combine flux with elements of connectedness and consistency, and to do so in new ways and with new kinds of equilibria. For to be protean does not in itself rule out—in fact, in its viable form requires—paths of cultural continuity. Any New History worthy of that name not only pits itself against, but draws actively upon, the Old. Only through such continuity can the young bring a measure of sure-footedness to their continuous movement. And to draw upon the Old History means to look both ways: to deepen the collective awareness of Auschwitz and Hiroshima and what they signify, and at the same time to carve out a future that remains open rather than bound by absolute assumptions about a "technetronic society" or by equally absolute polarities of "revolution" and "counterrevolution."

It is possible (though hardly guaranteed) that man's two most desperately pressing problems—nuclear weapons and world population—may contribute to the overcoming of totalism and psychism. I have written elsewhere of the pattern of nuclearism, the deification of nuclear weapons and a false dependency upon them for the attainment of political and social goals. Nuclearism tends to go hand-in-hand with a specific form of psychism, the calling forth of various psychological and political constructs in order to deny the technological destructiveness of these weapons.

Robert J. Lifton

Nuclearism and nuclear psychism have been rampant in both America and China. There are impressive parallels between certain Pentagon nuclear policies (grotesquely expressed in the John Foster Dulles doctrine of "massive retaliation") on the one hand, and the joyous Chinese embrace of nuclear weapons as further confirmation of the Maoist view of world revolution on the other. Similarly, Pentagon (and early Herman Kahn) projections of the ease of nuclear recovery—of what I have called the nuclear afterlife—bear some resemblance to the Maoist view of the weapons as not only "paper tigers" but even as a potential source of a more beautiful socialist order rising from the nuclear ashes. Now I think that young rebels, with their frequent combination of flexibility and inclusiveness, are capable of understanding these relationships. They have yet to confront the issues fully, but have begun to show inclinations toward denouncing nuclearism and nuclear psychism independently of their origins. Insights about nuclear weapons are of the utmost importance to the younger generation—for preventing nuclear war, and for creating social forms which take into account the radically changed relationship man now has to his world because of the potentially terminal revolution associated with these weapons.

To the problem of world population, young rebels are capable of bringing a pragmatism which recognizes both the imperative of technical programs on behalf of control and the bankruptcy of an exclusively technical approach. Looking once more at China, we find that a country with one of the world's greatest population problems has approached the matter of control ambivalently and insufficiently—mainly because of a Maoist form of psychism which insisted that there could never be too many workers in a truly socialist-revolutionary state. Yet this stance has been modified, and there is much to suggest that the inevitable Chinese confrontation with the actualities of population has in itself been a factor in undermining more general (and widely disastrous) patterns of psychism. Young radicals elsewhere are capable of the same lessons —about population, about Maoist contradictions and post-Maoist possibilities, and about psychism per se.

Are these not formidable problems for youngsters somewhere between their late teens and mid-twenties? They are indeed. As the young approach the ultimate dilemmas that so baffle their elders, they seem to be poised between the ignorance of inexperience, and the wisdom of a direct relationship to the New History. Similarly, in terms of the life cycle, they bring both the dangers of zealous youthful self-surrender to forms they do not understand, and the invigorating energy of those just discovering both self and history—energy so desperately needed for a historical foray into the unknown.

As for the "older generation"—those middle-aged Left-intellectuals I spoke of—the problem is a little different. For them (us) one of the great struggles is to retain (or achieve) protean openness to the possibilities latent in the New History, and to respond to that noble slogan of the French students, "Imagination in power." But at the same time this generation does well to be its age, to call upon the experience specific to the lives of those who comprise it. It must tread the tenuous path of neither feeding upon its formative sons nor rejecting their capacity for innovative historical imagination. This is much more difficult than it may seem, because it requires those now in their forties and fifties to come to terms with the extremely painful history they have known, to neither deny that history nor be blindly bound by it. Yet however they may feel shunted aside by the young, there is special need for their own more seasoned, if now historically vulnerable, imaginations.

For both the intellectual young and old—together with society at large—are threatened by violent counterreaction to the New History, by a restorationist impulse often centered in the lower middle classes but not confined to any class or country. This impulse includes an urge to eliminate troublesome young rebels along with their liberal-radical "fathers," and to return to a mythical past in which all was harmonious and no such disturbers of the historical peace existed. For what is too often forgotten by the educated of all ages, preoccupies as they are with their own dislocations, is the extent to which such dislocations in others produce the very opposite kind of ideological inclination—in this case a compensatory, strongly antiprotean embrace of the simple purities of the Old History.

If man is successful in creating the New History he must create if he is to have any history at all, then the formative fathers and sons I have spoken of must pool their resources and succeed together. Should this not happen, the failure will be shared as well—whether in the form of stagnation and suffering, or of shared annihilation. Like most other things in our world, the issue remains open. There is nothing absolute or inevitable about the New History—except perhaps the need to bring it into being.

BIBLIOGRAPHY

Arendt, H. (1963), *On Revolution*. New York: Viking Press.
Camus, A. (1954), *The Rebel*. New York: Knopf.
Cassirer, E. (1944), *Essay on Man*. New Haven: Yale University Press.

19. Our Permissive Society and the Superego: Some Current Thoughts about Freud's Cultural Concepts

HENRY LOWENFELD, M.D., AND
YELA LOWENFELD, M.D.

*It is easy, as we can see, for a barbarian to be healthy:
for a civilized man the task is hard* (Freud, 1938, p. 185).

AFTER PSYCHOANALYSIS had developed from a method of treating neurosis into a scientific psychology, Freud turned his interest toward cultural questions. However, his studies in this area—for instance, *Civilization and Its Discontents* (1929) —have not been completely accepted by many of his followers and disciples. Statements about cultural problems cannot easily be proved; the attitude that the individual assumes is largely dependent upon subjective views. But even if analytical statements about the development of civilization cannot be verified in analyses, they can encompass, though silently, predictions which are either confirmed or disputed by the evolution of civilization.

Freud's concept of civilization grew out of his clinical work. The conflict between the different agencies in the mind of the individual leads to neurosis; the conflict between the instinctual drives and the demands of civilization stands at the center of his cultural concepts. The present-day situation, the obvious change in the civilization and in our patients' behavior and experiences,

This is an expanded version of the paper "Our Permissive Society and the Superego; Some Current Concepts" which appeared in *The Psychoanalytic Quarterly,* 39(4):590–608.

challenges us to examine anew the questions of the discontent in the civilization posed by Freud. [1]

Freud has been accused of being a "pessimist," particularly in his works on society. Yet one of his predictions about what to expect in Russia was cruelly confirmed a few years later. In regard to the promises of the Bolsheviks, in 1929 he wrote: "One only wonders, with concern, what the Soviets will do after they have wiped out their bourgeois" (p. 115).

What then can be said of Freud's views today? The pictures of neuroses as well as of society show far-reaching changes. As early as 1910 Freud pointed out that certain neurotic manifestations, whose existence depended on the disguise and lack of recognition of the substitutive gratification of drives, would become impossible (p. 148). This prediction has been confirmed by the development of hysteria and the changes in this neurosis. But hysteria is not only changed because its symptoms have become transparent. As hysteria results from the repression of sexuality in the child's upbringing, the marked change in society's attitudes toward sex has made the conspicuous symptoms disappear. This can be confirmed by the occasional occurrence of the former symptoms of hysteria in areas where family upbringing has not changed. Where the environment has changed, the symptoms of hysteria have been replaced by a multitude of character neuroses and psychosomatic manifestations. Optimistic views, not shared by Freud, that liberation from sexual prohibitions would eliminate neurosis and make for a healthier society have proved to be wrong.

Freud's so-called pessimism consisted in seeing at the same time the dangers inherent in suppression of instinctual drives as well as the dangers accompanying their liberation. For many, the restriction of libidinal and aggressive drives is not possible without neurosis. Others save themselves from neurosis but feel impaired in the enjoyment of life. The ability of sublimation is not given to everyone to the same degree.

While drive restriction provokes hostility to civilization and thus endangers its continuity, Freud, at the same time, warned of

---

[1] It is beyond the scope of this paper to discuss the work of numerous sociological and psychoanalytical authors who have dealt with similar problems.

the danger that drive liberation also threatens civilization. He saw the drives as always ready to break out of their domestication. These thoughts appear in many of his works during different periods of his life. Freud said:

> In consequence to this primary mutual hostility of human beings, civilized society is perpetually threatened with disintegration [1929, p. 112]. . . . Human civilization rests upon two pillars, of which one is the control of natural forces and the other the restriction of our instincts. The ruler's throne rests upon fettered slaves. Among the instinctual components which are thus brought into service, the sexual instincts, in the narrower sense of the word, are conspicuous for their strength and savagery. Woe, if they should be set loose! The throne would be overturned and the ruler trampled under foot. Society is aware of this—and will not allow the topic to be mentioned [1924, p. 219].

In 1927 Freud remarked that every individual is virtually an enemy of civilization. Thus civilization has to be defended against the individual.

> For our mind . . . is rather to be compared with a modern State in which a mob, eager for enjoyment and destruction, has to be held down forcibly by a prudent superior class [1932, p. 221].
> In circumstances that are favorable to [aggression] . . . when the mental counter-forces which ordinarily inhibit it are out of action, it also manifests itself spontaneously and reveals man as a savage beast to whom consideration towards his own kind is something alien (1929, pp. 111–112). Civilization has to use its utmost efforts in order to set limits to man's aggressive instincts . . . hence, the restriction upon sexual life . . . [1929, p. 112].

Freud's concepts of the power of the drives led to the splits within the analytic movement, the new group more or less denying the dangers of the drives.

The question has to be asked here whether the drive-liberation in the education of the last decades (seemingly in agreement with psychoanalytic concepts) is not based on the same denial of the power of drives which had led to the splits in psychoanalysis. In place of the denial of infantile sexuality we have the "permissiveness" which, as it were, does not take the drives seriously.

Freud hoped that the "effects of repression" (namely, a relative control of the drives) could be replaced "by the results of the rational operation of the intellect. . . . In this way our appointed task of reconciling men to civilization will to a great extent be achieved." Freud was not in favor of religious education. He assumed that the "relative atrophy of the radiant intelligence of a healthy child" is caused by the education which inhibits the child from thinking clearly. The essential to him was the development of the mind of the child: ". . . we have no other means of controlling our instinctual nature but our intelligence" (1927, pp. 47–48).

Freud was critical of the sexual mores of his time and wished for more sexual freedom, but his view of the dangers of instinctual drives was not essentially different from that of former thinkers. Without regret he saw the inevitable dwindling of religion and advocated a rational education which would lead to the control of drives and the preservation of civilization. If this failed, he would have to say: ". . . man is a creature of weak intelligence who is ruled by his instinctual wishes" (1927, p. 49).

But although Freud saw "civilized society perpetually threatened with disintegration," apparently he did not foresee how far society would go in the liberation of instinctual drives. It is not easy to estimate to what extent his discoveries have contributed to the change of the cultural climate. In this development psychoanalysis may be only one factor among many others. The rapid growth of the physical sciences, of technology and communication, and the resulting decline of religious belief, the exploitation of human instincts in commercial advertising, all have contributed decisively to this change.

Freud may not have foreseen that it would be a difficult task for parents to consciously recognize infantile sexuality without being seduced into the role of a participant. The incest taboo lost its firm ground with the lifting of the parents' repression and is now only halfheartedly observed, certainly without the former moral conviction. In large parts of the population there is little discipline over the pregenital, and particularly the oral, drives of children. The aggressive drives meet with weak control. Television, in itself a constant passive-oral indulgence, stimulates and satisfies sadistic fantasies; at the same time it blunts responsiveness to one's sadistic impulses. In these factors are the root of the regressive trends in adolescence and in adult life.

Another consequence of the changed upbringing is a less marked latency period in many children. Freud emphasized the importance of the latency period for the cultural development of the individual, and hence the society. He pointed out that the latency period is absent in primitive society and is found only in higher cultures.

The discontent with our civilization has obviously grown in the last four decades. Freud attributed this discontent to the inevitable suppression of drives and hoped that a greater freedom of drives and a greater satisfaction of human needs through technical development might facilitate reconciliation of man with civilization. Yet the liberation has apparently not led to acceptance of civilization; rather in many layers of society, particularly the affluent ones, it has led to an intensification of restlessness and discontent.

The liberation of drives which is a consequence of the fact that the older generation exercises much less pressure on the younger generation, rather than having diminished the conflict between the generations, has heightened it. Sexual liberation and the easier opportunity of sexual gratification for today's youth have not produced a lessening of aggression.

We are aware of concentrating here mainly on one aspect of a complex development; there is not only a change in relations to instinctual drives but also a tremendous technical development that has influenced life and the growth of youth immensely. One aspect of these changes is the fact that they make so many little tasks of the daily life of a child easier. Thus the technical development is not helpful in the learning to master difficulties and to endure frustrations. The change in the total psychological climate in which a child grows up today can hardly be measured. [2] It is

[2] Cf., Henry, J. (1963), *Culture against Man.* New York: Vintage Books.

noteworthy that Freud, as early as 1929, many years before the first atomic bomb, concluded *Civilization and Its Discontents* with the following words: "Men have gained control over the forces of nature to such an extent that with their help they would have no difficulty in exterminating one another to the last man. They know this, and hence comes a large part of their current unrest, their unhappiness and their mood of anxiety" (1929, p. 145).

Instinctual drives themselves do not change in a short span of time, but the superego and ego are greatly exposed to environmental influences. No doubt the superego has gone through decisive changes in recent decades. We have a striking historical example of the changeability of the superego in what happened in Germany during the Nazi rule. [3]

The transformations taking place in today's youth are by far more complex. To understand them we have to explore their roots in early childhood. Freud reminds us in many of his works that the superego is the heir of the Oedipus complex. The superego draws its strength from the power of the infantile drives against which it is directed: ". . . [the conscience] is a real contrast to sexual life, which is in fact there from the beginning of life and not only a later addition." The installation of the superego can be described as a "successful instance of identification with the parental agency." It is of decisive importance that "the superego is stunted in its strength and growth if the surmounting of the Oedipus complex is only incompletely successful" (1932a, pp. 61–64).

All moral rules, it seems, derive their strength from the original incest taboo and lose their reliability if this taboo is weakened. Comparing the consequences of an unresolved Oedipus complex today with the same phenomena in Freud's time results in a markedly different picture. Implicit in this observation is a question; i.e., how has sexual liberation in family and society altered the development of the superego? "Permissiveness" has reduced the father's role as the strong and forbidding one. The contemporary father acts much more like a weak older brother. We have always seen that the milder father does not lead to a milder superego in

---

[3] A great part of the population put the Führer's superego in the place of their own. (Göring remarked: "My conscience is Adolf Hitler.")

NBC

VISITOR'S

TEMPORARY

PASS

NAME: _Father OOyd_

COMPANY: _for Mr Cordona_

DESTINATION: _315 W_

PLEASE RETURN TO SECURITY UPON LEAVING

SV — 1207   (12/75)   _C. M._

childhood but rather to an increase of fantasies and projections. For the development of the superego the projections are decisive; power and cruelty of the parents are magnified by the fantasies, as shown, for example, by castration anxiety.

There has always been a wide discrepancy in the superego between the infantile image of the parents and the later one in which the characteristics of the real parents predominate. The changes in our civilization have considerably enlarged this discrepancy. The image of the real parents contrasts more and more with the early infantile one, and this contrast includes others who became part of the superego, teachers and other authority figures.

The core of the superego is determined by the earliest parental images (Freud, 1932a); the later influence of parents is less on the superego and more on the ego. Thus today we have the following problem: the inhibiting, controlling, limit-setting and guiding function of the superego, which largely merges with the ego, is weakened through the weakness of the parents, through indulgent education which fails to train the ego, and through the general social climate of permissiveness. The sexual and aggressive instinctual drives are much less under the guidance of rules but the severe superego of early childhood still lives in the individual's unconscious. The result is restlessness, discontent, depressive moods, and craving for substitute satisfactions.

Freud stressed that the superego is the carrier of tradition and undergoes changes only slowly. This assumption, apparently sufficient in a stable civilization, has to be modified today. The controlling function of the superego, which draws its strength from the identification with strong parental figures and which can protect the individual from conscious and unconscious guilt feelings, functions poorly; its punishing and self-destructive power seems still to affect many.

We have not only a dwindling of the latency period, as mentioned above, but also a changed situation in adolescence. The final stage of the genital phase, the decision for health or neurosis, and the essential character formation occur in adolescence. So does the maturing of the superego.

The youth of today are being deserted by their parents in regard to superego development. The ego alone—particularly when not strengthened in the upbringing—can hardly solve the task of control and sublimation. Parents seem to have abdicated; schools and colleges also fail in this task. Youths, therefore, have no other choice than to strive for group formations, to support one another, to find new rules, to create new ideals. For many young people the organizing strength of an ideology is necessary. They need ideas and ideals that have the power to express and to channel their unconscious stirrings, still interwoven with infantile conflicts. This task, the creation of new constructive ideals, has hardly ever been accomplished by youth alone. Ideals have always developed over long periods of time as the result of historical evolutions and through exceptional personalities.

Thus, young people feel cheated by their parents without really knowing of what they have been deprived. Their heroes reflect their psychological needs; disappointed by the weak father, they not only look for a strong one but try to identify with men who fulfill at the same time infantile sadistic fantasies, such as Che Guevara or Mao Tse-tung. It is also characteristic that group formations encompass increasingly younger age levels, as the parental authority declines early. In contrast to former days, group influence today has become so powerful so early in the child's development that the psychoanalyst now has to concern himself with problems of group psychology in order to understand the problems of the individual. Such modern phenomena as encounter groups, Esalen, etc., may also spring from the needs that the "fatherless" society engenders.

The disappointment in the parents, the justified reproach that they do not get from parents what they need, leads to youth's contempt for civilization, for cultural tradition, while giving them grounds for their opinion that there is nothing to be learned from the history of human development. [4] Today's revolutionaries show

---

[4] It is interesting to note that about 150 years ago Goethe composed these lines in *Faust II*:

BACHELOR OF ARTS: Experience! Mere foam and fluff!
A peer of mind? No trace of that is showing.
Confess: what men have ever known is stuff
And absolutely not worth knowing . . .

little interest in earlier revolutionaries. Therefore they also lack the narcissistic satisfaction provided by the cultural ideal which facilitates reconciliation with society.

In connection with this attitude of contempt for history we see a kind of primitive animism, a regression to infantile theories. Whereas primitive man personified the incomprehensible forces of nature, today's youth is inclined to personify the incomprehensible social forces. Instead of attempts to study them, all evils are attributed to wicked individuals. The weakening of the father's role and the decline of monotheism seem to create a return to a kind of idolatry, and inclination toward primitive Eastern religions, mysticism, astrology, etc. [5]

The neuroses and their analyses reflect this situation. Nowadays one can say, though this is oversimplifying, that the decisive repressions concern not the id but the superego. The constant verbalization of the id impulses in today's culture makes their repression less possible and also less necessary. Therefore, in analysis, their exploration is less difficult, whereas the guilt feelings are repressed or denied. To uncover and analyze the repressed parts of the superego is difficult in a social climate where the superego is thought of as a superfluous appendix. [6] This development seems to be one of the main reasons that analyses require more and more time.

The specific problems of the superego configuration seem to be characteristic of a type of neurosis found frequently nowadays.

MEPHISTOPHELES (disguised as Faust): I long have thought so,
But I was a fool,
Now to myself I seem right flat and dull.
BACHELOR: What have you done? Thought, nodded, dreamed away,
Considered plan on plan—and nothing won.
It's certain! Age is but an ague cold,
Chill with its fancies and distress and dread.
If more than thirty years a man is old,
He is indeed as good as dead.
MEPHISTOPHELES: The Devil, here, has nothing more to say.

(Translated by George Madison Priest)

[5] Cf., Gordon, L. (1970), Beyond the Reality Principle: Illusion or New Reality? *American Imago*, 27:160–182.

[6] Cf., *New York Times Book Review*, Feb. 23, 1969, Interview with Philip Roth: "There is certainly a personal element in the book, but not until I had got hold of guilt, as you see, as a comic idea . . ."

H. Lowenfeld and Y. Lowenfeld

In 1965, the authors made a study of the applications for treatment at the New York Psychoanalytic Institute. The majority of the applicants had the same complaints: dissatisfaction, self-hatred, tension, depressed moods, no motivation in life, a feeling of emptiness, and an inability to love. It could be argued that in all these cases the diagnosis is discontent with civilization. There seems to be a typical development: the Oedipus complex is not fully resolved; the superego, incompletely developed, cannot sufficiently support the weak ego. The social superego is also ineffectual and its representatives give no support. Thus the ego is not capable of successful integration with the other components of the psychic apparatus. Consequently, the individual does not gain the narcissistic gratification, which can be derived from fulfilling the demands of one's ego-ideal; this adds necessarily to the general unhappiness. The affects are governed by guilt feelings, not accessible to the conscious mind. Here we have a repetition of the childhood in which the parents' weakness contributed to the unconscious need for punishment.

"But everybody hates his mother," remarked one of these applicants as a commonplace not worth talking about. This defense mechanism is freely provided by the present environment, serving as an effective denial of the oedipal situation. It apparently impedes the necessary separation from the parents (which Anna Freud compared to the mourning work), a variable which might be a significant factor in the inability to love. Although these patients are capable of sublimation through their work, such activities are soon felt as meaningless and are carried out without free libido, probably for the same reasons that impede their ability to love. (Most of them were considered not analyzable within the framework of the Institute.)

There is another problem where the changes in the superego have been influential. Sexual satisfaction itself, it seems, has lost its value for many young people. In 1912 Freud wrote:

> But at the same time, if sexual freedom is unrestricted from the outset the result is no better. It can easily be shown that the psychical value of erotic needs is reduced as soon as their satisfaction becomes easy.

An obstacle is required in order to heighten libido. . . . In times in which there were no difficulties standing in the way of sexual satisfaction, such as perhaps during the decline of ancient civilization, love became worthless and life empty . . . [pp. 187–188].

This development appears to explain why so many young people seek their happiness in drugs. They obviously have not found it elsewhere and have lost their faith in happiness through love.

Frequently we have not only a weakening of the father's role but also a lessening of the distinction between the father's and the mother's role, a kind of merging of the parents. The father who feeds and diapers the child is, in the infant's mind, not clearly distinguished from the caring mother. It is rather likely that such a shift in the nursing functions influences the child's development and makes normal and stable identifications more difficult. This merging of the parental images may be a decisive factor in the conspicuous increase of active homosexuality.

Heretofore we have emphasized the problems incurred by a superego which is deficient in giving the ego the necessary support. But the ego itself has, in many young people, not fully developed the functions that are needed in the grown-up's life. There is often an amazing lack of fear where any reasonable evaluation of the reality would require prudence and caution. For example, they are seemingly unafraid of venereal disease, pregnancy, are without hesitation willing to buy drugs from any stranger on the street and accept blindly what they are given, not knowing what they receive, the strength of the dosage, etc. This attitude is very different from that of former generations, where there was either a realistic or overcautious appraisal of danger or a neurotic enlargement and distortion. In neurotic symptoms real dangers are exaggerated and anxiety is rationalized, thereby hiding the underlying unconscious meaning (e.g., in the fear of venereal disease, the castration anxiety). Hypochondriacal, phobic or obsessional symptoms are also built upon real dangers about which the ego is aware. Thus, in neurotic anxiety the ego is regressed and experiences real dangers on an infantile level. In these young, fearless people we have another kind of problem.

H. Lowenfeld and Y. Lowenfeld

Freud said that education can be described as a conquest of the pleasure principle and its displacement by the reality principle. Reality testing and anticipating danger are learned in this process and become an essential part of a mature ego. The development of the reality principle seems to start when the infant experiences disappointment in its attempts at hallucinatory gratification. Further growth is largely determined by the parental attitude, particularly the father's, and the resolution of the Oedipus complex. Frustration of the infantile drives and the child's fear of losing the parents' love by disobeying their demands may be necessary for a healthy development of the ego's capacities to test the dangers of reality and to anticipate them realistically. Although the behavior of today's youth is self-destructive and masochistic in some cases, this interpretation does not hold true for most of them. Youthful rebellion may play a role in it, but the lack of fear remains strange. The ego has not reached the maturity which is expected in the grown-up.

In this connection it is interesting to observe in these days a particular attitude of some college students to their "alma mater" (the "nourishing mother"). In the past the college's "in loco parentis" included the father as the principle of the superego, but the decline of his role has increased the college's mother image in the student unconscious. After having left their mother's house (that is the way they usually refer to their parental home), they soon feel disappointed in their alma mater. This disappointment frequently drives them into seeking fulfillment of their wishes in (drug-induced) hallucinations. Unprepared to bear the inevitable frustration, they often attack the alma mater in an unrestrained rage.

A few fragments of case histories may illustrate the present psychological climate. [7]

I

A. was a young girl, the only child of a prominent pediatrician in an affluent suburb. Her development was warped by her par-

---

[7] These cases were analyzed by Dr. Yela Lowenfeld.

ents' permissiveness and their overidentification with the child's drives. The atmosphere was one of general social indulgence. After treatment of several months with an analyst, she had been diagnosed as schizophrenic, and hospitalization was recommended. On the way to the hospital she convinced her parents with reasonable arguments that she did not belong in an institution. She was sent to me for a last attempt at psychoanalytic treatment.

When I saw the patient for the first time—a couple of years before the "anything goes" sentimentality had taken hold—I was ready to agree with the previous diagnosis. She looked bizarre and disheveled with her tight-fitting pants and a man's pajama top. Her long uncombed hair hung loosely around an unwashed face, accentuated by the remainder of drastic eye makeup. Exquisite jewelry contrasted strangely with her neglected sorry appearance. To my surprise she emerged as an intelligent, articulate young woman with whom contact was easily established. Her main complaints were emptiness, frustration, and an indefinable feeling of guilt.

Her enlightened parents fully understood the nature of a child's sexual desires and the justification of the Oedipus complex. But it was this very knowledge that prevented them from curbing the girl's sexual wishes. More unfavorable was the fact that the parents themselves were sucked into a climate, not uncommon today, in which the incest taboo was observed without the power of conviction. The girl's sex life started at the age of 14 without any inner involvement. All sexual encounters were accidental and meaningless. They were carried out at home, diminishing to a degree the tension in the family. Although the father was unhappy about his daughter's loose love life, he did not trust his disapproval, always suspecting his motives as an expression of his possessive jealousy. The mother made only one condition, that the girl's sex life was to take place in her own house where it was "clean and safe." (She was entirely unaware of her own feeling of triumph in the competition for her husband.)

A period of promiscuity was followed by a clinging attachment to a young man who was basically homosexual. When he eventually succumbed in the struggle, she was left in a state of shock and despair. Her next attachment was a young man who, needing a wife to avoid the draft, proceeded to marry her and, after she had served the purpose, promptly abandoned her. She reacted with violent despair to the ending of this make-believe marriage, which to her was another traumatic repetition of the false promises of her childhood. A period of entirely indiscriminate promiscuous life with drunkards, hoodlums, and addicts followed, now no longer under her parents' roof. All attempts to continue her education beyond high school ended in failure, as she was unable to tolerate frustration and intellectual discipline. There was an intensification of depressions between her sexual bouts, and her total lack of self-preservation in a dangerous environment frightened her. In the course of her analysis, with rich dream material, it became apparent that her basic problem was built around typical oedipal conflicts. She was subsequently able to gain insight into her neurotic mechanism and to improve rapidly.

This case illustrates how unresolved oedipal problems (which formerly might have produced a typical hysteria) may today lead to a state of unrestrained and self-destructive acting out, and to delinquency, simulating a picture of psychosis, as the ego remains weak and the superego ineffectual in the face of uncontrolled drives.

II

B. was an adolescent boy whose loving parents failed to help their son cope with his instinctual drives.

The boy was sent for treatment at the age of 12 (on the insistence of the high school principal) because of the sudden onset of a school phobia which coincided with his transfer from a small elementary boys' school to a large coeducational institution. The child was a shy boy with a cherubic face and an ingratiating manner. In contrast to his appearance, he suffered from self-hatred, shame, continuous self-damaging behavior, and an overwhelming fear of being found out—for what he did not know. What emerged in the course of treatment was that the presence of girls made it impossible for him to repress his secret incestuous past. From the age of six until recently he had lived a free sex life with a sister five years older who had seduced him, thereby fulfilling his oedipal wishes. In that the sister had assumed all responsibility, he was able to repress any guilt. When he was 12, she left him for college and a boy friend, as a result of which he regressed into the original oedipal situation without having developed any of the mechanisms for solving the problem. He began to cling to his mother like a three-year-old, unable to bear any frustration. The permissive and indulgent father gave the boy no support to cope with his drives and sadistic fantasies. Thus, totally lacking in any kind of defensive equipment, he became increasingly paralyzed by guilt and anxiety. When, after the sister's departure the boy suffered from nightmares, the father would leave the marital bed to join his son for the night.

During the treatment the boy joined a Communist youth group, became more masculine and energetic, and participated in protest marches and picketing, even daring to wear the party button in school. However, when his father confided in him that he too was a Communist, the interest in the cause dwindled, and the boy soon exchanged the party button for a series of buttons with obscene words. These attempts to find sublimations helped him to ward off his homosexual fears. The contrast between the easy availability of the unconscious material and his understanding of it on the one hand, and the helplessness of the weak ego in coping with his conflicts on the other created special problems in the treatment of this adolescent. The analysis and working through of his anxieties eventually freed him from his phobias and enabled him to finish high school and enter a college out of town.

One can speculate that this boy might some day become one of the rebellious students who fight the establishment in an astonishingly infantile way, expecting at the same time not to be punished and to be granted full amnesty for their transgressions, just as a small child would expect from an indulgent parent.

The following case may illustrate the impact of the peer group and the social superego on today's youth, which can be enormously effective even where the upbringing in the family has not been different from earlier times.

III

The patient was the third of six daughters born into a family which maintained strict religious beliefs and practices. Aggressive behavior was highly disapproved of. When the children fought with each other, they were bodily punished by the father and had to make up by embracing each other. The patient was a pretty, sensual, sexually precocious child who experienced her father's disapproval of her seductive behavior as a great humiliation. She managed to be mother's favorite by becoming prudish and at the same time intellectually slow and vague. In spite of her attractive appearance she was socially a failure with girls and boys.

At 20 she married a young student who had taken her virginity against her will; marriage seemed the only way to quiet her shame and disgrace. As her complete frigidity threatened the relationship which both wanted to save, she hoped analysis would offer a cure and thereby save the marriage. During the analysis she remembered the wild outburst of jealousy against her mother that she had experienced when her future husband visited her family for the first time. This experience was obviously a revival of her infantile conflict with mother. One could have anticipated that the patient would have solved her sexual problem after analyzing, understanding, and working through the mechanism of the development of her frigidity as a reaction formation to her bold childhood desires for her father, his rejection, and the fear of competition with her mother and sisters.

And indeed, she was freed of her frigidity. She became more intellectually alert, lost her vagueness, and I fully expected her either to achieve satisfaction in her marriage or, if this relationship were too burdened by the neurotic beginning, to leave her husband and find a more suitable partner. Yet the rebellious youth groups into which she happened to fall encouraged her to live out all childhood fantasies. She became promiscuous and entirely indiscriminate in choice and number of her sex partners. I was unable to keep up with all the individuals she slept with at first meeting, young ones, old ones, worthless characters, decent ones, perverts, always with the feeling of enriching her life by sexual orgasm. There was no trace of guilt, shame, or fear. "I could shriek with joy over my liberation," she used to say.

It took a long time to convince her of the pathology of her sexual behavior and of the danger she exposed herself to constantly. I seemed to have become as prudish and forbidding as her pious parents. Had I not been afraid that she might perish any day, I might have ended the treatment with the cure of her frigidity. Yet to protect her from being destroyed, I made an effort to reinstate a discarded superego which would help her to master the uncontrolled drives, by showing her that a total lack of self-preservation was a form of self-punishment out of guilt, and not a proof of total liberation.

IV

M. was a young girl of 19 years in whose treatment some insight could be gained into the discrepancy between a total lack of reality fear and an overwhelming neurotic anxiety.

M. had come to New York for the completion of her college education. She had just graduated from the junior college of her home town, a small provincial place in the Middle West. Never before had she been away from home.

Ever since she was obliged by the rules of the New York college to spend her nights in the dormitory she found herself overwhelmed by night terrors and insomnia. The inability to cope with her nights made it impossible for her to function adequately in her courses—she frequently fell asleep during class—and she finally was advised to seek analytic treatment.

M. was a tall, willowy girl with delicate, intelligent features, which strangely contrasted with her ragged appearance. She often wore, on cold winter days, dirty canvas sneakers with holes at the big toe as part of the "uniform."

It had been her own desire to come to New York, the city of unlimited stimulation and vice. At home the girl had lived a double life ever since the age of 12. Her friends were mostly maladjusted youth, some dropouts from school, some drug addicts, all united by a goal to destroy the establishment, to love each other and to help each other against the hostile bourgeois world. M.'s nights were quite different from her bold and carefree days. Although she came home at all hours of the night, she used to crawl into the bedroom of the mother with whom she shared a double bed, the former marital bed. She clung to her mother with ambivalent tenacity. The mother, displeased with her daughter's disorderly life, did not dare to express any opinion; her friends' children were not any better and at least her daughter remained an excellent student throughout her school years.

M. was an only child of very loving parents. She remembered her earlier years as harmoniously happy, showered by the parents' love. The family life collapsed abruptly when her father, an ardent revolutionary, developed contempt for bourgeois family life. He learned a trade and left for an Eastern country to serve the cause, vaguely encouraging his daughter to join him later. She never saw him again.

Some of M.'s friends had come with her to New York. They quickly joined a circle of young people who had the same destructive ideals and an insatiable desire for pleasure. There was a great deal of promiscuity but little interest in mature sexual relationships.

M. felt very puzzled by the unbearable anxiety at night; why should she who knew no fear in the daytime experience this nocturnal terror? She used to roam the city from one end to the other, frequently without an escort, attended wild parties, participated in pilfering with her friends, accepted drugs from strangers without thinking for a moment that they might be harmful. She accepted them as a child accepts candy from a grown-up.

M. tried to cope with her night terrors by staying away from the dormitory at night as much as possible, sleeping over with any one of her crowd who was willing to share his pad with her.

It was still early in the treatment when M. was informed by the college authorities: she had to adhere to the dormitory rules or be suspended. M. used a brief vacation from the analysis to find a quick solution as she was unable to wait for a psychological understanding of her problems. Her solution was to marry one of her friends as marriage was the only way to live away from the campus. The young man, a "psychedelic" musician, owner of a shabby apartment, was agreeable to sharing his cot with her. He too suffered from bouts of anxiety which he quieted down with heroin. They lived in incredible squalor, yet it did not appear to bother her. Why mind helpless little insects? She had been dabbling in Eastern philosophy and felt now that vermin had the same right to live as humans. Instead of exterminating them like bourgeois people she left little food particles in the corners of the kitchen. When inner conflicts and reality problems interfered with their style of life, drugs would help.

The marriage had a calming effect on M. She attended college regularly and graduated with a high average. She never missed an analytic session, relating to me throughout the treatment like a trusting beloved child. In the course of the analysis she was able to free herself from her infantile fixation to her parents and to understand the nature of her night terrors as a regression to the vulnerable state of a deserted, helpless infant. It also became clear to her that her affinity to the rebellious, undirected youth arose from the longing for her father, as she in her immature way had identified them with his enigmatic image. At the same time, in her style of life she expressed revenge on mother whom she held responsible for the father's desertion. She understood that her young husband represented an early mother, the lost father and a helpless child like herself.

Eventually she gave up her marriage to find a maturer relationship. Yet a complete analytic cure proved to be impossible, as she was not willing to give up the pleasure of drugs. Her investment in Eastern religions, as she understood them, justified the drug culture and fortified her resistance to the necessity of reason in analysis. At this stage we terminated the treatment. She left with the feeling that it was the generation gap that ultimately separated us. I was left with the insight that where hallucinatory pleasure rules over the reality principle, psychoanalysis loses its power.

Up to now we have only briefly touched upon the aggressive drives. In the light of rapid cultural change the whole problem of frustration and aggression demands more scrutiny. Poverty leads to aggression, but so does affluence. Although it may still be correct to assume that frustration stimulates aggression, we must determine which constellations actually produce the feeling of frustration? Frustration does not only result from unsatisfied drives; it results from more complex processes in the individual psyche, and depends more on the disequilibrium of the different psychical agencies. This is an important task for further psychoanalytic research.

At the present time the aggressive drives are much less controlled in early childhood than was true in the past. An inevitable consequence is an increased ambivalence of the parents and of adults in general toward the unruly children, which lessens the children's trust in their love. Parents also avoid the formerly typical confrontations with their children in adolescence. Of course they had other standards than those of their children and hoped that the children would follow their example. But nowadays parents anxiously try to imitate their children. Youth has a natural need to create a world of its own before entering into adult life. Grownups today intrude into adolescent life by imitating their language, using their slang, dressing like them (women in particular try to affect the appearance of little girls). Aggression on the part of young people, which does not meet with resistance, leads to frustration. In vain they search for a contrast with the adult world in the family which is constantly yielding and running after them. Thus, to block out the adults, youth is often driven to absurd behavior and appearance.

In the case of sexual gratification, man's aggressiveness also remains unsatisfied. Rape, strangely frequent in a time of easily available sexual satisfaction, then becomes the last resort. As aggression becomes increasingly unnecessary in the sexual sphere and does not find any outlet in it, instinctual drives can no longer fuse properly and unmixed aggression grows. The glorification of pure aggression has given those philosophers who advocate destruction, in the service of accommodating a new culture, a charismatic role among the young.

Society has also developed a new attitude toward pregenital drives, which are given a special value and are highly esteemed.

Whereas formerly only a few writers (such as de Sade and Sacher-Masoch) propagated their practice, today they play a decisive role in the literature, art, music, theater, and movies of our culture. The freedom in the growing up of the child allows fixation on the pregenital phase and facilitates regression to it. Today many young people do not fully outgrow the phallic stage. They fail in the task of maturing into the genital phase in adolescence, a process which apparently needs much time. The separation of sexuality and love can be understood in the same way, today widely disseminated as a new "Weltanschauung."

Another aspect of our changing values which requires much further investigation is the conspicuous disappearance of the feeling of shame in situations where formerly people's pride was tremendously affected. As the feeling of shame originates in infancy in connection with the sexual organs and the pregenital drives the change in our attitude towards them seems to affect the later development of the feeling of shame or the lack of it in many other social situations.

The development during the last decades is too complex to be understood in its multiplicity of causes. But one aspect appears of greatest importance in studying the superego problems. The generation of fathers who drew their standards from religion, thus speaking in the name of divine laws, possessed an entirely different strength in the education of their offspring from the following generation. It was also easier for their children to bear the religiously founded superego, by which the father made his demands not only out of his own choice but in the name of a higher being to whom he himself had to submit as the child had to submit to him. A generation which follows a religious one still develops a superego deriving its strength from the identification with the unshaken father. [8] Thus Freud (and his generation) could say: "Morality is always a matter of course." This saying seems to have lost its validity today.

[8] The religious moral commands derive their strength in the last analysis from the same root: the infantile situation is transferred to God (father); the ethical rules lose their power in the fatherless society.

H. Lowenfeld and Y. Lowenfeld

In former times parents considered it their task to teach children moral values. Although infantile sexuality was not consciously perceived and therefore denied, nevertheless the child was considered impulsive and unbridled; the educational task consisted in changing the child from a savage into a valuable member of civilized society. Upbringing was a positive task. In recent decades parents and educators, insecure in this task, have been mainly afraid of harming the next generation and of losing its love.

SUMMARY

Freud's ideas about the development of civilization and its dilemma between freedom and restriction of drives, which derived from his study of the conflict in neurosis, have been remarkably confirmed by the events and the changes in the cultural climate over the last 50 years.

Sexual freedom has, in accordance with Freud's conception of repression, considerably transformed the manifestations of the neuroses; however, rather than having produced greater mental health it has led to new neurotic constellations. The lesser repression of infantile sexuality has, as he feared, reduced the control of aggression. The indulging upbringing with the constant gratification of pregenital drives results in a fixation on these stages. The hostility against the culture which forces the individual to restrict his libidinal and aggressive drives has grown, although the repression of drives has significantly diminished. The task of "reconciling man to civilization" is not made easier through the liberation of drives. The permissiveness in family and society has impaired a healthy resolution of the Oedipus complex, with a consequent weakening of the superego.

In a period of cultural stability, the infantile, irrational demands of the superego could be worked out in the analytic process. The protecting and controlling function of the superego could be left to the influence of the surrounding society. The narcissistic gratification which derives from fulfilling the ego-ideal's demands is lacking. The present cultural chaos confronts psychoanalysis with entirely new tasks. Culture is based on a balance of psychological forces and is threatened if this balance is impaired by losing one of its supports. The decline of the superego disturbs the equilibrium to a dangerous degree.

BIBLIOGRAPHY

Freud, S. (1910), The future prospects of psycho-analytic therapy. *Standard Edition*, 11:139–151. London: Hogarth Press, 1957.
_____ (1912), On the universal tendency to debasement in the sphere of love (Contributions to the psychology of love II). *Standard Edition*, 11:177–190. London: Hogarth Press, 1957.
_____ (1924), The resistances to psycho-analysis. *Standard Edition*, 19:213–222. London: Hogarth Press, 1961.
_____ (1927), The future of an illusion. *Standard Edition*, 21:5–56. London: Hogarth Press, 1961.
_____ (1929), Civilization and its discontents. *Standard Edition*, 21:59–145. London: Hogarth Press, 1961.
_____ (1932a), New introductory lectures on psycho-analysis. *Standard Edition*, 22:5–182. London: Hogarth Press, 1964.
_____ (1932b), My contact with Josef Popper-Lynkeus. *Standard Edition*, 22:219–224. London: Hogarth Press, 1964.
_____ (1938), An outline of psycho-analysis. *Standard Edition*, 23:141–207. London: Hogarth Press, 1964.

20. Psychoanalysis and Jurisprudence: Revisited

ALAN A. STONE, M.D.

THOSE WHO have been interested in the origins of psychoanalysis (Bernfeld, 1949) as they can be discerned in the life of Sigmund Freud have noted and commented on the significance of his early inclination toward a career in law and political affairs. Harking back to these aspirations in his later years Freud tended to emphasize their importance and minimize his predilection for medicine: "My self knowledge tells me I have never really been a doctor in the proper sense. I became a doctor through being compelled to deviate from my original purpose, and the triumph of my life lies in my having, after a long and roundabout journey, found my way back to my earliest path" (Jones, 1953, p. 28). This original path has been characterized by Bernfeld (1949) as a "search for power over men," and by Jones (1953), with his reverence for the master, as a "search into the meaning of humanity and human relations" (p. 28). Despite Jones' careful qualification of this "search for power," it seems reasonable to conclude that it held some fascination for Freud and that what he in fact eventually succeeded in doing was to make this early subject of his interest the object of his creative achievement (psychoanalysis). Out of this synthesis came Freud's several studies of the irrational and archetypal aspects of man's striving for power over man.

An analysis of Freud's later productivity demonstrates the extent of his final synthesis. Such contributions as *The Future of an Illusion* (1927), *Civilization and Its Discontents* (1930), and others, not only analyze the distribution of power within society, but also bypass the medical audience and are addressed to all those interested in the regulation of human affairs. Given this background, it is not surprising to learn from Anna Freud (1966) that her father had very much hoped there would some day be a major rapprochement between psychoanalysis and law. That rapprochement, despite some initial efforts, has not yet occurred, and in fact there may be reasons to believe that its prospects are now less promising than they were 30 years ago.

Joseph Goldstein (1968) recently presented a much more optimistic prospect. His scholarly effort and the comprehensive collection of readings assembled by Professor Goldstein and his collaborators, Professors Katz and Dershowitz, (Katz, Goldstein, and Dershowitz [1967]) will together serve as a point of departure in much of what follows.

Unlike Goldstein who, as a professor of law, is entitled to take the definitional complexities of the concept of jurisprudence for granted, it has seemed appropriate here to set them out at least vaguely. This can only be done in a limited way, but hopefully it will be sufficient to lead first to an examination of the broad conceptual dilemma of psychoanalysis and jurisprudence. Next I shall examine two specific instances of rapprochement where Goldstein believes progress has and can be made. Finally, I shall discuss what is perhaps most intriguing, the relationships between psychoanalysis and morality and its implications for morality and the law.

I

Some Definitions of Jurisprudence

Jurisprudence like psychoanalysis is a word that has different connotations depending on its linguistic context and the user's frame of reference. Etymologically its derivation suggests the wisdom of law; in academic usage it commonly refers to the philosophy of law; rhetorically it is used as equivalent to The Law with a capital L; sometimes without apology its meaning is given as the science of law. If, *arguendo,* it is the last of these, a science, then it most certainly is a science in search of an acceptable scientific method. Indeed, whether there is "a method" to jurisprudence is dubious since there is apparently no agreement as to the areas or even the issues to be studied (Dworkin, 1969).

Jurisprudence as taught in American law schools seems to be a composite discipline which borrows its methods from philosophy, history, the social and behavioral sciences. The relative emphasis found in different classrooms often depends on the professor's particular interests and the trends of the time.

The field and the methods of jurisprudence may be difficult to define, but the subject is pervasive in legal education since in one sense it can be said that it seeks in a variety of ways "to illuminate the meaning of law" (Schur, 1968). Professorial interest in jurisprudence is ubiquitous, therefore, and it is not unusual for what are called "jurisprudential questions" to be the subject of classroom dialogue in every law school class.

Over the years a variety of "schools of jurisprudence" have evolved (Schur, 1968): Natural law theorists trace their lineage to Aristotle and Aquinas, their interests are in the area of the relationship between law and morality. Formalists such as Austin and Kelsen tend to limit jurisprudence to the study of legal concepts and legal reasoning. Sociological jurisprudence emphasizes the social purposes and significance of law, viewing legal institutions as social processes. The realist school seems to have originated in a sense of skepticism about the judicial process, challenging the *"ratio decidendi"* as rationalization rather than reason and probing the "real" impact of the law on society and of society on law. This highly abridged account of some of the more important schools of jurisprudence is meant only to attest to the diversity of jurisprudential interests and points of view. Moreover, it should be noted that teachers of jurisprudence and legal philosophers resist simple classification into membership in schools.

Despite this diversity, there has been a contemporary tendency in jurisprudence to view law as dynamic rather than static, and as interactional rather than as a separate element. Lon Fuller (1934) a noted professor of jurisprudence, has cast this interactional aspect into the following analogy:

> In dealing with the problem we can employ with advantage Cohen's principle of polarity. Law and Society are polar categories. Though we are under the necessity of opposing them to one another we must recognize that each implies the other. If we deny one, the other becomes meaningless. We may picture Law and Society as the two blades of a pair of scissors. If we watch only one blade we may conclude it does all the cutting. Savigny kept his eye on the Society blade and came virtually to deny the existence of the Law blade. With him even the most technical lawyer's law was a kind of glorified folkway. Austin kept his eye on the Law blade and found little occasion in a book of over a thousand pages to discuss the mere "positive morality" which social norms represent. Blackstone shifted his eye from one blade to the other and gave us the confused account in which, on the one hand, he bases the common law on custom, and, on the other, informs us that the authoritative statement of this custom is to be found only in court decisions. As if to add to the confusion, he then lays down rules for determining when a custom should be recognized by the law. We avoid all these difficulties by the simple expedient of recognizing that both blades cut, and that neither can cut without the other [p. 452].

This interactionalist conception is a red thread running through much of the tangled skein of contemporary jurisprudence (e.g., it is obviously an implicit feature of the sociological and the realist schools). It suggests a view of law as in some important respects an ongoing, mutating, and mutative force. In keeping with this perspective on law as dynamic rather than static, American jurisprudence has often focused on what one might call the leading edge of the law and that is to be found in the courts' written decisions in controversial or difficult cases. [1] How courts decide most cases will of course depend on statutes and legal precedents.

[1] The leading edge of the law is also to be found in the legal aspects of major social problems and in legislative action. However, the testing of fundamental legal concepts is primarily achieved in the written decisions of the various courts.

· 401

Alan A. Stone

These are the professional platform of the judicial process. The difficult case, however, resists simple resolution, and the question arises as to the nature of the *ratio decidendi* if the judge does more than simply apply existing rules. Here is jurisprudence in *statu nascendi*!

A Psychoanalytic Jurisprudence?

The 'twenties produced a number of legal scholars (many in the realist school) whom one might assume from their writings had at least some familiarity with the psychoanalytic concept of the unconscious. These scholars addressed themselves to the question of whether the judge's explanation of his *ratio decidendi* could or should be accepted at face value. Benjamin Cardozo (1921) articulated this with particular clarity in a discussion of "The Nature of the Judicial Process."

> I have spoken of the forces of which judges avowedly avail to shape the form and content of their judgments. Even these forces are seldom fully in consciousness. They lie so near the surface, however, that their existence and influence are not likely to be disclaimed. But the subject is not exhausted with the recognition of their power. Deep below consciousness are other forces, the likes and dislikes, the predilections and the prejudices, the complex of instincts and emotions and habits and convictions which make the man . . . There has been a certain lack of candor in much of the discussion of the theme, or perhaps in the refusal to discuss it as if judges must lose respect and confidence by the reminder that they are subject to human limitations. I do not doubt the grandeur of the conception which lifts them into the realm of pure reason, above and beyond the sweep of perturbing and deflecting forces. Nonetheless . . . They do not stand aloof on these chill and distant heights, and we shall not help the cause of truth by acting and speaking as if they do [p. 167].

This statement of Cardozo's might be considered a beginning of a psychoanalytic school of jurisprudence. It is at least a school for candor. One of its major exponents was Judge Jerome Frank (1930). Assuming the importance of unconscious factors in decision making, he went further than Cardozo and questioned the whole structure of the case-law precedent system.

> Lawyers and judges purport to make large use of precedents; that is, they purport to rely on the conduct of judges in past cases as a means of procuring analogies for action in new cases. But since what was actually decided in the earlier cases is seldom revealed, it is impossible in a real sense to rely on these precedents [cited in Katz, Goldstein, and Dershowitz, 1967, p. 30].

Frank quotes one authority (Yntema, 1928):

"The most salient [aspect of the judicial process] is that decision is reached after an emotive experience in which principles and logic play a secondary part" (cited in Katz, Goldstein and Dershowitz [1967], p. 30).

The point of view of "psychoanalytic jurisprudence" as represented in the above quotations has been extremely difficult for the law to assimilate. One implication to be drawn from Cardozo's brilliant and literate statement is that in difficult cases judicial decisions will be based in some measure on forces outside consciousness. Thus they are potentially blindly biased rather than blindly objective, as Justice has been symbolically depicted for centuries. For the psychoanalyst "blind justice" must always seem enigmatic since we know how often the blotting out of external reality serves to permit the emergence of unconsciously derived "internal realities."

Irrationality in Judicial Decisions

This element of unconscious judicial bias is apparently acknowledged by lawyers (if it is acknowledged at all) with the same evasiveness and uneasy distaste that met Freud's emphasis on the reality of infantile sexuality. Although it is difficult to prove a negative, the combined wisdom of a score of noted professors of law was insufficient to produce a single example of a judicial decision in which a judge reversed himself on the basis of candid recognition that his previous decision was "fatally infected" [2] by pre-

[2] "Fatally infected" is one of those choice but standard pieces of judicial rhetoric.

conscious or unconscious bias which he has since confronted. Justice Cardozo's own decisions were apparently singularly lacking in any such evidence of public candor.

It is instructive to consider one example of a judicial explanation of previous error. It is found in a concurring Supreme Court opinion of Justice Jackson (1950), in a case which is a classic among lawyers. If there are ever opportunities for judicial candor of even the most superficial sort, this must have been one of them.

The case involved a Danish citizen, Mr. Kristensen, who came to this country in 1939 to attend the World's Fair in New York and to visit relatives. His 60-day visa was extended because of the outbreak of World War II and he was permitted to remain in the United States. On March 30, 1942, in the darkest days of the war, Kristensen secured exemption from the draft on the grounds that he was not a citizen or an applicant for citizenship in the United States. At the conclusion of the war in 1946 an attempt was made by then Attorney General McGrath to deport Kristensen, who was by then married to an American citizen. Attorney General McGrath interpreted the statutes as requiring deportation because of Kristensen's previous application for relief from military service.

McGrath based his brief for deportation in part on the opinion of Justice Jackson who had in 1940 been Attorney General. As Attorney General when war clouds were thick on the horizon and a new Selective Service and training act had been passed, Jackson had broadly construed the responsibility of almost any alien to serve in the military or else lose his eligibility for citizenship. In 1950 there were many reasons—social, political, and personal—which allowed him to make more precise distinctions. Perhaps since the motives in these two instances of decision seem almost transparent, he might have acknowledged with candor some of the forces at play in the background of his new and different opinion. Instead, he took refuge in a humor which emphasized his intellectual limitations as opposed to what Cardozo would have called his "human limitations."

> I concur in the judgment and opinion of the Court. But since it is contrary to an opinion which, as Attorney General, I rendered in

1940, I owe some word of explanation. 39 Op. Atty. Gen. 504. I am
entitled to say of that opinion what any discriminating reader must
think of it—that is was as foggy as the statute the Attorney General was
asked to interpret. It left the difficult borderline questions posed by
the Secretary of War unanswered, covering its lack of precision with
generalities which, however, gave off overtones of assurance that the
Act applied to nearly every alien from a neutral country caught in the
United States under almost any circumstances which required him to
stay overnight.

The opinion did not at all consider aspects of our diplomatic history, which I now think, and should think I would then have thought,
ought to be considered in applying any conscription act to aliens.

. . . Precedent, however, is not lacking for ways by which a judge
may recede from a prior opinion that has proven untenable and perhaps misled others. See Chief Justice Taney, *License Cases*, 5 How.
504, recanting views he had pressed upon the Court as Attorney General of Maryland in *Brown v. Maryland*, 12 Wheat. 419. Baron Bram-
well extricated himself from a somewhat similar embarrassment by
saying, "The matter does not appear to me now as it appears to have
appeared to me then." *Andrews v. Styrap*, 26 L.T.R. (N.W.) 704, 706.
And Mr. Justice Story, accounting for his contradiction of his own
former opinion, quite properly put the matter: "My own error, however, can furnish no ground for its being adopted by this Court . . ."
United States v. Gooding, 12 Wheat. 460, 478. Perhaps Dr. Johnson
really went to the heart of the matter when he explained a blunder in
his dictionary—"Ignorance, sir, ignorance." But an escape less self-
depreciating was taken by Lord Westbury, who, it is said, rebuffed
a barrister's reliance upon an earlier opinion of his Lordship: "I can
only say that I am amazed that a man of my intelligence should have
been guilty of giving such an opinion." If there are other ways of
gracefully and good-naturedly surrendering former views to a better
considered position, I invoke them all [340 U.S. Reports, 1950, pp.
176–177].

*Psychoanalysis, Social Science
and the Jurisprudence of Despair*

One must stop and reflect before one applies Cardozo's appraisal to Justice Jackson personally. That is, that he wishes to

Alan A. Stone

retain a personal posture as though he were "above and beyond the sweep of perturbing and deflecting forces." This may in fact be the case, but it is also possible that this posture is an institutional phenomenon inherent in the law. Psychoanalysis can discern the irrationality of the lawgivers, perhaps even help unmask some of the inequities of law, and yet there is a significant cost paid for such insights, a cost minimized by Frank and Cardozo. The possibility of justice as opposed to arbitrary law and order rests on the possibility of rational authority. Rational authority in turn rests on the possibility of certainty and finality. Paul Bator (1963) of Harvard Law School addressed himself to one aspect of this problem in a consideration of *habeas corpus* when he argued that we need a procedural system in law which at some point finally embodies the judgment "that we have tried hard enough and thus may take it that justice has been done."

If psychoanalytic insight introduces into the procedural system the likelihood of judicial irrationality in decision making, we confront the law and those who must obey it with a kind of doubt about its certainty and thus may vitiate the acceptance of "rational authority." We bring forward a kind of critical flaw in rational authority over which the law can have little control. This problem of uncertainty in law was dealt with at length by jurisprudential scholars in the 'thirties [3] and we shall return to it later. However, at this point it is important to recognize that psychoanalysis is not the only scientific discipline concerned with human affairs that casts a shadow of uncertainty over the legal process. All of the social sciences seem to create this same problem which can best be understood in the context of efforts at interdisciplinary research.

Since the turn of the century the dry format of pure legal research has been intermittently lubricated by efforts at interdisciplinary collaboration with the social sciences. Professor Harry Kalven, Jr. (1968) has characterized the history of this collaboration as one of "oscillation between simplistic optimism followed by chilling skepticism followed by a decade or so of silence and

[3] See, for example, Fuller, L. (1934), American legal realism. *Univ. Pennsylvania Law Rev.*, 82:429–462.

406 ·

inaction with the cycle repeating" (p. 56). Although he qualified this description as neither a serious nor a fair history, his subsequent comments do little to mitigate its impact. Perhaps most telling is one rather crucial conclusion that deals with the problem of uncertainty created by science and the law's reaction to it. Kalven suggests that if Law had "to wait until science had (all) the knowledge that was said to be rationally required . . . before making credibility judgments or handling criminals," then what had been a hope for productive collaboration becomes, and here he quotes Philip Mechem (1935), the "jurisprudence of despair." From the perspective of science, it is predictable that research in any field will reveal how much more there is that is unkown, but the law is an ongoing system of great power and implied rectitude which is deemed necessary and assumed to be rational in every civilized society. For it to be confronted by vast regions of uncertainty about what it does and why it does it, is an almost unacceptable burden.

Geoffrey Hazard (1967) of the University of Chicago Law School has been even more despairing in his essay, "Limitations on the Use of Behavioral Science in the Law." He argues that the law's primary concern is with *authoritative decision making in the context of disagreement.* He further asserts that the general principles of law are not questions of fact, but of policy. These he suggests are not the subject matter of behavioral science. However, he concedes that such principles can be broken down into fact components which can be studied, but in the process become trivial for law.

> Behavioral science, like any other science, can illuminate only questions that are in form ones of fact. I believe that most, if not all questions of legal principle can be reduced to a series of constituent questions of fact. The task of doing it is laborious, and not all the questions of fact so formulated are susceptible of investigation yielding reliable results. In any event, the process of reduction entails retraction of the generality and therefore the practical interest of the propositions under consideration. Indeed, when the process of reduction has advanced far enough to make the question scientifically meaningful, it

usually results in making the proposition trivial for an immediate legal purpose.

In the end, as against the exigencies of the law's processes, the uses of behavioral science are relatively remote, its methods relatively expensive, and its results relatively inconsequential. Its findings are, of course, more satisfying to the modern mind than the conclusions advanced from authority. That, however, is not much consolation for law men, whose concerns are for immediate, cheap, and significant decisionmaking. For them there are continuing attractions in the Delphic Oracle [pp. 76–77].

Unfortunately, the rational authority of the oracle of Delphi cannot yet be derived from social science or psychoanalysis.

Hazard's reference to the Delphic oracle is perhaps only sardonic in its intention, but it deserves to be taken very seriously. The implication is that if the law maker has sufficient mystical religious or customary authority, his decisions will be accepted and the system will work whether it is rational (fair) or not. It can be contrasted with Bator's notion that if the procedural system carries forward the issues with sufficient diligence, it is at some point entitled to rest and be accepted; again, it would seem whether it is rational (fair) or not. Hazard's authority is oracular where Bator's is based on entitlement, but both seem to accept that ultimately justice cannot be rationally and/or scientifically derived while suggesting that somehow the law must present itself as though it were. Going further, Bator might be read as follows: If the courts strive to be rational and strive long enough, and if the men of the court are good and true, eventually they should be accepted as rational, the "legal system" requires this. [4]

[4] It is, of course, possible to conceive of a system of law which is at least fair both as to its substance and procedure although it does not produce final rational judgment. For example, if a system of law can be devised in which it is understood that to determine absolutely the responsibility of criminals will require enormous expense and delay, the creators of the system might argue that the alternative of coming to an earlier, less costly judgment, knowing that it is not absolutely fair or absolutely rational, is still a rational alternative. This is only the case if the cost of not reaching a final rational decision is shared equally by all the participants in the legal system. That is, if there is great cost to the system to proceed to the point of an absolute rational judgment, a rational decision can be reached not to go that far if the cost of not going that far is equally borne. Such a system, however, to avoid bias must ensure that the cost is *evenly divided* throughout society. If the cost is not evenly

There can be little comfort for such a view of legal process in the psychoanalytic assertion that true rationality derives from a recognition of the irrational and not alone from further refinements of rational discourse among honest men.

The law is based on a view of man able to choose freely and rationally—both the man in the dock and the man on the bench. Psychoanalysis discovers that neither are as free to choose as the law would believe. A rapprochement between such views seems unlikely. As one judge (1965) put it: "The law's conception, resting as it does upon an undemonstrable view of man, is of course vulnerable. But those who attack it cannot offer a view which is demonstrably more authentic. They can tear down the edifice but have nothing better to replace it" (Weintraub, cited in Katz, Goldstein and Dershowitz [1967], p. 362). Freud, the great skeptic, seems to have put his own limited faith in science as a polestar for man. For law, psychoanalysis seems at this point to offer little guidance, and yet in the light of this polestar, the arbitrary nature of law and the judicial process is revealed as though in a harsh glare.

In a time of social change that borders on revolution, a discipline like psychoanalysis which exposes the arbitrary nature of law and order may well become an ideological weapon. If this is so, and Marcuse and Fanon give every indication that it is, "psychoanalysis" will have come full circle from a healing method to an instrument in the "search for power over men" in a way that Freud could never have imagined.

II

Some Comments on Professor Goldstein's Optimism

Having suggested that some of the basic assumptions of law and psychoanalysis are incompatible, I have placed this discussion in

---

divided, then such a system, though apparently rational, conceals an injustice. Bator's argument would seem to assume that in the current legal system the cost is equally shared, while Hazard ignores this issue entirely. Hazard's system may need to be Delphic partly to obscure its inequities.

opposition (at least in its emphasis) to Professor Goldstein. Professor Goldstein has in fact demarcated mutual borderlands of Law and Psychoanalysis and has even mapped out some of these as fertile territories. Thus Goldstein sets out the following areas of useful collaboration between psychoanalysis and jurisprudence.

1. Psychoanalysis can "press the law in theory and in practice to focus more sharply on those decisions for which the individual must be decategorized and perceived as the highly complex human being that he is."

2. Psychoanalysis can help explain the complexity of results that the same "law-created event" has on different individuals.

3. He emphasizes the importance of psychoanalytic theory and psychoanalytically oriented research on child development for child custody; that is, psychoanalysis can contribute to the court's understanding of what is best for the child.

4. He gives an example of how psychoanalytic insight into the significance of unconscious guilt can be used in evaluating rules of evidence. Thus he suggests that the jury may be instructed that feelings of guilt "which are present in many innocent people, do not necessarily reflect actual guilt."

The first two points in this (admittedly too simplistic) summary are general and theoretical, but they essentially emphasize ways in which psychoanalysis can critically inform the law and thus they are compatible with the thesis I have already advanced; namely, that psychoanalysis serves to confound and complicate rather than to simplify legal deliberation. The second two points are, however, quite specific and suggest something which does more than "tear down the edifice."

Goldstein emphasizes the contribution that psychoanalysis can make to problems of custody and implicitly to adoption, foster home care, and so forth. "To the extent that legal decisions regarding child custody are to comply with an official policy preference for the *child's best interest,* psychoanalytic theory and research findings have a contribution to make to both substantive guides and procedures for decisions" (p. 1073). The problem to be analyzed here derives from the qualification "to the extent that." Decisions in the application of adoption and custody laws, as

Professor Goldstein implies, are not made simply on the basis of what is perceived as the child's best interest. Psychoanalysis must therefore first demonstrate that it has something important to say about what is in the best interest of the child. And then, secondly, this new information must somehow be weighted against other considerations; this is not an easy task. There is first the problem of assessing the validity of the psychoanalytic claim to knowing what is in the child's best interest and then balancing the validity of this claim against other legitimate claims. For the purpose of what follows, we shall assume the validity of the psychoanalytic assertion and focus on the latter problem. The inherent diffculties can best be illuminated by an examination of a particular adoption case which has the advantage of having been discussed by Anna Freud. To highlight the underlying policy conflicts, I have set in parentheses what I construe to be some of the social policy issues.

In January of 1960 a Mr. and Mrs. Andrews paid an obstetrician $500 to cover "médical fees" and took from a hospital nursery the infant Cindy whom they planned to adopt. (Policy: private adoptions may have some value and should be allowed.) As required by law, their attorney filed a "Petition to Adopt" and the County Clerk then notified the County Welfare Department who were licensed to process independent adoptions. (Policy: private adoptions should be supervised by the state.) Before the legal formalities were completed, however, two things happened. First, the natural mother left the state without signing the required consent for adoption, and the Andrews, who had planned to adopt, separated and set about getting a divorce. The County Welfare Department investigated Mrs. Andrews' home and, as the facts suggest, quite justifiably found it unsuitable. They thus began an unsuccessful search for the natural mother in order that other arrangements might be made. (Policy: natural parents should have every opportunity to deliberate and retain or delegate the adoption of their natural children.)

At this point there was a judicial hearing, with a resulting decision that Cindy be removed from Mrs. Andrews' care and placed in a foster home since she could not yet be adopted until consent of the natural parents was obtained. Cindy was then approximately 10 months old, and already showed the kind of psychomotor retardation associated with maternal neglect. The foster parents however were excellent and gradually began to repair the damaged psyche of little Cindy.

Cindy's natural mother still had not made herself available, but there was a hint from her lawyer that she might want the child. However, by the time Cindy was 15 months old, the natural mother did legally relinquish her child and a court hearing was held so that the natural father, who, it turned out, had never legally married the natural mother, [5] could also be relieved of any custody or control. Although Cindy was blossoming in the foster home, she was now free for adoption and the agency carefully went about the selection of a permanent adoptive parent. The transfer to the adopting parents was accomplished when Cindy was approximately 28 months old. This was done with care, but not without hardship to Cindy.

These are the bare facts of the situation. Miss Freud, in her comments on the case, focused on the transfer of the child from the foster home to the adopting home at 28 months. "The agency's action to seek further placement for Cindy seems to me an unenlightened, dangerous, and unwarranted step" (Goldstein and Katz [1965], p. 1053). Miss Freud suggested that "more knowledgeable planning" would have omitted the interim foster placement and allowed for immediate adoption. Miss Freud, in summarizing her reasoning, pointed out that the three basic needs of the child are the need for affection, the need for stimulation, and the need for continuity. The agency, she indicated, had particularly disregarded the third. It is fortunate that the County Welfare Department, an enlightened group, were given the opportunity to respond to Miss Freud's critique. They proved themselves familiar with her work and accepted all three of her points. Although they seem to have exaggerated their own helpfulness in bridging the transfer from foster to adoptive parents, they did, however, sug-

[5] One might speculate that Cindy's mother delayed signing papers because of a vain hope of marrying the natural father. This vain hope might be one to which the law as an instrument of social policy might wish to lend support.

gest other factors as well. First, since there had been no legal relinquishment by the natural parents, adoption was not possible when the child was removed from Mrs. Andrews' care. Second, though the child's psychomotor retardation proved to be correctible, they were faced with the possibility of irreversibility and therefore felt that Cindy might not have been adoptable. (Policy: adopting parents ought not be expected to accept the responsibility for children who are defective in some significant or irremediable way.) Third, although there was no mention in the available material, it was later revealed that the foster parents were given the opportunity to adopt, but decided they would not.

Thus, the agency's actions in this case went counter to the child's interest at one point, not because of an ignorance of psychoanalytic principles, but rather because of practical difficulties and certain policy considerations which derive from the variety of social values that are legally and administratively applied to the adoption situation.

It becomes apparent from specific cases like that of Cindy, that psychoanalytic considerations can be given only limited weight both because of practical limitations and conflicting policies. When the weighting operation occurs, it will be the obligation of the court to inquire into the significance of the continuity of affection, and the validity of the psychoanalytic assertion, as contrasted with the right of a natural mother to claim her child. Psychoanalysis can perhaps contribute to these weighing operations, but it cannot answer the crucial question.

This analysis of the Cindy case is substantially in accord with Hartmann's (1960) conclusion that the place of psychoanalysis in morality (as applied here to legal decision making) will be found not in ultimate principles, but "it can contribute in the domain of means-ends relationships toward the realization of personal, social or cultural values."

Professor Goldstein is well aware of Hartmann's argument in this respect and the case of Cindy, which is taken from Goldstein's work (1965), is explicated here to emphasize that even "means-ends" applications can be hazardous as they are drawn into the moral nexus of law.

Alan A. Stone

The value of the judge informing the jury about unconscious guilt feelings seems to me an ambiguous advance in jurisprudence. The case referred to by Goldstein (1967) occurs in a decision by Judge Bazelon (1963):

> Bazelon, Chief Judge.
> [Appellant's robbery] conviction rested on the testimony of the complaining witness, Cornell Watson. In its brief the Government described this testimony as follows:
> "Watson testified that . . . he was en route home from work and boarding a bus at 7th and Florida Avenue, Northwest in the District of Columbia. His wallet . . . was in his left hip pocket at the time. As he was boarding the bus he felt a slight jostle and subsequently discovered his wallet was missing. As a result of a conversation with persons on the bus [The record indicates that he was told that "they had observed two people running down Florida Avenue (who) had gotten off] Watson got off the bus . . . into an alley. Upon entering the alley Watson observed four or five men, including the appellant, who was looking through a wallet described by Watson as belonging to him, and the one he had on his person prior to boarding the bus. Watson yelled, "Hey, that's my wallet. Give it back to me," and gave chase to the appellant who ran away still holding the wallet. The chase lasted a number of blocks and suddenly appellant stopped and came back toward Watson who caught hold of him. Watson testified that he asked appellant for his wallet and appellant replied, "Here, man, take this dollar and my ring and I will go back and get your wallet." Watson took the dollar and about that time Police Officer Mitchell appeared and took appellant into custody. During the ensuing excitement an unkown citizen returned Watson's wallet to him. Watson testified he did not see anyone take his wallet or see anyone throw it away."
> The Government sought to link appellant to the alleged crime by inferences of guilt from . . . flight.
> Two factual assumptions underlie the legal relationship between flight and guilt: (1) that one who flees shortly after a criminal act is committed or when he is accused of committing it, does so because he feels some guilt concerning that act; and (2) that one who feels some guilt concerning an act has committed that act. [6] Both assumptions purport to rest on common experience, not moral principles.

[6] Wigmore puts it as follows: "There are two processes or inferences involved—from conduct to consciousness of guilt, and then from consciousness of guilt to the guilty deed." 1 Wigmore on Evidence §173 (1940).

. . . Thus, although some courts recognize that flight may be prompted by something other than feelings of guilt, judicial opinion seems to assume that if flight is prompted by feelings of guilt, the accused is certainly the guilty doer.

But available empirical data suggest the wisdom of caution concerning this assumption. Many years ago Sigmund Freud warned the legal profession:

"You may be led astray . . . by a neurotic who reacts as though he were guilty even though he is innocent—because a lurking sense of guilt already in him assimilates the accusation made against him on this particular occasion. You must not regard this possibility as an idle one; you have only to think of the nursery, where you can often observe it. It sometimes happens that a child who has been accused of a misdeed denied the accusation, but at the same time weeps like a sinner who has been caught. You might think that the child lies, even while it asserts its innocence; but this need not be so. The child is really not guilty of the specific misdeed of which he is being accused, but he is guilty of a similar misdemeanor of which you know nothing and of which you do not accuse him. He therefore quite truly denies his guilt in the one case, but in doing so betrays his sense of guilt with regard to the other. The adult neurotic behaves in this and in many other ways just as the child does. People of this kind are often to be met, and it is indeed a question whether your technique will succeed in distinguishing such self-accused persons from those who are really guilty" [*Collected Papers* (1959), Vol. 2, p. 13].

The observation that feelings of guilt may be present without actual guilt in so-called normal as well as neurotic people has been made by many recognized scholars and is a significant factor in the contemporary view of the dynamics of human behavior.

It is not suggested that guilt feelings may not reflect actual guilt, but only that they do not always reflect it, and that Wigmore's commonly accepted opinion that "guilty consciousness" is "the strongest evidence . . . that the person is indeed the guilty doer," should not be elevated to an immutable principle either of law or human behavior.

When evidence of flight has been introduced into a case, in my opinion the trial court should, if requested, explain to the jury, in appropriate language, that flight does not necessarily reflect feelings of guilt, and that feelings of guilt, which are present in many innocent people, do not necessarily reflect actual guilt. This explanation may help the jury to understand and follow the instruction which should then be given, that they are not to presume guilt from flight; that they may, but need not, consider flight as one circumstance tending to show feelings of guilt; and that they may, but need not, consider feelings of guilt as evidence tending to show actual guilt.

○   ○   ○

[Burger, Circuit Judge (dissenting)]

. . . Fact issues and the reasonable inferences from accepted fact are for juries—not judges—in criminal trials and if we trust the jury system we do not need to attempt to guide every detail of jury deliberations. Let alone with a minimum of basic instruction juries can infuse the law with a sense of reality and can temper judicial technicality with the leaven of the common experience and community conscience. We should not attempt to limit the scope of jury deliberations by telling jurors to ignore their own experience and common sense, and in a case like the one before us, denigrate other evidence in the case which plainly suggests that flight was indeed indicative of guilt.

The desire to minimize if not eliminate flight as a source of reasonable inferences represents a futile attempt to require jurors to "unring the bell" of their individual and collective experiences . . . The "fuller instructions regarding flight" urged by Judge Bazelon may be appropriate to a philosophical interchange between judges, lawyers, and experts in psychology, but they are totally unnecessary to a jury and add nothing whatever to what the instruction conveyed to the jury . . . °

At best jurors get only a few general impressions from the trial judge's charge. I think it is fair to say that they understand such concepts as presumptions of innocence, burden of proof, criminal intent and credibility. Beyond these fundamentals and description of the specific elements of a particular crime, most instructions probably

---

° The full instruction on flight was as follows:

"There is a further doctrine of law that becomes pertinent in this case, and this is the testimony of the complaining witness, Cornell Watson, that the defendant fled from the alley where he was first confronted and ran for a period of several blocks. This brings into the case a *presumption* or an element of consideration which hinges around the principle that flight may be considered by jurors as evidence of guilt. In other words, you are entitled to draw from testimony which you accept as credible a conclusion that flight on the part of a defendant was or is evidence of guilt. You are instructed, however, as a matter of law that flight means not merely a leaving, but means a leaving under a consciousness of guilt and for the purpose of evading arrest. Therefore, if you find that the defendant's conduct was induced by fear of arrest, then it is a flight from justice and you may consider it as a circumstance indicating guilt. If, on the other hand, the defendant has explained his presence at the point where he said he was first accosted by the complaining witness to your complete satisfaction, then the element of flight is not a factor to be considered by you."

become confusing and blur the juror's recollection of the really vital elements of the charge.

The disagreement between Judge Bazelon and Judge Burger (now Chief Justice of the United States) is of particular interest to psychoanalysts. Judge Bazelon takes note of unconscious guilt and its significance in producing a guilty attitude or seemingly guilty behavior in an accused. He asserts that this is a universal enough phenomenon that a court may, if requested, so inform the jury to assist it in weighing the facts. Judge Burger seems wary of such data on irrationality and worries that it will only confuse the jury.

I cannot attempt to resolve this judicial dispute, but I would emphasize the following. Psychoanalytic recognition of unconscious and irrational guilt is, it seems to me, a demonstrable feature of the human experience. However, its relative significance in any individual defendant cannot be assessed theoretically. The only psychoanalytic assumption which is justified here is that conscious and unconscious guilt tend to be commingled; the extent of this commingling can only be determined clinically. Furthermore, Bazelon's quotation from Freud in this context seems slightly out of joint. The quote is excerpted from a lecture given by Freud to a group of law students in 1906. Freud at the time was enchanted with Jung and spent much of his lecture on the word association test. He contrasted it with a magistrate's interrogation of the accused. The law students had been conducting "experiments" in interrogation and studying minutely the reactions of the subjects. It was within the context of *such experimental interrogation* that Freud warned of unconscious guilt. If one reinserts in the paragraph quoted by Bazelon the language which has been omitted, the extent of the "dislocation" becomes blatant. You may be led astray *"In your examination"*[7] (p. 23) by a neurotic, etc. Thus, read in its original context, it is clear that Freud was focusing on a special situation in which an emotional reaction is the issue rather than some further, perhaps purposeful, reaction to the emotional reaction (like running away). Surely when a child is confronted by

[7] Emphasis added.

a parent his emotional reaction may well include all of the charged conscious and unconscious feelings of guilt. The same may be true of a confrontation with such obvious parent figures as a teacher, a policeman, or a magistrate, but the case in point was a man running from the scene of a crime. Thus both the specific situation and the specific response are different from those Freud emphasized. At any rate, it would seem that no other jurisdiction has embraced Judge Bazelon's view. Furthermore, Wigmore's classic presumption may, even in the light of psychoanalysis, be quite correct; that is, the significance of unconscious guilt may not be great in most instances of a guilty attitude and the flight inspired by such guilty attitudes. Wigmore's assumption may from another perspective serve an educative function. That is to say, from the point of view of law enforcement a widely accepted assumption that an attitude of guilt together with flight will be construed as actual guilt can serve to induce the innocent (no matter how much unconscious guilt they are harboring) not to run. If such assumptions do affect behavior, then Wigmore's rule may be more broadly functional, and this emphasis is vitiated by Bazelon's instruction as to unconscious guilt.

There is, however, in this case an entirely different question, to wit, the question of relevance.

The facts of this case involve an alleged robbery in a ghetto area. A black man runs from the scene of a crime and the significance of his attitudes and his flight are to be considered by the court. Given the social context of the events, one wonders whether the presence of unconscious guilt is as important for the jury to consider as are other factors. For example, might the judge more relevantly inform (middle class?) jurors that ghetto blacks tend to expect police brutality, false arrest, and humiliating stop-and-frisk procedures? Certainly these can be as pressing considerations in taking flight from the scene of a crime of which one is innocent. Furthermore, there may be a strong cultural value placed on such noncooperative behavior. Against a fabric of social forces such as these, the significance of unconscious guilt may, as Justice Burger suggests, be more appropriate to a philosophical discourse.

Based on the above interpretation it may be quite in order to reexamine the classic Wigmore presumption on the significance of flight. That is, the jury might genuinely profit from the knowledge that flight from the scene of a crime under certain circumstances is motivated by social factors. Thus, Bazelon's instructions, which tend to increase the jury's latitude, may move in the right direction though not for the right reasons.

III

Moral Obligation to Obey the Law

Perhaps the most controversial issue for jurisprudence today is related to the oldest subject of inquiry; that is, the relationship between morality and law (cf. Dworkin, 1969). The reasons for this are quite obviously related to the contemporary social context. The assumption of many antiwar, radical, revolutionary, and minority groups is that moral rectitude is on their side, and that the law as it currently operates is often immoral and oppressive. The concept of law and order is regarded by these groups as a euphemism for oppression by the establishment. But these groups are not alone in their dissatisfaction with traditional legal authority. The police in many cities have lost confidence in the support of the courts and now some base their strategy of crime prevention not on criminal justice, but on a go-it-alone system of "aggressive patrolling." The legal profession finds its own role bewilderingly radicalized by its younger members who question the basic integrity of the legal process as well as the lawyer's part in it.

Particularly impressive are the dissatisfactions of a large segment of the young intelligentsia. Not only are they united with urban blacks in their resentment of police brutality, they also desperately resent the legal institutions responsible for the enforcement of the draft and drug laws.

The Supreme Court finds itself at the center of many of these and other controversies. In the area of racial justice the Court's "principled" decision in *Brown v. School Board* has been thwarted

Alan A. Stone

first by conservative whites who are now joined by radical blacks. The Court's series of decisions that dealt with criminal procedure (e.g., Escobedo and Miranda, etc.) have become the target of the police and apparently of the Nixon Justice Department. The pornography decisions have been blamed by many public prosecutors for the current flood of pornography—a flood predicted by Justice Harlan in his dissent in the Roth case. Perhaps most damaging, however, is the taint attached to "the rational authority" of these ultimate interpreters of the Constitution by the circumstances which surrounded the resignation of Justice Fortas.

All of this suggests that American society has become deeply divided in what Sorokin (1962) called its ethico-juridical mentality. Sorkin's descriptive emphasis on the "heterogeneity of ethico-juridical mentality," despite its cumbersome phraseology, seems more accurate than what has been popularly called the polarization of American society. Sorokin's phrasing suggests a diverse breakdown in customary law, social traditions, and acceptance of the authority of the state. Polarization suggests more unanimity than in fact exists, while implying that solutions can be found by moving in one of two directions.

One of the tangible manifestations of this heterogeneous ethico-juridical mentality is the surge of principled disobedience of law, disobedience based on moral convictions. This disobedience, although it originated in a variety of reform movements which were in themselves politically nonradical, rapidly became a tactic of the radical left. However, in recent months the tactic of principled disobedience, including intentional disruption of procedural amenities, has spread throughout many sectors of society. Thus, to cite only one example, when public school teachers lead prayers in the Northeast, in open opposition to the Supreme Court, we are forced to acknowledge that principled disobedience has reached what in recent tradition was one of the bastions of the law abiding and law respecting.

Obviously we shall not here attempt to deal with the many implications of principled disobedience for jurisprudence. Instead we shall consider as carefully as a nonlawyer can the formulations

420 ·

of a rather dramatically radical point of view, that of Ronald Dworkin (1968). I shall attempt to extract and isolate his psychological assumptions in "On Not Prosecuting Civil Disobedience" and examine these from a psychoanalytic point of view. The arguments Dworkin presents will be dissected in their particulars, but because they intermesh with complex legal and constitutional issues, it may be appropriate first to orient the reader to the basics.

The Constitution, through its first amendment, guarantees among other things freedom of religion. At several points in time the Supreme Court in interpreting the clause on religion has made a distinction between religious beliefs and religious practices. The former seem to have absolute protection, but the latter can be interdicted. The problem, of course, is in determining what standards will be used in deciding which religious practices to interdict. Most authorities have suggested some form of balancing test which places the Government's secular interest on one side and the significance and sincerity of the religious practice on the other side of the scale. However, inevitably the Government's secular interest will be tangible and real while the value of a religious practice will consist only of the unweighable substances of unswerving faith and moral obligation. Dworkin takes this argument, framed in terms of religious belief and practice, a giant step forward. He urges the same sort of balancing test for Government interest and politico-moral conviction. He asks, what should be done with men who, based on politico-moral conviction, oppose the Government.

Dworkin's Arguments

1. The law frequently invokes discretionary power, [8] therefore it can use this discretion with those who out of moral principle disobey the law. This is a strong argument and needs only to be amplified by an analysis of when and why courts use their discre-

---

[8] Both the prosecutor and the judge enjoy considerable discretionary powers in our legal system.

tionary powers. The examples given by Dworkin suggest that prosecutors and courts invoke a variety of reasons for discretion; e.g. the youth of a criminal offender, repentance, turning state's evidence, etc. As Dworkin well knows, however, discretion invoked in good faith must be seen as serving some aim of the system of justice. Thus he suggests that those who disobey the draft law do so out of "better motives than those who break the law out of greed or a desire to subvert government."

From a psychological point of view one is immediately struck by Dworkin's emphasis on motive and his *a priori* assumption that he knows why that heterogeneous group of men who oppose the draft do so. Psychoanalytic familiarity with human behavior would suggest that the motives of such men are quite complex and varied. Perhaps, however, Dworkin uses motive in a different sense; that is, in a nontechnical face-value sense. But even on that basis he must be guilty of overstatement since there are many draft dissenters today who consciously argue that they are bent on subverting government. Unless Dworkin intends only to be hypothetical, there is implicit at least in his first argument the assumption that he can speak for people's motives without empirical inquiry. The negative pregnant of this tactic is that there are others who also without empirical inquiry will speak as if they knew the motives for such dissent. They will insist that this same group are cowards or "effete intellectuals," etc. It is by the way typical of lawyers and professors of law that they assume "motive" with what seems at first blush to be extreme naïveté. As I understand this phenomenon as exemplified by Dworkin and others, it is a retroactive attribution of motive defined not by the psychic context, but by the legal-political context. Thus if opposition to the draft serves a politically important goal and one which appeals to Dworkin's political-moral sense and legal arguments, he will assume that political-moral convictions were the motive for this dissent. Defined in this way motives are not internally derived, multiply determined epigenetic phenomena; they are another variety of legal fiction which in this instance may or may not be misleading. As we shall argue below, Dworkin's failure to consider the internal matrix from which motives derive is a potentially hazardous omission in his thinking.

2. Dworkin's next argument is that draft dissenters may not have broken valid laws because these laws may be constitutionally invalid. It is probably fair to argue that for the radical interpreter of law every question of incompatibility between law and morality becomes a "constitutional issue." Thus it is transformed into a question of law vs. higher law rather than law vs. morality. In fact, for Dworkin, due process, freedom of speech, equal protection, and other legal doctrines become conduits of morality. This morality, if not preexistent in the Constitution, emerges as an inevitable result of the legal process.

Dworkin, for example, easily shifts from the argument that men who break the draft law out of moral constraint ought not be punished (i.e., discretion is appropriate), to the argument that such moral opposition to the draft is condoned by the Constitution. Thus what begins as an argument dealing with the response of the legal system to morally inspired criminal behavior is transformed into a constitutional question. Dworkin goes further in his suppositions than many other authorities would, however. Thus he suggests, "In the United States at least, almost any law which a significant number of people would be tempted to disobey on moral grounds would be doubtful—if not clearly invalid—on constitutional grounds as well. The Constitution makes our *conventional political morality* [9] relevant to the question of validity" (pp. 14–15). Dworkin focuses on political morality because he deals particularly with draft dissent, but his arguments, it seems, can easily be adopted by those who espouse principled disobedience in other areas. In the case of *U.S. v. Leary* (1968), the Fifth Circuit Court decided: "It would be difficult to imagine the harm which would result if the criminal statutes against marijuana were nullified as to those who claim the right to possess and traffic in the drug for religious purposes. For all practical purposes the anti-marijuana laws would be meaningless and enforcement impossible."

[9] Emphasis added.

Alan A. Stone

At this point, given Dworkin's loose criteria for what is to be deemed unconstitutional, one has the impression either (1) that he views *"conventional* political morality" as rather fixed and/or (2) alternatively assumes that the Constitution can fairly readily translate dramatic changes in conventional political morality into new law. The former supposition brings us back as psychologists to a developmental consideration of individual and group political morality as mutable phenomena. The latter supposition implies an uncertainty in law and a disregard for precedent which is in a very radical tradition. Dworkin omits from consideration the first of these, but recognizes this latter problem of disregard for precedent which forms the substance of his next argument.

3. When a citizen believes a law is unclear and thinks it allows what others do not, "he may follow his own judgment, even after a contrary decision by the highest competent court," if his judgment is made on moral grounds. Dworkin suggests that men should dissent even in the face of precedent because courts, even the Supreme Court, may *reverse* a prior decision. He then cites a case in which the Supreme Court in 1940 ruled that it was constitutional to require students to salute the flag. In 1943 "it reversed itself and decided that such a statute was unconstitutional after all." Dworkin asks what was correct behavior for dissenters between 1940 and 1943, particularly since the Court held retroactively that refusal to salute was justified during this interim. He concludes, "If the dissenters had obeyed the law while biding their time, they would have suffered the irreparable injury of having done what conscience forbade them to do" (p. 17).

This reasoning brings us back to the earlier discussion in this paper of final rational authority. Dworkin's argument would suggest that men in the area of political morality should never assume that there is final rational authority. He therefore introduces a degree of uncertainty and ferment into the system which if generalized to other kinds of principled disobedience is incompatible with traditional legal doctrines.

Dworkin's statement that the flag saluters would have suffered irreparable injury contains another series of psychological assumptions which must be dealt with. If by this he means some abstract legal injury, his statement would seem irrefutable. However, even abstract legal concepts of injury are based on some common-sense notion of injury, and in this case there can only be some mental suffering assumed as the underpinning of the "irreparable injury." [10] Dworkin therefore not only presupposes motives, he also presupposes irreparable mental suffering. The latter presupposition, like the former, assumes something about human nature which may or may not be of functional value to law. That is, it may in the area of political morality be very important to emphasize a legal fiction of irreparable injury when in fact the individual involved suffered not one bit. However, if the implication to be drawn is that one kind of suffering is in fact particularly to be avoided on humane as distinct from politico-legal grounds, then empirical data is necessary. In addition, if there is no significant mental suffering in the flag salute case and it is entirely a question of political priorities, then this fact should not be obscured by invoking nonlegal notions of irreparable injury.

As Dworkin unravels his thesis it seems he has a very special kind of man in mind. That is, a man who knows enough about law to believe that a particular law is unclear despite precedent, and whom Dworkin knows to be swayed solely on political moral (i.e., constitutional) grounds. This, however, proves not to be the case; it seems that knowledge of the law is not a requisite. According to Dworkin, if men are unfamiliar with law, but are basing their dissent on political morality, they are entitled to the same protection as their hypothetical "more knowledgeable colleagues." This seems a particularly weak link in his argument since it widens still further the significance of the nature of motive for dissent, which is assumed *a priori*, while narrowing the rationality requirement. In other words, he asks the law to make no distinction between those who dissent on moral grounds and bother to define the constitutional questions, and those who simply dissent on moral grounds regardless of constitutional niceties. He can only succeed by convincing himself of his previously implied equation

[10] The concept of injury in law can be constructed quite abstractly, for example in tort cases, but even in these cases there seems to be an implication of mental suffering. (Cf. *Morningstar v. Lafayette Hotel Co.*, 211 N.Y. 465, 105 N.E. 656 (1914) Cardozo, J.

of moral justification and constitutional justification. Thus for Dworkin eventually every moral political response is potentially a "reasonable judgment" that a law is invalid.

Dworkin goes on to consider how the Government should deal with draft dissenters as he has defined them. In doing so he makes an effort to distinguish between different types of political-moral convictions. For example, he emphasizes the special nature of draft dissent vs. integration dissent. This is important for the current inquiry since it deals with the possibility of generalizing Dworkin's arguments to the many other areas of principled disobedience.

4. "Every rule of law is supported, and presumably justified, by a set of policies it is supposed to advance and principles it is supposed to respect" (p. 19). These justifications he asserts have a hierarchical order. Thus, a "moral right to be free from harm" is more important than "the alleged utility of the economic and social policies [the laws] promote." Having set up this proposition, he argues that the segregationist who blocks the schoolhouse door deprives children of their "right not to be segregated." The draft dissenter on the other hand only interferes with classifications "arranged for social and administrative convenience . . . They presuppose no fixed rights."

Here is a strange legal calculus indeed. Clearly to the extent that draft dissent is allowed, those who do not dissent face an increased risk of being drafted and therefore an increased risk of injury and death. Whether or not they have a legal right to be protected against such increased risk is never established because of the way the questions are framed. Drafting people implies that all not excused for specific reasons face death and injury equally. Exempting those who dissent increases that risk. Dworkin ignores this. "If these men had encouraged violence or otherwise trespassed on the rights of others, then there would be a strong case for prosecution" (p. 19). If the cost of nondissent is increased likelihood of death and injury while the cost of dissent is forgiveness and protection, there will indeed be a high premium on changing one's political moral convictions. Clearly Dworkin's calculus either ignores or omits this aspect of the problem.

This exhausts my dissection of Dworkin's arguments [11] and I shall now attempt a summary and evaluation.

Acts defined by lawyers as political are motivated by political-moral convictions and not by unconscious self-interest or other complex motives. People who are thus politically motivated are entitled to lenient treatment when their moral convictions lead to action which comes in conflict with the law. These politically motivated acts are of great importance to the persons who espouse them, and if forced to negate the acts based on these convictions, they will suffer irreparable harm. Thus the psychological aspect of this argument asks the law to identify a certain kind of moral conviction and, based on its presence, allot to the holder special treatment. The special treatment seems to be based not only on constitutional grounds, but also on the nature of the motive and the quality of the suffering if such motives are frustrated. That is, to the extent that Dworkin has said no more than that the Constitution must respect and protect political dissent, whatever its origin, there is no conflict. When, however, he argues that there is a special motive for political dissent which entitles its holder to preferential treatment, he has advanced a psychological thesis which is in issue. Dworkin's effort in this respect is reminiscent of the efforts made by interpreters of the Supreme Court's decision in the Seeger case.

The Seeger Court held that a man need not be a member of an established religious group such as the Quakers to be accorded the status of a conscientious objector. The test they propounded was that the pacifistic beliefs of the individual hold the "same

[11] Part of Dworkin's argument, and perhaps the most interesting part, has been neglected. It is not sophistry to lawyers to suggest that the Supreme Court needs cases so as to be able to interpret or reinterpret the constitutionality of various laws and statutes. Those who by their principled disobedience challenge a law with the expectancy of finding support or even possible support in the Court, therefore, present our society with an opportunity for change. In this context it would seem that Dworkin needs only to reward those who provide test cases to challenge specific laws. To do this, of course, the Court theoretically requires only one case which relates to an issue which is ripe for judicial decision. However, when Dworkin shifts his argument to embrace anyone who dissents on political moral grounds, no matter how little he knows of law, he has abandoned this criterion. His main argument, therefore, relates to the source of the conviction, a criterion vague and uncertain in its application when read against the mutability of "moral convictions" and the current heterogeneity of ethico-juridical mentality suggested earlier.

• 427

place" in his life as "an orthodox belief in God holds in the life of one clearly qualified for exemption."

Goldstein (1968), who reviewed the Seeger decision in some detail, concluded that its reasoning was compatible with the most sophisticated psychoanalytic theory. However, it is unclear how he reached this conclusion. If the Court had held only that because authentication of religious conviction through psychological means is exceedingly difficult, we will not inquire into how a man reaches a pacifist conviction but rather ask only whether his conviction is "truly held," it would have been congruent with the psychoanalytic theory cited by Goldstein. However, the test is its correspondence to the place held in the life of a theistic believer, a simplistic and probably psychoanalytically meaningless definition. Although Goldstein quite correctly suggests that beliefs have a complex and diverse origin as revealed empirically in psychoanalysis and spelled out theoretically by Hartmann (1961), the Court significantly departs from its intuitive recognition of this by its neotopographical "place" test. Goldstein apparently discounts the "place" test since he suggests that the Seeger decision tends "virtually to obliterate the distinction between 'religious,' 'philosophic,' and a 'merely personal moral' pacifism."

Thus Goldstein argues that because psychoanalysis demonstrates the difficulty of identifying the origin of convictions in the course of a man's life, it may enable the Court to recognize that they cannot draw a clear line between objections to war in general and objection to a specific war. (Some of Goldstein's logic has been echoed in the recent Sisson decision, 297 F. Supp. 902 [D Mass. 1969]). However, the Supreme Court's place test seems on its face to be somewhat removed from these psychoanalytic nuances. In fact, the simpler interpretation of it might be as follows: Most men believe in God; if they don't, then they adopt some other belief which takes the same place in their lives or minds as a kind of religion. It is unconstitutional to discriminate against these latter people no matter how bizarre or individualistic their religious beliefs may be. But then comes the task of constructing a test of this proposition, and not unexpectedly the Court finds itself stumbling: "In no field of human endeavor has the tool of language proved so

Psychoanalysis and Jurisprudence

inadequate." The Seeger decision rather than being consistent with psychoanalytic sophistication, as Goldstein suggests, seems instead only to be a poorly articulated attempt to interpret the draft laws in a way which would not seem to give precedence to established religions.

It is interesting that the implicit psychological assumptions of Dworkin and the explicit interpretation of Goldstein, despite their different theoretical orientation, produce conclusions which turn out to have a strong family resemblance; i.e., political-moral convictions resist analysis in the legal context, therefore, the Government cannot distinguish between categories of dissent and has to treat all alike. The Government in effect is helpless in its capacity to question or test in any way the significance of a psychological belief once the decision to give it some weight has been made. All it can do is balance its own interest, for example, in raising an army against its interest in allowing conscientious objection. Since the Government cannot discriminate between different kinds of conscientious objectors based on this type of analysis, it is suggested by some that all dissenters might draw lots with the Government allowing only so many places to be filled.

There are two rather unsatisfactory aspects to this sort of conclusion. First, intuitively a psychoanalyst must take note that the sense of moral rectitude and the tendency to object are highly contagious, as witness the contemporary scene. Furthermore, there is no doubt that although the Government may be unable to distinguish completely between moral convictions, there is some value in trying to do so. Surely an enlightened government may want to treat a man deeply committed to his moral convictions differently than it treats a man who has no such major conviction. Psychoanalysis and common experience both suggest that moral, ethical, and religious convictions are held with different intensity by different individuals. The Dworkin-Goldstein argument blurs this distinction as did the old law which treated in the same way a devout Quaker and a Quaker by birth.

This challenging problem has been dealt with to great effect by Morris Clark (1969), a recent graduate of Harvard Law School. Clark suggests after careful scrutiny that Seeger is a difficult test to apply, that it is essentially a "psychological" test, that it is "largely intuitive," and "therefore to some extent necessarily arbitrary." He applauds it, nonetheless, and sets about providing a solution of the dilemma it creates. Using in part psychoanalytic arguments which will be expanded below, he suggests that Seeger is a test of the extent of psychological compulsion which attends a given belief.

Psychoanalyzing Morality for Jurisprudence

Psychoanalysis would seem to support the following series of assumptions about the psychological compulsion attendant on the moral claims of adults. The development of morality, like other important psychological elements, is an epigenetic process shaped by the interaction of the personality core and life experiences. In the case of moral development, considerable mutability remains as a possibility throughout life, and due to the phenomena of reaction formation and negative identity, dramatic shifts are not impossible or even unusual. Research on adolescent development has highlighted the cyclic swings of moral standards which are considered typical. It is also rather well known to clinicians that peer group pressures can profoundly affect the superego and its moral imperatives. Furthermore, the sophisticated theoretical elaboration of Freud's work by Hartmann (1961) and Rapaport (1958) provides a framework for understanding the constant interaction occurring at the interface between internalized relatively fixed moral belief and life experiences which either may nourish, transform, or erode moral convictions. Thus Rapaport's notion of superego nutriment implies a more sophisticated awareness among ego psychologists (at least) of the constant potential for mutability of the structures of the superego and therefore of moral convictions.

From the perspective of the psychoanalytic study of the individual, the evidence suggests that neither a fixed nor a stable morality can be assumed or expected as an inevitable human occurrence. Indeed, Freud (1927, 1930) insisted that many of society's basic moral values are never internalized by large segments of the population, and particularly is this the case for those who are oppressed. Without this process of internalization, there is no moral imperative other than the evasion of punishment or suffering.

What follows from these psychoanalytic developmental constructs about morality is that some, though not all, moral convictions can be rapidly transformed by political force, by significant changes in law, by propaganda, by group support and identification, by charismatic leaders, by social and economic pressures, and by a variety of other emotional forces that transcend the individual socialization experience.

None of these psychoanalytic observations are meant to imply that natural morality or hierarchical orders of morality do not exist in some latent form. It is not offered as a contradiction of the theory of natural law. But it is to say rather definitively that psychoanalysis has found empirically that as a psychological phenomenon there is no consistently internalized natural morality, nor is individual morality a constant. Thus, when a man claims a moral conviction at one point in his life, he may well later repudiate his claim and act in such a way as to suggest that his prior claim is no longer an imperative producing guilt. The same is true for groups of men. This is not to say simply that men are hypocrites; rather, it suggests that the force and thrust of morality as a psychological configuration are neither naturally nor inevitably fixed in one direction. Indeed, it may be legitimate to suggest that those elements of moral conviction which affect man's interaction with other men in the social context (as opposed to the family setting) are the latest learned, the least solidly internalized, the most consciously rational, and the most readily altered. The full significance of this mutability was missed by a tendency of earlier psychoanalysts to emphasize the inherited components of the superego and to equate the family superego with the wide variety of moral convictions affecting social intercourse. Surely the early superego plays an important part in later superego development, particularly as to religious beliefs and anthropomorphic theism. However, the continuity of childhood and adult superego is disrupted by the adolescent experience in which there has been a great increase of cognitive and abstract capacity. The concrete imperatives of childhood become more abstract, and as Jacobson

(1961) emphasizes, in successful maturation the superego moves closer to ego and further from id. During this transition the quality of psychological compulsion may alter noticeably.

If one accepts the validity of these psychoanalytic constructs, one is forced to conclude that the significance of moral convictions varies enormously from person to person. This variation depends both on the extent of internalizations in childhood and the degree of restructuring which is most notable in adolescence. It is important to note that draft dissenters are invariably late adolescents or young adults. Thus they are at a point in their lives when moral convictions are most in flux. Frequently this is also a time of religious conversion and a massive transformation of all moral convictions. To create a legal test for the validity of individual moral convictions at this age is a staggering possibility, and yet to ignore the distinctions seems mindless.

Most notable in the current social context is the proclivity to righteous indignation and blaming the other, a psychosocial response at least part of which has its psychoanalytic explanation in the work of Anna Freud (1946). She describes as one early stage of superego development the sequence of "identification with the aggressor," supplemented by the "projection of guilt." "An ego which . . . develops along this particular line introjects the authorities to whose criticism it is exposed . . . and projects . . . its prohibited impulses outward." "Vehement indignation at someone else's wrongdoing is the precursor of a substitute for guilty feelings . . ." "This stage in the development of the superego is a kind of preliminary phase of morality." "It is possible that a number of people remain arrested at (this) intermediate stage" (p. 129).

As we well know in psychoanalysis every stage of development leaves its traces in human personality. It is likely that this type of superego functioning is a potential response in all humans. I would suggest that in times of social disorder when there is a breakdown in conventional law, when authority is challenged, when anxiety and uncertainty are high, this type of regressive superego functioning proliferates. In the area under discussion it would clearly promote the kind of moral conviction which contributes to principled disobedience. This is not to suggest that all principled disobedience derives from regressive superego functioning. I do hypothesize, however, that in a climate of social change there is an increased likelihood of such behavior. It would be mediated for example as follows:

A group of young draft dissenters vociferously challenge their elders for embarking on an immoral war. The elders, threatened by the free expression of angry criticism, respond with anxiety and guilt. Some further react by identifying with the angry tone of the young authorities and counterattack, denying their own sense of guilt and turning on the young with increasingly vehement accusations about the lost generation whose behavior is contrasted with their own lives of sacrifice and hard work. The young, frightened and provoked by the condemnation of their parent figures, in turn react by overemphasizing their own idealism and still more vehement condemnation. Thus the sequence of criticism and countercriticism mounts with neither side developing an increased awareness of their own part in the struggle. Since attacking is an antidote to guilt, there is no easy solution to this dilemma. Perhaps the reader will tolerate an even further speculative leap. When a young draft protester dissents on the basis of sincere moral conviction and he is labeled a criminal, it is quite likely that he and those who identify with him will be tempted, perhaps through identification with the aggressor, to attack the system which so labels him. They may subsequently deny their own moral responsibility for acts of violence which may be destructive of life and property, while they violently condemn similar behavior in others. On the other hand, if the legal system treats all dissenters equally without regard for their depth of conviction and real justification, it will present an appearance of moral bankruptcy which is almost as unfortunate.

A potential solution to such a dilemma (besides ending a war which many deem immoral) is for the system of law enforcement to develop strategies which respect genuine moral conviction without promoting moral vindictiveness.

Clark (1969) offers a remarkably sensible approach to a solution of this dilemma which seems to me compatible with the psychoanalytic theory discussed above, although it may be somewhat visionary from the legal point of view. He realizes, of course, that there will be great difficulty in detecting the amount of psychological compulsion attached to an act of principled disobedience such as draft dissent *ab initio*. Therefore, he sets out a series of guidelines to be applied by the Court to the free exercise clause which (again it would seem to me) create an ongoing test of moral conviction.

The legal response is a complex one, but makes distinctions between acts and omissions, sets out the principle of false conflict, the principle of alternative burdens, civil remedies vs. criminal remedies, the use of juries rather than administrative boards in the finding of fact as to conscientious objection. He discusses methods of evaluating the cost of privileged inaction to Government, etc. In effect, he creates a balancing technique which realistically (although not without difficulty) attempts to assess the worth of a moral conviction to a person who asserts it.

I shall at my own risk translate one part of his legal strategy into my own language. The degree of psychological compulsion which attaches to a belief cannot be decided in advance by the Court. However, the Government is not prevented from responding to dissent in a clear-cut and orderly fashion that makes crucial distinctions and forces the individual to detect within himself that which he does out of self-interest and that which arises out of moral conviction. If a man refuses to fight in a war out of what he sincerely believes to be moral conviction, the Government, instead of immediately labeling him a criminal, might allow him to present his views to a jury who would evaluate his claim; then, if the jury felt the situation warranted it, the Court would levy some civil penalty. That is, he might be given the choice of four years of alternative service as opposed to two years of military service. If his motivation is only self-interest, then he may under that circumstance choose the military alternative. The Government in such an approach recognizes the admixture of self-interest and moral conviction, but creates a test which potentially sorts out the diverse motivation of the dissenter without creating a sense of narcissistic entitlement or deprivation in all other draft-age citizens. Clearly the alternatives set up by the Government must be carefully chosen for such a system to work fairly.

In this and other ways Clark suggests a kind of balanced governmental reaction which would respect all dissent under the free exercise clause at the same time that those who practice principled disobedience or dissent will be encouraged to weigh the significance of that dissent in light of the alternatives that confront them. Clark's reasoning embodies the logic that a moral conviction cannot be weighed in advance and that either rewarding or stifling moral dissent is a dangerous business for society. Nonetheless, Clark suggests it may be possible to construct an orderly system that respects human integrity without destroying governmental authority.

Apologia

Obviously a psychoanalyst who ventures as deeply into constitutional waters as I have done does so at his own risk. However, it was not my intent to solve constitutional arguments; rather, my discussion is meant to suggest only that psychoanalysis has something to say about the feasibility of certain legal judgments based on what we know psychoanalytically of human nature. Nor do I mean to imply that I oppose draft dissent or other instances of principled disobedience. It has only been my intention to emphasize that the law cannot escape the problem of difficult social policy decisions by either ignoring or hiding in the darker forests of the psyche.

BIBLIOGRAPHY

Bator, P. (1963), Finality in criminal law and federal *habeas corpus* for state prisoners. *Harvard Law Rev.*, 76:441.
Bernfeld, S. (1949), Freud's scientific beginnings. *Amer. Imago*, 6:163–196.
Cardozo, B. (1921), *The Nature of the Judicial Process*. New Haven: Yale University Press.
Clark, M. (1969) *Harvard Law Review*, in press.

Alan A. Stone

Dworkin, R. (1968), On not prosecuting civil disobedience. *New York Review of Books*, 10:14–21.

———— (1969), Morality and law. *New York Review of Books*, 22:29.

Frank, J. (1930), *Law and the Modern Mind*. New York: Brentano.

Freud, A. (1946), *The Ego and the Mechanisms of Defense*. New York: International Universities Press.

———— (1966), Personal communication.

Freud, S. (1906), Psychoanalysis and the ascertaining of truth in courts of law. *Collected Papers*, 2:13. London: Hogarth Press, 1948.

———— (1927), The future of an illusion. *Standard Edition*, 21:3–56. London: Hogarth Press, 1962.

———— (1930), Civilization and its discontents. *Standard Edition*, 21:59–145. London: Hogarth Press, 1962.

Fuller, L. (1934), American legal realism. *Univ. Pennsylvania Law Rev.*, 82:429–462.

Goldstein, J. and Katz, J. (1965), *The Family and the Law*. New York: The Free Press.

———— (1968), Psychoanalysis and jurisprudence. *Yale Law Journal*, 77:1053.

Hartmann, H. (1960), *Psychoanalysis and Moral Values*. New York: International Universities Press.

———— (1961), Ego psychology and the problem of adaptation. In: *Organization and Pathology of Thought*, ed. D. Rapaport. New York: Columbia University Press.

Hazard, G. (1967), Limitations on the uses of behavioral science in the law. *Case Western Reserve Law Rev.*, 19:71–77.

Jacobson, E. (1961), Adolescent moods and the remodeling of psychic structures in adolescence. *Psychoanalytic Study of the Child*, 16:164–184.

Jones, E. (1953), *The Life and Work of Sigmund Freud*, Vol. I. New York: Basic Books.

Kalven, H., Jr. (1968), Quest for the middle range: empirical inquiry. In: *Law in a Changing Society*, ed. G. Hazard. Englewood Cliffs: Prentice-Hall.

Katz, J., Goldstein, J., and Dershowitz, A. (1967), *Psychoanalysis, Psychiatry and Law*. New York: The Free Press.

McGrath v. Kristensen (1950), *U.S. Reports*, 340:162–178.

Mechem, P. (1935), The jurisprudence of despair. *Iowa Law Review*, as cited in Kalven, H., Jr. *op. cit.*

Miller v. U.S. (1963), 320 F. 2d 767 (D.C. Cir. 1963), as cited in *Psychoanalysis, Psychiatry and Law*, *op. cit.*

Rapaport, D. (1958), The theory of ego autonomy—a generalization. *Bull. Menninger Clin.*, 22:13–35.

Schur, E. (1968), *Law and Society: A Sociological View*. New York: Random House.

Sorokin, P. (1962), *Social and Cultural Dynamics*, Vol. II. Totowa, New Jersey: Bedminster Press.

State v. Sikora, (1965), 44 N.J. 453, 210 A 2d 193; as cited in *Psychoanalysis, Psychiatry and Law*, *op. cit.*

U.S. v. Leary (1968), 392 U.S. 903.

Yntema, H. (1928), *Yale Law Journal*, 37:468, 480; as cited in Frank, J., *op. cit.*

21. Sin and the Sense of Guilt

VIVIAN FROMBERG, M.D., AND
SALO ROSENBAUM, M.D.

THE ANALOGOUS development of civilization, religion and individual maturation has been much elaborated upon in Freud's writings. We are familiar with his formulations in relation to religious evolution in terms of primitive drives, oedipal strivings, father murder, and the return of the repressed (Freud, 1913, 1927, 1930, 1939). It is not the purpose of this presentation to review or dispute various aspects of Freud's contentions, but rather to explore the concept of sin and its transformation in the early Judaic and Christian literature, in terms of Freud's hypotheses and current psychoanalytic formulations regarding the superego and its ultimate internalization (Hartmann and Loewenstein, 1962; Lampl-de Groot, 1962). In the use of the term superego, we will refer to Arlow's and Brenner's (1964) definition of that "group of mental functions which have to deal with ideal aspirations and with moral commands and prohibitions. It owes its origin as an organized division of the mind to identification with parental figures, ethical and moral aspects. This identification is primarily a consequence of the violent mental conflicts of the phallic, oedipal phase of development" (p. 39). By internalizing the prohibitions of the parental figures, the child is able to summon defenses against as well as gain control of his instinctual impulses. This process in the face of intense conflict or inadequate defense mechanisms, is a reinstinctualization of mental functions, or a "re-externalization" of those commands and moral prohibitions which have been more or less incorporated in the individual's personality. The authors reaffirm the thoughts of David Beres (1966) communicated verbally as well as in his writings that the "sense of guilt" (as distinguished from expressions of guilt feelings, remorse, fear of punishment, loss of love, etc.) is the by-product of the oedipal struggle and its resolution, and the heritage of a relatively internalized superego.

We use the word "sense" (Lewis, 1966) derived from the Latin "sensus" (meaning knowledge at first hand, or by experience) as an inner awareness, a combination of thought and feeling, an "internalized" experience. The sense of guilt is then the developmental product of those same functions, autonomous, and defensive, which comprise the mature, i.e., internalized superego.

So too the words "conscience" and "conscious" are derived from the prefix "with" or "together" and the verb "to know" or "to know well." C. S. Lewis (1960), in tracing the derivation of the word "conscience" from the Latin "conscire," points out the implicit implication of an inner observing self as well as the acting one. The Hebrew word *ladaht* "to know" implies intimacy, or experience beyond intellectual recognition; thus the word is often used in conjunction with heart, *lev. Jeremiah*, for example, reads: "I will give them the heart to know me."

In this paper we will attempt to demonstrate the vicissitudes of the superego development of a religious people, as reflected in their shared concepts of sin, morality, and relationship with the father, i.e., God. While there is much contradiction, spurts of progression, and regression throughout, and more seriously, much dispute as to the chronology of biblical literature, the following trends and observations seem valid. In the Torah which is "the literary product of the earliest stage of the Israelite religion" (Kaufman, 1960), "sin" is primarily a legalistic religious, ritualistic code of behavior rather than a moral conception (Moore, 1966). With the exceptions of passages, mainly from *Deuteronomy* (the last of the five books of Moses), which will be elaborated upon, sin was regarded as any lack of conformity to the will of God. While the greatest offenses are against his holiness, e.g., blasphemy, and idolatry, the latter being "the crucial national sin" (Kaufman, 1960), even minor infractions are dangerous since they are indicative of rebelliousness and lead to greater sins, the cardinal sins of heathenism, unchastity, and homicide. The invasion of God's sphere has to do with man's self-assertion and the unconscious wish to replace him. In this context we may look upon the laws of God as parental superego admonitions against incest and patricide.

There is, nevertheless, a clear distinction even in the Pentateuch between violating a statute and moral wrongdoing, between social sins (against man) and sins against God. Their sameness lies in that all are violations of the revealed will of God. There is also a special ritual expiation for sins committed unwittingly (*Lev.*, 4.5; *Num.*, 22.31), the intent of which is to mitigate the remorsefulness of the sinner, and not to satisfy God. However, for willful sinning there is no such expiation. The person who does anything willfully, blasphemes the Lord. Then that person shall be cut off from the midst of his people, "for he despised the word of the Lord and nullified his commandment, that person shall be cut off, his guilt is upon him" (*Num.*, 15. 30. 31; *Ps.*, 19. 14).

"The primacy of morality was not reached before classical prophecy" (Kaufman, 1960), the first of those utterances having been attributed to the prophet Amos. As Kaufman states, "He never speaks of murder but of every day moral sins of exploitation, oppression, perversions of justice, such as were perpetrated by the rulers and the rich" (Kaufman, 1960, p. 366). In the books of *Isaiah* and *Jeremiah* national cult, ritual and sacrifice are rejected in favor of morality and social justice.

According to Arlow (1951), "The prophet symbolizes a stage in the historical evolution of the moral conscience of his people" (p. 396). Moreover, the prophet conquers his ambivalence and overcomes his aggression through identification with a prohibiting but occasionally tolerant God. This stage represents a more highly developed identification with the father whose "moral" values are to be incorporated into "the heart and mind *(Deut.*, 29. 3) of his children and to become their own."

It is Freud's suggestion in *Moses and Monotheism* (1939) that the Jewish people remain in a state of torment because "it was a case of 'acting out' the great misdeed of primaeval days rather than remembering." In the wishful fantasy of a Messiah, the Jews longed to undo the deed and absolve their guilt. "The poor Jewish people," says Freud (1939), "with their habitual stubbornness continued to disavow the father's murder, atoned heavily for it in the course of time (p. 90). Whether Moses was murdered by the Jewish people is a matter much disputed by scholars, but this does not refute Freud's contention if the wished-for murder is equated with the deed.

Freud attributed the success of Christianity and its appeal to the multitudes to the murder of Christ and his transfiguration, through which the son was put in the place of the father. In the sacrifice of Christ who was without sin, the sins of Christians were exculpated. Moreover, the Christians in admitting their "guilt" (i.e., inherent sinfulness), could hope for absolution. Freud in the same paper (1939) speaks of the return of the repressed and refers to the fact that in "some respects the new religion meant a cultural regression as regularly happens when a new mass of people, of a lower level, break their way or are given admission." It is the opinion of the authors that the Christian concept of sin represents a partial ego and superego regression to more primitive levels of identification, and a merging with the bisexual parent as represented by God and the Virgin Mary, primarily through oral incorporation.

At this point it behooves us to examine sin in biblical history. In its Hebraic roots the Bible expresses no antipathy to sex, nor does the sin of Adam and Eve have any special connection with sexual activity. In fact the word sin is not used in any of its Hebraic forms in the account of the Fall. It was man's refusal to submit to God's prohibition against eating from the tree of knowledge that led to his expulsion from the Garden of Eden.

Adam and Eve, having been rebellious, were punished to avoid the greater crimes of aggression and acquisitiveness "lest he put forth his hand" and indeed gain the omnipotence of his father. Adam and Eve were not punished by death (mortality), since presumably they never had the gift of eternal life, God's anxiety being "lest" they "take also of the tree of life" *(Gen., 7. 22)*.

With their new knowledge of good and evil, Adam and Eve became embarrassed by their nakedness. It is to be noted that the Hebrew word *arom,* nakedness, is not too dissimilar from the word *arum,* meaning deceitfulness. What was previously natural to them became a source of shame. "The eyes of both of them were opened and they knew they were naked" *(Gen.,* 3. 7). It would seem that their forbidden acquisition of knowledge led to the sins of voyeurism and exhibitionism. In any case, although man suffers in consequence of Adam's guilt, [1] i.e., he toils for his bread, and woman bears children in pain *(Gen.,* 3. 19, 16), it is nowhere suggested that this guilt is transmitted from generation to generation.

The classic concept of original sin was conceived in the New Testament, beginning with Paul, and formally crystallized by Augustine. Before the Fall of Man, Augustine taught, sexual activity was totally under control, and obedient to the will, never striving independently. Adam and Eve, through their willfulness and pride, became "conscious of new and destructive impulses," namely lust generated by their act of rebellion, inordinate awareness of the new disobedience of their genitals, no longer innocent, or docile, no longer amenable to the will. Shame followed upon this demonstration of unruliness" (Feldman, 1968). William Graham Cole (1955) believes that while the Apostle Paul is highly inconsistent regarding the evils of the flesh, and although Paul believed that sin is transmitted from generation to generation through the flesh, he did not state that the sexual act is evil nor responsible for original sin, although he made it clear that celibacy was preferable to marriage. It was Augustine who equated original sin with lust, so that every child can be said to be conceived in the sin of its parents.

Early Christianity departs from Judaism in its attitudes towards worldly pleasures, and particularly towards sexual gratification. Spiritual perfection is achieved through renunciation of the world and the bodily appetites, but most important "the decisive test, the critical discipline was that of sexual abstinence. This cult of virginity followed inevitably from the ethical dualism implicit in Saint Paul's comparison of the married with the single state to the advantage of the latter" (Bailey, 1959 pp. 19–20).

According to the New Testament, man is in a constant state of sin. This is not to be equated with specific acts of sin, but can be described as "the tendency of man to build the world around him-

[1] In this context guilt is used in the general sense of being responsible for a transgression, not in the psychoanalytic sense.

self, to corrupt even his best achievements by being conscious that they are his achievements. . . . It is the activity of man which is done apart from faith and which therefore is not done only for God and neighbour but also for self" (Dillenberger and Welch, 1954, p. 29) that constitutes sin.

The Old Testament on the other hand encourages marriage. It is for this purpose that Eve was created. "It is not good for man to be alone; I shall make him a help meet for him" (*Gen.*, 2. 18). "Therefore doth a man leave his father and mother and cleave unto his wife and they shall become as one flesh" (*Gen.*, 2. 24).

In *Ecclesiastes* (9. 9) man is enjoined to seek pleasure in conjugal love. "Enjoy life with the wife whom thou lovest all the days of the life of thy vanity which God has given thee under the sun . . ."

The first mention of sin in the Pentateuch is in reference to the legend of Cain and Abel. Cain displeased God by his sacrificial offering which in contrast to Abel's showed a kind of niggardliness or lack of generosity. While Abel chose the choicest of the "firstlings of his flock and of the fat thereof" as an offering, it is to be noted that Cain merely "brought of the fruit of the ground" (*Gen.*, 4. 3, 4). God had no respect for Cain's offering and "Cain was very wroth and his countenance fell" (*Gen.*, 4. 5). "And the Lord said unto Cain, Why art thou wroth? and why is thy countenance fallen?" "If thou does well, shalt thou not be accepted? and if thou does not well sin lieth at the door, and unto thee is its desire but thou canst rule over it."

The Hebrew word in this context is *het*, meaning transgression —and clearly it is within Cain's will to make amends. However, Cain in his envy of his brother slew him, the punishment for which is exile. Cain then acknowledged his responsibility pleading, "My sin is greater than I can bear." Here the biblical word is "avon" which means both iniquity and guilt, not punishment as it is usually translated (*Gen.*, 4. 13). It is after this that God protects him from death by placing his mark upon him "lest any finding should kill him" (*Gen.*, 4. 15).

The next major reference to sin occurs in the legend of Noah where God sees and condemns the wickedness of men. The sins of man again have to do with aggression, corruption and violence.

Only Noah was gentle and just, and God saved him because he was righteous.

There are many Hebrew words indicating the varying severity of sins: for example, *pesha* is conscious rebellion, a revolt against God and consequently is viewed as a most profound sin. The word *averah,* on the other hand, refers to overstepping or transgressing the word, command or law of Yahweh *(Num.,* 14. 11). The word *shgaga* means erring through ignorance, or by mistake.

It is interesting to note that the more profound sins, *pesha* and *avon,* are translated and used interchangeably with "guilt." These are the sins of conscious rebellion.

Although there is a hierarchy of sins, all sins are considered transgression against the law and the covenant, and consequently against the father himself.

To some extent the essence of sin in both the New and the Old Testaments is not merely transgression or disobedience, but a "condition of dreadful estrangement from God, the sole source of well being" (Buttrick, 1962). The Bible deals with man's suffering and the painful effects of sin and salvation through God. While the sinfulness of estrangement from God pervades both the Old and the New Testaments, Christianity diverges considerably from Hebrew ideas about the nature of sin and the mode of salvation therefrom. Hebrew literature deals primarily with the sins of rebellion, violence and aggression towards the father, as well as aberrant or perverse sexual behavior, the punishments for which are excommunication and death. It is made plain that man is endowed with two inclinations, "yezer ha-ra" *(Gen.,* 8. 21) the evil impulse, or tendency, incorrectly translated as imagination, and its counterpart, conformity to the laws of God. Conflict and temptation are recognized as inherent to man from early childhood; yielding to his "yezer" is a matter of personal will. The evil impulse in man converts the invitation to sin (from within or without) into a temptation. It is not in itself sinful, only in that it leads to sin. The concept of "yezer" is related to the idea of intrapsychic conflict, bears no resemblance to Hellenistic dualism, nor to the carnal evils expatiated upon later by Paul. Man's salvation according to Judaism lies in the recognition of his responsibility for transgression, repentance, and

V. Fromberg and S. Rosenbaum

forgiveness by God. "Man is ready for union with God by virtue of his human essence, and needs no renewal in order to participate in eternal life" (Guttman, 1964). However, the Hebrew religion never thoroughly resolved the problem of guilt and salvation, but rather pondered and questioned the ways of the Lord, particularly in the books of *Job* and *Ecclesiastes*.

The elaboration of sin in the Christian religion embraces many of the iniquities and transgressions of the Old Testament with the additional emphasis on fornication, and the sinfulness of sexual pleasure. However, the profound points of departure lie in the concept of original sin and the separation from God. In Christianity the nature of man is depraved by original sin, and must be changed by the Grace of God to be united with Him. Redemption is granted by repeated identification with the person of Jesus who deliberately chose the cross. It is the goal of man to be wholly transformed in God, and divine perfection is achieved through this mystical reunion. The consequence of sin (separation from God) is abandonment; separation anxiety, the earlier prototype of castration anxiety, is all-pervasive.

As has been stated, in reference to Cain's crime, the word *avon*, "iniquity," willful disobedience, bears the connotation of guilt as well. The effect of sin upon man is to make him afraid. Thus both in the Garden of Eden, and in the making of the Golden Calf, when Moses came down from the mountain, the people were afraid *(Gen.,* 3. 8; *Exod.,* 34). Implicit in this is the fear of retaliation, and while the Bible speaks of guilt, it refers to the awareness of having transgressed rather than to the sense of guilt as understood psychoanalytically.

Nevertheless, in *Leviticus* the concept of morality in terms of identification is clearly expressed in the lines, "Also thou shalt not oppress a stranger for Ye know the heart of a stranger, seeing Ye were strangers in the land of Egypt" (*Exod.,* 23.9), and in many passages in *Deuteronomy* (15, 9. 10 ff.) Beres (1965) in referring to the continued influence of Hebraic ethics in the Western world, asks in his paper on the History of Morality: "Was there in fact among the Hebrews a greater degree of internalization?" (p. 19). We are of the opinion that the inner awareness of guilt as opposed to the talion and fear of punishment is expressed mainly in texts dating from later periods of Israel's religious development, much as the sense of guilt, as an internalized experience, is a later product of the child's superego development. Thus in the *Prophets* and *Psalms* the weightiness of guilt becomes more than a man can bear. The need is expressed for confession as a relief from the inner tension. "When I declared not my sin my body wasted away through my groaning all day long. . . . For day and night my strength was dried up as by the heat of summer" *(Ps., 32. 3, 5)*. The effects of guilt are a drain upon psychic energy, ensuing conflict and depression. The resultant experience of sinfulness is no longer simply fear, or shame, but rather depression. This conclusion would accord with Beres' (1966) concepts of depression. One can think of no more eloquent a description of depression than Isaiah's, "We grope for the wall like the blind, and we grope as if we had no eyes; we stumble at noon day as in the night; we are in desolate places as dead men. We roar all like bears, and mourn sore like doves: we look for judgment but there is none; for salvation, but it is far from us. For our transgressions are multiplied before Thee, and our sins testify against us; for our transgressions are with us; and as for our iniquities, we know them" *(Isa., 59. 8, 12)*. In *Deuteronomy*, parts of which very much resemble the style of *Jeremiah* (Kaufmann, 1960), Moses expounds upon the depressive effects of wrongdoing. "The Lord will give you an unquiet mind, dim eyes, and failing appetite. Your life will hang continually in suspense, fear will beset you night and day, and you will find no security all your life long" *(Deut., 29. 66)*.

In *Moses and Monotheism* Freud (1939) speaks of the sense of guilt almost as though it were a mechanism of defense serving to ward off anxiety of losing the loving, omnipotent father. In reference to the Hebrews, according to Freud, when misfortune befell them time and again, "they did not allow themselves to be shaken in their convictions; they increased their own sense of guilt in order to stifle their doubts of God." *In Civilization and its Discontents,* Freud (1930) wrote, "When the great father caused misfortune after misfortune to rain down upon this people of his, they were never shaken in their belief in his relationship to them, or questioned his power of righteousness. Instead they produced the prophets who held up their sinfulness before them; and out of this sense of guilt they created the overstrict commandments of their priestly religion" (p. 127).

Freud's statements are not entirely historically valid, and in the light of current psychoanalytic formulations of superego development (Beres, 1966, Hartmann and Loewenstein, 1962, Lampl-de Groot, 1962) they seem somewhat oversimplified. First, it is to be noted that throughout post-Mosaic biblical literature the righteousness and omnipotence of God are questioned, although there is no satisfactory solution. The Jews were haunted by their doubts, and alleviated them through the prophetic promises of forgiveness and the salvation of a remnant of the people (*Isa.*, 38.32), exculpation through repentance, and the later doctrines of resurrection. It is perhaps in contrast to this failure to provide an adequate solution that Christianity, with its explanation of the origin of sin and promise of salvation, was so appealing. The accusations of the prophets can be more easily understood as projections of man's own aggression onto the father. The prophets arose in a time of political unrest, fear of war, and desire for vengeance, a time when fear, confusions, and aggression permeated the Jewish people. Thus the Hebrews in their disappointment and rage against God for having abandoned them, endowed God with these passions. The exhortations of the prophets against man's sinfulness reflect the child's fantasies and fears and the ways in which he is dealing with his own aggression. The prophets attempted to resolve their anxiety through identification and internalization. It is during this period that we also see evidence of higher forms of identification with God and the formation of internalized superego regulations as expressed in their exhortations. Rituals and the outer manifestations of righteousness, sacrifice, etc., were held in contempt, in contrast to inner remorse and an inner sense of justice. Thus Jeremiah composed the New Covenant suggestive of internalization, as opposed to the regressive resolution through introjection and incorporation, techniques which are more characteristic of early Christianity.

According to Jeremiah's prophecy: "After those days saith the

Sojourners Mag

1029   Vermont
         Ave, NW.

    Wash, DC
         20005

    $12/yr

Lord, I will put my law in their inward parts, and write it in their hearts; and will be their God. No longer need they teach one another to know the Lord; all of them, high and low alike, shall know me," etc. *(Jer.,* 31. 32, 33, 34).

The above would conform to Lampl-de Groot's (1962) fourth phase of the development of the ego-ideal, i.e., "Formation of ethics and ideals as attainable goals after disillusionment by the idealized parents," and to a transitional stage between stages three and four in the development of the restricting superego. Stage three is described as "Internalization of single demands through identification with some parental demands during the preoedipal phase," and stage four: "Inner conscience and internal acceptance of restrictions and punishments imposed by the parents and the wider environment in order to guarantee a social relationship within a certain class or group or milieu" (pp. 99–100).

We may look upon the religious development of the Hebrews not only in terms of man's oedipal strivings, but in the light of his infantile bisexuality as well. The Yahweh of the Hebrews was clearly a masculine God, father and king. Most often the relationship is that of a father to his children, sometimes that of a lover. We have described one more way in which the Jews dealt with their aggression, i.e., by projection of their own fantasies, and to this we might add the concept of identification with the aggressor (Freud, A., 1946), as well as Freud's formulation of turning the aggression onto one's self. Another mechanism of defense which frequently appears is that of displacement onto the siblings. Thus fratricide is a major preoccupation in the Old Testament, beginning with Cain and Abel, Isaac and Ishmael, then Esau and Jacob, etc. The Hebrews killed thousands of their brethren, presumably in the service of their wrathful God, as for example after the incident of the Golden Calf. We view this both as an identification with the vengeful father and as a displacement of the children's aggression against the father onto their brothers.

But after all the Jews loved their father as much as they feared him. And while they attempted to resolve their oedipal conflict through identification with the omnipotent father, they also offered themselves to him as passive homosexual love objects. This

• 447

represented not only a denial of aggression, but an identification with the beloved mother. They yearned to be loved, and precisely at the time when they were faced with external danger and loss of love, we see many references to the femaleness of the children of Israel. Hosea compared the breach of the covenant to adultery *(Hosea,* 2. 2, 5 and 9. 1). Throughout the *Prophets* the disloyal Jews are referred to as harlots *(Jer.,* 3. 1), and Jeremiah lyrically describes Israel's youthful relationship with God as that of a bride and her loved one *(Jer.,* 2. 2 and 3. 32).

It is our contention that at the time of the exile the communal religious fantasies of the Jewish people as expressed in prophetic literature represented a progression in superego development. Following the fall of Jerusalem (568) the spirit of prophesy waned. With the further undermining of their relationship to God, (i.e., abandonment by the love object), an attempt at restitution was made through the regressive revival of priestly laws and rituals, as well as the building of the Second Temple and the crystallization of the Torah books (Kaufmann, 1960, p. 448).

In the postexile period, we see evidence of superego regression, beginning with the Pharisees and culminating in Pauline Christianity. To understand this regression, or at least speculate as to its origins, we must briefly review the historical background of the Jews at the time of the birth of Christianity.

After the Fall of the First Temple, and the expulsion from Jerusalem by the Babylonians in the Sixth Century B.C., not all of the Jews "wept by the rivers of Babylon." Most of them acclimated themselves and prospered in the Babylonian culture. Alexander the Great defeated the Persians in the Fourth Century, at which time the Jews came under Grecian rule and Hellenic influence; it was in the next century that the Bible was translated into Greek. The Jews, having absorbed Greek culture and philosophy, also made important spiritual contributions. They rose to high places in the government and the intellectual world, assumed Greek names and wore Greek garments. Tradesmen began to socialize after working hours; Jewish youths frequented Greek cabarets and gymnasiums, and would strip naked for Greek athletic games. As Jewish youth succumbed to Greek pleasures, Jewish intellectuals feared the spell of Greek philosophies. To the Stoics pity and compassion was weakness; they advocated indifference to suffering, a philosophy which was repugnant to the prophets. The Epicureans maintained that it was man's duty to free himself from the superstitions of punishment and reward. Consequently the principles of morality yielded to the pursuit of pleasure and the philosophy of Epicurus was distorted into licentiousness and immorality. The name "Apikoros" or "Epicurean" was affixed to those free-thinking Jewish youths and has remained a cursed appellation to this day.

The Hellenism that reached Palestine "was not the Hellenism of classical Greece that flourished in the genius of Pythagoras, Socrates, Aristotle, Plato. It was a debased kind of Hellenism, decadent, wily, voluptuous" (Epstein, 1959, p. 90). The nadir of corruption, brutality and rapacity was reached in the First Century B.C. For the Jews those last centuries were fraught with internal and external harassment. From within, the danger was deneutralization or reinstinctualization of aggressive and sexual drives; from without there was the real threat of annihilation by their enemies. We will direct our attention primarily to the internal dissent.

With the temptations and threat of Hellenization, a strong party of anti-Hellenists arose among the Jews, known as the Hasideans. Their members were almost totally demolished when Antiochus marched into Jerusalem and slaughtered 10,000 inhabitants. By outlawing the Sabbath and forbidding circumcision, he recruited for the Hasideans many Jews who were formerly pro-Hellenization. The consequence of this was the great Maccabean victory and the establishment of the Kingdom of Judeah in 143 B.C. The Hasideans, torn with internal conflict and external oppression, split into three separate parties, the Sadduceans, the Pharisees, and the Essenes. The last two, with the help of the Apocalyptics, gave rise to Christianity.

Judea had been fairly secure and largely prosperous under the rule of Simon who expelled the Syrian overlords. However, his son, Hyrcanus, in the last part of the Second Century B.C., adopted an increasingly aggressive attitude towards the countries around him. Hyrcanus forced circumcision upon the vanquished pagans, converting them to Judaism by the sword. It was to the Galileans, who were to become his first converts, that Jesus Christ initially preached his doctrines. The militant nationalistic ambitions of Hyrcanus, and the Sadducees to which he belonged, approached megalomania, much to the antipathy of the Pharisees who comprised the other principal party of the time. The Sadducees were primarily of the aristocratic and priestly class. They believed in a nationalistic God, the Temple, the Priests, and Sacrifice—in short, in prepprophetic Judaism. The Pharisees, on the other hand, believed in a universal God, the Synagogues, the Rabbis, personal repentance and prayer.

The Pharisees continued their religious brotherhood, divorcing themselves from politics, but not from the workaday world. While first and foremost they advocated a ritualistic doctrine, it was never to the exclusion of worldly possessions and social reward. Intensely concerned with ritual, they segregated themselves further from the ritually impure. As is the case with obsessional neurosis according to Hartmann and Loewenstein (1962), their "superego regression was prompted by the regression of their instinctual drives" under the pressure of violence and sexual stimulation to which they were exposed.

The pursuit of purity, and the retreat from worldly temptation, went even further with Essenism which probably began as a radical Pharisaic sect: where the mechanism of defense characteristic of obsessive compulsive neuroses (i.e., isolation, reaction formation and undoing) failed, the instinctual drives, as well as superego functions regressed further, finding expression in the asceticism of the splinter group, the Essenes. The strict and monklike Essenes go back to the Second Century B.C. "Secular enjoyment was objectionable, and all study except law and scriptural cosmology was considered Pagan and therefore dangerous. . . . They shunned trade and rejected possessions. They considered rage and all passions as demoniacally instilled traits. Theirs was a pacifistic ethic like early Christianity" (Weber, 1952). Whereas at no time before in the history of Judaism was coitus within marriage restricted (with the exception of the menstrual taboo)—rather, celibacy was frowned upon—among the Essenes copulation was disdained. Intercourse was at first restricted to once a week, on Wednesdays, and celibacy was extolled. For the sake of self-perpetuation, however, like Paul they allowed, "that it is better to marry than to burn." Evaluating the withdrawal and asceticism of the Essene Jews, Epstein (1959) says:

> The Essenes were intrigued with mysteries, foretelling of the future, casting out demons, and resorting to supernatural invocations for curative purposes. They also held to a rigid predetermination which denied man all freedom of action and effort. The Essenes, in departing from the Pharisaic teaching, lost that sense of harmony between life and religion, with the result that they withdrew from the world, and sought to make up by the strictness of their asceticism for the failure to take a share in facing the temptations and sufferings of life [pp. 102–103].

In psychoanalytic terms, according to Hartmann and Loewenstein (1962) "as a result of superego regression" or regression to a more archaic superego as evidenced in the harsh punitive superego of the Essenes, "we see early identifications, and early object relationships taking the place of the contents and functions of the superego."

From the evidence in the Dead Sea Scrolls, and the Copper Scrolls discovered five years later, it may now be questioned whether the Essenes were indeed the "missing link" between Judaism and Christianity, and whether Jesus spent some period of his youth in the Essene monastery discovered in the neighborhood, in which, according to the New Testament, he spent his youth. The Essenes carried the words of the prophets to extreme, believing that "perfection of way" was the remedy against the disease of sin and "guilt," and that mortification of the flesh was the vehicle of healing and life in anticipation of the Messiah. The Dead Sea Scrolls refer to the historical period beginning with the accession of Antiochus in 175 B.C., and ending with the fall of Hercanus II in 40 B.C. The period in which they lived is referred to by the Essenes as the "age of wrath" in the Damascus rule (Vermez, 1962). In the First Century B.C. the Jewish philosopher Philo of Alexandria, the historian Flavius Josephus, and the geographer and naturalist Pliny the Elder referred to this sect of ascetics whose common life and severe discipline they seem to have admired. The resemblance to the Christian doctrine which followed is evident from the Community Rule, so similar to Christian Church Orders, ritual baptism, the sacred meal, etc. The extension of physical suffering and mortification of the flesh is seen in Paul's appeal to the Roman Christians to present their bodies "as living sacrifice holy and acceptable to God" (*Rom.*, 12).

After his visit to Jerusalem at the age of 12, Jesus disappears from the pages of the Gospels until somewhere between 28 and 30 A.D. At the age of 30 he is baptized by John the Baptist, who in accordance with the Essene creed believed that men should cleanse their souls symbolically through immersion in water. The purification ritual had its precursors in Jewish practice, and John, who proclaimed that his passion was to usher in the Kingdom of God, was not blasphemous. However, since sexual abstinence and asceticism were so antithetic to the nature of Judaism, the Essene cult in its brittle structure and its exclusive pursuit of "perfect holiness" had neither the pliancy to survive within the Jewish culture, nor the strength to exist apart from it.

Jesus spoke and acted like a Jewish prophet, never deviating from Jewish practices. While he announced the speedy advent of the Kingdom of God, he never applied the term "Messiah" to himself, nor did he refer to himself as the "Son of God." These appellations belong rather to the language of Hellenized Christians such as Saint Paul, author of the fourth Gospel. Jesus was a Galilean who won over relatively few Jews outside of several hundred Galileans, many of whom were pagans who had been forcibly converted at an earlier time.

The reasons for Jesus' failure are apparent, both in terms of the Jewish political and intellectual climate at the time, as well as the limitations of the rewards he offered. He preached self-examination, love of neighbor, humbleness of heart, and a son's faith in his Father "to a people who were expecting an appeal to arms and announcement of the final struggle, preceding everlasting triumph. He did not say, 'Arise, the Messiah of Yahweh is in your midst' but 'Prepare yourselves by repentance to make a good showing in the Judgment which is at hand' " (Guignebert, 1927).

According to many Christian scholars, were it not for the trusting faith of the Apostles in their master's restoration to life, and the publication abroad, there would have been no Christianity. This may be disputed but certainly Paul's faith in Jesus' resurrection is of first importance, both in the establishment of Christianity, in the offer of a divine way of salvation, and in the separation of Christianity from Judaism.

While resurrection had some role in the Jewish eschatology, the resurrection of Jesus according to Saint Paul holds more in common with those oriental cults in which the initiate in dying and being reborn partakes of the divine nature of the god and thus becomes immortal. In performing these rites the initiate was mystically cleansed of sin either by bathing in sacred water, or as in the religions of the Great Mother, Cybele, by the blood of a bull, the taurobolium through which the initiate was "reborn forever" (see Walker, 1959, p. 10). According to Walker, the religions of the Great Mother which originated in Asia Minor reached Rome in 204 B.C., and that of Isis and Serapis with its emphasis on regeneration and immortality was established by 80 B.C.

The fundamental rites and essential ideas of Eastern mythology typically involve the death of the hero at a certain period of the year, and his restoration to life shortly thereafter, consequently inundating his adherents with grief followed by ecstatic joy. In his restoration to life the initiate has absorbed the very essence of God. This union is often obtained or at least renewed by a sacred repast at the tables of the Gods. In all of these myths the ultimate reward for mankind is the offer of hope in, and the means of securing a blissful immortality. Freud (1913) referred to the emergence of divine figures such as Attis, Odonis, and Dionysius as demonstrations of man's incestuous desires and defiance of the father. He states, "But the sense of guilt which was not allayed by these creations, found expression to those youthful favorites of the mother-goddess and decreed their punishment by emasculation or by wrath of the father in the form of an animal" (p. 152). Freud believed that the totem animal which was killed and eaten was indeed the father, and that the Christian Eucharist, i.e., the communion in which the flesh and blood of the son are consumed, is essentially "a fresh elimination of the father" (p. 155), as well as an identification with him. We suggest that a disheartened and frustrated segment of people, overwhelmed by instinctual drives and lacking the ego strength to harness them, yielded to the primitive panacea of oriental syncretism. In the light of later psychoanalytic formulations, the preoedipal nature of the sacred meal is more blatant than the incestuous components. Moreover, the promise of transformation or rebirth through the mystical union with the divinity, is the antidote to separation anxiety to which castration anxiety is the heir.

Let us reexamine the Phrygian cult of Cybele and Attis in which we find the unique ceremony called taurobolium which formed part of the mysterious initiation rites exclusively reserved for believers.

> A deep pit was sunk in the precincts of the temple, into which the initiated descended, and it was then covered over with a grating upon which a bull was solemnly sacrificed; its blood flowed like rain into the pit, and fell on the naked person of the novitiate. . . . After this baptism the animal's genital organs were deposited in a sacred vessel to be presented as an offering to the goddess, after which they were buried beneath a memorial altar [Guignebert, 1962, p. 71].

The aim of the rite was originally to obtain the cooperation of Cybele and Attis, who, it is believed, governed nature, just as the Dionysiac initiatory rites were intended to draw the bacchanals of both sexes into partnership with the fertilizing work of Dionysus. By the beginning of the Christian era, however, an "evolution took place which converted the taurobolium into an efficient means of achieving immortality." The regressive features of this achievement are self-evident in the following elaboration (Guignebert, 1962):

> The pit signifies the kingdom of the dead, and the mystic, in descending into it, is thought to die; the bull Attis, and the blood that is shed is the divine life-principle that issues from him; the initiate receives it and, as it were, absorbs it; when he leaves the pit he is said to be "born again," and milk, as in the case of a new-born infant, is given

him to drink. But he is not born the mere man again he was before; he has absorbed the very essence of the god and if we understand the mystery right, he has in his turn become an Attis and is saluted as one. Then, in order to follow in the footsteps of the sacred history the further stage which makes Attis the lover of Cybele, he must also effect a union with the goddess. The offering of the genitals of the bull of Attis of whom he is now a colleague symbolizes this union, which is carried out in mystic fashion in the nuptial chamber of the Great Mother. The mutilation of the bull also recalls the similar acts of Attis who, it is said, castrated himself under a pine tree and died as a result.

The initiate is assured, at any rate for a considerable period of time,* that his fate will be the same as that of Attis at his inevitable death and a happy resurrection and survival among the gods his portion. In many of the cults of these saviors and interceding gods, such as those of Cybele, Mithra, the Syrian Baals, and still others, the beneficial union obtained by means of initiation is renewed or at any rate revivified, by sacred repasts which the members, assembled at the table of the gods, ate [pp. 72–73].

In the Mysteries of Mithra there is a ceremony in which the initiate is presented with bread and a cup. In the Mysteries of Cybele and Attis "the initiate takes part in a mystic repast. Its conclusion enables him to say, 'I have eaten of that which the dulcimer contained, I have drunk of that which was in the cymbal; I have become a myste (initiate) of Attis.' The dulcimer was the attribute and instrument of Cybele, the cymbal that of Attis, and there is reason to believe that the sacred sustenance placed therein was probably bread or the flesh of sacred fish, and wine" (Guignebert, ibid., p. 73).

Since the name Attis presumably means "corn" or grain in general, Guignebert in 1910 concluded that "the act performed in this communion is the eating of the god himself and thus becoming fully impregnated with his immortalizing essence . . ." Both Guignebert (1927) and Walker (1959) believe that Christianity was influenced by these Oriental mystery religions. The former states, "From the First to the Fifth Centuries, from Saint Paul to Saint

* "It seems as if the taurobolium were repeated after a lapse of twenty years; at any rate, this was so toward the end of the Roman Empire."

V. Fromberg and S. Rosenbaum

Augustine, there is abundant testimony to prove that the fathers of
the Church were struck by them" (p. 73).

It is to be noted that there is a fundamental difference between
the Christian Eucharist and the biblical peace offering which has
been *erroneously* interpreted along pagan models. Kaufmann
(1960) demonstrates that the Hebrew peace offering was eaten
"before" or "in the presence of" (the Hebrew word *lifneh*), never
"with" YHWH. The bible makes no reference of communion, nor
to the notion that he who partakes of the flesh shares the deities'
divine rank, or partakes of the life of God. "Joy, not mystic union,
is the basic emotional content of the Israelite cult; this joy too is
"before," not "with" YHWH. *(Deut.,* 12. 12, 18).

The Pharisees' pursuit of purity through ritualistic adherence as
an undoing of their instinctual desires, has been alluded to above.
Freud (1939) states in *Moses and Monotheism,* "It appears as
though a growing sense of guilt has taken hold of the Jewish people, or perhaps the whole civilized world of the time, as a precursor to return of the repressed material" (p. 86). Although the anal-
ly regressive aspect of the scrupulous ritualism of the Pharisees
is evident, they were perhaps, through obsessive compulsive defense mechanisms, able to maintain a harmony between their instinctual drives and the real world around them. They did not
withdraw to ascetic self-denial, nor were they generally vulnerable
to the more profoundly regressive fantasies of the Pagan myths.

From the members of the relatively pacifistic Pharisees, Saul of
Tarsus was born, the son of a wealthy Jew from whom he inherited Roman citizenship. Tarsus was the seat of Stoic teaching, and
while Paul remained a devout observant Jew until his conversion,
it is unlikely that he was not opposed to Hellenic ideas and political atmosphere (Walker, 1960).

The following portrait is taken from Dimont's *Jews, God and
History* (1962):

Throughout his life, he (Paul) was overwhelmed with an all-pervasive
sense of guilt which pursued him with relentless fury. From early
paintings and from descriptions in New Testament accounts, both his
and others', we have a rather repellent physical portrait of him . . .

Paul was of slight stature, bowlegged, blind in one eye, and had some deformity of body. He was given to recurrent attacks of malaria, and repeated hallucinations, and some scholars believe he was subject to epileptic seizures [p. 141].

A celibate himself, he exhorted others to a life of renunciation and chastity. But as Freud (1930) stated, "Instinctual renunciation is not enough for the wish persists and cannot be concealed from the superego . . . This constitutes a great economic disadvantage in the erection of a superego, or as we have put it in the formation of conscience" (p. 127). Paul's aggressive impulses found expression in his violently anti-Christian zealousness. He had stoned Saint Stephen to death, and applied to the high priest for the arrest of all Jews who confessed to following Jesus. It was this mission which culminated in his hallucinatory encounter with Jesus (whom he had never seen in the flesh) as a result of which he was temporarily blinded, and was led helpless to Damascus. Here, Ananias, a Jew of the Christian sect, by laying his hands upon him, cured his blindness and converted him to Christianity. We will refrain from expatiating here on the hallucinatory experience and the resurrection, as phenomena relating to ego regression, and as attempts at reconstruction and restitution.

The Pauline Epistles are a striking conglomeration of thoughts and reactions, sometimes contradictory, emanating from the influence of Paul's personal history and the milieu in which he lived. These are, mainly, Jewish ideas, memories of Gospel ideas, Eastern myths, Hellenistic dualism, and Greek philosophy. Although he never studied at the University in Tarsus, he was undoubtedly influenced by the Stoicism in which it was engrossed. The professors at the University were primarily Stoics who believed in justice, prudence, courage and temperance. They regarded soul as a very refined form of matter that was literally transmitted in tainted form from generation to generation. Although a materialistic system, its highest principle was "spirit," a kind of "fiery vapour, inherent in all things." But this basic divine stuff was also called "Logos" or reason; it was thought of as an active imminent principle holding all things together and directing their development in a purposive harmony" (Wiles, 1966). Identification with Christ in his death and resurrection was accomplished, according to Paul, by faith. While the Stoic also emphasized the importance of faith, the profound mysticism whereby man is united to his God through faith, and his life divinely transformed, was absent before Paul's interpretation.

Paul discarded the Torah as legalistic and mechanical, substituting the Laws of the Spirit for the Laws of Moses. In this respect he spoke of "conscience" rather than law. To some extent this was a reiteration of the prophets beseeching an inner morality rather than ritualistic practices. However, Paul had other reasons as well, the most obvious being the encouragement of pagans to join the Christian movement. Thus he removed the hurdles of circumcision and *kashruth*. But he also recognized that the laws were stimulants to instinctual drives, that the prohibition invited the temptations against which he was constantly warring. "Therefore [he said] by the deed of the law there shall no flesh be justified in his sight: for by the law is the knowledge of sin" *(Rom.,* 3. 20).

The Jews believed that man's sinfulness is a natural consequence of his mortality, whereas the Christians believed that mortality is the consequence of his sin. In the Old Testament it is clear that Adam was mortal from the time of his creation. His disobedience led God to predict the further defiance of man, i.e., his eating from the tree of life, thus replacing the immortal father. The Christians interpreted the text to mean that man was once immortal in the Garden of Eden and that "Death entered the world of sin" *(Rom.,* 5. 112). It was necessary to believe in man's sin in order to believe in salvation through man's virtue. In Paul's words: "For as by one man's disobedience many were made sinners, so by the obedience of one shall many be made righteous" *(Rom.,* 5. 19), and "That as sin hath reigned into death, so might grace reign through righteousness unto eternal life by Jesus Christ our Lord" *(Rom.,* 5. 21).

Christ s perfection lies in his freedom from original sin, having been born exclusively of the uncontaminated mother. Through his death he assumed the carnal guilt of all humanity. By incorporating his body all those conceived in sin become the body of Christ

(I. *Cor.*, 12. 17), and are thus transformed, reborn in his perfection. This rebirth through death suggests the reunion with the unsullied mother-goddess (reminiscent of the Great Mother cults) as well as reconciliation with the father. While all religions may be regarded as elaborations upon earlier mythologies, the concept of apotheosis which is inherent to pagan mythology is clearly absent in the Judaic religion. Insofar, as it reappears in the Christian religion, it represents a return to collective fantasies of a more archaic nature.

Religion is thought of in the context of this paper, in the manner in which Arlow defines the myth, i.e., "a particular kind of communal experience," a "shared fantasy which serves to bring the individual into relationship with members of his cultural group" (Arlow, 1961). At various moments in history these fantasies undergo progressive or regressive elaborations as expressions of the neutralization of instinctual drives or the reactivation of repressed wishes.

The authors believe that the vicissitudes in the development of ancient Judaism and the rise of Christianity parallel the increase or decrease of ego autonomy, which in turn fluctuates with the relative internalization of aggression and consequent superego functions. In keeping with Hartmann, Kris and Loewenstein's (1969) formulations, we support their contention that "cultural conditions should be viewed also with the question in mind, which and what kind of opportunities for ego functions in a sphere free from conflict they invite or inhibit."

The effects of deneutralization of instinctual drives are evident in the regressive means by which the various religious sects resolved their conflicts. Saint Paul's struggle against his uncontained aggression reached its pinnacle when he was about to act out a fantasy of fratricide. This culminated in the restitutive hallucinatory experience.

The authors are aware of the pitfalls in drawing parallels between the religious development of a society and the development of the individual. Moreover there have been men throughout history whose individual development has transcended that of other members of their culture. We know too that in the last century and a half religious concepts have been modified and advanced,

V. Fromberg and S. Rosenbaum

and that insofar as modern biblical interpretations are directed towards further independence from instinctual drives, they are in greater harmony with the psychoanalytic concept of the sense of guilt.

BIBLIOGRAPHY

Arlow, J. A. (1951), The consecration of the prophet. *Psychoanal. Quart.,* 20:374–397.

——— (1961), Ego psychology and the study of mythology. *J. Amer. Psychoanal. Assn.,* 13:371–393.

——— and Brenner, C. (1964), *Psychoanalytic Concepts and the Structural Theory.* New York: International Universities Press.

Baily, D. S. (1959), *Sexual Relations in Christian Thought.* New York: Harper and Brothers.

Bates, E. S., ed. (1936), *The Bible.* New York: Simon & Schuster.

Beres, D. (1965), Psychoanalytic notes on the history of morality. *J. Amer. Psychoanal. Assn.,* 13:3–37.

——— (1966), Superego and depression. In: *Psychoanalysis—A General Psychology,* ed. Loewenstein, R. M., Newman, L. M., Schur, M. and Solnit, A. J. New York: International Universities Press.

Bouquet, A. C. (1962), *Comparative Religion.* Baltimore: Penguin.

Bridger, D. and Wolk, S. J. (1962), *The New Jewish Encyclopedia.* New York: Behrman House Publishers.

Buttrick, G. A., ed. (1962), *The Interpreter's Dictionary of the Bible.* New York: Abingdon Press.

Cole, W. G. (1955), *Sex in Christianity and Psychoanalysis.* New York: Oxford University Press.

Dillenberger, J. and Welch, C. (1954), *Protestant Christianity Interpreted through Its Development.* New York: Charles Scribner's Sons.

Dimont, M. I. (1962), *Jews, God and History.* New York: Simon & Schuster.

Epstein, I. (1959), *Judaism.* Baltimore: Penguin.

Feldman, D. M. (1968), *Birth Control in Jewish Law.* New York: New York University Press.

Freud, A. (1946), *The Ego and the Mechanisms of Defense.* New York: International Universities Press.

Freud, S. (1913), Totem and taboo. *Standard Edition,* 13:1–161. London: Hogarth Press, 1955.

——— (1927), The future of an illusion. *Standard Edition,* 21:5–56. London: Hogarth Press, 1955.

——— (1930), Civilization and its discontents. *Standard Edition,* 21:64–105. London: Hogarth Press, 1955.

——— (1939), Moses and monotheism. *Standard Edition,* 23:3–140. London: Hogarth Press, 1955.

Guignebert, C. (1962), *The Early History of Christianity*. New York: Twayne Publishers.

Guttman, J. (1964), *Philosophies of Judaism*. New York: Holt, Rinehart & Winston.

Hartmann, H., Kris, E. and Loewenstein, R. M., (1962), Notes on the superego. *The Psychoanalytic Study of the Child*, 17:42–81. New York: International Universities Press.

——, —— and —— (1969), Some psychoanalytic comments on culture and personality. In: *Man and his Culture: Psychoanalytic Anthropology after "Totem and Taboo,"* ed. W. Muensterberger. London: Rapp and Whiting, pp. 230–270.

Holy Bible. King James Version (c. 1600), Philadelphia: A. J. Holman Co., 1970.

Jewish Encyclopedia (1901–1905), Vol. 9. New York: Ktav Publishing House.

Kraeling, C. H. (1956), *The Excavation of Dura Europos* (Final Report VIII, Part 1. The Synagogue). New Haven: Yale University Press.

Kaufmann, Y. (1960), *The Religion of Israel*. Chicago: The University of Chicago Press.

Lampl-de Groot, J. (1962), Ego ideal and superego. *The Psychoanalytic Study of the Child*, 17:94–106. New York: International Universities Press.

Landman, I., ed. (1948), *The Universal Jewish Encyclopedia*, Vol. 9. New York: Charles Scribner's Sons.

Lewis, C. S. (1960), *Studies in Words*. London: Cambridge University Press.

McGiggert, A. C. (1953), *A History of Christian Thought*, Vol. 1. New York: Charles Scribner's Sons.

Moore, C. F. (1966a), *Judaism*, Vol. 1. Cambridge: Harvard University Press.

—— (1966b), *Judaism*, Vol. 2. Cambridge: Harvard University Press.

New Catholic Encyclopedia (1967), Vol. 8. New York: McGraw-Hill Book Co.

Noonan, J. T. Jr. (1965), *Contraception: A History of Its Treatment by the Catholic Theologians and Canonists*. Cambridge: Harvard University Press.

Sholem, G. (1941), *Major Trends in Jewish Mysticism*. New York: Schocken Books.

Spencer, S. (1963), *Mysticism in World Religion*. Baltimore: Penguin.

The New English Bible. Old Testament (1970). New York: Oxford University Press.

The Torah. A New Translation of the Holy Scriptures according to the Traditional Hebrew Text (1962). Philadelphia: The Jewish Publication Society of America.

Vermes, G. (1962), *The Dead Sea Scrolls*. New York: Heritage Press.

Walker, W. (1918), *A History of the Christian Church*. New York: Charles Scribner's Sons.

Weber, Max (1952), *Ancient Judaism*. Glencoe: The Free Press.

Wiles, M. (1966), *The Christian Fathers*. New York: J. P. Lippincott.

22. Psychoanalysis and Faith:

The Thirty-Year Debate between Sigmund Freud and Oskar Pfister

MARTIN GROTJAHN, M.D.

THE STORY of the correspondence and of the friendship between Sigmund Freud, the professor in Vienna, and Oskar Pfister, the parson in Switzerland, reflects accurately Sigmund Freud's attitudes towards religion, and moral values in psychoanalysis. Freud's development and final position is well documented in this 30-year correspondence.

Oskar Pfister was born in February 1873 and died in 1956. In the early days of psychoanalysis he became interested in the work of Sigmund Freud and, as was customary in those years, following the establishment of a personal friendship, a regular correspondence developed between the two men. The parson from Switzerland became a respected friend of Freud and beloved by the entire family.

Anna Freud described the parson as a strange figure in Freud's home which was so turned away from all religious and church beliefs. Pfister differed from other visiting analysts by virtue of his

---

This essay was written after the correspondence between Sigmund Freud and Oskar Pfister had been published in the original German text by S. Fischer Verlag, Frankfurt, Germany, 1968, but before the publication of its English translation (1970). No direct quotation from this translation has been used here.

warmth, his enthusiasm and his ability to be interested in the most minute details of any member of the Freud family. In the eyes of the Freud children he was not a holy man but more like the Pied Piper of Hamelin. The children were always enthusiastic about the clergyman, and always eager to visit and go mountain climbing with him.

THE 30-YEAR DEBATE

The correspondence between Sigmund Freud and Oskar Pfister spans a period of 30 years. From the 135 Freud letters, only 100 were published; the majority of Pfister's letters were written after 1927 when Freud, at Pfister's request, destroyed most of the clergyman's previous letters. More than half of these published have been shortened.

It is a special delight to have both sides of this correspondence available for study. Even when the difference in the stature, style and depth of the two letter writers becomes obvious, it still remains true that both men stand their ground well. Their affection for each other remains unchanged through these years.

Freud's first letter, dated 1909, indicates his delight in having interested a minister in psychoanalysis. He considers the parson's therapeutic position as fortunate, since he may guide his patient's transference from the therapist toward God. Freud is surprised that he had not realized before how well psychoanalysis could be handled by an understanding clergyman. From the beginning Freud admonishes Pfister not to shy away from sexuality, since all censorship is bad and cuts deeply into the body of psychoanalysis. Freud had reason to be watchful in this respect after his bad experience with the inhibited and puritan analysts from Switzerland, even when they were not ordained ministers.

Some of the early letters are written with great patience and in considerable detail, as though Freud were giving a seminar in writing. For instance, he protests against Pfister's use of tests: every word spoken to the patient interferes with his free associations. Freud never disguises his impatience or disagreement. He warns against philosophy and religion: all fundamentals should be left in that semidarkness where they look so well in our present state of knowledge.

In 1911 Freud warned against Adler's theories and tried to clarify matters in the language of the parson by claiming that Adler forgot the words of the Apostle Paul when he pleaded for love. According to Freud, Alfred Adler had created a system without love and Freud planned to unleash upon him the vengeance of the insulted goddess of libido.

Several years later, in 1927, Freud debated a technical controversy: according to his opinion, people are inclined to take the rules of psychoanalysis too literally and then by overdoing them follow them ad absurdum. One of the rules which is often overdone refers to the analyst's passivity. There are analysts who spoil the efficiency of analysis through a certain moody indifference. In this way they lose their opportunity to uncover resistance which they cause by their own behavior. Sometimes when a transference neurosis cannot be completely dissolved it leads to a genuine interpersonal relationship.

On May 10, 1909, Freud confesses to Pfister that he has analyzed his "father complex" (a term which he credits to Jung) and has decided to correct his compulsion to be more financially successful than his father. His freedom from this compulsion he attributes to his relationship with Oskar Pfister.

There are no letters between March 1913 and October 1918, but then the correspondence resumes with a deepened warmth and recognition of Pfister's loyalty, his love for truth and humanity, his courage, devotion, understanding, and optimism. As could be expected, Freud's tragic sense of reality remained unchanged. Although he no longer tortured himself about good and evil, he found little good in people.

Only once in these one hundred letters did Freud vary the customary salutation of "Dear Doctor" to "My dear Man of God" (October 4, 1909)—a salutation he never repeated. The deepest expression of mutual understanding and respect is reached in the famous letters of October 1918, already quoted by Ernest Jones (1955, Vol. II) in his biography of Freud:

In the first place you are not a Jew, which my endless admiration for Amos, Isaiah, Jeremiah, with the men who composed Job and the Prophets makes me greatly regret; and in the second place you are not so godless, since whoever lives for the truth lives in God and whoever strives for the freeing of love "dwelleth in God." If you would fuse your own contribution with the great world harmony, like the synthesis of notes in a Beethoven symphony into a musical whole, I could say of you, "There never was a better Christian" [p. 199].

Freud admires the mild and tolerant tones of Pfister's writings which are so little directed against the enemy. He confesses that he himself could not write that way but rather must write to free his soul and to express his emotions. Since his enemies would be pleased to see him angry, he prefers not to answer them at all. Compared with the parson: "a good, loving man, incapable of injustice," Freud calls himself terribly intolerant toward fools.

Pfister considered a world without religion, without art, without poetry, as a Devil's Island fit only for Satan. If psychoanalysis offers such a gruesome, icy climate, he cannot blame people for preferring sickness. Both men discuss matters of religion with ease because, as Pfister explains with Swiss directness: the danger is not great that you will apply for baptism or that I will come hopping down from my pulpit.

After the publication of *The Future of an Illusion*, Freud (1927) tells Pfister that it is not his intention to become a successor to Jesus Christ even if he must admit that he would love to be able to say believingly: "Your sins are forgiven you. Arise and walk." Freud wonders what would happen if the patient were to ask: "How do you know that my sins are forgiven?" Freud could not simply answer: "I am the Son of God." He could not invite such unlimited confidence, he would have to say: "I, Professor Sigmund Freud, forgive you your sins." This, Freud admits, would not work well.

This letter (November 25, 1928) culminates in a remarkable confession. Freud did not know whether or not Pfister had guessed the secret bond between the two books by Freud on *Lay Analysis* and *Illusion.* In the first one Freud sought to protect analysis against physicians; in the latter, against priests. Freud wanted to place psychoanalysis into the hands of professionals who do not yet exist, i.e., a group of physicians of the soul, who do not need to be physicians and should not be allowed to be priests.

On February 4, 1921 Freud mailed an angry post card: there had been some trouble between Pfister and Otto Rank, as there had been between Pfister and Hans Sachs previously. The trouble was about the publication of Georg Groddeck's novel *Der Seelensucher,* by the Viennese psychoanalytic publishing house. Freud declared that he was going to defend Groddeck with all his energy against Pfister's respectability.

Oskar Pfister, who was reprimanded occasionally in strong terms by Freud, took the reproof well, answered undisturbed, as a man from Switzerland might be expected to do (March 14, 1921). He did not expect Freud to react differently than he did. The spirit which prompted Freud to advocate Groddeck must have been the same spirit in which Freud accomplished his great discovery and became a pioneer of psychoanalysis. Still Pfister could not take Freud's judgment as his own and continued his opposition against publishing this kind of book. Pfister also pointed out that there is a big difference between Rabelais and Groddeck: The former remains in the role of the satirist and avoids the mistake of being taken as a scientist. Groddeck, however, vacillated between science and literature. Moreover, Pfister was very disapproving of the excessive punning in which Groddeck indulged. Finally, in the spirit of the argument, Pfister made his position quite clear: he liked clean writing paper and he also liked rich butter—but butter spots on a clean sheet of paper neither pleased his eyes nor satisfied his stomach.

Freud answered almost immediately (March 20, 1921) and was greatly pleased about Pfister's honesty and steadfast position. It was a sign of their friendship that these two men were capable of telling each other the truth as they saw it, "rudely," while still remaining on good terms.

In later years Freud allowed a certain melancholic mood to break through (May 26, 1926). He no longer thought that life was easy, nor was he certain as to its meaning. He could not see why anyone should be grateful for having reached 73 years of age and mused that perhaps sometime the parson would explain to him why one should be grateful for a long life.

A few years later Freud discussed the death instinct with Pfister. He realized that the dissimilarities in their respective philosophies remained unchanged over the 30-years of their correspondence. Freud did not have an emotional need to postulate the death instinct, but he did want to explain that puzzling reality which is beyond ourselves. Comparing Pfister's optimism with a marriage based on good, rational reasons, he hoped that Pfister's "marriage" was happier than his own.

Finally come letters from the last, bitter years in Vienna, when Freud began to worry about his family and wrote with tired resignation (May 28, 1933). Freud realized that Switzerland did not belong to the hospitable countries. His judgment about the nature of man, especially about the Christian-Aryan man, had little reason to be changed.

A deeply moving letter from Pfister to Mrs. Freud after her husband's death concludes this remarkable documentation of a lifelong friendship.

The Development of Protestant Ethics from Martin Luther to Sigmund Freud

Once, rather early in the correspondence, Oskar Pfister remarked that the Protestant Reformation was nothing but psychoanalysis of Catholic sexual repression. Freud accepted the remark and called himself and his friend "sexual Protestants."

The development of religion leads from the visible God of early times to the invisible God of Jewish-Christian religion. The Jewish God was a portable God who could be packaged and introjected into the soul of the Eternally Wandering Jew. Out of it grew the image of Jesus Christ, the symbol of the son who wanted to live in peace with fathers and brothers. A new turn of ideology was reached when Martin Luther found the words of prayer to a God who "lived in us." It was a prayer in which Luther tried to express what he really meant—a prayer directed at the God within us. This is where Martin Luther left off and Sigmund Freud continued.

Where Martin Luther made man responsible for what he really meant in a prayer, Sigmund Freud wanted to make man responsible for an honesty which included a new dimension: namely, the dimension of the unconscious. Where Luther talked about faith, Sigmund Freud championed the new religion of reason.

Luther postulated the ethics of honesty, and Freud included the unconscious in this honesty and made man truly responsible for his destiny. Freud postulated the existential man. The moral man of Martin Luther was joined by the psychological man of Sigmund Freud. The integration of both will lead to the free man of the future. According to Luther, to be free meant to be free from dogma; according to Freud, man must be free from all self-deceit —including unconscious, or defensive deceit. Sigmund Freud would not have been possible without the freedom postulated by Martin Luther 400 years earlier.

Freedom from dogma and self-deceit is a prerequisite for the freedom to be one's self. This is the heavy burden man of today has assumed. Having almost destroyed Martin Luther, this burden led Sigmund Freud to his despairing, tragic outlook on life. Man's ethical behavior is now guided by "the reverence for life." The new free man needs courage to be himself in the sense of Martin Luther and in the sense of Sigmund Freud, both of whose systems have many parallels.

Luther's fight for his soul was symbolized in his experience in the Tower of the Wartburg when he encountered the devil. Freud had a similar experience albeit less dramatic and less symbolized —i.e., his struggle through self-analysis for the conscious control of his unconscious. Both helped man to find, to confirm, and to develop his ego-identity. Luther wanted to speak to his God directly, without an intermediary and by himself, "without shame and embarrassment" (as Nietzsche once said). He wanted an intimate, personal relationship to his God. He wanted to feel as if God were a part of man's soul. In this way man progressed from a state of being dominated by dogma to an acceptance of his individual responsibility.

Psychoanalysis is an appeal to honesty at the level of the unconscious; it is an appeal to live without illusion but not without faith and virtue which is what makes a man to be a man. Psychoanalysis offers a method of studying the human propensity for self-deception. It aims at an acceptance of man as he is, which includes his striving to grow and mature.

God did not die—the devil did. Satan, who was so well known to Martin Luther, did not exist for Sigmund Freud, who placed psychoanalysis beyond good and evil and therefore made possible, genuine human understanding.

As Erikson (1958) points out, Luther protested against the age of absolute dogma while Freud protested against the age of absolute reason. Luther proclaimed a meaningful, personal faith and Freud proclaimed an individual, unconscious basic trust. His faith was in science. Luther introduced a new spirit into prayer whereas Freud introduced a new technique and a new method in the service of contemplation, introspection and insight. Psychoanalysis discovered in the unconscious a new dimension of integrity. Where Martin Luther aimed at ethics of honesty, Freud continued with psychological investigation. Both men were bound to their times (which Jesus Christ was not).

Luther took a fresh look at himself and the experience proved almost fatal, practically destroying his faith and belief in God and the church.

Freud's reappraisal of the unconscious meaning of honesty gave us insight into the ethics and dynamics of protest, making a person responsible for his unconscious. The next generation, slated to experience the coming age of mastery, will hopefully accept this new responsibility and develop a new maturity.

CONCLUSION

It would be as misguided to conclude that Sigmund Freud was a Lutheran as it would be to assume that Martin Luther was an early Freudian. It would be equally inappropriate to conclude that although Freud was not a God-fearing Christian he meant well and therefore can be excused. He was nothing of the sort; rather he was a reluctant Jew who considered himself Godless and declared religion an illusion.

Luther, 450 years ago, and Freud 50 years ago, worked in the same direction, helping to clarify the future, and offering clues to what has become the current assignment. Both men increased the margin of man's inner honesty and freedom by introspective means. Luther instituted the technique of meaningful prayer. Freud's contribution was a technique that opened the way to honest introspection, and which extended into the new dimension of the unconscious.

Luther advocated an appeal to God that He grant the good intention with which the prayer was started, and Freud postulated an analogous rigor for genuine introspection, demanding that one take an "honest look at one's honesty." According to Erikson (1958), Luther's faith in God led to Freud's faith in man.

Neither Luther nor Freud aimed at self-sacrifice but they did aim at a certain self-acceptance as a basis of tolerance and love for one's self and one's neighbor.

Freud always thought that if man could gain insight into the depth of his unconscious and into the true nature of his motivation, he would be a free man again and could make good decisions, for him good and evil become self-evident. Nobody is voluntarily bad.

BIBLIOGRAPHY

Erikson, E. H. (1958), *Young Man Martin Luther, A Study of Psychoanalysis and History*. New York: W. W. Norton.
Sigmund Freud-Arnold Zweig: Briefwechsel (Letters), ed. E. L. Freud. Frankfurt am Main: Fischer Verlag, 1968. *The Letters of Sigmund Freud and Arnold Zweig*, ed. E. L. Freud; trans. E. and W. Robson-Scott. New York; Harcourt, Brace & World, 1970.
Grotjahn, M. (1962), A psychoanalyst looks up to Albert Schweitzer. In: *Albert Schweitzer's Realm*, ed. A. A. Roback. Cambridge: Sci-Art Publ.

____ (1963), Review of *Sigmund Freud-Oskar Pfister, Briefe. Psychoanal. Quart.*, 32:574–578.

____ (1967), The protestantism of Martin Luther and Sigmund Freud. Paper presented at the 450th Anniversary Convocation, The Lutheran Hospitals of California, October 30, 1967.

____ (1971), *The Voice of the Symbol*. Los Angeles: Mara Books.

Jones, E. (1955), *The Life and Work of Sigmund Freud*, 3 Vols. New York: Basic Books.

Rieff, P. (1959), *Freud: The Mind of the Moralist*. New York: Viking Press.

23. Morality and
the Population Explosion

ALEXANDER WOLF, M.D.

I HAVE ONLY two kinds of patients: one, the unmarried in endless and frustrated search for a spouse; two, the married who want a divorce. How we manage to have a population explosion under these circumstances is some testimony either to man's versatility or to my limited practice.

Occasionally, when an actress has found herself in an unplanned-for pregnancy, she has claimed freedom from her contract to perform on the grounds of the Act of God doctrine; but the *law* has always judged that God was otherwise engaged in each instance. There are medical and public health, social and economic, national and international, political and military, cultural and anthropological, ethnic and sociological, religious and irreligious, ecological and societal (i.e., class position), mathematical and biological, instinctual and sexual, ethological and psychological explanations for the population explosion. Poverty and ignorance are equally culpable allies in contributing to the enlarging masses of misused and unwanted children and aging adults. Probably all, other than the psychological, are more basic factors in any attempt to assess the many forces at work in the threatening multiplication of peoples. This paper will, however, concern itself principally with the *unconscious* need on the part of men and women to produce large families. It will review also the questions of love and responsibility in the creation of multiple offspring. If the world population continues to expand unchecked, we may yet suffer not merely from lack of food and water, not only from in-

Read at the Society of Medical Psychoanalysts, Symposium on Moral Values and Superego Functioning, New York City, March 4, 1968.

creasing air and water pollution, but from a teeming mankind. It has become not merely a physical problem to provide for the bodily needs of man, but an ethical question as well. It is said that every fetus is a potential human being whose life must therefore be preserved at any cost. But when does life become sacred? At birth? As a fetus? As a fertilized ovum?

If all life must be preserved should not every spermatozoon and every ovum—full of the promise of life—be so venerated? If we are so dedicated to life, do we not then also have a moral responsibility to every infant to see that he is born into a world in which the crowded living do not stifle him to death in their numbers? Must life be frenetically and limitlessly sponsored no matter how much we suffocate one another? Can we not more appropriately control our numbers to the end that we may make a good place for every man? As long as man has striven for the preservation of life he has been equally engaged in promoting death, whether by military means, epidemic infection, robbing the poor, exploiting the weak, impoverishing his neighbor, or murdering his imagined enemies. Will his moral responsibility to love his neighbor triumph over his immoral irresponsibility to exterminate him prevail? Will the forces of destructive self-interest triumph? Scientists and humanists and political leaders have the keys to save us or eliminate us. Or we may simply crowd one another to death in a population explosion. The psychoanalyst has a very small part to play in the menace of an overcrowded mankind. But he can tell us something of why so many men and women want so many children, why some want none, what is normal in the wish for children and what is abnormal in the limitless promotion of offspring. If misdirected sexuality is at the heart of the neurotic and psychotic dilemma, the analyst ought to be able to divulge the pathological misuse of human intercourse which threatens to multiply the population of man to such proportions that he becomes engulfed by the swarm he has spawned.

In my reading articles and books on the population explosion I find that there are two camps. One camp is optimistic, feeling that the earth can handle the population's growth for millennia; that very shortly we shall have plenty of room under the seas, on the moon, the other planets and the endless stars for our infinite propagation. The other camp is quite pessimistic, believing that we are in a population explosion now, that if we do not seriously limit the number of children in a family to two or three, we shall be hopelessly overcrowded by the year 2000. Between these two camps what is the reality? And who am I to say?

While others may decry the population explosion on the grounds that the earth can no longer feed its multiplying people, the psychoanalytic position is not one opposed to childbirth. Others can provide good and sufficient reasons to limit the size of families in an increasingly overcrowded world. The analyst's province is to inquire into the unconscious factors motivating parents to produce large numbers of children. This is the moral position. The psychoanalytic view is one of consciousness, of increasing awareness as to why we need to have offspring, and why so many. Lebensraum and poverty are not psychoanalytic issues. But consciousness of motivations and values are psychoanalytic issues.

Psychoanalytic therapy would seem almost irrelevant in a population of 7½ billion in the year 2,000. There would be no room to lie down—certainly not on a couch. And "how can we solve the population explosion if we continue to have these power blackouts?" (Manna, 1967). The population explosion has been explored, studied and reported on widely. So I do not believe that I am about to uncover much in the way of virgin territory.

THE MEGALOPOLIS

"In *small* communities, visitors are invariably asked two questions as soon as they arrive: which church denomination they belong to, and how many children they have; and anyone who happens to be a sterile atheist might as well go back where he came from as soon as possible" (Harris, 1967).

Tom Wolfe cites experiment after experiment of overcrowding among animals demonstrating that although ample food was available, where the population exploded, chaos, disease and death inevitably followed" (Wolfe, 1967). ". . . [Chombart de Louve and his wife] found a direct relationship between crowding and general breakdown. In families where people were crowded into the apartment . . . social and physical disorders doubled . . ." (Wolfe, 1967).

In the megalopoli of the United States one observer declares that ". . . parental control [has] evaporated. In those great impersonal, dehumanized hives rising skywards in New York, Chicago, Boston and other big cities, family life, so far from acquiring new dignity (has) simply disintegrated. Nor [have] family ties endure[d] elsewhere" (Green, 1966).

In a cartoon I saw recently, a mother, father and child are looking over an endless parking lot filled with automobiles. The mother says to the father, "He is already five years old and he has never seen a parking space" (see Bibliography, URS).

Some Psychodynamics

According to Wolfenstein (1957) there is a grandiose yet impotent self-deception about our sense of security in the face of the population explosion. There is an illusory safety in not taking seriously cautionary predictions of the impending calamity. The anxiety repressed in the face of such warnings may in fact lead to more sexual indulgence in an attempt to neutralize the underlying uncertainty. Represented in such behavior is an escape into the pleasure of the here-and-now with little concern for future perils. There is an unconscious setting aside of the danger as not applicable to us as individuals. The average man believes he has little to offer in the face of such a world problem. If, however, he is unconsciously hostile to proliferating mankind he may project onto the growing masses his own resentment.

Feelings of culpability and dread of retribution may stir a fear of a disastrous population explosion, particularly if we have made a contribution to it. We may see the future calamity as a corrective chastening directed by God or the forces of nature. Our sense that we are exempt from the dangers of the population explosion are particularly prevalent if we believe we are helpless to prevent it. If we believe we can avert it, we are more likely to concede that we are in jeopardy and take some action to check it.

Should we agree that a population explosion would be highly undesirable, the inclination to refuse to believe there is a threat is augmented. The reluctance to take precautions to elude such a catastrophe thereby enlarges the trend toward disbelief that it can come to pass. Americans tend to reject any anticipation of an unfortunate outcome. We reject anxiety, vexation, fear and trembling. We expect our people to be brave, unafraid, to see things through. We urge one another not to be afraid of risk. If we do not, the hazard looms large and we feel correspondingly inadequate. So we repudiate the danger of a population explosion. We ridicule it. If we are men enough, there is no peril we cannot overcome. The danger is, if we are men and women enough, we create the very danger we would avoid.

Another characteristic some of us share is our reluctance to provide against the possibility of our vulnerability. That would make us look irresolute, or worse, impotent. We might appear alarmed or frightened to others. We demand of ourselves the resources to contend without any advance precautionary measures. In all of this we must remain unruffled, not become agitated. To look overwrought would be unseemly. It would offer our children a poor model with which to identify. Besides, any internal agitation might well bring on the very external danger we hope to avoid. It is like our trying to walk calmly by a big, growling dog lest he smell our anxious sweat and attack us.

By rejecting the existence or imminence of a population explosion and by suppressing our anxiety about it, we manage to diminish or control any daydreams or nightmares about it as a possibility. We reject overwhelming images of disaster. The acceptance of a prediction of actual or coming misfortune might precipitate anxiety over the weakening of affective competence or ascendancy. It might even produce panic. Instead of denying the peril, a more effective alternative is the preparation of a realistic plan to cope with the danger and thereby offer a bulwark against the outbreak of unforeseen affect and shock.

The more evidence and certainty of our precarious position in an expanding population, the more abnormal our dissent becomes. As the population demonstrably expands, we deny it and produce more children as guarantors of our indestructibility, as proof of our unbeatable virility, as evidence of our persistence and durability. In the face of uncertainty, we return again to more sexual gratification.

As the menace of the population explosion grows (whether or not we take some appropriate action), there is likely to be an increase of impulsivity. Anxiety and bewilderment about the future are forerunners of acts of atonement. If the future is clearly discerned, impulsivity is more likely to follow as a way of warding off any anxiety. The rejection of a new adaptation in the face of an obvious and increasing population explosion is a way of continuing to renounce the existence of the danger.

Our fantasy is: If we merely keep an unswerving eye on the fact that there is a dangerous population explosion with worse to come, we shall surely survive it unscathed. That our watchfulness will still the threat is an illusion of omnipotent magical power.

PATHOLOGICAL MOTIVATIONS FOR HAVING A LARGE FAMILY

I am limiting myself in this discussion to the pathological motivations for having a large family. Obviously there are also healthy reasons for creating a considerable tribe of one's own. There is social value, prestige and applause placed on aging parents who, as one example, are the source of 12 children, 124 grandchildren and, as of the latest available count, 22 great grandchildren. It is probably one of the few rewards of being a grandparent to look down with pride from the pinnacle of patriarchy or matriarchy on the pyramid of descendents that one has initiated. The religious practice of venerating one's forebears fosters the desire for increasing descendents. There is also in such a productive line something of the wish not to be forgotten.

There are parents who must show, must exhibit their fertility, their worthiness. Sometimes the state, the church and industry will demand, sponsor or reward such productive citizens. There is, for example, world-wide interest and esteem for parents at the birth of quadruplets and quintuplets. Parents sometimes need to demonstrate their versatility. If the first three, four or five children are all girls, or all boys, there is often a wish to try again and again for a child of the other sex.

There seems then to be a need for large numbers of children to carry on the faith, whether it be in the service of the family line, the nation or the religious group. There is a perpetuation of self in having many children, a wish for immortality, perhaps compensatory for an underlying fear of extinction, death or castration.

Children may be seen as objects, as investments that will guarantee a commitment of support for the aging parent. Here the children are exploitatively groomed and misused as parents to their actual parents.

A parent may use a counterphobic response against the threat of a population explosion by denying that there is any such danger and having as many children as possible. Such a mechanism is probably related to the schizoid maneuver. The fear of being crowded to death may be a displaced claustrophobia. The fear of declining population may be a displaced agoraphobia. The fear of a population explosion may be a displaced fear of cannibalism.

Among impulse-ridden parents, psychopathic parents, or parents with inadequate superegos, there is little thought of consequences. Only the pleasurable feeling of the moment counts. Only the excitement of the here-and-now is meaningful. The pregnancy to come is forgotten. This is an acting out of sociopathic irresponsibility. For such parents, the children to come are unimportant, accidental by-products of sexual pleasure. The rebellion of teenagers against the sexual prohibitions as well as sexual encouragement by parents, motivated by their own unconscious sexual conflicts, not infrequently results in unwed motherhood.

Children may be used as parental or sibling substitutes on whom revenge is taken for the poor treatment one endured from one's own parents. The vendetta may be perpetuated by turning the aggression on the self. Or one may surround oneself with children to be unreservedly and unequivocally loved by them to compensate for this lack in the original family.

Some people feel greater security within the family they have evolved than with strangers. They live with and within their own families and avoid the nonfamilial. The more members of the family they procreate, the more they feel safe and at home. They are made anxious by the unknown, the nonfamilial, the strange.

A parent may want many children as a way of warding off or binding the spouse, husband or wife. If either is afraid of being abandoned by the other, having a large family of dependent children may be a way of holding on to a mate who threatens to desert.

A man may try to keep his wife pregnant and busy with many children, so that he may engage in extramarital affairs, or prevent her from having extramarital affairs. It seems to me that a man who keeps his wife pregnant most of her reproductive life must be, at the very least, *unconsciously* hostile to her.

A woman may also seek repeated impregnation to ward off intercourse with her husband or, its opposite, to enjoy nine months of sexual relations. It may be, in some instances, because she cannot enjoy sex with the use of contraceptives. A woman may make a husband less the object of her love than before there were children. Such a mother may have many children in order to evade her husband, using the children's needs to ward off contact with their father.

There are oral, anal and phallic motives for having large families. Some parents have children because they can accept children but not adults, not even the adults their children become. In part this is because the parents are themselves regressed children and can understand, enjoy and play only with their own kind. This inability to relate comfortably to adults almost demands a succession of babies.

The parental expression of love toward their children "I love you so, I could eat you up," is at least orally aggressive and incorporative, if not orally sadistic.

An anal attitude towards one's children is to produce as large a number of them as possible, and then to accumulate, exhibit or hide, possess and control them, while at the same time expecting to be loved, admired or accepted for having produced such an ample brood.

Children are sometimes seen as multiple phallic extensions of the parent, evidence of his virility or her religiosity. A large num-

Alexander Wolf

ber of children may confer prestige, implying vigor and a love of children. There is narcissism and grandiosity in wishing to see oneself so limitlessly reproduced. It is important, however, to remember that "only one man in a thousand is [such] a leader of men. The other 999 are followers of women" (Brande, 1961).

A pregnant woman or mother may unconsciously use the fetus or child as a phallic incorporate and executive hitherto unavailable to her. There are women who have to be pregnant to feel well. Otherwise they feel useless, empty, hollow, that is, without a phallus. The fetus is for them a symbolic penis to keep the husband out of the vagina. Intercourse is resisted because it makes them feel they have only a vagina and no penis. Intercourse is a painful confrontation with the reality that they are, in fact, women.

To quote Rainwater (1965):

> At a deep level, one of the functions of having many children may be to moderate reciprocal Oedipal attachments; from the parent's point of view, several children lessen the intensity of incestuous involvements and diffuse them in ways that result in less anxiety. Not uncommonly, parents mention as advantages of the large family that one is protected against loss should one of the children die, and that one has children around longer in the life cycle. This suggests a greater continuity of Oedipal gratifications on the parents' part at the same time that these gratifications are made safer by diffusion. They are not only safer for the parents (in the sense of producing less guilt and anxiety), but also for the children, since the large family, many people believe, prevents pathological attachments to and dependence on the parents. This too, assuages parents' guilt, since they can feel that they have created a situation in which their incestuous desires are not damaging to their children [pp. 190–191].

There may be death wishes against one's own children, particularly if they are too many, needy, hungry and demanding, and do not fulfill the parents' expectations. The family may keep growing in the parental hope that maybe the next child will be "better," more gratifying than the previously disappointing ones. There is a sadistic Sgt.-Major Syndrome which may be exercised by a parent.

To be a Sgt.-Major in one's family needs a regiment of children. Multiple children may be a way of trying to create an intrafamilial society that will love, adore, obey, submit and execute the will of the parent—unlike the real world.

Some parents would unconsciously develop a brood of sociopaths, sadomasochists or id-dominated and superegoless army to act out the parents' repressed wishes. Out-of-wedlock or even multiple in-wedlock pregnancies are a way of submitting to or defying the parental expectation. Some masochistic parents overload themselves with large numbers of sadistic children who reinforce the masochistic depression of the martyred parents.

A child may be lost in too large a family, too large a class at school, in too large a therapeutic group, or as an adult in too crowded a society. Having a large family is, then, a way of coping with such loneliness and isolation, and providing warmth and security. The parents who have many children, in order to avoid the re-experiencing of the painful sense of abandonment of their own childhood, inappropriately bind their children to them in guilt or create thereby the very flight they hoped to avoid.

MORALITY

On the question of morality it has been said that, "It is by the goodness of God that in our country we have those three unspeakably precious things: freedom of speech, freedom of conscience, and the prudence never to practice either of them" (Twain, 1967). Or that "soap and morality (my word—Twain said "teaching") are not as sudden as a massacre, but they are more deadly in the long run" (Twain, 1955). Shaw counselled us, "first (to) secure an independent income; and then practice virtue" (Shaw, 1947). And Wilde thought that, "Morality is simply the attitude we adopt towards people we dislike" (Wilde, 1954).

The issue of morality arises only where there is choice. As long as we know that in reality we have the freedom to choose the number of children we want, our choice is more likely to be ethical and responsible. Release from blind dictation, whether from within or without, permits the flowering of the freedom to be moral. Freedom is not limitlessness. I deplore limitlessness which the unknowing believe to be freedom. Freedom needs to be mutual and requires moral obligation, and that is one of the reasons why most of us shrink from it. There are no irresponsible children —only irresponsible parents who have not outgrown their own childhood. Freedom is the observance of moral standards which we can follow because *we* have chosen them without restraint.

In the sphere of morality man is expected to check himself, to ask himself whether in good conscience the action he is about to take is ethical or not. What is our responsibility to the generation and the society that follow us? Ought we not to have some foresight, some reasonable plan for their future? To have an open-ended number of offspring is an irrational pursuit of limitlessness, a search for permanence in the face of our aging and inevitable death.

The parent who loves his or her many children is an admirable and popular figure, for a value is set upon fertility and motherhood as good and infertility as bad. Infertility, like idleness or impotence, is taboo. A woman is expected to be productive of children or creative in some other way. There is a view of contraception as sinful to which large masses of people subscribe and rebel. Some see contraception and abortion as murder. Others regard family planning as lifesaving for the mother—sometimes even of the overworked father.

Is it ethical to escape involvement in the face of the threat of our population explosion? Is it proper to allow oneself to be lulled by optimistic dreams of colonizing the planets and stars? Is it right to rely on predictions which assure us of science's future ability to synthesize enough protein to feed the world's starving millions? Is it fair to assume that we shall survive on the minute animals and plants drifting in our seas? Is it fitting to have an acre to oneself now but expect our grandchildren to stand forty to the acre? Is this a *moral* heritage?

Reason acknowledges and respects the morality of law. Primitive self-gratification would satisfy personal pleasure. An ethical choice is a preference for reason against regressive blind impulse or compulsion.

When we love our children we feel responsible for their welfare. There is no love where there is no responsibility. We ought to have no more children than the number for whom we can be morally accountable. And we cannot shift this obligation to others. A moral choice appears when our selection involves other people as having children does. An ethical choice emerges when there is a hierarchy of alternatives, as when we ask ourselves whether it is better or worse in this time and place and in this society to have two or three children or three or four.

While I believe we need to see and act on the necessity of limiting the expansion of population, I do not believe we ought to pass laws limiting the number of children a family may have. Prohibition for man is an invitation to illegality. Strategies need to be developed for freedom to choose, leaving room for dissent, for openings for amendment, for reform, for revised estimates based on new developments (Kahn & Weiner, 1967).

Some parents are too compulsively responsible. It is, like overprotection, an attempt to deny their negative feelings towards children by having too many in order to prove their responsibility.

SOME IRRATIONAL SOLUTIONS TO THE POPULATION EXPLOSION

According to McClain (1967):

A sociologist was lecturing to a women's club on the crisis arising from the world population explosion. "Do you realize that somewhere in the world a woman is giving birth to a child every minute, day and night?" he said. "What are we going to do to solve this problem?" A woman in the back row raised her hand. "I think the first thing we should do is find that woman," she said, "and *stop* her!" [pp. 89–90].

Pathological solutions to the population explosion have been proposed—like war, genocide, child murder, homosexuality, masturbation, limits on heterosexual relations, limitless sexuality and, more recently, exposure to the rays from color TV sets.

It has been predicted that in the twenty-first century "the tendency to expose the female body will continue to ever greater degree, until woman regains her Garden of Eden freedom and

· 483

grace. Progressive nakedness, contrary to puritanical thinking, progressively lessens the curiosity of the male and slows the baby-production rate. It was not until Eve put on her leaf that baby-making started" (Fuller, 1968).

Methods of fertility regulation have been vigorously resisted because they help the users to avoid the punitive responsibility that it is generally assumed should follow sexual indulgence. This need for punishment may be displaced from oneself to others. An individual's guilt may be alleviated, his conscience satisfied if he sees others victimized and overburdened by too many children. Parents may, indeed, use their own children for this purpose.

A parental sense of guilt may be atoned for by assuming the increasing burdens of bearing and supporting successive children. With the birth of each infant, the superego is temporarily satisfied by the suffering endured, and the parents are momentarily freed to seek personal gratification previously prohibited by guilt. Self-punitive asceticism may result in no marriage, marriage with no children or with too many children. Self-punitive asceticism is related to moral masochism.

Daily coitus or coitus t.i.d. may be a way of solving the population explosion. A patient of mine was told by his physician that his daily cohabitation kept his sperm immature and his sperm count too low to impregnate his wife.

Not long ago the "Attorney-General . . . urged the U.S. Congress to restrict the sale of guns, claiming they have killed more Americans in peace time than in all the nation's wars" (*The Ocean Times,* 1967). Evidently we are not armed well enough to reduce the population explosion in our private feuds. Some of this aggression is turned to self-destruction in drug addiction, alcoholism, LSD-induced psychoses, masochism, depression, despair and suicide. But none of these foundering people, whether murderers or suicides, will make a dent in the population explosion. The 300–500 million spermatozoa in a single ejaculation and the increasing female freedom to engage in intercourse far outweigh our ability to kill ourselves or one another off.

Homosexual men may try publicly to show they are men and homosexual women that they are women by a marriage productive of children. Underneath their union they can continue their secretive homosexuality. As mentioned above, masturbation has been suggested as a solution to the population explosion, as well as homosexuality. What the psychoanalyst's role in such a society would be can hardly be predicted. We may then be consulted by some homosexuals with doubts about their femininity.

A RATIONAL SOLUTION TO THE POPULATION EXPLOSION

Clarence Darrow (1942) when asked at a women's club meeting what he thought about birth control for the masses replied: "My dear lady, whenever I hear people discussing birth control I always remember that I was the fifth" (p. 825).

"If (Lenica and Sauvy, 1962) were asked to designate a single key to the problem, (they) would reply without hesitation, *the education of women.* An educated woman ceases to be the slave of man and nature. Education is, in the fullest sense of the word, emancipation" (p. 106). If *I* were asked this question I would say, the sexual education of *women and men.*

Flugel (1945) advocated a movement "from egocentricity to sociality," when we are inspired by an ideal of commitment to a group, the acknowledgement of the rights of others as well as our own. And by these others I mean the right of children to the most favorable conditions for self-realization.

A rational solution would promote family planning through fertility regulation. We need to train corps of counsellors in family planning to teach couples the various forms of contraception so that they can choose that method which is most effective and agreeable. Such a plan should be a part of community mental health programs.

"If parents would have only the children they want, we'd be off to a good start . . ." (Mead, 1968). Despite many others' gloomy predictions, I remain optimistic, because I believe in the resources of consciousness, in man's freedom to choose the reasonable alternative to the population explosion, namely planned parenthood. It is immoral to have children if we cannot assure them of survival. Moreover it is immoral if we cannot provide them with some success, happiness and those conditions necessary for gratification in this complicated world.

CONCLUSION

Do we really have the freedom to choose or are we puppets of necessity, fate, providence, God's will? (Lamont, 1967). I am not as cynical as Feiffer who sees "Escalating war, rising poverty, rising racism, riots in the ghettos, crime in the streets, drugs on the campus, a spreading disillusionment with electoral politics. In November, in order to solve these problems, "I can," he says, "vote for Richard Nixon or Lyndon Johnson. In a free society there is always choice" (Feiffer, 1968). Freedom is a consequence of the recognition or awareness of the existence of choices and then acting on them in reality. If the reality is that mankind is threatened by our increasing numbers, we must make a commitment to family planning.

For the psychoanalyst the analysis of resistance and finding the nature of the predetermined behavior is a first step toward the recovery of freedom. An understanding of the psychopathological operations is a step toward liberty from them. To have insight enables the patient somewhat to control the outcome, to unseat the governing neurosis and use his energy, not in self-defeat, but in promoting his potential. The limits and extent of our freedom is determined by three co-existing conditions: first, a relative degree of determinism; second, elements of chance; and third, some freedom of choice. As the patient recognizes these three, his relative freedom to choose increases. Chance and choice constantly set determinism in motion. For example, if an ovum is fertilized by a spermatozoon by chance or by choice, determinism is set in motion, that is, fertilization initiates the orderly development of a fetus.

The freedom to choose is derived from man's unique individuality, his potentiality, his initiative and his ability to take advantage of opportunity presented by chance events. Animals lower than man do not have the same freedom to choose. Through the exercise of consciousness, reason and free choice, he can modify, control and redirect predetermined events, external and internal. He can manipulate procreation and plan whether or not, when, to what extent and in what number, he wants children.

In fostering consciousness, the analyst sponsors freedom. In promoting freedom he enables his patients to make reasonable choices. And reasonable choice leads to limiting the number of children each family has. The analytic position is that it is immoral to be unconscious of the implications and consequences of one's behavior. The analyst is for *conscious* motherhood and fatherhood. If he were for unconscious parenthood, he would promote parentage among psychotics whether in or out of mental hospitals. If parents were conscious of their own needs, of their parental role, of their children's needs, conscious of themselves and others (of whom their children are a part), they would plan more appropriately. The analyst strives to help his patient, whether mother, father or child, to be more aware of his own, his family's and his community's needs. Of what must a married couple be conscious? Among other things, whether to have or not to have children; of what it means to be a first, second, third or fourth child—or a parent of such numbers; of their responsibility to bring up a child in the best possible way.

Analysis is concerned also with the question of *limits*. Freedom decreases with limitlessness. Freedom is the recognition of necessity. It is necessary to make parents more conscious of the role of parenthood, part of which means a consciousness of limits. Limitlessness permits of no family planning.

As a psychoanalyst I believe that despite the existence of necessity, every human being has or should have the freedom to choose among a series of alternatives. The freedom to choose may be lessened by a restraining outer reality or by intrapsychic pathology. The analyst focuses his treatment on resolving the unconscious disorder enabling the patient to deal more realistically with the external reality. As a therapist I reject absolutism in any form, for such a view embraces the inevitability of fate and the nonexistence of choice. Absolute freedom rejects the laws of determinism. Therefore, I must reject absolutism which makes man ethically irresponsible. And unless we can help our patients out of the bondage to which their psychopathology enslaves them, we ought to give up our profession.

If we were absolute determinists, we would all be secure that "God's in His Heaven—all's right with the world." There would be no tension, no responsibility, no choice and no work—for psychoanalysts. The therapist's freeing the patient to choose gives him anxiety, responsibility to differentiate the good from the bad, to develop his unique resources, to give up the illusion of certainty for the reality of uncertainty.

Thought, intelligence and consciousness are necessary in order to enable one to make an appropriate, i.e., a reasonable choice. But thought, the use of intellect and consciousness require patience, the imposition of some self-restraint, of limits. This rational, freely chosen self-control is self-discipline, not inhibition *nor* predeterminism. Freedom of choice in psychoanalytic therapy is a consequence of the uncovering of the unconsciously repeated psychopathology, its origins, its outmoded uselessness and finally the conscious choice of the freeing healthy alternative in reality.

Freedom to choose and determinism are not mutually exclusive. Each is not absolute but relative. They coexist. Man's study of nature has revealed to him certain scientific laws, that certain causes produce inevitable effects. But the free use of his intellect has enabled him to manipulate natural phenomena so that they serve his interest. He exercises a freedom to choose in a determined context.

The more aware a parent is of his freedom to determine the number of children he will have, the more adequate and high-spirited he becomes. *He,* not fate, is his master. His freedom to choose builds his self-respect, his feeling of effectiveness, his ego.

To take a stand against the population explosion is like criticizing motherhood. Despite my daily experience with patients critical of their parents and parents critical of their children, I believe motherhood and fatherhood are here to stay. I believe in the family and the human right, the privilege and the necessity to have children—within limits.

Man needs more food, shelter and clothing, more room and less air pollution, less noise. While we need each other, at some point in our increase there will just not be enough land space for the peace and beauty of nature. And in the lives of all of us there are times when for each of us there ought to be a Walden.

Love between man and woman, between parent and child, makes life worth living. It is only the limitless consequences of the living products of their union in large numbers that threaten to exterminate us—and the future possibility of loving fulfillment which I believe to be life-exterminating—and therefore immoral.

A time-honored precept engraved on the temple at Delphi said, "Nothing to excess" (Plato, 1960). If we can avoid the excesses of war, we shall have more time to love one another with care, caution—and precaution not to overdo a good thing.

BIBLIOGRAPHY

Brande, J. M. (1961), *Speaker's Encyclopedia of Humor.* Englewood Cliffs, N.J.: Prentice Hall, p. 132.

Churchill, S. (1967), Variation of a remark made on the TV "Tonight Show," NBC.

Darrow, C. (1942), In: *The Public Speaker's Treasure Chest,* ed. H. V. Prochnow and H. V. Prochnow, Jr. New York: Harper & Row.

Feiffer, J. (1968), Cartoon. In: *The Village Voice,* Vol. 13, No. 164.

Flugel, J. C. (1945), *Man, Morals and Society.* London: Penguin Books, pp. 295–298.

Fuller, B. (1968), Why women rule the world. *McCall's,* Vol. XCV, No. 6, 11.

Green, C. M. (1966), *The Rise of Urban America.* London: Hutchinson University Library.

Harris, S. J. (1967), *The Miami Herald,* 7a.

Kahn, H. and Wiener, A. J. (1967), *The Year 2000.* New York: Macmillan & Co., pp. 586–587.

Lamont, C. (1967), *Freedom of Choice Affirmed.* New York: Horizon Press.

Lenica, J. and Sauvy, A. (1962), *Population Explosion.* New York: Dell Publishing Co.

Manna, C. (1967), A remark on the TV "Tonight Show," NBC.

McClain, J. (1967), The New York Journal-American. In: *Reader's Digest Fun and Laughter.* Pleasantville, New York: The Reader's Digest Assn.

Mead, M. (1968), Variation of a remark made on the TV "Tonight Show."

The Ocean Times (1967), In: the S. S. Queen Mary (eastbound).

Plato (1960), *Protagoras.* In: *The Penguin Dictionary of Quotations,* ed. J. M. Cohen and M. J. Cohen. Baltimore, Md.: Penguin Books, p. 8.

Rainwater, L. (1965), *Family Design: Marital Sexuality, Family Size and Contraception*. Chicago: Adline Publishing Co.

Shaw, G. B. (1947), Nine plays by Bernard Shaw with prefaces and notes. New York: Dodd, Mead & Co., pp. 831–931.

Twain, M. (1955), Education, In: *Bartlett's Familiar Quotations,* ed. J. Bartlett. *13th Centennial Edition.* Boston: Little, Brown & Co., p. 674.

—— (1967), Europe and elsewhere. In: *The Great Quotations,* ed. G. Seldes. New York: Pocket Books, p. 217.

URS, Cartoon by *Nebelspotter*, Rorschach, Switzerland.

Wilde, O. (1954), An ideal husband. In: *Penguin Plays.* Baltimore: Penguin Books, Inc., pp. 147–244.

Wolfe, T. (1967a), Oh rotten gotham—sliding down into the behavioral sink. In: *Best Magazine Articles 1967,* ed. G. Walker. New York: Crown Publishers, pp. 95, 100.

Wolfenstein, M. (1957), *Disaster.* Glencoe, Ill.: The Free Press, pp. i–xv and 1–42.

Name Index

Name Index

Gill, M. M., 186
Gitelson, M., 187, 220
Glover, E., 25, 71, 149, 181, 219
Goblot, E., 205, 214
Goffman, E., 192
Goldstein, J., 399, 403, 409–414, 428
Green, C. M., 475
Greenacre, P., 33, 112, 121, 254, 255–256, 272
Greenson, R. R., 230, 242
Greenwald, H., 131
Grotjahn, M., 464–473
Guevara, C., 352, 359, 382
Guignebert, C., 452, 454, 455

Hammerman, S., 115
Harlow, H., 129
Harlow, M. K., 129
Harris, S. J., 474
Hartmann, H., 1, 47, 54–57, 74, 75, 81, 83, 84, 88, 89, 90, 114, 119, 121, 169, 192, 210, 219, 220, 228, 242, 413, 428, 430, 437, 450, 459
Hayden, T., 345, 359
Hazard, G., 407–408
Himes, C., 188
Himmelweit, H., 180
Horney, K., 108
Huxley, J., 207

Isaacs, S., 38
Isakower, O., 41, 233, 234

Jackson, Justice, 404–405
Jacobson, E., 14, 29–30, 31, 33, 44–46, 88, 99, 112–114, 121, 268, 431
Johnson, A. M., 255
Jones, E., 38, 101, 109–110, 398
Jones, L., 348

Kahn, H., 483
Kalven, H., 406, 407
Kanzer, M., 254, 255
Kaplan, A., 53
Katz, J., 399, 403
Kaufman, Y., 438, 439, 445, 448, 456
Kelsen, H., 277
Keniston, K., 96–97, 98, 173, 345
Klein, G. S., 89
Klein, M., 36–37, 39, 109
Kluckhohn, C., 170
Knight, R. P., 81
Koestler, A., 93

Kohut, H., 120
Kraepelin, E., 286
Kramer, P., 34–35
Kris, E., 47, 75, 459
Kris, M., 76

Lalande, A., 206
Lamont, C., 486
Lampl-de Groot, J., 46, 108–109, 437, 447
Lederer, W., 88
Lenica, J., 485
Levin, S., 185
Lévy-Bruhl, L., 222
Lewin, B., 27, 42, 232–233, 269
Lewis, C. S., 438
Lifton, R. J., 342–376
Loewald, H., 148, 149
Loewenstein, R. M., 28, 47, 74, 88, 89, 90, 114, 119, 437, 450, 459
Lorenz, K., 63, 275
Lowenfeld, H., 377–399
Lowenfeld, Y., 377–399
Lustman, S. L., 5, 148
Luther, M., 467–470

Malmquist, C., 98
Manna, C., 474
Marcuse, H., 357, 358, 359
Masserman, J. H., 210
McClain, J., 483
Mead, M., 92, 485
Mechem, P., 407
Menninger, K., 220
Mertens, R., 66
Meth, J., 277
Michaels, J. J., 185, 221
Modell, A., 34
Money-Kyrle, R. E., 210, 217
Muslin, H. L., 101–125

Nagel, E., 212
Nass, M., 90
Nielsen, N., 210
Nunberg, H., 26, 31–33, 147

Offer, D., 98
Orbach, C. E., 135
Orwell, G., 186
Ostow, M., 323–341

Parson, I., 277
Pfister, O., 462–467
Pieper, W., 122

Pierce, C., 91
Piers, G., 28–29, 48, 114, 120
Pious, W. L., 34
Poincaré, H., 213
Post, S. C., 255–276

Rainwater, L., 480
Ramzy, I., 57–59, 63, 207–227, 237
Rapaport, D., 186, 430
Read, H., 207
Redlich, F. C., 220
Reich, A., 7, 14, 30, 42–43, 268, 269
Reid, J., 207
Rieff, P., 207
Ritvo, S., 74–86, 99
Roazen, P., 197, 198, 199–206
Robbins, B. S., 129
Rosenbaum, S., 439–463
Rosenfeld, H., 37
Rosenthal, R., 180
Rudd, M., 348, 349
Russell, B., 49–50, 209

Sachs, H., 33, 110–111
Sandler, J., 46, 89, 98
Sartre, J., 345, 347, 356, 358
Sauvy, A., 485
Schaefer, R., 35, 90
Schur, E., 400
Sharpe, E., 219
Shaw, G. B., 481
Shor, J., 210
Singer, M. B., 28–30, 48
Solnit, A. J., 75, 79, 99
Sorokin, P., 420
Spender, S., 359, 360
Spiegel, H., 277
Spiegel, L., 87, 255
Spitz, R., 36, 39
Stein, M. H., 89, 228–241
Sterba, R., 148, 149, 158

Stone, A. A., 400–438
Stone, L., 27, 90
Strachey, J., 25, 26
Szasz, T. S., 177, 184, 245
Szurek, S., 255

Thernstrom, S., 173
Tinbergen, N., 66
Titchener, J., 96
Trilling, L., 207, 349, 359
Twain, M., 481
Valenstein, A. F., 63–73
Von Holst, E., 375

Waelder, R., 228, 235
Walker, W., 453, 455, 456
Wangh, M., 253, 255
Washburn, S. L., 68
Weber, M., 450
Weigert, E., 37
Weiner, A. J., 483
Weisman, A., 190
Welch, C., 442
Wexler, M., 230
Whitehorn, J. C., 179
Wilde, O., 481
Wiles, M., 458
Winnicott, D. W., 37
Wittels, F., 71
Wolf, A., 474–489
Wolfe, T., 474
Wolfenstein, M., 475
Wolff, R. L., 179
Woodcock, G., 356

Yankelovish, D., 182
Yntema, H., 403
Yurick, S., 356

Zilboorg, G., 220
Zinberg, N., 171–198

Subject Index

498 ·

Subject Index

Real experience, need for, and acting out, 253–273
Reality, detachment from, 332
Reality testing
  ego in, 17, 48, 386
  superego in, 32, 90
Regression
  to identification, 151, 153
  to narcissism, 145, 149–150, 151, 154, 159, 161, 269
Relevance, and youth rebellions, 365
Religion
  ambivalence toward, 323
  and antinomianism, 332, 334–338
  as defense against depression, 327–332
  and development of Protestant ethic, 467–470
  and family practices, 322–324
  father figures in, 445–448, 453–454
  Freud's views on, 437, 439–440, 445–446, 453, 456, 462–470
  and immortality, 453, 458
  and jurisprudence, 421, 427–429
  and mysticism, 333–334
  and mythology, 453–456, 459
  and obsessive-compulsive neurosis, 324–326
  and other-worldliness, 332, 334–339
  psychoanalytic view of, 321–339
  as response to distress of mental illness, 324–334
  as response to specific event, 324
  and schizophrenia, 333
  sin and sense of guilt in, 437–460
  and superego, 35, 326–327, 395, 448
Renunciation
  of identification with therapist, 154, 155–156, 159, 161–162
  in neuroses, 156–160
  in psychoses, 160–161
  and superego formation, 149–152
  in therapy, 144–147
Repression
  and ego-ideal, 13
  superego related to, 12
Revenge, as motivation for homicide, 307–308
Revolution and rebellion. See Youth rebellion
Rituals, in primitive societies, 278

Sadism, anal, and homicide, 308–309

Schizophrenia
  catatonic, 275–288
  and detachment from reality, 332
  object cathexis in, 160
  religious ideas in, 333
  superego in, 34, 37
Seduction, and acting out, 255, 258
Self-awareness, and New History, 341
Self-destructive acts, and guilt, 141
Self-esteem
  concepts of, 46
  and narcissism, 13–14
Self-observation, as superego function, 41–42, 47, 89, 148
Sexual behavior
  and acting out, case reports of, 257–268
  attitudes toward, 92, 245–246, 248–249, 378–379, 387
  control of, 127
  frustration in, as motivation for homicide, 306–307
  promiscuous, 131–132, 387–388, 390–391
  and religious ideas, 441
Sexualized identification, 152
  and desexualization, 151, 152, 164
Shame, feelings of, 114, 120
  after criminal act, 300, 307
  and guilt feelings, 28–29, 48
  lack of, 395
Sin
  biblical concepts of, 440–444
  and sense of guilt, 437–460
Slogans, in youth rebellions, 346, 348, 351, 364, 365
Social change
  and psychoanalytic values, 188–195
  and value systems, 172–176
Social sciences, and jurisprudence, 405–409
Society
  and adolescent development, 90–93
  and childhood development, 180
  ego-ideal and group psychology in, 16
  and feminine superego development, 119–120
  laws in, 50–51
  middle-class status in, and value conflict, 182–188
  motives for rejection of, 333–334
  needs of, and individual gratification, 128, 129–130
  permissive, and superego formation, 375–397